Working Stiffs, Union Maids,
Reds, and Riffraff

WORKING STIFFS, UNION MAIDS, REDS, AND RIFFRAFF

AN ORGANIZED GUIDE TO FILMS ABOUT LABOR

TOM ZANIELLO

ILR PRESS AN IMPRINT OF
CORNELL UNIVERSITY PRESS

ITHACA AND LONDON

First published 1996 by Cornell University Press.

Printed in the United States of America

∞ The paper in this book meets the minimum requirements of the
American National Standard for Information Sciences—Permanence
of Paper for Printed Library Materials, ANSI Z39.48-1984.

Library of Congress Cataloging-in-Publication Data

Zaniello, Tom, 1943–
    Working stiffs, union maids, reds, and riffraff : an organized guide to films
about labor / Tom Zaniello.
        p.   cm.
    Includes bibliographical references and index.
    ISBN 0-87546-352-5 (cloth: alk. paper). — ISBN 0-87546-353-3 (pbk.: alk.
paper)
    1. Working class in motion pictures.   I. Title.
PN1995.9.L28Z36   1996
791.43'655—dc20   95-47514

In memory of Bill Worley—
artist, film fan, and friend

Contents

Introduction

If you are searching for a labor-related film, this guide will help. If you are an experienced viewer of such films, this guide is likely to expand the list of titles available for consideration.

Many viewers have seen the pro-labor films I like to call the Big Three: "Harlan County U.S.A.," "Norma Rae," and "Matewan." Another group, the Problematical Pack, have been marked by controversy: "Salt of the Earth," "The Molly Maguires," "Roger & Me," and "American Dream." Still others—such as "The Grapes of Wrath" and "On the Waterfront"—are Historical Hits; they are cited in standard film surveys as classics.

These nine films would form the core of any list of labor-related films. But what other films should be recommended for viewing or study, a semester's film course, or a public labor-related film program? Do we include the proletarian classics of the 1930s, when working-class characters, explicit political allegiances, and labor issues were considered mainstream material ("Our Daily Bread" or "Riffraff")? Do we include only non-Hollywood independents? Or only documentaries? Or only films made by politically self-conscious collectives? And what of the labor-related films from Mexico and Canada, not to mention Britain, other parts of Europe, Asia, Africa, and Oceania?

Developing a canon of film classics is hard enough. It is not surprising, therefore, that constructing a list, much less a canon, of labor-related films raises as many questions as it answers, especially when one considers that Hollywood, the production and distribution systems, as well as our viewing habits all conspire to limit access to the tremendous variety of films that are available.

Working people, their unions, labor issues in general, and political movements involving the working class have always been a part of Hollywood (and other independent and national) filmmaking. But some of the most popular films about labor have presented their subjects in an unfavorable light, while lesser-known titles with more balanced or even positive views go unseen and unnoticed. Yet, because we live in a culture that receives so much of its information (and ultimately derives so many of its opinions) from visual media, it is especially important to see, to understand, and to study a variety of media images.

As a result of the revolution in videocassette (home) viewing and the explosion in cable and other made-for-TV offerings in the last ten years, we no longer receive our most influential images of labor from the classics, such as "On the Waterfront" or "The Molly Maguires." Millions of viewers now see a new interpretation of the murder of United Mine Workers officer Jock Yablonski in "Act of Vengeance" or the tragic heroism of the workers in "The Triangle Factory Fire Scandal" on cable or network television or on videocassettes rented at a local video store.

Even our access to the classics has increased significantly, so that independent Academy Award winners, such as "Harlan County U.S.A.," circulate in numbers never dreamed of by the filmmakers. Others that have virtually been hidden away, such as "Salt of the Earth" (a blacklisted film about miners in the Southwest) or "Business as Usual" (a little gem featuring a British union's struggle against sexual harassment in a small dress shop) are much more accessible. And, if one is so inclined, one can see at least *four* different interpretations of the controversial career of Teamster leader Jimmy Hoffa.

Who Is This Guide For?

Viewers looking for a film about working people, labor activism or history, and related economic and sociological issues should find this guide helpful. It is currently the only comprehensively annotated guide that includes critical commentary and sources for further reading and research. Film students and teachers will discover, once such classics as "On the Waterfront" and "Harlan County U.S.A." are duly noted, a much wider range of films about labor than most such books cover.

At the same time, any guide like this must be selective. I have tried to include films that are relatively accessible; consequently, I have not included every labor-related film. Feature films are covered most comprehensively. Because of their limited availability, documentaries and independent films are represented less thoroughly. (A little more than 20 percent of the titles in this guide are documentaries.) I have tended to include documentaries that received major release in theaters or on videocassette. I have also given preference to documentaries that pair well with a feature film I have included. Teachers and film programmers should find such pairings particularly useful. Perhaps another fifty documentaries are excluded, not because of their subject matter, but because they are not always easily accessible.

Each entry includes a mini-essay. This format afforded me the flexibility to cover films that are so well known ("The Molly Maguires") that it is a bit of a dare to say something new about them (although I have tried) and films that have received very little critical attention ("The Killing Floor"). This format also enabled me to discuss new films ("Germinal") and recently rereleased films ("Nothing But a Man") in a way that was both efficient and flexible.

Most viewers of labor-related films will have a special interest in the historical and cultural issues surveyed in each entry. But, where relevant, I also explore issues of cinematic tradition and artistic style. Some films, such as "Matewan," have a wide audience not only because the subject is compelling but because the material is presented so artistically. In feature films, the quality of the acting can sometimes overshadow other aspects of the production. Thus, "On the Waterfront" became a classic in large part because of Marlon Brando's acting style, whereas "The Killing Floor," which involves vastly more complex economic and political issues, remains relatively unknown in part because of the low profile of most of its actors.

Some of the entries in this guide are substantially longer than others, especially if the film being profiled is controversial ("American Dream"), foreign ("Germinal"), has received little critical attention ("Newsies" and "Nothing But a Man"), or has a somewhat complicated production history ("Look Back in Anger," "A Raisin in the Sun," and "Metropolis").

How Were the Films Selected?

As a result of teaching and lecturing about film for twenty years and developing a very specific course (Images of Labor in Film) for the College Degree Program of the George Meany Center for Labor Studies, I was often pressed to recommend "a really good film about labor." I soon discovered that no current or comprehensive list of titles was available, although book-length studies and essays offered useful surveys.

I have selected the films for this guide based on the recommendations of trade unionists and labor educators, who reviewed a proposed list of approximately 125 films. This core list was expanded to the current total of 150 titles.

For a film to be listed, it had to satisfy one or more of five criteria. Films that met the first two criteria—(1) films about unions or labor organizations or (2) films about labor history—were relatively easy to identify. Choosing films that met the remaining three criteria, however, involved a number of judgment calls. These films had to satisfy one of these criteria:

(3) They had to be films about working-class life in which an economic consideration is important. "Marty" and "A Catered Affair," in which workers strive to become "owner-operators" or self-employed, are therefore included, but "Moonstruck," which has similar ethnic characters, is not.

(4) They had to be films about a political movement tied closely to the interests of organized labor. The Polish film "To Kill a Priest" is included because of its subject's ties to the Solidarity movement, but "Romero" (on a similar topic in Latin America, the assassination of a priest) is not.

(5) They had to focus on production or the struggle between labor and capital from a "top-down"—either entrepreneurial or managerial—perspective. "Tucker"

is included, but "Citizen Kane" (in part a portrait of newspaper mogul William Randolph Hearst) is not.

The third category includes several left-wing films because the subjects of these films have historically been associated with certain sectors of the labor movement, but such films have not been included simply because of their politics. *Cineaste*, a journal that specializes in the political analysis of films, published a list of the "Ten Best Political Films, 1967–1987" (16.2, 1987–88): two of the films on the list, "Harlan County U.S.A." and "Man of Marble," are included in this guide; eight other excellent films, including Bernardo Bertolucci's "The Conformist" and Constantine Costa-Gavras's "Missing," do not satisfy any of the five criteria and are not included here.

A selection of foreign films (but not an exhaustive list by any means) is included, but the majority of films in the guide were "made in the USA." Several that are not available on video are included as well. I have also included several important documentaries, both those released as theatrical feature films (such as "Roger & Me") and nontheatrical titles (such as "The Willmar 8") that have special labor—and labor history—significance. (Although police officers, cowboys, and professional athletes are certainly "working" in virtually every film in which they appear, films about characters in these occupations are not listed in this guide.)

The decision to include films that are not currently available on video was based on several considerations. Some of these films are routinely discussed in studies of labor-related film. Others occasionally show up on cable TV. And a few may become available on video in the near future. Perhaps this guide will even exert some influence in bringing unavailable titles back into distribution.

Trends and Themes

Important studies of labor-related films have been published over the years and are cited in various entries in this book. The most extensive is Peter Stead's *Film and the Working Class: The Feature Film in British and American Society* (London: Routledge, 1989), which charts the portrayal of working-class life from silent-era films through the Hollywood features of the 1970s. The films from the 1930s that are included in this guide (the American "Black Fury" and the British "The Stars Look Down," for example) support Stead's contention that the "social realism" of the early decades—when "working people who were drawn into picture-houses were not surprised to see the kinds of communities in which they lived, the kinds of homes in which they reared their families, and even occasionally the kind of workplace where they spent their days depicted in the movies"—was gradually supplanted in Hollywood and elsewhere by the glamorous "world of entertainment" represented in comedies, romances, and adventures.

When we are confronted by the contradictions of "Gold Diggers of 1933"—leggy chorus girls dancing with neon-lit violins and homeless veterans—Stead's survey is a good reminder that "it is always dangerous to generalize about the content of Hollywood's output because the industry could always afford to experiment, to cater for sectional interests, and to indulge eccentric or visiting European directors," but that when working-class people went to the movies, "they no longer expected to see that real world with which they were so familiar."

Surveying fewer films than Stead and concentrating almost exclusively on Hollywood films through the 1980s, William J. Puette in *Through Jaundiced Eyes: How the Media View Organized Labor* (Ithaca, N.Y.: ILR Press, 1992) argues that "with few exceptions, [the portrayal of unions in the media, particularly in movies] has been both unrepresentative and virulently negative." Films such as "On the Waterfront" from the 1950s and "The Molly Maguires" and "Blue Collar" from the 1970s all support Puette's argument that the common refrain in Hollywood is that "unions are by nature violent and mired in corruption." Peter Rottman and Jim Purdy's *The Hollywood Social Problem Film* (Bloomington: Indiana University Press, 1981) also provides an excellent survey of many of the films in this guide from the 1930s throught the 1950s.

Ken Margolies's pioneering essay, "Silver Screen Tarnishes Unions," which appeared in *Screen Actor* (Summer 1981), covered some of the same ground as Puette's survey and, like Puette, noted some of the exceptions to "Hollywood's common refrain," such as "Norma Rae." A somewhat more narrow essay but fascinating in its original research was Francis Walsh's "The Films We Never Saw: American Movies View Organized Labor, 1934–1954," published in *Labor History* 27 (1986). Using manuscript sources, Walsh tracked the production history of such films as "Black Fury" from the 1930s and "How Green Was My Valley" and "An American Romance" in the 1940s. He argues that the pro-labor militancy of these films was constantly compromised in their early stages (e.g., during scriptwriting) by studio heads who consistently caved into pressures from censors, government officials, and manufacturers' organizations.

Although this book is intended to be a guide and not a general study of labor-related films, it should supplement the previous studies as well as expand their field of coverage. By including both documentaries and foreign films, this book encompasses a wider range of film images of labor produced both within and outside Hollywood. Furthermore, it reflects three significant changes in film production since the 1970s that are resulting in more varied, less stereotypical images of labor.

First, there has been an explosion in labor-related documentary filmmaking which made the selection of the thirty-two documentaries in this guide difficult. Some of these films have established themselves as classics ("Harvest of Shame," Edward R. Murrow's investigative report on migrant workers, and "Salesman," the

Maysle brothers' breakthrough in cinema verité), while others ("With Babies and Banners" or "The Life and Times of Rosie the Riveter") offer new (often feminist) perspectives on labor history sorely missed in early documentaries. Barbara Kopple won two Academy Awards for her "purely" labor films ("Harlan County U.S.A." and "American Dream"), an unprecedented accomplishment, while Michael Moore's spoof on the chairman of General Motors ("Roger & Me") was the first major labor-related documentary to make real money in commercial theaters.

But even after these obvious half-dozen or so titles were included, the list of possibilities remained immense. In the end I selected documentaries partly because of their venerable status ("The Inheritance"), partly because of their status as pieces of investigative journalism ("Who Killed Vincent Chin?"), and partly because they made an interesting pairing with a feature film ("Hoffa: The True Story" with "Hoffa" or "Collision Course" with "Wall Street").

Second, the number of independent filmmakers working *close to* and sometimes *in* but never totally *as part of* Hollywood grew significantly in the 1980s. To a major extent, the explosion described above has occurred for this reason. Most documentary filmmakers operate outside the Hollywood system and develop their films with the help of foundations, patrons, labor and other community organizations, and even personal funds. Another group of independent filmmakers has evolved, however, who would have to be described as mavericks. This group would include John Sayles ("Matewan"), Julie Dash ("Daughters of the Dust"), and Charles Burnett ("Killer of Sheep" and "To Sleep with Anger"). Their work is quasi-independent of Hollywood studios, but they sometimes enter into alliances with the studios either for budgetary reasons or after they have achieved a reputation for their filmmaking.

Third, the made-for-TV films included in this guide to a certain extent fit one stereotype of labor films: they are violent in nature and gangster-related. "Act of Vengeance," "Blood Feud," and "Teamster Boss" also follow the trend among labor-related docudramas to deal with actual incidents in the lives (and deaths) of such figures as Jock Yablonski of the United Mine Workers, and Jimmy Hoffa and Jackie Presser, both of the Teamsters. Combining gangsterism with virtually any other favorite TV topic (for example, the Kennedys) is also typical of this group.

The number of films devoted to African-American struggles is perhaps surprising then. Possibly because of the success of "Roots," both cable and public broadcasting stations sponsored a wider range of such films. In this group I would include two films about slavery ("Half Slave, Half Free" and "Uncle Tom's Cabin") and two about black family life and economic survival ("The Killing Floor" and the second version of "A Raisin in the Sun").

Although no list of labor-related films is likely to be complete, certain trends in subjects are nonetheless obvious. More than 10 percent of the films included here are about mining and miners' communities; only the auto industry and waterfront workers, which have eleven and seven films, respectively, come close. Barbara Kopple, Martin Ritt, and King Vidor have the most titles represented here (four each). Clearly, Teamster leader Jimmy Hoffa is the labor leader about whom a significant number of films have been made (four). Although union struggles are featured prominently in several films, not all identify actual AFL-CIO unions. Images of labor continue to appear in major Hollywood films (Danny DeVito's "Hoffa" and John Turturro's "Mac"), but cable and made-for-TV films ("Teamster Boss" or "The Burning Season") may eventually dominate the cultural arena.

How Is This Guide Organized?

Each of the entries in this guide includes essential information about the production, cast lists, and other relevant data, such as the film's rating. I have tried to refine the overbroad classification of "R" films to make the rating as clear as possible. It simply is not helpful to classify both Michael Moore's "Roger & Me" and Oliver Stone's "Natural Born Killers," for example, as R-rated films, since the only thing possibly offensive in Moore's film is his attitude toward General Motors and his hometown of Flint (and perhaps the president of the United Automobile Workers). "Last Exit to Brooklyn," also included in this guide, should be R rated, however, because of, among other things, an extended scene of a gang rape.

For each entry I included a brief list of related print material and films, and most of these films are also discussed in this guide; titles that are bracketed are not entries in the guide but are of interest nonetheless. When a film or topic is particularly controversial ("The Molly Maguires," for example, or "American Dream"), I have tended to include a longer reading list.

Because many of the issues addressed in certain films—not to mention the films themselves—are controversial, I have tried to provide background materials and interpretations from many different popular and scholarly sources. One of the easiest sources of reviews is the *New York Times*, since most libraries contain bound volumes of selected reviews and back issues on microfilm. Likewise, I refer to some reviews from *Variety*, one of Hollywood's trade newspapers, because they are also easily available in bound volumes or on microfilm in many libraries. (All *Variety* reviews are cited in this guide by date from the bound volumes.)

If the *Times* and *Variety*, are too predictable for some tastes, many libraries have other reference materials, in both hard copy and computer-based forms. Documentary films are always harder to research, although both the computerized Info-Trac (for example) and the venerable *Reader's Guide to Periodical Literature* will lead the reader to articles about the subject of the documentaries if not the documentaries themselves.

An Evolving List

I have tried to strike a balance in my commentary between studied objectivity and bemused partisanship. Some films, although they are about important topics, need warning labels ("Blue Collar," for example); others are so controversial—some individuals think "American Dream" is taboo—that my commentary can only suggest the range of differing opinions.

Almost every entry includes a plot summary, the historical and cultural context surrounding the subject of the film, critical commentary, and personal judgment. How successful the latter will be in guiding the reader to titles that meet his or her needs can be put to a simple test: read my entry on a film you have never seen, rent it, then compare your judgment with mine. If it is a match, you have the right guide! If it is not a match, I hope you will at least see why I have made the comments I have.

Certainly there are arguments for including other films and excluding some that I have included, not to mention some I may simply have overlooked. If certain combinations of films or a film and a reading have worked successfully for you in the classroom or in film programs, let me know. Please send your comments and suggestions to Tom Zaniello, Literature and Language, Northern Kentucky University, Highland Heights, KY 41099, or FAX me at 606-572-5566, or E-mail me at zaniello@nku.edu.

Availability of the Films

The majority of films listed in this guide are available in VHS format at major videocassette rental outlets. I have rated the ease of rental access (and any special circumstances) according to the following key words:

Easy: available at major videocassette rental chains like Blockbuster
Not currently available: not currently available in any format
Selected collections: available at unusually well stocked rental stores, public libraries, universities, and through labor unions and archives
16 mm: available in reel-to-reel, 16-millimeter film only

Several entries also list a rental source: check the "Address List of Film Rental Sources."

Because videocassettes go in and out of "print" quite regularly, consult a video guide or your rental source before making any assumptions about availability. Movies Unlimited has many of the films in this guide for sale, while Evergreen Video and Facets have many of them for sale or rental.

A Note on Abbreviations

I have used the standard Motion Picture Association codes (R, PG, PG-13, G) as well as the following abbreviations:

TVM = TV movie
M = mature audience (a TV movie rating)
B & W = black-and-white film

Acknowledgments

The students and faculty of the George Meany Center for Labor Studies have been important allies in constructing the list of films in this guide and have discussed many of them with me. Many thanks for all of the suggestions and ideas. Several students were especially helpful in locating titles: Michelle Kikta, Rick Moralez, Terry Nicoludis, and Cosmo Mannella.

David Alexander, senior staff associate at the George Meany Center, read an early draft of this guide and made very helpful suggestions. Director Bob Pleasure, associate director Jeff McDonald, College Degree Program coordinator Diana Linton, and program assistant Claudette Lewis have all created an environment that has made teaching at the center a truly stimulating experience.

Paul Reichardt, chair of the Literature and Language Department at Northern Kentucky University, and my colleague Bob Collier have been very supportive over the years: without their recent help, this project could not easily have been completed. I have also used material in this book for my classes at Northern Kentucky University; thus, my students and colleagues there have often been unacknowledged collaborators in my study of these films.

Several reviewers for ILR Press also made important recommendations. I am grateful for all their advice: Joseph Agonito, Judy Ancel, Ken Margolies, Robb Mitchell, William J. Puette, Jim Rundle, and Alan Harris Stein. Dexter Arnold made valuable suggestions as well. If I have not always followed their advice, I have only myself to blame. John Alberti of Northern Kentucky University made a number of very helpful suggestions on an earlier draft of this book.

I am very grateful to Sharon Taylor of the Interlibrary Loan Office and Nancy

Hands of the Educational Media Service, both of Northern Kentucky University, who have been helpful on numerous occasions. The librarians and staff of the Cincinnati Public Library (especially the Film and Recordings Desk) and the Northern Kentucky University Library (especially the Periodicals Room) have been (as always) wonderfully helpful.

The AFL-CIO Film/Videotape Library, Appalshop (especially Carolyn Sturgil), California Newsreel, the Cinema Guild, Filmakers Library, the former New York State School of Industrial and Labor Relations AV Center (especially Steve Truesdail), and Women Make Movies have facilitated my research in many kind ways. The National Film Theatre of London has, by its innovative and eclectic programming, always been an inspiration.

A very special "thank you" goes to Frances Benson, editor-in-chief of Cornell University Press, whose interest in this project has been exemplary.

T. Z.

Address Lists of Sources

Film Rental Sources

AFL-CIO Film/Videotape Library
815 16th St. NW, Room 407
Washington, DC 20006

Appalshop
306 Madison St.
Whitesburg, KY 41858

California Newsreel
149 Ninth St., #420
San Francisco, CA 94103

Cinema Guild
1697 Broadway, Suite 506
New York, NY 10019-5904

Films Inc.
5547 N. Ravenswood Ave.
Chicago, IL 60640-1199

Filmakers Library
124 East 40th St.
New York, NY 10016

ILR Media
Media Services Resource Center
7–8 Business and Technology Park
Ithaca, NY 14850

Indiana University Audio-Visual Center
Bloomington, IN 47405-5901

New Day Films
22-D Hollywood Ave.
Hohokus, NJ 07423

Swank
350 Vanderbilt Motor Parkway
Hauppange, NY 11787

Third World Newsreel
335 W. 38th St., 5th floor
New York, NY 10018

Women Make Movies
462 Broadway, Suite 500C
New York, NY 10013

Sources of Videocassettes for Sale

Ambrose Video
1290 Sixth Ave., Suite 2245
New York, NY 10104

Evergreen Video
228 West Houston St.
New York, NY 10014

Facets Video
1517 West Fullerton Ave.
Chicago, IL 60614

Kino Video
333 W. 39th St., Suite 503
New York, NY 10018

Movies Unlimited
6736 Castor Ave.
Philadelphia, PA 19149-2184

Act of Vengeance

Act of viciousness

1986, 96 mins., TVM, M
Director: John MacKenzie
Screenplay: Scott Spenser, from Trevor
 Armbrister's nonfiction book of the same
 title
CAST
Jock Yablonski = Charles Bronson
Margaret Yablonski = Ellen Burstyn
Charlotte Yablonski = Carolyn Kava

Ken Yablonski = Alf Humphreys
Chip Yablonski = Joseph Knell
Paul Gilly = Robert Schenkkan
Annette Gilly = Ellen Barkin
Tony Boyle = Wilford Brimley
Terrance Madden = Raynor Scheine
Claude Vealy = Maury Chaykin
Buddy Palmer = Keanu Reeves

On 30 December 1969, Jock Yablonski, his wife, Margaret, and their daughter, Charlotte, were murdered by three men who were hired by intermediaries for Tony Boyle, the president of the United Mine Workers of America (UMWA). Although he had worked for Boyle for years, Yablonski had decided six months earlier to challenge him for the presidency.

Trevor Armbrister's book and the film argue that Yablonski might have had to tolerate Boyle's lack of sympathy after one mining disaster too many. In November 1968, a Farmington, West Virginia, Consolidation Coal Company mine had trapped seventy-eight miners after a coal gas explosion. Two days after the blast, Boyle appeared in Farmington and called it "an unfortunate accident." Although Consolidation had received numerous federal safety citations, Boyle announced that it was "one of the better companies to work with as far as cooperation and safety [were] concerned." The company's "reply" was to seal up the mine a week later, after many more explosions. The trapped men were given up for lost.

John L. Lewis, the UMWA's president for many years and a popular and influential leader, had selected Boyle as his assistant in 1948. In 1963, Boyle succeeded this man whose bushy eyebrows and powerful voice made him virtually an icon of tough and dedicated union service. Boyle had little or none of Lewis's charisma—his dyed reddish-brown hair was not a folksy touch.

The film opens with three parallel-edited sequences at different locations. It is an obvious but effective way of developing an uneasy "triangle": Jock Yablonski's happy home life with his extended family, Tony Boyle giving a speech following a performance by a sexy African-American singer at a UMWA testimonial dinner, and miners in a pit facing a deadly explosion. In short (and perhaps too obvious): the good, the bad, and the dangerous.

Bronson, playing Yablonski, seems to have wandered onto the set from his usual action picture. He seems uncomfortable as the union go-fer for Boyle and married to an intellectual. (Unlike Jock, who stopped school in the tenth grade, Margaret Yablonski was college-educated and aspired to be a writer.) The film has scenes of union politics, on both the local and the national level, but the director was clearly in a hurry to introduce Yablonski's killers and to make this more of a TV crime film (filled with violence and scuzziness) than a film about union politics.

The first two killers are incredibly inept, stupid, and dangerous yet terrifyingly brutal specimens of riffraff. They are so real they are genuinely scary. (The more repulsive one at one point brags, "I f—— shot my old lady, and she didn't press charges!") They are also cowardly. After the arrival of the third killer, however, played brilliantly and diabolically by Keanu Reeves, the film becomes a "real" Bronson movie (like his "Deathwish" series), that is, one filled with senseless shooting and the slaughter of innocents, although, as in real life, the Bronson character does not survive.

See also: "Harlan County U.S.A."
Availability: Easy.
Further reading: Armbrister, Trevor. *Act of Vengeance.* New York: Saturday Review Press, 1975. The source book for the film.
Geoghegan, Tom. *Which Side Are You On?* New York: Farrar, Straus, 1991. A union lawyer's reminiscences, including some about the Boyle years.
Zieger, Robert H. *John L. Lewis, Labor Leader.* New York: Twayne, 1988. Includes background on the Yablonski-Boyle struggle in the context of Lewis's ailing last years.

∾
Adalen 31

Romance and the picket line

1969, 115 mins., Swedish (with English subtitles), X (some disturbing violence, but film should be an R)
Director: Bo Widerberg
Screenplay: Bo Widerberg
CAST
Kjell = Peter Schildt
Kjell's Mother = Kerstin Tidelius
Kjell's Father = Roland Hedlund
Ake = Stefan Feierbach
Martin = Martin Widerberg
Anna = Marie De Geer
Manager = Olof Bergstrom
Manager's Wife = Anita Bjork
Nisse = Jonas Bergstrom
Strikebreaker = Olle Bjorling
Foreman = Pierre Lindstedt

The somewhat unusual title of this film refers to the year 1931 (14 May 1931 to be precise), when five sawmill workers were killed during a demonstration in Adalen, Sweden. A bitter strike had dragged on for months before the authorities called in strikebreakers and eventually the army.

Sawmill workers march for their rights in Adalen, Sweden, in 1931. Courtesy British Film Institute Stills, Posters, and Designs.

A sensitive young worker, Kjell, spends a lot of time with the sawmill manager and his family—they wish to cultivate his talents—until he falls in love with their daughter, Anna. Once she becomes pregnant, crossing over class lines is no longer possible. When Kjell's father is then killed during the demonstration, all options for Kjell are narrowed considerably.

The strike of 1931 has been credited with bringing the Social Democrats into power in Sweden and with the permanent exit of the Conservatives. The titles at the end of the film acknowledge that the events in a sense created Sweden's "welfare state." Leonard Maltin, in his *Movie and Video Guide*, accurately observed that, despite the political weight of the film's subject, "no one will ever mistake Widerberg . . . for a gritty filmmaker of social realism."

The essence of Widerberg's art seems to be in his protrayal of doomed but heroic lovers, at least two of whom (Kjell in this film and Joe Hill in the film of that title) are no less romantically inclined than the officer in Widerberg's apolitical film of thwarted love, "Elvira Madigan." Critic Stig Björkman has argued in Widerberg's defense that his heroes are romantics who are rebelling against the domination of the upper classes, so that it does not matter whether the struggle is played out on the factory floor or in army barracks (as in "Elvira Madigan").

"Adalen 31" has the mixture of politics and "poetic" imagery that is characteristic of Widerberg's filmmaking. Children on the roof of a barn in the northern Swedish town of Norrland jump off, flapping little homemade wings. Fortunately for them, there is a haystack below. With seduction of the local young women in mind, a young man takes a correspondence course in hypnotism. When he finally induces a trance in one young lady, he doesn't know what to do next. These are small but lovely touches. When Kjell's father is killed, however, wearing the clean shirt his wife just readied for him, Kjell tears up the shirt and side by side with his brothers and mother begins to clean some dusty windowpanes. The detail here is visually strong, but its message is more charged with significance than the other more poignant incidents.

Widerberg's young man (like the director himself, argued Vincent Canby), is "slightly schizoid," torn apart by loyalties to two conflicting classes. But in a Widerberg film, even this conflict becomes lyrical: at Anna's house Kjell learns to play Chopin; later he will go to the People's House and practice the "Internationale" with the workers' band.

See also: "Joe Hill."
Availability: 16 mm; Films Inc.
Further reading: Björkman, Stig. *Film in Sweden: The New Directors.* London: Tantivy Press, 1977. A thorough survey of Widerberg's career and films.
Canby, Vincent. "Adalen 31." *New York Times*, 20 Sept. 1969, 21. Emphasizes the clash between Widerberg's political interests and his "barely controlled passion for visual images so lush they are intoxicating in a numbing way."
Note: The title is sometimes rendered with an apostrophe, as "Adalen '31."

∿
Alamo Bay

Vietnamese immigrants as Mexicans in Texas

1985, 98 mins., R (not really: suitable for mature children)
Director: Louis Malle
Screenplay: Alice Arlen
CAST
Shang = Ed Harris
Glory = Amy Madigan
Dinh = Ho Nguyen
Wally = Donald Moffat
Ben = Truyen V. Tran
Skinner = Rudy Young
Honey = Cynthia Carle
Luis = Martino Lasalle
Mac = William Frankfather
Ab Crankshaw = Lucky Mosley
Sheriff = Bill Thurman
Wendell = Michael Ballard

Glory (Amy Madigan) and Shang (Ed Harris) disagree in "Alamo Bay" on whether Vietnamese immigrants should be allowed to work in the local fishing industry.

The struggle between "native" Texan fishermen and recent Vietnamese immigrants on the Texas Gulf Coast lasted for three years (1978–81), during which the Texans and the Klan attacked the Vietnamese for taking away their livelihood. Although the Vietnamese were anticommunist Catholics, the Texans treated them as if they were a battalion of the Viet Cong.

The film is a loose interpretation of the shooting of Billy Joe Aplin by Sau Van Nguyen in Seadrift, Texas, in 1978. The Catholic Vietnamese immigrant was acquitted because the jury (apparently) believed he fired on Aplin after the Texas fisherman repeatedly beat him. (Aplin's family had also wandered the South for a number of years in search of work.) The trial was the culmination of a form of guerrilla war in which Texans and Vietnamese cut each other's crab pot lines, let moored boats go adrift, and fished illegally at night (although both sides said they were only out to protect their lines from the *others*). The violence, however, was mostly one-sided, as the Vietnamese were often the victims of racist attacks, eventually led by the Klan.

The filmmakers simplified this complex story. Shang, whose behavior and attitudes resemble Aplin's, is at first a fairly passive villain. He clearly reflects the sentiments of most of the Texas fishermen who taunted the Vietnamese at every opportunity. Only Glory, the daughter of a waterfront fish wholesaler, and Dinh, a recent Vietnamese immigrant, have the nerve to stand up to the Klan. Unfortunately, Glory has also been romantically involved with Shang, who becomes an angry leader of a group of Vietnam vets the Klan is recruiting. His jealousy when Glory sides with the Vietnamese (and he cannot have her as his girlfriend) makes him murderous. When the proceeds from his daily catch cannot support the payments for his new boat, he blames the Vietnamese for stealing his fish and launches a bay "lockout" against the Vietnamese and Glory's business. The result is a vicious parody of a workers' action to protect their jobs.

The Klan and the fishermen, most of whom are armed Vietnam vets, make a frightening combination in the film. When a flotilla of fishing boats, each dotted with a robed Klansman and a vet riding shotgun, sail into the harbor to police and intimidate the Vietnamese, Louis Malle's almost cartoonish vision of American violence seems more than vindicated.

The film's Klan leader is modeled closely on the real-life Klan organizer that Ross Milloy profiled in his article on the incidents on which the film is based. This leader's attempt to organize "his people" would be ludicrous if it were not so murderous in its implications: "We are already aware of Communist agents among the refugee community who are actively stirring up trouble between blacks, Mexicans, and Vietnamese in Houston and elsewhere in the United States. There are a number of Vietnam veterans like myself who might want to do some good old search and destroy right here in Texas. They don't have to ship me 12,000 miles to kill Communists. I can do it right here. They trained me for it, and with sufficent motivation, I'm ready."

Perhaps because of Malle's outsider status—he had already been successful in France as a director before he made films in the United States—he likes to portray complex actions with simple symbols: the vets fly their American flag upside down as a sign of distress, but new immigrant Dinh affects a ten-gallon hat to look more American; Shang's boat (confiscated for his failure to keep up with the payments) is named *American Dream Girl*, while Dinh's first boat (really just a dinghy) is named *Glory* (as Shang points out, Dinh didn't know it is bad luck to name a boat "after a girl").

The film is an engrossing if uneven exploration of the competition for work, and some of the awkward moments may not seem that way to viewers with limited contact with immigrant workers. When Dinh is recounting to Glory all he had to do to escape the Viet Cong's murderous attack on his village in South Vietnam, she ignores the killings and says, "You had to eat grass?!"

Although there is no Alamo Bay in Texas, there certainly was a Battle for the Alamo, and Malle captures in his title the siege mentality of the Texas vets when faced with a wave of "Mexicans" they thought they had defeated. Besides the film's title, Malle points to the violent history of Texas in a brief scene featuring a worker named Luis. When Shang asks Luis what he thinks of the "Vietmanese" (sic) using up all the fish, Luis replies, simply enough, "I'm a Mexican," and refuses to comment further.

Screenwriter Arlen was also the coauthor with Nora Ephron of "Silkwood." Both screenplays demonstrate a feel for the frustrations of workers who are being "displaced," they think, by the manipulation of liberal do-gooders.

See also: "Who Killed Vincent Chin?"

Availability: Easy.

Further reading: Canby, Vincent. "Screen: 'Alamo Bay,' Ethnic Strife in Texas." *New York Times*, 3 April 1985, C23. A negative but comprehensive review: "Its mediocrity is especially surprising," considering the director's previous credits.

Milloy, Ross. "Vietnam Fallout in a Texas Town." *New York Times Magazine*, 6 April 1980, 39–56. A comprehensive article about the original events retold in the film.

New York Times. "Americans and Vietnamese Agree on Fishing Limits," 17 April 1980, 20; "Videotapes of Klan Leader Shown at Shrimper Hearing," 13 May 1981, A18; "750 Attend Klan Rally for Fishermen in Texas," 15 Feb. 1981, I.36. Samples of the news coverage of the Seadrift incidents and the Klan's involvement, highlighting (in the second article) "a fishing dinghy labeled 'U.S.S. Viet Cong.'"

American Dream

Local P-9 versus everybody in the Hormel strike

1989, 100 mins., PG-13
Director: Barbara Kopple
Unscripted documentary
PRINCIPAL FIGURES
Jim Guyette, president, Local P-9
Ray Rogers, consultant, Corporate Campaign, Inc.
Lewie Anderson, chief negotiator,

Meatpacking Division, United Food and Commercial Workers Union (UFCW)
Bill Wynn, international president, UCFW
Ron and R. G. Bergstrom, P-9 members and brothers
John Morrison, P-9 member and opponent of Guyette and Rogers

"American Dream" earned Kopple her second Academy Award for documentary; her first was for the classic "Harlan County U.S.A.," which, like many documentaries that focus on labor conflict, presents the perspectives of two groups: labor and management. In the case of "American Dream," the conflict was between Local P-9 of the United Food and Commercial Workers Union and Hormel Meats of Austin, Minnesota, but there were *three* sides to present: that of the local union, its international union, and management. And, just in case we want to avoid blaming the messenger, Kopple didn't make up the three sides. They were depressingly real.

Kopple and her crew worked on this film for five years, first as part of the action in Minnesota soon after the strike began in 1985. When asked how she felt about working on the same project for so long, she replied: "I feel really lucky. I feel lucky because I've been trusted by people. I've been able to go in behind closed doors and have people really trust me. I've had people pour out their hearts and souls to me and not feel awkward about doing it" (Di Mattia).

The strike began when Hormel requested a cut in pay and other givebacks during contract negotiations. This goaded Local P-9 into a strike, because of a complicated contract settlement in 1978, in which P-9 in a sense had agreed to subsidize a new $100 million plant (to keep Hormel in Austin) by putting workers' incentive pay into an escrow account that floated a $20 million loan to Hormel. Hormel had violated this contract by making new demands. Although the local had always been militant (a sitdown strike in 1933 had created the local), it had not had a strike since 1933.

Unfortunately, the local's new-found militancy did not meet with the approval of the United Food and Commercial Workers, whose leaders felt that the strike was ill timed and did not accord with their national strategy of pattern bargaining, which might involve some concessions. Further disagreements arose when P-9 decided to hire the controversial Ray Rogers, head of Corporate Campaign, Inc., as a consultant.

Kopple's approach in developing this complicated situation also helped to create controversy over the film. Because she so carefully presents the strengths and weaknesses of all three sides in the conflict and because she profiled three extremely strong participants (P-9 president Jim Guyette, Ray Rogers, and Lew Anderson of the UFCW), viewers are sometimes mystified as to her position.

Of course, the simple answer is that she supports no particular group: as a documentary filmmaker, she supposedly records; she doesn't judge. This has never been her style, however, but neither has she ever had to choose between two labor "allies," a local and its international.

Despite what appear to be Kopple's efforts to let her characters "speak" for themselves, I have always felt that Ray Rogers comes off much less positively than Guyette or Anderson. Rogers seems somewhat arrogant, more than a little disdainful of the gains international unions have made. Both Rogers and Guyette feel that the UFCW is selling them down the river, conceding too much to the company.

By the time the film ends, the gloom is pervasive. Brothers are enemies, and a rump caucus, nicknamed "P-10" by the P-9 loyalists, is criticizing Guyette's handling of the strike. Eventually, it gained control of the local. Rogers's strategy is shown at least in this instance to be unsuccessful.

At least three books have been written about the strike. Consulting some of them (or articles about it) may be necessary before viewers can make a final judgment on the struggles Kopple captures so well in the film.

See also: "Fallen Champ"; "Harlan County U.S.A."

Availability: Selected collections.

Further reading: Crowdus, Gary, and Richard Porton. "American Dream: An Interview with Barbara Kopple." *Cineaste* 18 (1991): 37–38, 41+. A detailed discussion of her access to participants in all aspects of the conflict.

Di Mattia, Joseph. "Of Politics and Passion." *International Documentary* (Winter 1990–91): 12–16. Another good interview with Kopple.

Geoghegan, Thomas. *Which Side Are You On?* New York: Farrar, Straus, 1991. A Chicago labor lawyer's memoir, it is melancholy and pessimistic about the labor movement but strong on its discussion of individuals; matches the mood of Kopple's film.

Green, Hardy. *On Strike at Hormel.* Philadelphia: Temple University Press, 1990. Anti-UFCW book by a former Corporate Campaign associate (now a *Business Week* writer).

Hage, Dave, and Paul Klauda. *No Retreat, No Surrender: Labor's War at Hormel.* New York: Morrow, 1989. A detailed, readable, fairly neutral account of the strike by two reporters.

Klawans, Stuart. "Films." *Nation*, 30 March 1992, 425–28. An excellent review: the film is "moving; it's absorbing; it understands everything but is too wise to pardon all."

Main, Jeremy. "The Labor Rebel Leading the Hormel Strike." *Fortune*, 9 June 1986, 105–10. A positive profile of Rogers, the controversial labor consultant, although the article states: "Consultant Ray Rogers looked like an organizing genius after his tactics helped force textile giant J. P. Stevens Co. to sign a union contract. Today he is leading Hormel's strikers to disastrous defeat."

" 'More' Is Less and Less: Thirties Tactics, Unions Learn, Don't Work in the Eighties." *Barron's*, 24 Feb. 1986, 11. An early gloating editorial in the business press about P-9 fighting the international.

Rachleff, Peter. *Hard-Pressed in the Heartland: The Hormel Strike and the Future of the Labor Movement.* Boston: South End Press, 1993. A leader of community support groups for the strike criticizes Kopple's film for being too pro-UFCW.

Roberts, Sam. " 'American Dream' Charts Labor's Loss." *New York Times*, 24 May 1992, II.16. Reviews the film as "a labor nightmare from real life."

Rule, Sheila. "A Film Maker Balancing the Inequities of Life." *New York Times*, 24 March 1992, B1, B3. Another interview with Kopple and a survey of her career.

Slaughter, Jane. "Ray Rogers: 'Workers Don't Have to Keep Losing.' " *Progressive*, June 1988, 26–28. An interview with Rogers: "There have to be reforms in unions like the UFCW. There are some awfully sleazy leaders at the top of the labor movement, and they are the biggest obstacles to workers winning."

∾
An American Romance

Labor and capital make nice.

1944, 122 mins., unrated, but suitable for all
  ages
Director: King Vidor
Screenplay: Herbert Dalmas and William
  Ludwig

CAST
Steve Dangos = Brian Donlevy
Anna = Ann Richards
Howard Clinton = Walter Abel
Anton Dubechek = John Qualen
Teddy Dangos = Stephen McNally

Having made two successful films with populist themes in the 1930s ("Our Daily Bread" and "The Citadel"), Vidor saw his predominantly progressive spirit apparently evaporate in the war years that followed. Perhaps his jettisoning the first script for "An American Romance," by Louis Adamic, the chronicler of American labor violence in *Dynamite* (1934), was a mistake; as Francis R. Walsh has argued, the new scriptwriter gave Vidor a Horatio Alger (rags-to-riches) story with a bizarre strike as its resolution.

Immigrant Steve Dangos starts out as a iron worker in the Mesabi Range of Minnesota, moves to an Ohio steel mill, and eventually gains control of his own auto company! Because the post-Adamic script eliminated a sit-down strike at his auto factory—in response to the Breen Office's censorship of the most important union tactic of the 1930s—Steve's workers miraculously disappear from the factory at one moment only to reappear with Steve's son, Teddy, as their bargaining representative. (He had been "learning the line" on the factory floor.) In a scene reminiscent of the father-son (brain-heart) unity of Fritz Lang's "Metropolis" and with some new lessons in fascistic collectivism (Teddy: "Why don't we have faith in each other?"), the strike is settled.

Vidor's faith in an "open-shop" industry is obvious, as is his belief in the intrinsic power and beauty of the American factory: documentary footage, shot by Vidor himself, of an auto assembly line and of an aircraft factory reinforce the view that the unions have a formidable job, especially if they choose the boss's son as their negotiator.

See also: "The Citadel"; "The Fountainhead"; "Our Daily Bread."
Availability: 16 mm; Swank.
Further reading: Dowd, Nancy, and David Shepard (interviewers). *King Vidor*. Metuchen, N.J.:
  Scarecrow Press, 1988. Among other things, discusses Vidor's inclusion of documentary-
  type industrial sequences in the film.
Walsh, Francis R. "The Films We Never Saw: American Movies View Organized Labor, 1934–
  1954." *Labor History* 27 (1986): 564–80. Contains an excellent short section on the produc-
  tion of the film.

ॐ The Angry Silence

Like murderous bees

1960, 95 mins., B & W, unrated, but suitable
    for all
Director: Guy Green
Screenplay: Bryan Forbes
CAST
Tom = Richard Attenborough

Anna = Pier Angeli
Joe = Michael Craig
Connolly = Bernard Lee
Travers = Alfred Burke
Davis = Geoffrey Keen
Martindale = Laurence Naismith

Faced with a walkout by his union local—unsanctioned by the national and led by an unscrupulous shop leader following the advice of an outsider (no doubt a communist)—family man Tom (played by Richard Attenborough, who also coproduced the film) says "no" to the strike and returns to work. For this act of defiance, he is sent "into Coventry" (given the silent treatment) by his mates, bullied by the shop steward, and betrayed by his best friend; furthermore, his son is injured (in a tarring incident) and Tom is attacked and loses an eye, all because of the forces of "union solidarity." The film ekes out a happy (at least a not too sad) ending, as some of Tom's workmates show guilt and sorrow.

Because the behavior of the union members in the film was so vicious, several British unions urged a boycott. Attenborough was incensed: "This sort of fascist behavior is just what the film is about. Mob rule by a few scheming communists" (Hill). But even the *New York Times* reviewer emphasized that "a particular and arbitrary set of circumstances has been organized in this film" and that even though it is "one of the best" films of the year from Britain, one must be careful with it, "lest one find oneself distrusting the entire working class."

See also: "I'm All Right Jack"; "On the Waterfront."
Availability: Not currently available.
Further reading: Crowther, Bosley. "The Angry Silence." *New York Times*, 13 Dec. 1960, 25. An
    appreciative American review.
Hill, John. *Sex, Class, and Realism: British Cinema, 1956–1963.* London: British Film Institute,
    1986. Discusses the film in the context of other similar British features.
Stead, Peter. *Film and the Working Class.* London: Routledge, 1989. Discusses the film in the
    context of British culture and makes some interesting comparisons with "On the Water-
    front."

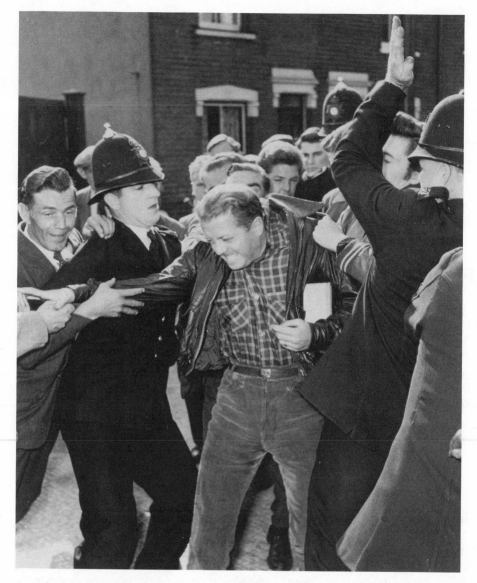

Coworkers attack strikebreaker Tom (Richard Attenborough) outside his workplace in "The Angry Silence." Courtesy British Film Institute Stills, Posters, and Designs.

At the River I Stand

"One more river to cross before I lay my burden down."

1993, 56 mins., unrated, but suitable for all ages

Directors: David Appleby, Allison Graham, Steven Ross

Scripted documentary inspired in part by Joan Turner Beifuss's nonfiction book of the same title

PRINCIPAL FIGURES

Coby Smith, community organizer and leader of the Invaders

Taylor Rogers and Clinton Burrows, sanitation workers

T. O. Jones, local union organizer

Henry Loeb, mayor of Memphis

Jerry Wurf, president, American Federation of State, County, and Municipal Employees (AFSCME)

Rev. Ralph Jackson, leader of boycott

Lewis Donelson and Bob James, city council members

Rev. James Netters, black city council member

Martin Luther King, Jr., head of the Southern Christian Leadership Council (SCLC)

Martin Luther King, Jr.'s famous "I have been to the mountaintop" speech was delivered on 3 April 1968 in Memphis, the day before he was assassinated. "At the River I Stand" reminds us that, although King went to Memphis as part of his Poor People's Campaign, he also went there because thirteen hundred sanitation workers had been on strike for higher wages and recognition of Local 1733 of AFSCME. The film is a persuasive and moving argument for the position that the Memphis sanitation strike was the culmination of the civil rights struggle in the South. In that King's assassination was a tragic part of that strike, the assassination also changed the strike's status from a local struggle to one of national significance. The assassination also signified the turn in the civil rights movement from nonviolent to violent protest (although the film suggests that that distinction may itself be problematical).

The film captures the complexity of the civil rights movement, especially its sometimes-contested leadership. There were at least four centers of leadership in Memphis as the struggle evolved: (1) the sanitation workers, strongly united behind union organizer T. O. Jones; (2) AFSCME's mostly white national leadership, especially Jerry Wurf; (3) the ministerial nonviolent civil rights leaders, including both those on the local scene and Martin Luther King, Jr.'s people; and (4) the militant youth of Memphis, including the Invaders, a black power group led by Coby Smith. Standing firm against these sometimes-united, sometimes-quarrelsome contenders for power was the Memphis establishment, led by the city's unyielding mayor, Henry Loeb.

The film carefully traces the various stages of the Memphis struggle, establishing clearly how the sanitation workers, always courted by various leaders, remained

Memphis sanitation workers on strike in 1968 in "At the River I Stand." Photo by Ernest Withers, courtesy California Newsreel.

steadfast in their determination to prove, as their most famous picket sign indicated, that they were "men." (Their signs read "I Am a Man," and they were often photographed by the national media with the tanks of the National Guard rolling down the Memphis streets behind their picket lines.)

The film, like Joan Turner Beifuss's *At the River I Stand*, took its inspiration from an oral history project involving 364 interviews done by the Memphis Search for Meaning Committee, a group formed by "progressive white Memphians" to try to understand what happened in their city.

See also: "Miles of Smiles, Years of Struggle."
Availability: Selected collections; California Newsreel.
Further reading: Beifuss, Joan Turner. *At the River I Stand: Memphis, the 1968 Strike, and Martin Luther King.* New York: Carlson, 1989. A very helpful narrative and analysis of the struggle, based on extensive interviews.

∾ The Best Years of Our Lives

If these are the best . . .

1946, 172 mins., B & W, unrated, but suitable for all ages
Director: William Wyler
Screenplay: Robert Sherwood, from MacKinlay Kantor's *Glory for Me* (a "novel in verse")
CAST
Sgt. Stephenson = Fredric March
Capt. Fred Derry = Dana Andrews
Homer Parrish = Harold Russell
Milly Stephenson = Myrna Loy
Peggy Stephenson = Teresa Wright
Butch Engle = Hoagy Carmichael
Marie Derry = Virginia Mayo
Hortense Derry = Gladys George
Wilma Cameron = Cathy O'Donnell

This drama about the reintegration of three World War II vets into their small midwestern city reminds us that this process almost always caused severe dislocations in both the men and their families who waited for them. The film, which won seven Academy Awards, offers a sensitive portrayal of how men from three different class backgrounds reestablished their lives at work and with loved ones. Postwar economic conditions affect our heroes' jobs because of gender and social class relations: Rosie the Riveter does not exist, for example, women are still mainly interested in marriage and family, and an independent woman is defined by the riffraff she hangs around with.

The film does not flinch from difficult issues in the veterans' lives: their feelings of helplessness in the face of a society that has moved on without them; the competition for jobs, especially with those "who did not go"; and the romantic and sexual tensions in their relationships with loved ones. The film was based on an unusual source—MacKinlay Kantor's best-selling "novel in verse." The book must have certainly had an incredible public reception, for a best-selling book of poetry is virtually a contradiction in terms.

Harold Russell plays Homer Parrish, a handless sailor who can handle war but is terrorized by the effect his new disability will have on his loved ones at home. Russell, who had such a disability, won one Academy Award for his role as a supporting actor and another special one for his courage. (Despite his first success, Russell never acted in a film again, preferring to work in veterans' organizations; recently, he announced he had to auction off one of his awards to raise money for his foundation for the handicapped.)

While Homer Parrish's neighborhood seems classless, those of the other returning men are more carefully situated. Fredric March plays a banker who is willing to give vets loans with just a handshake. Dana Andrews, by contrast, is a soda jerk. The social interactions of these and the other characters are complex, although easy to follow on the screen. The ironies of a war economy deflating itself are less comprehensively sketched though nonetheless convincing.

As the veterans approach their city, they see below them hundreds of war planes, some so new, they realize, that they will never be used. Later, Capt. Derry visits this graveyard of "his" old bomber planes. He is framed by the now-impotent shells of these engines of destruction, raising questions about what a warrior and a warring country do after gearing up for war. Somewhat fortuitously, Derry gets a job dismantling the planes so that the scrap metal can be recycled to make quonset huts. These huts will be used for homes as the country returns to peace.

Wyler's film was a significant step in strengthening his reputation as a popular but artistic director; two other films—"Mrs. Miniver" in 1942, about an English middle-class family during the war, and "Dodsworth" in 1936, an adaptation of Sinclair Lewis's novel about an American industrialist in Europe—were both critical and popular successes.

See also: "The Deerhunter"; "The Men."
Availability: Easy.
Further reading: Bazin, Andre. *What Is Cinema?* Trans. Hugh Gray. Vol. 1. Berkeley: University of California Press, 1967. An analysis of Wyler's cinematic techniques, which solidified his reputation as a film artist.
Crowther, Bosley. "The Best Years of Our Lives." *New York Times*, 22 Nov. 1946, 27. A glowing review—"catches the drama of veterans returning home as no film—or play or novel that we've yet heard of—has managed to do."
Kantor, MacKinlay. *Glory for Me.* New York: Coward-McCann, 1945: The source book by war correspondent Kantor, loosely adapted for the film.

Bitter Rice

Po Valley tales

1948, 107 mins., Italian with English subtitles, unrated, but suitable for mature children
Director: Giuseppe De Santis
Screenplay: Giuseppe De Santis, Carlo Lizzani, and Gianni Puccini
CAST
Silvana = Silvana Mangano
Francesca = Doris Dowling
Walter = Vittorio Gassman

Marco = Raf Vallone
Aristide = Checco Rissono
Beppe = Nico Pepe
Celeste = Adriana Silveri
Amelia = Lia Corelli
Gabriella = Maria Grazia Francia
Anna = Dedi Ristori
Irene = Anna Maestri
Gianna = Mariemma Bardi

Silvana (Silvana Mangano), one of the rice workers, in "Bitter Rice."

When earthy Silvana Mangano became internationally known for playing the doomed heroine of this film, her peasant look forced the *New York Times* reviewer to make a series of comparisons between her and other actresses: she was like "Ingrid Bergman with a Latin disposition and Rita Hayworth plus twenty-five pounds." The reviewer recognized that he was dealing with a very raw tale of migrant rice workers (*mondine*) in the Po Valley, but he appeared to miss the film's placement in the postwar Italian tradition of social realism (or *neorealism*), in which laboring folk, the criminal riffraff, and untrustworthy contract gang leaders vie for the viewer's attention.

Giuseppe De Santis, like other social realist filmmakers, often included numerous scenes with nonprofessional actors, in this case, rice field workers, whose migrant work camp, filled with women who choose to be on the make as well as the objects of leering men, has a caged-in look. Unity among the contract workers and scabs is achieved only after a spectacular brawl among the women in the rice paddies.

The melodramatic plot involves two couples joined in a lusty dance of death:

Francesca and Walter, on the lam after a jewelry theft, travel on the same train as the rice workers; at their destination, Francesca falls in love with Marco, while Walter inveigles the Hollywood star–struck Silvana ("Miss Rice Worker 1948"!) to help him steal the harvest. Silvana, with a characteristically tragic and farcical (operatic) gesture, shoots Walter, in part because he has given her a piece of worthless costume jewelry (it proves he's a liar) and then commits suicide. The climactic sequence is a classic of Italian *neorealism*: with the rice harvest safe, Silvana's companions in the fields file past her body, tossing handfuls of dry rice on her as the camera carries us away from their scene of tragic unity.

De Santis admired the films of such American directors as King Vidor ("Our Daily Bread") and John Ford ("Grapes of Wrath" and "How Green Was My Valley") for their portrayals of working people. For his film, Peter Bondanella argues, De Santis used Hollywood genres such as the gangster film (the jewel thieves), the musical (the *mondine* sing as they work), and the Western (the shootout) as models, but he also wanted to satirize the negative effects of Hollywood star ideology on working-class characters such as Silvana. Film is a fickle medium, however, and Silvana Mangano became the very type of international star De Santis thought he was satirizing.

The sequences of good, solid work in the fields almost always overshadow the Hollywood dreams in the *True Romance* magazines the rice workers read. Silvana wants to go to North America, where everything is electric, but her stolid friend Walter warns her that the *electric* chair is also American and he instead holds out the possibility of building a family in *South* America (the other destination of so many Italian emigrants in this century).

The masses of laboring women, sometimes beautiful but always strong, are the real heroines for De Santis's camera. He really can't bear to cut away from them to stick to his melodramatic plot.

See also: ["The Bicycle Thief"]; "The Organizer."
Availability: Selected collections.
Further reading: Bondanella, Peter. *Italian Cinema from Neorealism to the Present.* New York: Ungar, 2d ed., 1989. Analyzes the film and its place in Italian film history.
Crowther, Bosley. "Bitter Rice." *New York Times*, 19 Sept. 1950, 39. A very positive review—"hundreds of actual rice field workers appear in the beautiful and pulsing scenes of camp life and rice-field cultivation."

○ᴗ
Black Fury

An impossible terrorist

1935, 92 mins., B & W, unrated, but suitable for mature children	Harry R. Irving's play "Bohunk"
Director: Michael Curtiz	CAST
Screenplay: Abem Finkel and Carl Erickson, based on Michael Musmanno's and Paul Muni's screenplay "Jan Volkanik" and	Joe Radek = Paul Muni
	Anna Novak = Karen Morley
	Mike Shemanski = John Qualen
	Slim Johnson = William Gargan

It is hard to believe that Michael Curtiz directed this film and "Casablanca" just seven years later. The heavy-handed Joe Radek, who represents the miners' "black fury," will give way to Humphrey Bogart's suave and cynical Rick. Both men are fighting injustice, of course, but Joe is as good as he is dull. He has been a loyal union man, more out of friendship than solidarity. Thus, when he's drunk and jilted, he easily disrupts a union meeting by siding with a "rebel" group led by a company agent-provocateur.

Characteristic of Warner Brothers' more socially conscious productions, this was one of the first feature-length films to portray the tough life of the miners sympathetically. The story was based on a specific incident in 1929 in which a union man was brutally beaten to death by two Coal and Iron Policemen in western Pennsylvania. As a result of this murder, Ralph Musmanno, an appeals lawyer for Sacco and Vanzetti and later a crusading congressman, led a successful campaign to abolish the private armies the coal companies had considered their right for fifty years. The murder remains in the film, with its brutality intact. (See "The Molly Maguires" for another portrayal of the Coal and Iron Police.)

Many critics have commented on the unbelievable, terroristic ending: Joe sneaks into one of the main shafts of a mine, distributes dynamite, and phones topside. If the union and management don't stop the strike, he will blow up the mine and himself. He convinces them to stop the strike (it's back to business as usual, an arrangement that the union wanted in the first place), and the death of one of Joe's friends (like the historical incident) is avenged by the law. Joe even gets his girl back, "by golly."

Musmanno's original script ("Black Hell") got flack from the National Coal Association, whose executive secretary told the Hollywood Production Code Office (the so-called Breen Office, named after its chief censor) that Warner Brothers needed to be reminded that (among many other things) "the miners have little to complain" about. The conclusion of Walsh's excellent research on this episode was that "the Breen Office accomplished its goal."

See also: "How Green Was My Valley"; "The Molly Maguires"; "The Stars Look Down."

Availability: Selected collections.

Further reading: Higham, John. *Strangers in the Land: Patterns of American Nativism, 1860–1925.* 1963. Reprint. New Brunswick, N.J.: Rutgers University Press, 1988. Places racist, anti-foreigner, and anti-immigrant attitudes on the same historical and conceptual map.

Maltz, Albert. "Coal Diggers of 1935." *New Theatre,* 8–9 May 1935. Radical novelist Maltz criticizes the film's lack of realism and its ending as "a ridiculous, impossible, terroristic solution."

Musmanno, Michael A. *Verdict! The Adventures of the Young Lawyer in the Brown Suit.* New York: Random House, 1958. The autobiography of the state congressman who challenged the Coal and Iron Police.

Sennewald, Andre. "The Screen." *New York Times,* 11 April 1935, 27. "Warner Brothers exhibited almost a reckless air of courage in producing the picture at all."

"Story behind a Story." *New York Times,* 21 April 1935, X.3. Activist Musmanno meets actor Muni and the two collaborate on "Black Fury."

Walsh, Francis R. "The Films We Never Saw: American Movies View Organized Labor, 1934–1954." *Labor History* 27 (1986): 564–80. An in-depth discussion of the script, with details on behind-the-scenes maneuvering to "eliminate anything unfavorable to the coal mining industry" (Warner Brothers memo).

∽

Black Legion

A legion of racism and murder

1936, 83 mins., unrated, but suitable for
  mature children
Director: Archie Mayo
Screenplay: Abem Finkel and William
  Wister Haines
CAST
Frank Taylor = Humphrey Bogart

Ed Jackson = Dick Foran
Ruth Taylor = Erin O'Brien Moore
Betty Grogan = Ann Sheridan
Pearl Danvers = Helen Flint
Prosecuting attorney = Addison Richards
Tommy Smith = John Litel

This topical film was based on a Michigan incident involving a terrorist group called the Black Legion, which was responsible for the assassination of Charles Poole, a Works Progress Administration worker. The actual assassin, Dayton Dean, turned state's evidence at the trial and implicated the rest of his super-patriotic gang.

Bogart's fictionalized Dean, Frank Taylor, is an autoworker whose family is more than a little put upon by Depression problems, despite his decent wages. To get ahead, Frank wants to be promoted to foreman. His simple-minded anger makes Frank an easy target of a group of fascists, who recruit him when a "foreigner" named Dombrowski gets promoted instead of Frank. Film historian Peter Stead pointed out that Warner Brothers depoliticized the Black Legion by making the members more like racketeers than an overtly political group, although the studio obviously still succeeded in giving the film an authentic working-class look.

More disturbing was Warner Brothers' publicity plan (see Stead) to have hooded figures with torches in theater lobbies and even to have someone carried out of the theater to an ambulance by two of the hooded men. Although few theaters actually did this heavy hype, reviewers such as Frank S. Nugent of the *New York Times* certainly wanted the film to succeed: "I hope its message reaches the type of mind to which the Michigan's organization's aims appealed." (It may have been getting away with murder for years: Malcolm X, for example, believed that the Black Legion was responsible for his father's murder in Michigan in 1931.)

Warner Brothers in the 1930s was especially tuned to Nugent's desires. One of the screenwriters of "Black Legion," Abem Finkel, had just the year before also worked on "Black Fury," the equally hard-hitting film (for then) about miners and the fascistic Coal and Iron Police.

See also: "Black Fury"; "Fury."
Availability: 16 mm; Swank.
Further reading: "Black Legion." *Newsweek*, May 30, 1936, 9–10; 6 June 1936, 10; 13 June 1936, 10. A series of news articles on the Black Legion murder of Poole.
Davis, F. "Labor Spies and the Black Legion." *New Republic*, 17 June 1936, 169–71. Interprets the actual events in terms of labor unrest.
Nugent, Frank S. "At the 86th Street Casino." *New York Times*, 18 Jan. 1937, 21. "Editorial cinema at its best—ruthless, direct, uncompromising."
Sklar, Robert. *City Boys: Cagney, Bogart, Garfield*. Princeton, N.J.: Princeton University Press, 1992. Analyzes the film's use of a new kind of Hollywood hero—urban and tough.
Stead, Peter. *Film and the Working Class*. London: Routledge, 1989. Analyzes the film in the context of what he calls the "sociological punch" of the 1930s films.
Ward, Paul W. "Who's Behind the Black Legion?" and "Caliban in America." *Nation*, 10 June 1936, 728–29, 731. Contemporary political analysis on the upsurge in American fascism.

Blood Feud

Hoffa beats Kennedy at "Indian hand wrestling."

1983, 200 mins., TVM	JFK = Sam Groom
Director: Mike Newell	Lyndon Baines Johnson = Forrest Tucker
Screenplay: Robert Boris	J. Edgar Hoover = Ernest Borgnine
CAST	Edward Bennett Williams = Jose Ferrer
Jimmy Hoffa = Robert Blake	Hoffa's Attorney = Micaeh C. Gwynne
Robert F. Kennedy = Cotter Smith	Randy Powers = Danny Aiello

One has to acknowledge all the fuss paid to the so-called blood feud between Jimmy Hoffa and Bobby Kennedy, in part because American TV and Hollywood have placed it on the labor history agenda as virtually the only issue of note involving Hoffa (and of course it keeps films about Hoffa always leaning on the crime angle) and in part because Hoffa himself admitted in his autobiography that he was obsessed with the feud and said it was one of two "disastrous mistakes" in his life: "The first was coming to grips with Robert F. Kennedy to the point where we became involved in what only be called a blood feud." (The "second mistake was naming Frank Fitzsimmons" as his "successor.")

This film deserved most of the critical and public neglect it received. In addition to the primary characters, there are about forty others, ranging from a Capo di Capi (Mafia talk for Captain of Captains) and a Restaurant Captain (restaurant talk for a maitre-d). And Hoffa's attorney is called . . . "Hoffa's Attorney"! Is this the incredibly feisty Frank Ragano, he who must not be named? The subject of his own TV documentary on "Frontline," "JFK, Hoffa, and the Mob," as well as a book, *Mob Lawyer*, by Ragano and Selwyn Raab (New York: Scribner, 1994)? It must be, although presumably for reasons of libel, Rangano is not identified. (His libel suit would not be for accusations of gangsterism but for its bad lines.)

With a four-hour running time, it seems hardly credible for the filmmakers to expect us to take the opening title, which tells us that names have been changed and "other individuals and certain events have been altered or compressed for reasons of dramatic economy," seriously. *Variety*'s reviewer concluded that the film had to be a "sure TV attraction," as it had Hoffa, Kennedy, and the Mob. (The fourth sure thing, a disease, was missing.)

Robert Blake is not many people's idea of a Hoffa stand-in. If you come to this film after seeing Hoffa himself in the documentary "Hoffa: The True Story" or Jack Nicholson playing him in "Hoffa," Robert Blake will seem even more unbelievable.

There exists an extraordinary amount of negative information here about Hoffa, presented mostly from the government's (and Robert Kennedy's) point of view. At the height of the investigation against Hoffa, Bobby Kennedy had almost twenty lawyers working in the "get Hoffa" division of the attorney general's office. That they got Hoffa on so few of the things they said he masterminded is an enigma this film cannot answer. It certainly demonstrates how Hoffa seemed to crowd so much of the Kennedys' other agendas—civil rights, for example—to the side.

Clearly, Bobby Kennedy had the troops and Hoffa had the muscle, which, in this film, without a doubt, belongs to the Mafia. Unfortunately, our attitude could only be, So what else is new? Not much. (Unless you didn't know that Hoffa beat Bobby Kennedy at "Indian hand wrestling.")

Without trying to finesse an important issue, do we dare to ask if the "blood feud" might also be traced to the long internal cultural and class struggle between the Lace

Irish (the rich upper-class Kennedys) and the Shanty Irish-Dutch (the struggling Hoffas)?

See also: "Hoffa: The True Story"; ["JFK, Hoffa, and the Mob"].
Availability: Not currently available.
Further reading: Hoffa, James R. *Hoffa: The Real Story.* New York: Stein and Day, 1975. "The only authorized book of Hoffa's life . . . as told to Oscar Fraly"; also includes the "Indian hand wrestling" incident.
"Blood Feud." *Variety,* 11 May 1983. A snippy review that calls the film a "variation of 'The Untouchables' without the quality."

Bloodbrothers

Ties that blind

1978, 116 mins., R
Director: Robert Mulligan
Screenplay: Walter Newman, from Richard
  Price's novel of the same title
CAST
Stony de Coco = Richard Gere
Chubby de Coco = Paul Sorvino

Tommy de Coco = Tony Lo Bianco
Albert de Coco = Michael Hershewe
Marie = Lelia Goldoni
Dr. Harris = Floyd Levine
Annette = Marilu Henner
Cheri = Kristine DeBell

"Bloodbrothers" is another entry in the ethnic working-class sweepstakes, albeit a decade or two late: it is a drama of two pairs of brothers, old-guard construction electricians and union men, Tommy de Coco and his brother, Chubby, and Tommy's two sons, Stony and Albert. We have wives and lovers, too, but they are clearly subsidiary to this male-dominated Italian-American world. Tommy wants his son Stony to follow along in his union footsteps, but Stony's got other ideas. At first he does give it a try, and some of the best scenes involve his initiation into the world of high-rise building construction, where the regulars like to play tricks on the new boys to get them ready to booze and fight like real men.

Unfortunately for his father, Stony really wants a job in which he can be a nurturer—a teacher or a social worker or some other unproletarian career. Stony has been especially attentive to his brother Albert, who has to be the only *male* anorexic character in modern film history. The level of tenseness in the de Coco household would make anyone dysfunctional. On top of the usual macho Italian-American shouting just to make oneself heard, the father's exaggerated sense of importance has brought him into violent conflict with his wife (whom he beats when he hears about a particularly sordid incident involving a neighbor) and his sons (who in his eyes are just a pair of sissies).

The film clearly wants to do in hard-hat family values by showing most of the men as boozy whore chasers, who are disdainful of anything but justice by a punch in the nose. After a few of these incidents, the viewer will long for some of the Saturday-night boredom the characters in "Marty" complained about. Also targeted—we guess satirically—are the generosity and sentimentality of the men when they are among "their own kind." Thus, a party the hard hats throw for a bar owner who was crippled on the job makes sense only if we accept the cliché that soft hearts beat inside hard bodies. The director, Robert Mulligan, who is a seasoned Hollywood veteran ("To Kill a Mockingbird," for example) probably wanted this scene to be exactly what it seems to be on the surface: a male ritual to prove that men can bond and cry too.

The film's finale, with Stony lighting out for the territories (Queens?) in a taxi with his younger brother is a little unrealistic: even Stony suspects "they" will come after them and take Albert away. Before he picks up his brother, however, Stony's father and uncle stand on either side of the taxi and throw money in the windows for Stony's journey while screaming at him not to go. These gestures seem a lot closer to the real world of these impossible men than what Stony thinks he is about to experience, although most viewers will presumably want his escape to be successful.

See also: "Marty."
Availability: Easy.
Further reading: Price, Richard. *Bloodbrothers*. New York: Penguin, 1976. The source novel.
Schonberg, Harold C. "Bloodbrothers." *New York Times*, 29 Sept. 1978, 52. Finds the film too
    contrived and sentimental.
Note: Also known as "A Father's Love" in a 98-minute TV version.

ᖇ

Blue Collar

The tight blue collar

1978, 114 mins., R (for violence and sex)   CAST:
Director: Paul Schrader   Jerry = Harvey Keitel
Screenplay: Paul Schrader.   Smokey = Yaphet Kotto
                                                Zeke = Richard Pryor

Harvey Keitel, Richard Pryor, and Yaphet Kotto play a band of workers who unfortunately decide to rob the local office of their fictional American Auto Workers union. They find only $600 and a curious ledger book. When they discover evidence in the book that the local has been loan-sharking, they decide to blackmail the local officers. They are surprised when the local first announces that $10,000 was stolen and later raises the figure to $20,600 in an effort to cheat the insurance company. This gang, who couldn't rob straight, has some very dangerous knowledge, and soon our heroes' unity begins to crumble.

There's a combination of brutality and convincing reality in "Blue Collar," Schrader's first film, that sets it aside from many films in this guide. It's in part the feel for actual work that the film manages to convey: compare its auto-assembly lines with those in "Gung Ho," for example, to see the difference. The film tries to do a lot—explore racism, friendship, union corruption (there it is again!), the crushing of working-class militancy and spirit, and so on. Its scope is ambitious, its presentation often gross, especially a short but unpleasant sex and drugs party and a disturbing murder scene.

Overall, "Blue Collar" is a depressing portrayal of American unionism, although there are flashes of individual integrity. Unionism in this world, however, is an elaborate scam in which little attention is devoted to looking out for the welfare of the membership.

Smokey at one point makes a brief speech to his buddies, which is repeated as a voice-over at the end of the film after Smokey has been killed and the workers' unity has been destroyed: "Everything they do—the way they put the lifer against the new boy, the old against the young, the black against the white—is meant to keep us in our places."

Availability: Easy.

Further reading: Georgakas, Dan, and Marvin Surkin. *Detroit: I Do Mind Dying.* New York: St. Martin's, 1975. Insights into the political and nationalist struggles of black auto workers in the late 1960s.

Puette, Wiliam J. *Through Jaundiced Eyes: How the Media View Labor.* Ithaca, N.Y.: ILR Press, 1992. Using this portrayal of the United Auto Workers, Puette argues convincingly that Hollywood was attacking one of the three principal and powerful unions then outside the AFL-CIO (the other two being the Longshoremen in "On the Waterfront" and the Teamsters in "F.I.S.T.").

Bound for Glory

Another guerrilla folksinger

1976, 147 mins., PG
Director: Hal Ashby
Screenplay: Robert Getchell, from Woody
    Guthrie's autobiography of the same title

CAST
Woody Guthrie = David Carradine
Mary Guthrie = Melinda Dillon
Ozark Bule = Ronny Cox

Pauline = Gail Strickland   Luther Johnson = Randy Quaid
Locke = John Lehne   Liz = Elizabeth Macey
Slim Snedegar = Ji-Tu Cumbuka   Memphis Sue = Melinda Dillon

Although this is a relatively long film, it covers only a small portion (1936–40) of Woody Guthrie's autobiography (published in 1943); thus, we see the early clairvoyant Woody, the family Woody, and the footloose Woody, but only some of Woody the guerrilla folksinger, when he made his reputation. Some of the great songs that have become working-class anthems ("This Land Is Your Land") are included, but we don't see the politicized Woody, whose guitar had a big sticker that read, "This machine kills fascists." The film stops a little before he wrote the great Dust Bowl ballads (including "Tom Joad," which he wrote after seeing "The Grapes of Wrath") and his anti-Hitler songs and before he supported the communist left (drafted on the day Germany surrendered, he said, "I don't know if it was me or that big Red army or those few million Yanks there acrost his fence that caused [Hitler] to give in").

Woody's autobiography is a big book, and the film does not include the sharper political confrontations. There is thus no room in this somewhat romantic film for a revealing incident when Woody and Cisco Houston took on some anti-Japanese fanatics in Los Angeles after Pearl Harbor. Cisco tried to calm the crowd with such remarks as, "Nine-tenths of [the local Japanese] hate their Rising Sun robbers just as much as I do, or you do."

To fill in the missing pieces of Woody's amazing career, the documentary "Woody Guthrie: Hard Travelin'" (directed by his son, Arlo, also a folksinger) is helpful: it combines a view of Woody as a radical and as an inspiring figure for the generation of folksingers who came to prominence in the 1960s (such as Bob Dylan, Joan Baez, and Judy Collins).

But Ashby's film does capture the spirit of Woody's life and his commitment to poor and working people. We see the populist Woody, less committed to any political line, an "aw shucks" kind of guy who can't stand laboring people being pushed around by the big boys. His friendship and work relationship with Ozark Bule (presumably Cisco Houston in real life) is typical of the passive way David Carradine plays Guthrie: as a rule it is Cisco who hits the road while taking a break from their country-western radio show to talk up the union to stoop laborers, and it is typically Woody who is a bit slow on the drawl to clear out when the company goons come rushing in. It is Ozark who wants to paint slogans on a farmer's fence, but it is Woody who wants to take the time to make the lettering look just right. Nonetheless, Ashby's portrait is convincing, if not in its biographical completeness at least in conveying Woody's spirit. It is Ozark who organizes the radio show, but it is Woody who always dedicates his songs to the workers and whose lyrics irritate the program's sponsors.

Woody Guthrie (David Carradine) entertains farmworkers' children in "Bound for Glory."

Woody's life and songs captured the troubles and high-energy life he lived among the riffraff riding the rails during the Depression: "Men fighting against men. Color against color. Kin against kin. Race pushing against race. And all of us battling against the wind and the rain and that bright crackling lightning that booms and zooms, that bathes his eyes in the white sky, wrestles a river to a standstill, and spends the night drunk in a whorehouse." The young man from Okemah, Oklahoma, knew a lot of "hard travelin'," riding the rails.

At the age of fifty-five, Woody lay dying of a rare disease (Huntington's chorea), while faithful friends and new apprentices (such as Bob Dylan) paid deathbed visits. The film's title comes from one of his songs, and as usual it's about a train, a train "bound for glory."

See also: ["Woody Guthrie: Hard Travelin'"].
Availability: Easy.
Further reading: Canby, Vincent. "In Films, Acting Is Behavior." *New York Times*, 12 Dec. 1976, II.1. Celebrates Carradine's portrayal of Woody.
Green, Jim. "Bound for Glory." *Cineaste* 8 (1977): 36–37. Sees some positive aspects in the portrayal but concludes it fails to do justice to Woody's politics or his music.

Guthrie, Woody. *Bound for Glory*. 1943. Reprint. New York: Dutton, 1976. The later edition has an excellent introduction by Studs Terkel.

Hampton, Wayne. *Guerrilla Minstrels: John Lennon, Joe Hill, Woody Guthrie, Bob Dylan*. Knoxville: University of Tennessee Press, 1986. Discusses the reality and the myths associated with these radicalized folksingers.

༄

Boxcar Bertha

Hoppin' trains to hell

1972, 97 mins., R (a little nudity, a lot of shotguns)
Director: Martin Scorsese
Screenplay: Joyce H. and John William Corrington, from Boxcar Bertha's autobiography, *Sister of the Road* ("as told to" Ben L. Reitman)

CAST
Big Bill Shelley = David Carradine
Bertha = Barbara Hershey
Van Morton = Bernie Casey
Rake Brown = Barry Primus
H. Buckram Sartoris = John Carradine

Martin Scorsese's first Hollywood film was this exploitation (read: sexy, violent, and fairly stupid) imitation of the incredibly popular and successful "Bonnie and Clyde": both films tried to paint heroic and romantic portraits of Depression-era itinerant riffraff or hobo rebels. Eric Hobsbawm has called such popular heroes "social" or "primitive" rebels, because their banditry had a populist and inevitably antigovernment cast. (In many Hollywood films about railroads, the fired worker tries to get even with the company, as in "End of the Line," or in another film outside the scope of this guide, "The Wild Bunch," in which one of the outlaws says you can't pledge your word to a "railroad.")

Boxcar Bertha's exploits—she and "coauthor" Ben L. Reitman swear they were real—did not capture the popular imagination the way other "populist" outlaws did. Bertha was promiscuous and pro-union—a fatal combination in the 1930s South, but, unlike the men in her life, she lived to tell the tale. Further, she was a supporter of the International Workers of the World (the IWW), a Wobbly in deed and in spirit, as her "autobiography" makes clear.

Perhaps because it is a proto-Hollywood film (its producer was the speed king of exploitation films, Roger Corman), Scorsese has his male rebel take more of the lead, something readers of Boxcar Bertha's autobiography would find doubtful. This makes Barbara Hershey seem decidedly sluttish and more of a follower of riffraff than a leader. In any case, she outwits the law most of the time.

We follow Bertha and her gang as they move from supporting railway strikers to "robbing the rich to help the poor." Most of the time they're nonviolent thieves, unlike Bonnie and Clyde, but the law—in the form of two company thugs, the

McGivers—just keep on coming until the bloody end. Bertha's main man is called Big Bill Shelley, presumably a nod to the Wobbly leader Big Bill Haywood (in the film the union is called the Brotherhood of Workers, a reasonably close facsimile to the One Big Union or IWW). A black worker from Bertha's past (the mechanic at her dad's crop-dusting business) and an eastern gambler round out this improbable group of "primitive rebels."

Only Big Bill is bothered by the gang's criminal exploits. "I ain't no criminal. I'm a union man," he insists, and he decides to bring his share of a railway robbery to the union. Unfortunately for his pride, the union officer will take Big Bill's money but only after complaining that he is running with "whores and niggers"—"some company for a union man."

To salve their consciences, the gang "holds up" a railroad payroll office and makes the cashier slip an extra ten bucks in every worker's envelope. Bill is never comfortable with his role, however, while Bertha likes to wear a lot of rich folks' jewelry on her naked body.

A few scenes of discreet sex hardly prepare the viewer for what has now become a classic sequence in exploitation films: the company thugs crucify Big Bill on the side of a boxcar. If this makes Boxcar Bertha Mary Magdalene, then it's (almost) time to appreciate the virtually apolitical "Bonnie and Clyde."

See also: ["Bonnie and Clyde"]; "Bound for Glory"; ["End of the Line"]; "Joe Hill"; ["The Wild Bunch"].

Availability: Selected collections.

Further reading: Boxcar Bertha (Thompson). *Sister of the Road.* 1937. Reprinted as *Boxcar Bertha: An Autobiography.* New York: AMOK Press, 1988. Reads like fiction and folklore, but whether as a character or a real person, Boxcar Bertha got around.

Hobsbawm, Eric. *Primitive Rebels.* New York: Norton, 1959.

——. *Bandits.* New York: Dell, 1969. Hobsbawm's cultural studies develop the model of armed riffraff who are "social" or "primitive" rebels.

Thompson, David, and Ian Christie. *Scorsese on Scorsese* (interviews). New York: Faber and Faber, 1989. Discusses the film in the context of Scorsese's career.

Thompson, Howard. "Boxcar Bertha." *New York Times*, 18 Aug. 1972, 19. Celebrates the cast; calls the film "beautifully directed by Martin Scorsese."

❧ Breaking Away

Class struggle on the asphalt track

1979, 100 mins., PG	CAST
Director: Peter Yates	Dave = Dennis Christopher
Screenplay: Steve Tesich	Mike = Dennis Quaid

Cyril = Daniel Stern   Katherine = Robyn Douglass
Dave's Dad = Paul Dooley   Nancy = Amy Wright
Dave's Mom = Barbara Barrie   Suzy = P. J. Soles
Moocher = Jackie Earle Haley

The class distinctions in Bloomington, Indiana, home of Indiana University and a generation or two of quarry workers called "cutters," are sharp and inevitable. The golden men and women on campus have beautiful tans, drive nice cars, play frisbee, and occasionally study. Our four antiheroes look and act scruffy, have graduated from high school but refuse to take jobs, and were good enough to be sports stars in high school but received no scholarships for their pains. Although all four leads are played to perfection, one of them, the most disaffected and grumpy, Michael, sums up their dilemma: "These college kids are never going to get old or out of shape. And they're going to call us 'cutters.' To them it's just a dirty word. To me it's just another thing I never got to be."

Because the quarries are never going to return to their glory days, the boys could not even get jobs there if they wanted to. The most adjusted of the lot, or so it seems, is Dave, whose obsession with cycling and all things Italian has led him to integrate Italy into his daily life, so much so that his father, a former cutter and now a used-car salesman, is going crazy with all those "Eye-ty" (Italian) words that end in "inni"—zucchinni, Fellini (Dave's new name for his cat), and so on.

Furthermore, Dave's way of crossing the class barriers of Bloomington is to impersonate an Italian exchange student on the Indiana University campus. He falls into this deception innocently enough, trying to impress a campus queen, "Katarina," as he calls her, who is sweet and nice enough never to doubt that her serenading suitor is just a "cutter." After a disillusioning experience with the visiting Team Cinzano bicycle team, Dave gives up his Italian ways and divulges his true identity to his new girlfriend. She ditches him.

In the meantime, the class struggle continues. Cyril, Dave's guitar-playing accomplice in his serenade at the sorority house, is attacked by Katarina's slick frat friends; Dave's friend Michael, in turn, launches an attack on them at the campus student union. In an attempt to deflect the struggle onto the playing fields, the annual Little Indianapolis 500 bike race is opened to a "cutter" team for the first time. The excitement of the race tends to heal most of the wounds, and even the most obnoxious frat boy (who drives a Mercedes convertible and is a champion swimmer) warms to the spirit of the "cutters" in the end.

Tesich's screenplay won an Academy Award because he captured the bittersweet nature of being working class in a town dedicated to middle- and upper-class mobility. A third member of the foursome, Moocher, is very short and very sensitive. He is one of the first to break ranks and take a job. Unfortunately, in his first two minutes at work, his car-wash boss says, "Don't forget to punch the clock, Shorty," whereupon Moocher literally punches the clock to pieces.

On another occasion the "cutters" are frustrated when the golden lads and lassies intrude on "their" swimming hole—an abandoned quarry, once the source of the community's jobs. Dave tries to help out his father at the used-car lot but takes the side of a customer who feels he has been cheated by Dave's "papa," played brilliantly by Paul Dooley. When he recovers from what appears to be a heart attack, he tells Dave that he had a nightmare in which "everybody I ever sold a car to came back for a refund and you were handing back the money." Eventually the two are reconciled, and Dave and his father visit a campus building he cut the stone for. He urges Dave to join the college world.

In a comedy like this, we don't expect too many insights. Perhaps a few little ones are enough—and some low blows: when Dave's dad visits his old workplace, one of the men comments on his suit and big car, "I thought he was a safety inspector or a union organizer." A brief visit to the cutting shed suggests that workers don't wear safety goggles, ear protectors, masks, or hard hats. Where was OSHA when these guys needed it?

See also: "Rising Son."
Availability: Easy.
Further reading: Canby, Vincent. "A Comedy in Which Class Tells." *New York Times*, 9 Feb. 1979, II.13. Celebrates the film's ability to examine American class distinctions.

◌ The Burning Season

The fires are still on.

1994, 123 mins., TVM, unrated, but in effect an R for brief scenes of female nudity	Wilson Pinheiro = Edward James Olmos
	Ilzamar Mendes = Kamala Dawson
	Estate Boss = Luis Guzman
Director: John Frankenheimer	Steven Keyes = Nigel Havers
Screenplay: Ron Hutchinson, from Andrew Revkin's book of the same title	Darli Alves = Thomas Millian
	Darci Alves = Gerrado Moreno
CAST:	Jair = Esai Morales
Chico Mendes = Raul Julia	Orlavo Galvao = Tony Plana
Regina de Carvalho = Sonia Braga	

Chico Mendes, the leader of the rubber tappers union in the western Amazon state of Acre [*ah*-cray] in Brazil, was murdered in 1988 by a rancher and his son (Darli and Darci Alves), locals who routinely burned the forests to make way for agricultural expansion. Mendes led the "empates," or sit-down strikes of the rubber tappers of the Xapuri [shah-poo-*ree*] Rural Workers Union, as a nonviolent means of protecting their livelihoods and their forest.

Xapuri was a rubber-trading outpost (population: 5,000), where in 1977 Mendes helped found the local union of rubber tappers and other Indian workers who needed to stop the destruction of the forest. After a fairly successful campaign that slowed the chain-saw crews of the ranchers, Mendes was invited to the United States by environmental groups that hoped to persuade international development banks to stop financing the paving of roads into the Amazon.

Unfortunately, Xapuri was also a very dangerous place for union members. Mendes's mentor and friend, Wilson Pinhiero, president of Acre's first rural workers union, was murdered in 1980. The ranchers who were eventually convicted of killing Mendes had a ten-thousand-acre ranch in Acre and a formidable reputation for murdering anyone they chose. Darli's brother also worked in the office of the sheriff of Xapuri. The Alveses were convicted of murder in 1990 and sentenced to nineteen years in prison, but not long after reporters observed that the rules of their incarceration were extremely easy, the Alveses escaped.

The film stays close to Revkin's account of Mendes's life and death. It was originally to be a Brazilian film, but the rights were sold to Warner Brothers, which built a set in Ecuador. When this location shoot failed, its subsidiary, HBO, used Mexico as the new location for the film, with Mexicans playing Brazilians. Only one Brazilian, star Sonia Braga, became part of the final cast. Brazilian critics treated the film harshly, arguing that it was not surprising that a (North) American film with Mexican extras did not convey the Brazilian reality accurately.

Despite these (possible) problems, the film is remarkably sincere in its depiction of the interrelationships between the economic and social forces in the region and the competing demands of the cattle ranchers, rubber tappers, and Indian forest dwellers. Some scenes are also unnerving, deliberately so. For example, we see a murder that supposedly Mendes witnessed as a boy of a man who tried to organize the workers: a foreman poured gasoline on him and burned him to death.

Director Frankenheimer has been a noteworthy filmmaker for forty years. His first major film, "The Manchurian Candidate" (1962), a tale of paranoia and assassination, has rarely been equaled in its genre. More recently, with "The Year of the Gun" (1991), on Italian political assassinations, and "Against the Wall" (1994), on the Attica Prison uprising, he has returned to more topical and political subjects.

Film buffs will see in Chico's comic verbal duel with his future wife's father echoes of Zapata's courtship of his wife in "Viva Zapata!" On a much more disturbing note, they will recognize a "quotation" from the scene from Frankenheimer's "Manchurian Candidate" in which a senator is assassinated while holding a milk bottle to his chest. Chico's assistant is murdered while rubber-tapping, and the bullets cause the white sap to spurt from the container he is carrying.

The forest fires Mendes died trying to stop continue unabated to this day, raising concerns not only about local Brazilian workers but the literal survival of the earth's "lungs" in this crucial greenbelt.

See also: "Viva Zapata!"; ["Manchurian Candidate"].
Availability: Easy.
Further reading: Brooke, James. "Brazil Winces at a Film on its Hero." *New York Times,* 3 Sept. 1994, 9.
——. "Hostility in Amazon Drives Makers of Chico Mendes Movie out of Brazil." *New York Times,* 27 July 1991, 13. This and the article above explain the controversy surrounding the film's production and the Alveses' imprisonment.
O'Connor, John J. "The Little Guy as the Big Hero." *New York Times,* 16 Sept. 1994, B4. "The movie makes its points powerfully, although its anger can sometimes be simple-minded."
Revkin, Andrew. *The Burning Season: The Murder of Chico Mendes and the Fight for the Amazon Rain Forest.* Boston: Houghton Mifflin, 1990. This source book provides a thorough review of the case.

༄

Business as Usual

Sexual politics in the small shop

1987, 89 mins., British, PG	Josie Patterson = Cathy Tyson
Director: Lezli-An Barrett	Peter Barry = Eamon Boland
Screenplay: Lezli-An Barrett	Mark = James Hazeldine
CAST	Paula Douglas = Buki Armstrong
Babs Flynn = Glenda Jackson	Terry Flynn = Stephen McGann
Kieran Flynn = John Thaw	Steve Flynn = Mark McGann

Although this film did not find a commercial/theatrical audience in the United States, it is a very careful and entertaining look at a strike in a small dress shop in Liverpool, England. When a new line of clothing and a new hip look are to be introduced to a store in a chain, regional manager Peter Barry uses an excuse—that he has been falsely charged with sexual harassment of one of the "shop girls" who works for manager Babs Flynn—to fire Flynn and create a new ambience in his store: Babs, it seems, doesn't have the new "Aelita" look.

Neither Babs nor the shop workers belong to the Transit and General Workers Union (TGWU), but British law permits Babs to join and file a grievance. Her husband had belonged to a union-management team that tried to save his factory (a Tates-Lyle sugar refinery, most likely) from being eliminated by the demands of the new European Economic Community (EEC), formerly the European Common Market, for limits on an individual country's production. Protracted high-level

Babs Flynn (Glenda Jackson) on the picket line of the Aelita dress shop in "Business as Usual." Courtesy British Film Institute Stills, Posters, and Designs.

negotiations did not save his company or his job. (We see video interviews with his younger self as he tries to negotiate to save "his" factory.)

Babs's struggle is on a smaller scale, but she at least lets members of her family, friends, and union-mates talk her into fighting back by striking the shop. Meanwhile, her husband is becoming more and more discontented with his house-husband role. He is especially irritated by his wife's new militancy and his son's (old) socialist militancy.

Everything about "Business as Usual" is on a small scale, but it is nonetheless unusual filmmaking. More attention is paid to the details of the organization of a picket line, the rallying of unemployed workers and other sympathetic supporters, and the negotiations than in most films. Also of interest is the origin of the strike, since sexual harassment issues have only relatively recently entered workplace discussions in Britain.

The look of contemporary England—its potential for positive interracial relationships, the emergence of small businesses into international corporate sleekness, and the then-growing negative feelings toward Prime Minister Thatcher—mark this as an impressive feature film debut for director Lezli-An Barrett. Excellent performances by Cathy Tyson, Glenda Jackson, and John Thaw (who plays Inspector Morse on the PBS series named after his character) make this film a real sleeper.

The most disturbing scene in the film involves police brutality. After a humorous and energizing moment—Mr. Barry pops open a bottle of champagne and releases the curtains on Aelita's new opening day only to be faced by a massive picket line from the TGWU—the picket line settles into the usual ups and downs of confronting a public that is not yet aware of the issues involved in the strike. Suddenly, a flying squad of police officers pick off most of the leadership—Babs's family and friends—and hauls them off to jail. On the pretense that one woman, Paula, is hiding drugs in her dramatic post-reggae Afro, she is aggressively strip-searched by two women officers (who are pointedly shown putting on rubber gloves).

Eventually, this incident works in the strikers' favor as they gain much sympathetic publicity because of the disproportionate force used by the police. The women are acquitted of obstruction charges and provoke a Parliamentary inquiry into the strip-search incident. After three weeks of totally successful picketing, Babs addresses a socialist political rally: "I got sacked," she says, "because I stood up for myself and the girls in the shop." Most British viewers would no doubt recognize this rally as fairly typical of the activities of the Labor Party/socialist left in England, but it would not be clear to most American workers, who might be surprised by the somewhat open alliances that occasionally develop between trade union locals, the Labor Party, and various socialist organizations.

Actress Glenda Jackson is herself a Labor Party activist, having been elected a member of Parliament from a north London district in 1992.

See also: "Riff-Raff."
Availability: Selected collections.
Further reading: Barnes, Julian. "Letter from London." *New Yorker*, 4 May 1992, 78–92. On Jackson's political career.

The Business of America

. . . *used* to be business.

1987, 60 mins., unrated, but suitable for all ages
Directors: Larry Adelman, Lawrence Daressa, Bruce Schmlechen
Documentary scripted by the codirectors
PRINCIPAL FIGURES
Paul and Maureen Trout, former steelworkers
David Roderick, president, U.S. Steel
Ron Weiser, president, Local 139, United Steelworkers of America (USWA)
Jack Bain, grievance man, Local 1397, USWA
Marvin Weinstock, USWA staff
Mark Green, the Democracy Project
Stanley Aronowitz, City University of New York
John Naretto, narrator

U.S. Steel demolishes its steel mill in Youngstown, Ohio, in "The Business of America."
Photo by Paul Schell, *Youngstown Vindicator*, courtesy California Newsreel.

Which of these statements about the Reagan era are true?

(1) American corporations spent more money suing one another than doing basic research.

(2) U.S. Steel had only 25 percent of its assets in steel—the remainder was in plastics, real estate, and a Disney hotel.

(3) The National Association of Manufacturers once predicted the advent of the flying automobile.

All are true, despite Calvin Coolidge's oft-quoted observation that "the business of America is business." This film is a chronicle of the collapse of the steelworks of western Pennsylvania; it is also a study in the potential and actual absurdity of these three statements.

The steelworkers by and large were loyalists during the Vietnam War; they also voted for Ronald Reagan. By the 1980s their most famous work site—U.S. Steel's Homestead Works—was closing down and the workers were being laid off in record numbers; they were also literally besieging the corporate headquarters in Pittsburgh for help. These loyalists began to question the corporation, which seemed to have no loyalty to the region or to the people who had worked in their factories for years. Nearby, in Youngstown, Ohio, community groups in coalition with workers tried to buy the U.S. Steel plant with no luck. A smaller company, Weirton Steel, *was* purchased and became the model for new ways of combating community decline.

The film concludes with a follow-up report on several of the principal figures. Two steelworkers, Paul and Maureen, are now minimum-wage workers, the latter as a grocery clerk, the former as a night watchman. U.S. Steel is importing foreign steel for a local construction project. The only positive note is the creation of the Tri-State Conference on Steel, bringing together forces (labor, academic, community) to prepare a blueprint for regional development using the natural resources and expertise of the region's workers. One plan calls for developing new power plants that would utilize the region's resources (coal reserves, steelmaking capacity, skilled workers, and metalurgical research facilities).

See also: "Iron Maze."
Availability: Selected collections; California Newsreel.

The Catered Affair

The "Father of the Bride" is a cabbie.

1956, 93 mins., B & W, unrated, but suitable for all ages	Mrs. Tom Hurley = Bette Davis
Director: Richard Brooks	Jane Hurley = Debbie Reynolds
Screenplay: Gore Vidal, from Paddy	Uncle Jack Conlon = Barry Fitzgerald
Chayefsky's TV play of the same title	Ralph Halloran = Rod Taylor
CAST	Mr. Halloran = Robert Simon
Tom Hurley = Ernest Borgnine	Mrs. Halloran = Madge Kennedy
	Mrs. Rafferty = Dorothy Stickney

Like screenwriter Paddy Chayefsky's more famous "Marty," "The Catered Affair" is an ethnic, working-class, sentimental comedy that is filled with familiar conflicts—how much to spend on a wedding, who decides the guest list, and so forth. This is another story of a working-class guy who wants to be self-employed. He wants to buy his own cab and New York City medallion and make it on his own rather than continue to drive the company's car. No union affiliation is specified for this Bronx worker, but surely a company hack in the 1950s had one.

Bette Davis does an overacting star turn as the wife who never had a proper wedding reception and now wants to spend the money for the cab on one for her daughter. Barry Fitzgerald proves there will always be an Ireland if not an Irish ham, and Debbie Reynolds confounds skeptics by being a thoroughly convincing and modern young woman.

Like "Marty," this film was written as an original TV play by Chayefsky, who pioneered working-class family plays. Most of his ethnic plays were supposed to be about his own Jewish background (see the entry on "Marty'), which would explain why Mrs. Hurley has an extremely unbelievable Irish brother. Whether there is a universal (European) ethnic experience or not, certainly the drab utilitarian world of the working-class 1950s comes through here.

See also: "Marty."
Availability: Easy.
Further reading: Considine, Shaun. *The Life and Work of Paddy Chayefsky.* New York: Random House, 1994. An excellent survey of Chayefsky's career, emphasizing his innovative TV and film portrayals of working-class ethnic characters (and his autobiographical scripts).
Crowther, Bosley. "The Catered Affair." *New York Times*, 15 June 1956, 32. An "unsuccessful" film "of what amounts to a plain, low-down, drawn-out family brawl."

~

The Citadel

A doctor chooses: sick miners or the idle rich.

1938, 112 mins., U.S.-British, B & W, unrated, but suitable for all ages	Dr. Lawford = Rex Harrison
Director: King Vidor	Owen = Emlyn Williams
Screenplay: Frank Wead and others, from A. J. Cronin's novel of the same title	Toppy LeRoy = Penelope Dudley Ward
	Mrs. Orlando = Mary Clare
	Charles Every = Cecil Parker
CAST	Mr. Stillman = Percy Parsons
Andrew Manson = Robert Donat	Dr. Page = Basil Gill
Denny = Ralph Richardson	Mrs. Page = Dilys Davis
Chris = Rosalind Russell	

"The Citadel" depicts an unusual moment in British working-class history when Welsh miners had enough clout to employ (through a voucher system) their own doctors. Andrew Manson works *for* the miners, but as an intellectual and a scientist, he feels his research into lung disease—using the miners as guinea pigs as well as actual animals—will be more beneficial to them in the long run. In the short run, however, he runs afoul of miners who want quickie excuses not to work and truly sick miners used to a little medicine here and there to ease their pains. Manson's mini-research lab falls victim to one of the malingerers, who—using the cry of "no animal harmful experimentation"—destroys Manson's gradually successful research.

Forced to go to London, he and his wife become estranged as he begins to take on society patients who have minor ailments or none at all but pay big fees. After laboring at the bottom, he is more than ready to be top dog. Even the nurses at his new clinics have svelte outfits and high heels, not to mention the society ladies he caters to. (One of them tells him right away that he needs to "get a tailor.") Only the death of his best friend (who fails to sell Manson on a community health clinic scheme) and the love of his ever-patient wife (played with style and a confident air by Rosalind Russell) lead Andrew back to the path of righteousness.

The film mixes what Vidor could do best with some Hollywood imperatives. Since it keeps Manson's wife alive (she dies in the novel), she is by his side after his triumphant speech at his trial for helping an unlicensed practitioner work on a pneumonia case. And when he realizes that the incompetent surgeons of the rich he has been hobnobbing with have failed to save his friend, he roams the city at night and may even consider suicide until he hears the heavenly voice of his friend urging him to sit up straight.

If much of this sounds a bit too sentimental and moralistic, you would not be far wrong. But Robert Donat's ever-chirpy ironic style and the strength of the film's realism keep the viewer going during teary intervals. When Andrew wanders London, he sees people scrounging in garbage cans, the blind begging, and children playing in traffic. In short, he sees the have-nots and he stops wanting to be a "have." He returns to the radicalism of his earlier days—when he and his friend dynamited a horribly pestilential sewer to force the government to replace it—and challenges the stodgy medical establishment.

See also: "How Green Was My Valley"; "The Stars Look Down"; "Sullivan's Travels."
Availability: Easy.
Further reading: Cronin, A. J. *The Citadel.* There are numerous editions of this 1937 best-seller.
Nugent, Frank S. "The Citadel." *New York Times*, 4 Nov. 1938, 27. "A splendid transcription of
   a dramatic story, with strong performances to match a sensitive director's design."
Note: A later version of this film, a mini-series directed by Paul Bryant for British TV, is not
   currently available in videocassette.

∾
Coal Miner's Daughter

More music than coal

1980, 125 mins., PG
Director: Michael Apted
Screenplay: Tom Rickman, from Loretta
   Lynn's autobiography
CAST
Loretta Lynn = Sissy Spacek
Doolittle Lynn = Tommy Lee Jones

Patsy Cline = Beverly D'Angelo
Ted Webb = Levon Helm
Clara Webb = Phyllis Boyens
Moonshiner = William Sanderson

Most of Loretta Lynn's life has become an open book: married at thirteen, four children by twenty, just a country gal from Butcher Holler, Kentucky. It was a long way from the Saturday-night Grange Hall crowd to the Grand Ole Opry, but the film makes it seem like an inevitable if not a risky journey, despite the difficulties of rural poverty.

Making a film set in an Appalachian mining community is not an easy task: the visual imagination of most Americans is already filled with moonshiners, barefoot children, married teenagers, and miners coughing on coal dust. Michael Apted shows all of these too, but he manages to dispose of the moonshiner in the first five minutes. This is too bad, because he is a lively chorus on the difficulties of life in this neck of the woods. There are only three things you can do if you are from rural Kentucky, the moonshiner tells Doolittle, Loretta's future husband: moonshining, mining, or "movin' on down the line." Fortunately for Doolittle, he doesn't try moonshining, because the moonshiner is killed while trying to poach on a rival's still. Loretta's dad tells Doolittle that at least he was smart enough not to get mixed up with him; but it is characteristic of Apted's humor and vision for her dad to add: "But at least if you had, you would've had a job!"

Doolittle ends up trying options two and three. As for coal mining, he tells Loretta that if he stayed down in the mine he would have a "chest full of coal dust and be an old man at forty." He tries the third and takes Loretta off to Washington, where he gets a logging job and she starts to sing around the house. Doolittle decides to launch her as a professional singer, although she doesn't even know what the expression "pay your dues" means.

She gets more than a few breaks, and "Honky Tonk Girl" becomes a hit. Soon she is touring with the Patsy Cline Show and we have yet another story of a working-class gal who breaks into show biz. In this way, then, Apted is working within a tradition of music "biopics": the story of a star's rise from rags to riches, the old ways she leaves behind, the drugs she has to take (in Loretta's case, only headache pills), and the obligatory breakdown on stage when the pressures get to be too much. ("Lady Sings the Blues" and "The Doors," to name just two films, have precisely these generic elements.)

Apted seems to have wanted to do MORE and perhaps succeeded somewhat. Loretta's roots as a coal miner's daughter are shown to be co-opted into her role as "just a country gal": "If you're lookin' at me," she sings, "you're lookin' at country." When husband Doolittle tells her that coal dust caused her daddy's headaches but that he, Doolittle, caused hers, we are brought up short. Is Apted telling us that Loretta is—without knowing it—exploiting her working-class roots? Acting out a fantasy for her poor and working-class audiences? She's no union maid, that's fer sure: if the UMWA was in Butcher Holler, it kept quiet when Loretta's family was around.

Both Sissy Spacek and Beverly D'Angelo sing Loretta Lynn's and Patsy Cline's songs themselves and do so convincingly. When Spacek finally sings the title song, so much of Loretta's class resentment comes through that the references to washboards and bare feet don't loom as important: "He shoveled coal to make a poor man's dollar," she sings, but her father always tried to find the money to buy them at least one pair of shoes every winter.

See also: "The Dollmaker"; "35 Up."
Availability: Easy.
Further reading: Lynn, Loretta, and George Vecsey. *Loretta Lynn: Coal Miner's Daughter.* New
    York: Warner, 1976. Lynn's autobiography.
Maslin, Janet. "Coal Miner's Daughter." *New York Times,* 7 March 1980, C8. The reviewer is
    especially keen on the four leads.

ᖇᖇ
Coalmining Women

"If you can't stand by my side, don't stand in my way."—Hazel Dickens

1982, 40 mins., unrated, but suitable for all
  ages
Director: Elizabeth Barret
Documentary
PRINCIPAL fiGURES
Coal miners from Kentucky: Mavis
  Williams, Viola Cleveland, Marilyn
  Vanderfleet

Coal miners from Colorado: Nan Livermore,
  Linda Sexton, Pat Farnsworth
Other coal miners: Barbara Angle, Elizabeth
  Barret, Nancy Prater
Al Blankenship, general mine manager
Betty Jean Hall, Coal Employment Project,
  Oak Ridge, Tennessee
Helen Lewis, narrator

One of the historical "lessons" of this film is that women have worked in mines for decades, especially in Great Britain, where whole families went underground in the early nineteenth century, and in the United States during World War II, when they were employed mainly as surface sorters. ("Germinal" depicts women working underground in France well into the mid-nineteenth century.)

More recently, women in the United States have been in "support" roles, as wives and family members of miners, but also as militants on picket lines and at rallies (such as the Black Lung Rally in Washington, D.C., in 1981) and as grieving witnesses to mine disasters (such as the Scotia Mine Disaster in Letcher County, Kentucky, in 1976). The film documents these events and similar ones with archival footage.

When gender roles were challenged in other areas of society and the superstition that women were bad luck in the mines was defied, women and their supporters used the fact that organizations such as the Tennessee Valley Authority (TVA) had

Friends gather after work in "Coalmining Women." Photo by Earl Dotter, American Labor Educational Center, courtesy Appalshop Films.

federal contracts and could not discriminate in hiring as a legal wedge in opening the mines to women.

Women miners, the majority from Kentucky and Colorado, tell their stories in this film. Not surprisingly, safety issues are among the most important and recurring themes. One woman explains, as we watch her somewhat unconsciously moving her injured right arm with her good left hand, how dangerous operating a shuttle car can be. Another woman carefully tucks her long braid of hair into her jacket as she prepares to go underground.

The women also tell of harassment both petty and grand. Barbara Angle, a coal miner from Maryland, sums it up this way: "It's basically the last locker room in the world. These guys take a lot of pride in what they do, and justifiably so. But it's hard for them to accept the fact that women can do the same work." The film shows women doing "the same work": securing the tunnel ceilings, laying bricks for ventilation barriers, and shoveling coal.

See also: "Germinal"; "We Dig Coal"; "Moving Mountains."
Availability: Selected collections; Appalshop.

Collision Course

. . . even on the ground

1988, 47 mins., unrated, but suitable for all ages
Director: Alex Gibney
Scripted documentary by Alex Gibney
PRINCIPAL FIGURES
Frank Borman, chair, Eastern Airlines
Charles Bryan, president, District 100, International Association of Machinists (IAM)
Robert Cole, professor of business administration, University of Michigan

Leo Romano, chief steward, Logan Airport, IAM
Joe Lapointe, shop mechanic
John "Buddy" Sugg, chair, combined shop, Miami base
Jeff Callahan, director of labor relations, Eastern Airlines
Frank Lorenzo, president and owner, Texas Air
Peter Coyote, narrator

Although air passengers never like to think of a "collision course," it is an apt title for the struggle between Frank Lorenzo's Texas Air and the International Association of Machinists after his acquisition of Eastern Airlines in 1986. Two more unsuitable partners could hardly have been found: Texas Air (which owned Continental and New York Air) was traditionally anti-union, while the Machinists had begun a fairly radical restructuring of their relationship with Eastern in 1983, when the company, in very bad shape financially, agreed to a plan that gave the workers a 25 percent share in the company and created "work teams" that seemed to lead the way to a recovery.

The film reviews both the complicated history of airlines in the era of deregulation and the specific history of Eastern. In the wake of deregulation and the subsequent rise of about a hundred nonunion airlines such as People's Express, Eastern posted enormous losses in 1983. Both Braniff and Continental (with Lorenzo at the helm) went bankrupt. Eastern's move to counter the trend was to bring in former astronaut Frank Borman as chair.

To some, Borman had charisma. (Do all astronauts get charisma by being exposed to ultraviolet rays in space?!) To others, he was an unreconstructed military man used to a "strict chain of command." He openly referred to the workers as children and at first reacted to the proposal that management share governance with them as equivalent to letting the "monkeys run the zoo." Nonetheless, he accepted what appeared to many as a real alternative to most received traditions of corporate culture.

The deal was that management would "get" from the workers an 18 to 22 percent wage cut, productivity increases, and a change in the work rules management found too limiting; the workers would receive a 25 percent stock share, four seats on the board of directors, the right to open the company books, the "right to organize work" as they thought best, and pay increases if there was a rise in productivity.

By 1984, it looked as if the deal would work: Eastern went into the black, and all benefited. But the recovery was short-lived: a 1985 fare war, combined with the costs of maintaining Eastern's overlarge fleet, and soon management was demanding a 20 percent wage cut. Enter Frank Lorenzo, one of the models for Gekko-ism (see "Wall Street"): "We're airline builders not airline busters." After the sale, Borman resigned, but Eastern did not survive.

Most of the workers and a fair number of their managers at Eastern believed that they had broken through to a new level of labor-management cooperation that could be a model industrywide if not for corporations in general. They would have us believe that a collision course does not require a collision as its only outcome.

While Secretary of Labor Robert Reich was at Harvard, he was enthusiastic about the film's value (according to California Newsreel): "If up to me, I'd project it on a mountainside and have the audio boom over valley and stream." But don't let it interfere with the radar or the traffic controllers' jobs! Not to mention the flight attendants and the pilots, who are, perhaps unfortunately, but, given the film's focus, inevitably, not really major players in the film.

See also: "Wall Street."
Availability: Selected collections; California Newsreel.
Further reading: Robinson, Jack E. *Freefall: The Needless Destruction of Eastern Air Lines and the Valiant Struggle to Save It.* New York: Harper Business, 1992. Discusses Lorenzo and the unions that squared off against him (the pilots; the flight attendants; and the machinists).

Come See the Paradise

Come see the relocation camp.

1990, 138 mins., R (but not really)
Director: Alan Parker
Screenplay: Alan Parker
CAST
Jack McGurn = Dennis Quaid
Lily Kawamura = Tamlyn Tomita
Papa Kawamura = Sab Shimono

Mama Kawamura = Shizuko Hoshi
Charlie Kawamura = Stan Egi
Harry Kawamura = Ronald Yamamoto
Dulcie Kawamura = Akemi Nishino
Joyce Kawamura = Naomi Nakano
Mini (at different ages) = Elizabeth Gilliam,
    Shyree Mezick, Caroline Junko King

The detention of Japanese-Americans (including American citizens) in concentration camps during World War II has received very little attention in Hollywood, or elsewhere for that matter. Dennis Quaid's Jack is a union activist—first with the projectionists on the East Coast, then with the fish cannery workers on the West Coast—who falls in love with a Japanese-American woman whose family (from Little Tokyo in Los Angeles) is deported to an internment camp in 1942.

The difficulties of camp life—its politics and its jealousies—are presented very convincingly in this film. Lily's brother Charlie, for example, becomes a "no-no boy": he answers "no" twice to a loyalty oath ("Will you serve in the army?" "Will you forswear allegiance to Japan?") and is deported to Japan; his brother, Harry, by contrast, says "yes" twice, joins the army, and is killed in Italy (like Komoko's son, who saves Spencer Tracy's life in "Bad Day at Black Rock," one of the few other Hollywood films to deal with the camps and the anti-Japanese hysteria).

Jack was forced into "exile" on the West Coast because he objected to the more provocative direct actions of his union (firebombing a movie theater, for example, during a crowded showing) and is also constantly in trouble with both the law and the military. His wife and daughter provide the stability he needs, although he gets into more trouble with his union when he tries working in a cannery.

In the end the film's romantic and antiracist message is more satisfactory than its portrayal of union activism. Its celebration of the Supreme Court's release of the Japanese and Japanese-Americans from the camps short-circuits the historical record a bit, but that 1944 decision did lead to the inmates' release the next year.

The possible economic issues involved in eliminating "competition" from the Japanese at home is not developed in the film, but one of the lobbyists for the Salinas Grower-Shipper Association defended the evacuation: "We're charged with wanting to get rid of the Japs for selfish reasons. We might as well be honest. We do. It's a question of whether the white man lives on the Pacific Coast or the brown men. They came into his valley to work, and they stayed to take over" (Girdner and Loftis).

The Kawamura family at the Japanese relocation camp in "Come See the Paradise."

Only Alan Parker, a British director whose "Mississippi Burning" casts (totally improbably) white FBI agents as the heroes of the murder investigation of the civil rights workers Chaney, Schwerner, and Goodman in 1964, has had the nerve to make a beautiful film about a shameful period in American history.

See also: ["Bad Day at Black Rock"].
Availability: Easy.
Further reading: Bosworth, Allan R. *America's Concentration Camps.* New York: Norton, 1967. A little dated but a very good nonfiction book.
Girdner, Audrie, and Anne Loftis. *The Great Betrayal.* New York: Macmillan, 1969. Argues that the evacuation was economically motivated.
Hansen, Arthur A., ed. *Japanese American World War II Evacuation Oral History Project.* 5 vols. New Providence, N.J.: Saur, 1991–94. A monumental collection of reminiscences by internees, resisters, administrators, analysts, guards, and townspeople.
Houston, James, and Jeanne W. Houston. *Farewell to Manzanar.* Boston: Houghton Mifflin, 1973. The story of Ms. Houston's youth in the concentration camp at Manzanar in California.

James, Caryn. "Come See the Paradise." *New York Times*, 23 Dec. 1990, 42. "The heavily ironic title is the single overdone element in this restrained and moving work."

McWilliams, Carey. *Prejudice—Japanese-Americans: Symbol of Racial Intolerance*. Boston: Little, Brown, 1944. Contemporary radical analysis that argued that "race prejudice," not military security, was the reason for the internment.

New York Times. "F.B.I. in Raids Seize Alien Contraband" and "Coast Japanese Split on Ouster." 21 Feb. 1942, 1–2. Sample press coverage on East Coast roundup of Japanese, Germans, and Italian "spy" suspects and on a West Coast vigilante murder of a Japanese man in a county where a district attorney charged Japanese farmers with "planting tomatoes so that they formed a crude arrow pointing at an air training field."

Okada, John. *No-No Boy*. 1957. Reprint. Seattle: University of Washington Press: 1979. A very strong novel about a character like Charlie who refuses to sign the loyalty oath.

Payne, Robert. "The Color of Paradise." *Jump Cut* 27 (1992): 51–55. A fairly negative review of the film that includes some history of Hollywood's depiction of Japanese-Americans in other films.

"U.S. Uproots Jap Aliens." *Life*, 9 March 1942, 24. A representative sample of the anti-Japanese press that focuses on three Buddhist priests who were arrested for possessing "maps, a spotlight, and a mimeograph machine."

Computers in Context

Creativity not redundancy

1987, 33 mins., unrated, but suitable for all ages
Director: Jim Mayer
Documentary
PRINCIPAL FIGURES (VERY SELECTED)
Oslo Savings Bank
   Leif Johansen, president, Sparebanken Buskerud
   Knut Koe and Espen Trenoy, Norwegian Bankworkers Union
   Oyvinn Ottestad, Ann Sofie, Turid

Petterson, and Tom Johnrud, Fellesdata
Tor Andersen, secretary, Norwegian Labor Organization
Utopia Project
   Malle Ericsson and Walter Carlsson, Swedish Graphic Union
   Pelle Ehn and Susanne Bodke, Center for Working Life
Scandinavian Airlines (SAS)
   Ulf Lindstrom, production manager
   Torsten Bjorkman, consultant

The premise of this film is simple enough: most of us have assumed that computers will replace human workers. What if, the film asks, we see computers as tools for workers, as part of the process of human work and not as substitutes for workers?

The film surveys three Scandinavian companies involved in improving human-computer interaction, and in every instance the watchword is worker participation.

The workforce throughout Scandinavia is 80 percent unionized and government organizations such as Sweden's Center for Working Life, which fosters "codetermination," exist to facilitate worker-management interaction.

The three case studies share an approach that is referred to during a section on the Oslo Savings Bank as "treating the moment": studying and facilitating the interaction between the front-line worker and the computer with the customer. In the first case examined, it was important to involve the workers in deciding what computer hardware and programs would do the best job in meeting the customers' needs and deepening the front-line workers' authorization to carry on a fairly complex layer of business at the moment of customer interaction. The result transformed bank tellers into "personal account managers."

In the second case, graphic design workers from the Swedish Graphics Union went to the Center for Working Life for what was called the Utopia Project, which involved the design and implementation of new computer software that would enable designers of daily newspapers to continue to use their creative skills. The third case study involves Scandinavian Airlines maintenance shops, where an "expert" computer system at first increased the numerical turnover of items serviced but led to a decline in quality. A new system brought workers in as diagnostic experts and planners for repairs.

The film is somewhat overloaded with interview clips and could have provided a more detailed account of the unions' negotiations to achieve their goals in using computers to develop rather than eliminate jobs. (It does a better job on this point for the third case study.) Nonetheless, the film presents a convincing argument for more widespread "codetermination," avoiding, it is to be hoped, the end game that such an approach, in general, led to during the development of the Eastern Airlines–IAM agreement in the 1980s (see "Collision Course").

See also: "Collision Course."
Availability: Selected collections; California Newsreel.

Convoy

Truckers ticked off mightily

1978, 110 mins., PG	Melissa = Ali MacGraw
Director: Sam Peckinpah	Lyle Wallace = Ernest Borgnine
Screenplay: B.W.L. Norton, based on C. W.	Pig Pen = Burt Young
McCall's pop song of the same title	Widow Woman = Madge Sinclair
CAST	Governor Haskins = Seymour Cassel
Rubber Duck = Kris Kristofferson	

Let's hope that President Clinton's Rhodes Scholarship will be more relevant to his career than Kristofferson's was to *his*. No one should make a film with a character nicknamed Rubber Duck, but coming from a director like Sam Peckinpah, whose earlier films were depressing but impressive milestones of cinematic innovation and violence (e.g., "The Wild Bunch" and "Straw Dogs"), this film should have been more appealing. The truckers here are independent owner-operators who are wary of The Law and are the closest thing to open-road cowboys American culture is likely to have for a while. But a film as old-fashioned as "They Drive by Night," which emphasized the risks the drivers face more than their run-ins with the law, was superior to this film, based on a one-note hit country song.

The essence of the film is the mighty and only weapon the truckers have—their ability to form a convoy and make access to the nation's interstates hard for almost everyone, especially the bad guys, who in this worldview are, of course, the Smokies, the highway patrol. The leading Smokey is the crooked arch-villain of the film, played with a particularly silly scuzziness by Ernest Borgnine. Communicating by CB, the truckers can do almost everything, including pick up an incredible out-of-place middle-class fashion plate (Ali MacGraw), who is out on the road looking in all the wrong places for authentic photographs and maybe a turn or two in the back of Rubber Duck's cab. Breaker one-nine, cut loose this film!

See also: "They Drive by Night."
Availability: Selected collections.
Further reading: Canby, Vincent. "Truckers and Women." *New York Times*, 28 June 1978, C17. Assesses Peckinpah as someone who would "sell his grandmother for five percent of the gross" profits of a film.
Ouellet, Lawrence J. *Pedal to the Metal: The Work Lives of Truckers.* Philadelphia: Temple University Press, 1994. A participant-observer sociologist and part-time truck driver reports on the life and work of nonunion truckers.
Sayles, John. "I-80 Nebraska M.490–M.205." In *On the Job*, edited by William O'Rourke, 226–43. New York: Vintage, 1977. An excellent short story on the mythic aspects of truckers on their CBs.

The Corn Is Green

Educating Morgan

1945, 114 mins., B & W, unrated, but
   suitable for all ages
Director: Irving Rapper
Screenplay: Casey Robinson and Frank
   Cauett, from Emlym Williams's play of
   the same title

CAST
Miss Moffat = Bette Davis
Squire Treverby = Nigel Bruce
Morgan Evans = John Dall
Bessie Watty = Joan Lorring
Mr. Jones = Rhys Williams
Mrs. Watty = Rosalind Ivan
Miss Ronberry = Mildred Dunnock

Bette Davis re-created in this film Ethel Barrymore's role on stage as the mighty Miss Moffat, the reformer of a rural Welsh coal-mining village. What obviously worked well on stage—Miss Moffat's numerous cutting remarks and set speeches as she deflates whatever class status the self-satisfied locals have—makes the film look like elocution lessons in front of a cardboard set.

Miss Moffat is fortunate enough to have, as she puts it, inherited money and a house, so she opens a school to keep the local boys from going into the mines at the age of twelve. She concentrates on one star pupil, Morgan Evans, whose first composition about the mines knocks her woolen socks off: "When I walk in the dark, I can touch with my hands where the corn is green." (I'm not sure what this means either, but Miss Moffatt knows it's poetry.)

But Miss Moffat also has enemies, particularly Squire Treverby, who "owns the Hall" and a "half share" in the mine and doesn't take kindly to "his" workers speaking English (instead of Welsh) or even becoming literate. Looking and sounding like Sherlock Holmes's Doctor Watson (whom Nigel Bruce played for years), the squire questions everything about Miss Moffat, beginning with her degree, an M.A. "A female M.A.? And how long's that going to last?" Her reply: "Quite a long time, I hope, considering we've been waiting for it for two thousand years."

Miss Moffat is an early feminist and is never shy about her opinions. On why she never married, she says, "I've never talked to a man for more than five minutes without wanting to box his ears." So much of the satisfaction one gets from the old black-and-white British films comes from such exchanges that we almost forget that we are in a mining village. Actually, we almost always see the miners returning home—they never seem to go *to* the mines or spend time *in* the mines—and, of course, they are always singing, like their brother Welsh miners in "How Green Was My Valley." (Actor Barry Fitzgerald visits from that film as an uncredited—surprise!—bartender.) It may be that miners in Wales used to sing on their way home from work, but surely that activity occupied only a small percentage of their waking hours.

We are expected to believe that the squire is so dumb that he would agree to Miss Moffat's scheme to sponsor Morgan for an Oxford exam, even after hearing her response to his suggestion that she take up croquet. Her comeback sets out a reasonably witty class analysis of the countryside: "I know I shall be sticking a pin into a whale, but here are just two words about yourself. You are the Squire Bountiful, are you? Adored by his contented subjects, intelligent and benignly understanding, are you? I should just like to point out that there is a considerable amount of dirt, ignorance, misery, and discontent abroad in this world, and that a good deal of it is due to people like you, because you are a stupid, conceited, greedy, good-for-nothing, addle-headed nincompoop, and you can go to blue blazes."

Her assistant teacher says what everyone is thinking: "A miner can't go to

Oxford!" But Morgan does, after Miss Moffat deals with a potentially embarrassing subplot in which her star pupil gets one of the other students pregnant.

See also: "The Citadel"; "Educating Rita"; "How Green Was My Valley"; "The Stars Look Down."
Availability: Selected collections.
Further reading: Crowther, Bosley. "Corn Is Green." *New York Times*, 30 March 1945, 18. The reviewer applauds Davis but mocks the film's sets.
Williams, Emlyn. *The Corn Is Green.* New York: Random House, 1941. The film is a close adaptation of this playscript.
Note: Another version of "The Corn Is Green," directed by George Cukor in 1979 with Katharine Hepburn as Miss Moffat, is available on videocassette.

A Corner in Wheat

The labor theory of value dramatized

1909, 12 mins., B & W, silent, unrated, but suitable for all ages
Director: D. W. Griffith
Screenplay: D. W. Griffith, from Frank Norris's short story "A Deal in Wheat" and sections of his novel *The Octopus*

CAST
The Wheat King = Frank Powell
His Wife = Grave Henderson
His Assistant = Henry Bualthals
The Farm Family = James Kirkwood, Linda Arvidson, W. Chrystie Miller, and Gladys Egan

In 1909, D. W. Griffith released two short American Biograph Company films that he labeled "editorials." The first, "The Redman's View," although sentimental and condescending, was a rarity—the Indian wars as seen from the point of view of a vastly outnumbered and pacifist people. The second "editorial" was "A Corner in Wheat," a less sentimental, more sharply focused attack on capitalism, in which the rich get richer and the poor pay more for their bread.

Griffith's film was his contribution (as Scott Simmon has argued) to the muckraking decade at the turn of the century. Lincoln Steffens had already blamed big business for most of what he called "the shame of the cities," and Griffith had just finished "The Song of the Shirt" in 1908 (just three years before the Triangle Factory fire), in which a shirtwaist worker has her home-assembly work rejected and her sister dies in their tenement room because the shirtwaist worker is unable to earn any money.

"A Corner in Wheat" is potentially an even more radical film than "The Song of the Shirt." It combines a vision of farm labor, a wheat king's monopoly, and the failure of city relief (the breadline is suspended). Griffith, following Norris's original storylines closely, presents a grim class-conscious vision of a system that can benefit only a few. When the relief line is suspended, the city dwellers rush the bread shop. The shop owner calls the police, who deals the leader of the demonstration several sharp blows to the head and draws his revolver.

The title, however, is a pun: as the Wheat King gains a "corner" on the market— even ruining some of his fellow capitalists—he accidentally falls into his own grain shaft and is buried in *a corner* of the cascading wheat. This death scene, while memorable, is not the only important sequence in the film. In the midst of the Wheat King's triumph, Griffith inserts a freeze-frame of a breadline, as if to emphasize the hopelessness of the poor. And in the first and last shots of the film, as a farmer is sowing wheat (he should, as a contemporary reviewer noted, be *planting* the wheat), Griffith deliberately re-creates a famous painting of the nineteenth century, Jean François Millet's *The Sower*. The lingering final shot of the landscape is a futile gesture toward the agrarian source of wealth, ruined (as the film demonstrates) by monopolies and trusts.

Griffith's popular reputation as "a racist and reactionary" (based mainly on "The Birth of a Nation"), as Simmon has demonstrated, is not applicable to his entire career. His "urban films" and "Intolerance" ("The Modern Story") indicate he was a more complex director who would have had to have been blind not to notice the increased number of breadlines in New York City after the Panic of 1907.

See also: "Intolerance" ("The Modern Story").

Availability: Selected collections; Kino Video (its 1992 release is titled "A Corner in Wheat and Selected D. W. Griffith Shorts, 1902–1913").

Further reading: Norris, Frank. *A Corner in Wheat and Other Stories of the New and Old West* (1903) and *The Octopus: The Epic of the Wheat—A Story of California* (1901). Norris's short story was published posthumously; both story and relevant sections of the novel are available in Pratt and in many other editions of Norris's work.

Petric, Vlada. *D. W. Griffith's "A Corner in Wheat": A Critical Analysis.* Cambridge: University Film Study Center, 1975. A pamphlet that includes a detailed shot analysis of the film.

Pratt, George C. *Spellbound in Darkness: A History of the Silent Film.* New York: New York Graphic Society, 1973. A reprint of the fictional sources for Griffith's film and some contemporary reviews.

Simmon, Scott. *Films of D. W. Griffith.* New York: Cambridge University Press, 1993. Essential discussion for the study of "A Corner in Wheat" and Griffith's other "muckraking" short films.

Steffens, Lincoln. *The Shame of the Cities* (1904). An important muckraking classic—"In all cities, the better classes—the business men—are the sources of corruption." Numerous editions are available.

The Crime of Monsieur Lange

The killing of a capitalist cad

1935, 90 mins., French (with English
   subtitles), unrated (suitable for adults)
Director: Jean Renoir
Screenplay: Jacques Prévert and Jean Renoir
CAST
Lange = René Lèfevre
Batala = Jules Berry

Valentine = Florele
Estelle = Nadia Sibirskaia
Edith = Sylvia Bataille
Young Meunier = Henry Guisol
Concierge = Marcel Levesque
Concierge's Wife = Odette Talazac
Charles = Maurice Baquet

Film historians often credit Jean Renoir with two classics of world cinema—"Grand Illusion" and "The Rules of the Game." Both involve revealing big truths after an intense scrutiny of personal relationships and in the midst of important settings. War, or, more precisely, the "grand illusion" of honor in war, is the subject of the first film, while the class structure of bourgeois society informs the second.

Less well-known but almost in the class of these two films is this story of love and justice set in a publishing firm in Paris. Its owner, Batala, is a notorious ladies' man who has seduced almost every woman within reach. He is also a capitalist cheat who is flimflamming his way through one publishing contract to the next. Monsieur Lange is one of his duped employees, who writes a successful dime-magazine serial about his dreamy alter-ego, the Arizona Kid. When Batala uses a train crash as an excuse to escape the law, Lange and the other employees establish a democratically run cooperative business, encouraged by the political climate of the Popular Front government in mid-1930s France.

But Batala comes back, smelling profits, and pursues further lechery. The Arizona Kid has to come to life, and Lange shoots Batala. Lange escapes with his girlfriend, a successful worker-owner of a laundry, to the French-Belgian border. As he rests in his room, she pleads his case with the occupants of a border inn where they have fled from the law. These rough-and-ready country folk must be Lange's judge and jury. Will they agree that killing Batala is justice, or will they turn Lange over to the police?

"The Crime of Monsieur Lange" anticipates the moment in French political history, from 1936 to 1938, when communists, socialists, and other radicals formed an antifascist coalition government. Several films celebrated the politics of this Popular Front: cooperatives with worker control were just one part of the movement, which also included forty-hour weeks and other benefits.

See also: ["Grand Illusion"]; ["Rules of the Game"].
Availability: Selected collections.

Publisher Batala (Jules Berry) flimflams his workers in "The Crime of Monsieur Lange." Courtesy British Film Institute Stills, Posters, and Designs.

Further reading: Bazin, André. *Jean Renoir.* Edited by François Truffaut. New York: Simon and Schuster, 1973. Contains an analysis of the film by France's leading critic and a draft of the screenplay.

Strebel, Elizabeth Grottle. "Jean Renoir and the Popular Front." In *Feature Films as History*, edited by K. R. M. Short, 76–93. Knoxville: University of Tennessee Press, 1981. Analyzes the film and Renoir's career in the context of the French political scene in the 1930s.

Vincendeau, Ginette, and Keith Reader, eds. *La Vie Est à Nous: French Cinema of the Popular Front, 1935–1938.* London: British Film Institute, 1986. A collection of essays on Renoir's films and others made during the Popular Front period.

Daughters of the Dust

The power of the African-American past

1991, 114 mins., unrated, but suitable for all ages	CAST
Director: Julie Dash	Nana Peazant = Cora Lee Day
Screenplay: Julie Dash	Eula Peazant = Alva Rodgers
	Haagar Peazant = Kaycee Moore

Eli Peazant = Adisa Anderson
Iona Peazant = Bahni Turpin
Yellow Mary = Barbara O
Viola Peazant = Cheryl Lynn Bruce

Trula = Trula Hoosier
The Unborn Child = Kai-Lynn Warren
Mr. Snead = Tommy Hicks

Julie Dash's first major feature is a complex, beautiful, fascinating historical drama. She centers her story on a Gullah family, the Peazants, who are descended from slaves from West Africa. It is 1902 and they are now living on the Sea Islands off the Georgia/South Carolina coast. The family and their community, cut off from white America by the remoteness (plus insects, heat, and disease) of their island world, are maintaining many African customs and rituals while simultaneously becoming part of the economic system of the post–Civil War period, especially cotton cloth production and indigo dying. Their dialect is also unique: the film uses both English and this dialect, Geechee (employing subtitles in English when necessary).

The Peazants are about to leave their isolated world and move north. Although maintaining their African culture through the slavery period has been heroic, the twentieth century and its inevitable breakup of immigrant families of all ethnic backgrounds may yet destroy the family. At least that is the primary fear of the matriarch, Eula, who is most in touch with her community's Yoruba roots.

Although this film is perhaps more mystical than logical, it demands and rewards re-viewings. Several plot complications and narrative strategies become much clearer with each viewing.

The film opens with a series of images—Nana Peazant's hands covered in sand and what appears to be a wooden sculpture floating in the water. The "sculpture" actually is the "African" figurehead of a ship, and it suggests the legend of Ibo's Landing, when the enslaved Ibos of Africa disembarked on the Sea Islands. According to the legend, they took one look at what their slave masters had in store for them and either walked on the water back to Africa or tried to and drowned. It is a legend of stoic and suicidal defiance or of magical survival, like so much of this film.

Completion and distribution of the film were difficult. Dash's refusal to tell a straight narrative was one problem, but her insistence on getting period details such as costumes correct also led to some criticism. This is surprising given the Hollywood tradition of paying great attention to such details. The film industry newspaper *Variety* summed up some of the resistance this way: "Only intended as an investigation into a very little-known African-American culture, 'Daughters of the Dust' plays like a two-hour Laura Ashley commercial." Such a comment ignores the film's portrayal of an unusual if not unique cultural and economic system.

See also: "To Sleep with Anger."

Availability: Easy.

Further reading: Dash, Julie. *Daughters of the Dust.* New York: New Press, 1992. Essential reading for viewers of the film, this book includes the script, a preface by writer Toni Cade Bambara, and a "dialogue" with critic bell hooks.

Georgia Writer's Project (Savannah Unit). *Drums and Shadows: Survival Studies among the Georgia Coast Negroes.* 1941. Reprint. New York: Doubleday, 1972. Stories and customs, including the Ibo Landing legend.

Rule, Sheila. "Director Defies the Odds, and Wins." *New York Times,* 12 Feb. 1992, B3. Background on the director's struggle to make her film.

Holden, Stephen. "'Daughters of Dust': Tradition's Demise." *New York Times,* 16 Jan. 1992, B5. "A film of spellbinding visual beauty."

∿
The Deer Hunter

"The violent bear it away."—Flannery O'Connor (from Matthew 11:12)

1978, 183 mins., R (accurate)	Nick = Christopher Walken
Director: Michael Cimino	Linda = Meryl Streep
Screenplay: Derek Washburn, partly	Steven = John Savage
inspired by James Fenimore Cooper's	Stan = John Cazale
novel *The Deerslayer*	John = George Dzundza
CAST	Axel = Chuck Aspergren
Michael = Robert De Niro	

One of the two now-classic Vietnam films of the late 1970s (the other is "Apocalypse Now"), "The Deerhunter" dramatized what only a few Vietnam films ("Coming Home"; "In Country") dared to tackle: the way the war altered and sometimes ruined the lives of those left behind—wives, loved ones, friends, and family. It is more a film about veterans and veterans' scars than about war itself. One of the returning vets is wheelchair bound—Michael Cimino's gesture toward the most-decorated film about returning vets, "The Best Years of Our Lives" or perhaps "The Men," Marlon Brando's first successful film, in which he plays a maladjusted wheelchair-bound vet.

The film alternates between Vietnam and America, specifically a predominantly Ukranian-American steel town in western Pennsylvania. The first part in America itself alternates between the men's world and the women's—the men at work in a steel plant and at play after work at their bar, while the women prepare for a wedding. The next section, in which American and South Vietnamese POWS are in a Vietcong holding tank (literally: they are semisubmerged), and a later section, in a collapsing Saigon, have some of the most controversial footage of any Vietnam film—GIs (and others) at first forced by their captors (and then later semiwillingly) to play Russian roulette as spectators gamble on the result.

When the action takes place again in Pennsylvania, America has become a different and bitter place. Linda's job at a grocery store seems particularly pathetic when the "wrong man" comes home: instead of Nick, who is truly lost in Vietnam, she welcomes Michael, a hero who is now lost in America.

Remarkable peformances by the leads help to carry the sometimes overweighty notion of the primitive American hero, the deer hunter/slayer, who makes his kill "with only one shot." When Michael chooses at the end of the film to let a deer escape although it is in his sight, we know that he is on the way to healing. Cimino's insistence that the war was fought mainly by working-class men like Michael is evident in the bar scene in which everyone gathers to drink a toast to Nick's memory after he has been killed in a final game of Russian roulette in a doomed Saigon. When one of the men starts singing "God Bless America," they all join in. It is a tribute to Cimino's hard-won vision of the ambiguity of the American experience in Vietnam that no two viewers usually agree on whether this scene is intended to be seen as straight or ironic.

See also: ["Apocalypse Now"]; "The Best Years of Our Lives"; ["Coming Home"]; ["In Country"]: ["The Men"].
Availability: Easy.
Further reading: Canby, Vincent. "Blue-Collar Epic." *New York Times*, 15 Dec. 1978, C5. Welcomed the film as "both deeply troubling and troublesome" but with the "vision . . . of an original, major new film maker."
———. "How True to Fact Must Fiction Be?" *New York Times*, 17 Dec. 1978, II. 1. Praises the film, despite its "serious lapses in common sense," such as the Russian roulette sequences.

Desk Set

When UNIVAC was king

1957, 103 mins., unrated, but suitable for all ages	CAST
Director: Walter Lang	Richard Sumner = Spencer Tracy
Screenplay: Phoebe and Henry Ephron, from William Marchant's play of the same title	Bunny Watson = Katharine Hepburn
	Peg Costello = Joan Blondell
	Mike Cutler = Gig Young
	Sylvia = Dina Merrill

Since "Desk Set" was made with the "cooperation and assistance of IBM," one should not expect a sharp satire on the computerization of office life in the 1950s.

The efficiency experts, led by Richard Sumner (Spencer Tracy), stand with their computer between the workers (the Women) and management (the Men) in "Desk Set."

Potential satire is included, however, in part because the threat of computers taking away jobs from workers is a theme of the film. Spencer Tracy plays a "methods engineer" ("efficiency expert" sounds too threatening) who is called in to introduce computers to a major broadcasting corporation in general and to Katharine Hepburn's information department—staffed by herself and three women—in particular. Since the women simply deal in facts, they should be easily replaceable by a machine whose specialty is facts. When the computer gets hung up on differentiating "Corfu" from "curfew," the women—who are clearly smarter than both the men and the machines—do their stuff.

Although the satire about computerization is light, the film inadvertently provides a window on office politics and gender roles in the 1950s. Hepburn's Bunny is waiting endlessly for a marriage proposal from her supervisor, played with pleasant smarminess by Gig Young, but in the meantime she ghostwrites his important reports. The other women spend a lot of time worrying about men, marriage, and their jobs, often in that order. Office parties with too much booze, workplace fashion, and witty conversation fill up a good part of their days.

The film has a few giggles, but the real story—automation and layoffs/firings—is not so funny. IBM no longer misses the fact that the joke may be on it.

See also: "Computers in Context"; "The Efficiency Expert"; "9 to 5."
Availablity: Selected collections.
Further reading: Crowther, Bosley. "Desk Set." *New York Times*, 16 May 1957, 28. "The next time they bring up automation, they'll have to pick someone less formidable than Kate [Hepburn]."

ᚥ
The Devil and Miss Jones

Fantasy on 38th Street

1941, 92 mins., unrated, but suitable for all ages	John P. Merrick = Charles Coburn
	Joe O'Brien = Robert Cummings
Director: Sam Wood	Hooper = Edmund Gwenn
Screenplay: Norman Krasna	Elizabeth Ellis = Spring Byington
CAST	George = S. Z. Sakall
Mary Jones = Jean Arthur	

This impossible labor union fantasy has a "Miracle on 34th Street" air about it: John P. Merrick, "the richest man in the world," is burned in effigy outside his department store on 38th Street in Manhattan, becomes a humble clerk to catch the culprits, and ends up on the committee of the local to negotiate with himself! In the meantime, he discovers love and union solidarity and rents an ocean liner to take all his employees on his honeymoon cruise.

What is going on here? With a slickness and collective nose for topicality, Hollywood used real-life situations—an organizer is discharged and blackballed from other department stores, for example—and gave them a comic twist. Robert Cummings plays Joe O'Brien, an all-American union man and organizer, who handcuffs himself to the pipes in Merrick's store in order to make speeches to the employees cowed by Merrick's anti-union tradition. Joe's girlfriend, played by the very popular Jean Arthur, works at the store and is always ready to provide the "women's point of view" for Joe's organizing campaign: these are "moral issues," she always insists.

Joe is very sincere; he plays the straight man to everyone's jokes. When he is arrested at one point, the police have to decide whether it is worth the trouble to keep him in jail since he is driving them crazy about his rights. "When they start reciting the Constitution," a police sergeant says, "Look out!" It's a great comic scene, because these fantasy police officers are of course more concerned about maintaining peace and quiet in their station house than in the streets. Joe really doesn't mind being arrested because then he can test the system.

While the audience is chuckling over the various love affairs and new-found friendship between the (secret) millionaire and the average Joe, a few progressive points are made about the oppressive anti-union atmosphere of the store and the need for improved wages and conditions. As a comedy, however, the real issue is how to reunite the feuding couples. In the end, the millionaire with the opulent mansion out of "Citizen Kane" (it looks like the studio recycled the giant fireplace) finds a companion in the sweet staff woman who loves him "for what he really is," a nice guy who happens to be "the richest man in the world." But she didn't know that!

See also: "The Pajama Game."
Availability: Selected collections.
Further reading: Crowther, Bosley. "The Devil and Miss Jones." *New York Times*, 16 May 1941, 21. The reviewer celebrates this "frothiest" of comedies.

The Dollmaker

The great inland Appalachian migration

1984, 150 mins., TVM
Director: Daniel Petrie
Screenplay: Susan Cooper and Hume
   Cronyn, from Harriet Arnow's novel of
   the same title
CAST
Gertie = Jane Fonda
Clovis = Levon Helm
Mamie Childres = Amanda Plummer
Mrs. Kendrick = Geraldine Page

Reuben = Jason Yearwood
Enoch = David Brady Wilson
Clytie = Starla Whaley
Amos = David Dawson
Anne = Nikki Creswell
Victor = Bob Swan
Max = Ann Hearn
Sophronie = Susan Kingsley
Taxi Driver = Studs Terkel

"The Dollmaker" makes an interesting companion piece to "The Killing Floor": just as rural blacks moved to Chicago in search of jobs during World War I, Appalachian whites moved to Detroit and other midwestern cities during World War II. Fonda plays the title character, Gertie, a rural Kentucky woman with a great talent for making wooden dolls and animal figures. She follows her husband north after he moves to take a factory job as a mechanic, although she really wants them to stay in Kentucky and buy a farm. The Detroit housing project they move to is pretty dispiriting, even if a whimsical taxi cab driver (played by Studs Terkel) ferries them over from the railroad station to the unpromised land.

Kentucky begins to look awfully good, despite its poverty and lack of medical facilities. One of the most dramatic scenes, back in Kentucky, involves a medical emergency, as Gertie is called upon to give her choking son a tracheotomy by the side of a road. After cutting a passage into his throat, Gertie sticks a hollow reed into his windpipe. A passing army vehicle stops, but the men aren't much help; in fact, the captain faints. So much for menfolk. Gertie, as ever, carries on.

The slummy conditions of Detroit project life do get to her, however, as do her husband's poor pay (when he manages to be working), sneers at her Appalachian traditions, incidents of fascist behavior, and the layoffs as the war work slackens. She really begins to lose her spirit when her daughter, Cassie, is killed by a train.

In both the novel and the film, Gertie's final act of indignation is her destruction of her block of cherry wood, a kind of mystical and artistic talisman, which she breaks up to make smaller "whittled" objects for sale. The screenwriters made a major alteration in the novel's ending, in which Gertie must accept staying in depressing Detroit. The film places her in a pickup truck heading joyfully back to Kentucky.

See also: "Coal Miner's Daughter"; "The Killing Floor."
Availability: Easy.
Further reading: Arnow, Harriet. *The Dollmaker.* New York: Macmillan, 1954. The filmmakers significantly whittled Arnow's great novel down to size.
"The Dollmaker." *Variety,* 23 May 1984. "Certainly one of the finest telepics of the season."
Farber, Stephen. "'It's as Far from What I Am as Anything I'll Ever Play,'" *New York Times,* 13 May 1984, II. 33. Extensive discussion of Fonda's role and details about the production of the film.
O'Connor, John J. "Jane Fonda, Gritty Mountain Woman." *New York Times,* 11 May 1984, C30. Fonda's "performance . . . is nearly always spellbinding, even when the film becomes a bit too reverential about Gertie."

❧
Edge of the City

An interracial contender, also "on the waterfront"

1957, 85 mins., B & W, unrated, but suitable for mature children	CAST
Director: Martin Ritt	Axel North = John Cassavetes
Screenplay: Robert Alan Aurthur, based on his own TV play, *A Man Is Ten Feet Tall*	Tommy Tyler = Sidney Poitier
	Charles Malik = Jack Warden
	Ellen Wilson = Kathleen Maguire
	Lucy Tyler = Ruby Dee

Martin Ritt's career in labor-related feature filmmaking began with this impressive debut. He acquired a ready-made controversial story from TV and kept Sidney Poitier as Tommy Tyler, a black dock worker who befriends Axel North, a fairly unpleasant new white worker, played by the usually semisnarling John Cassavetes. Add Jack Warden as an evil and racist foreman and the mix is clearly explosive.

Warden plays Charlie Malik, a foul-mouthed bully who discovers that Axel North has something to hide (his imagined responsibilty for a brother's death) and blackmails him. After a friendship develops between Tommy Tyler and Axel North, the Tylers invite North to their apartment, where we see a fairly rare moment in a contemporary film: social life across racial lines.

Tyler steps in during an inevitable fight between Malik and North, and although Tyler has Malik at a disadvantage, Tyler "turns the other cheek" and is stabbed in the back and killed. Tyler's wife has to awaken North's sleeping conscience and convince him to go to the police so that Malik can be brought to justice. Critics have commented (see Johnson) that too often the price of integrating African-Americans into mainstream film in the 1950s was death or the threat of death.

Poitier's sacrificial status was apparent in another unusual interracial "friendship" drama, "The Defiant Ones" (1958), in which a white convict (played by Tony Curtis) spends a good part of the picture shackled to another convict, played by Poitier.

See also: ["The Defiant Ones"]; "On the Waterfront."
Availability: 16 mm; Swank.
Further reading: Cripps, Thomas. *Making Movies Black.* New York: Oxford University, 1993. Discusses the film's critical reception and its role in Poitier's career.
Crowther, Bosley. "Edge of the City." *New York Times*, 30 Jan. 1957, 33. Applauds a few of the moments of "brotherhood" in the film but finds it too derivative of "On the Waterfront."
Johnson, Albert. "Beige, Brown, or Black." *Film Quarterly* 13 (Fall 1959): 39–43. Analyzes roles for African-Americans in 1950s films, including "Edge of the City."

∾
Educating Rita

. . . to become middle class

1983, 110 mins., PG-13	Dr. Frank Bryant = Michael Caine
Director: Lewis Gilbert	Brian = Michael Williams
Screenplay: Willy Russell, from his play of	Trish = Maureen Lipman
the same title	Julia = Jeananne Crowley
CAST	Denny = Malcolm Douglas
Rita = Julie Walters	Rita's Father = Godfrey Quigley

This is the English version of the story of the working-class kid who makes good by giving up her/his roots and making it into the middle class. Since one's accent is such an obvious class marker in England and a college education is limited to only a few percentage points of the population, Rita's heroic attempts to become independent and "intelligent"—just like "real" college students—are full of humor and spunk.

Rita (Julie Walters) is a "returning student" at the university in "Educating Rita."
Courtesy British Film Institute Stills, Posters, and Designs.

The walk she walks, the talk she talks . . . all make it clear that in most people's eyes (including hers at first) she's just a good old gal from the corner pub. But Rita wants more, and she forces the system to deliver it.

Fortunately for her, the British university system has opened a few more doors to working-class students with its adult education program, the Open University, which combines aspects of our public TV education network with on-campus tutorials. The film celebrates the value of such programs for those with enough energy and self-confidence to try them.

The film makes it clear that Rita also educates her alcoholic middle-class tutor, played admirably by Michael Caine, who in real life jumped out of the working class into the acting classes but with his accent more or less intact. Rita's enthusiam for literary study reignites her tutor's passion for it, although he becomes upset because she's "done" the poet William Blake at a summer session without his help.

Although Rita's class origins are played at first for big laughs—shots of her teetertottering in heels and a mini-skirt on the stones of Dublin's austerely traditional

Trinity College grounds set this tone early on—the film wants us to believe that Rita will be the better for having shared the experiences of two social classes. Like Willy Russell's other comic heroine, Shirley Valentine (filmed in 1989, also by Gilbert), Rita is a survivor who is not about to be held back by anything as dubious as a one-thousand-year-old class system.

Rita is hard to classify. She refuses to go "off the pill" and have a baby. Her alienation from her husband and the rest of her family is inevitable. Further, she is so impressed with Rita Mae Brown's *Rubyfruit Jungle* that she gives up her name of Susan and takes the novelist's first name. No academic jungle would be able to contain her either.

See also: "The Corn Is Green"; "How Green Was My Valley"; "Look Back in Anger"; ["Shirley Valentine"]; ["This Sporting Life"].
Availability: Easy.
Further reading: Canby, Vincent. "What Makes Audiences Fond of Rita?" *New York Times*, 13 Nov. 1983, II.17. Mocks the film's spunk but indicates its part of the tradition of "valentines to literacy."
Maslin, Janet. "Learning." *New York Times*, 21 Sept. 1983, C21. This reviewer found film "an awkward blend of intellectual pretension and cute obvious humor."

∽
The Efficiency Expert

"Reduce unnecessary contact among employees."—First Law of Efficiency

1992, 97 mins., PG	Fletcher = Dan Wylie
Director: Mark Joffe	Robert = Bruno Lawrence
Screenplay: Max Dann and Andrew Knight	Cheryl = Rebecca Rigg
CAST	Kim = Russell Crowe
Wallace = Anthony Hopkins	Jerry Finn = John Walton
Carey = Ben Mendelsohn	Gordon = John Flaus
Wendy = Toni Collette	Ron = Jeff Truman
Mr. Ball = Alwyn Kurts	

In the last twenty years the New Australian Cinema has produced a series of notable films—the mystery "Picnic at Hanging Rock," the young girl's coming-of-age film "My Brilliant Career," and the historical drama "Breaker Morant." But with the exception of the video release of a TV mini-series called "Waterfront," we have not seen films of comparable merit on labor and work-related topics. It is thus with high hopes that we encounter "The Efficiency Expert," directed by Mark Joffe, who made the well-received thriller "Grievous Bodily Harm," which was not released in the United States.

The opening titles strike a whimsical note that will run throughout this comic look at an "efficiency expert," played by Anthony Hopkins in his usual intense and sympathetic style. He doesn't like to be called a "time and motion man" because his company surveys a client's "whole corporate picture," including its financial health. When he takes a look at Ball's Moccasins in Spotswood, a "small, shabby industrial suburb of Melbourne," he finds a paternalistic boss and a utopian workplace: the employees work as much as they want, when they want, and have time to gossip, to manage the company's "slot car" racing team, and to dance to "Heart of Texas" when the mood strikes them.

And it does, because Ball's Moccasins hasn't made a profit in decades: the owner has been selling off assets (parcels of his real estate, for example) and cooking the books to make it look like everything is fine. He cannot bear to make his employees unhappy. He ignores the failure of such sales campaigns as "Mocc and Roll" and treats them all as business coups.

In a parallel plot, the efficiency expert, Mr. Wallace, has just recommended to an auto parts factory that it cut a quarter of its staff. When a fellow efficiency expert leaks an inflated layoff figure to the unions, all hell breaks loose and the auto workers try to storm their plant. Whimsy wins the day, however, and Mr. Wallace ends up helping Ball's Moccasins survive with its (obviously) impossible work culture. (The auto parts factory ends up cutting "only" five hundred jobs.)

In Australian films, so often both the whimsical and the impossible are celebrated as realistic and necessary, so that we leave the expert in the end with his new-found soul intact and the old cohort of workers streaming back into Ball's Moccasins.

The original screenplay (and perhaps the British Commonwealth version, which I have not seen) called for a bittersweet ending in which the titles read: "Ball's Moccasins closed two years later. / Arthur Ball died three months after that. / The Moccasin Factory now houses an arts collective." Apparently American moviegoers (who do not see these end titles) need to be reassured that all's well in Aussie-Land.

Although the film is supposed to be set in the 1960s—Donovan's song "Catch the Wind" is featured over the end credits—the film shows two post–high school youngsters, Carey and Wendy, happily biking off to work as if time stood still in 1955. They should fall in love, we know that almost immediately, but Carey has to fall for the boss's beautiful daughter before he comes to his senses and realizes that homespun Wendy (who, like her counterpart in "Peter Pan," may be able to fly) is the gal for him. Carey also has to realize that being an apprentice to an efficiency expert is a sure way to destroy workplace friendships.

This is a PG film that is suitable for mature children, and it may help teach such youth about the evils of corporate maneuvering for profits. Mr. Wallace's suggestion that Ball's become a cooperative in which the workers hold the shares in the company may also teach them about another kind of corporate ownership, however rare. If they ask you for an airplane ticket to Australia so they can get a job at Ball's Moccasins, then Australian whimsy has won again.

See also: "Waterfront."
Availability: Easy.
Further reading: Dann, Max, and Andrew Knight. *Spotswood.* Sydney: Currency Press, 1992. The original screenplay includes brief essays by the director and a critic.
Murray, Scott. *Australian Film: 1978–1992.* London: Oxford University Press, 1993. Includes a review of the film, emphasizing its "utopian" attitudes toward the factory.
Note: The original title in British Commonwealth countries was "Spotswood."

◑ El Norte

No pasar.

1983, 139 mins., some Spanish (with English subtitles), R, but suitable for mature children	Enrique Xuncax = David Villalpando
	Arturo Xuncax = Ernesto Gomez Cruz
	Lupe Xuncaz = Alicia del Lago
Director: Gregory Nava	Pedro = Eraclio Zepeda
Screenplay: Gregory Nava and Anne Thomas	Josefita = Stella Quan
	Ramon = Rodolfo Alejandre
CAST	Nacha = Lupe Ontiveros
Rosa Xuncax = Zide Sylvia Guiterrez	

"The North" is the promised land of the poor and oppressed children of Guatemalan Indian coffee workers who dare to organize to improve their conditions. When a young man, Enrique, discovers that his father has been decapitated for his union activities, he kills a government soldier. When his mother is disappeared as well, he and his sister, Rosa, escape on a trek to "el Norte."

The film is divided into three "acts": (1) life and death in Guatemala, (2) travel in Mexico from Oaxaca to Tijuana, and, finally, (3) life as illegal "Mexican" immigrants in Los Angeles. Each stage is filled with horrors and difficulties. To leave Mexico, for example, Enrique and Rosa must find a "coyote" to lead them across the border. The first one attacks them for their money, but the second one—a "friend of a friend"—sends them successfully through an old sewer tunnel, but it is overrun with rats.

Some moments of sick comedy enliven the siblings' difficult lives. To pass as Mexicans, they are told to add an extremely vulgar Mexican phrase to their oral vocabulary. When they are detained by the "Migra" (immigration police) after their first failed attempt to cross the border, Enrique fools the interviewer by casually cursing every third word. At the overly high-tech home of her new employer, Rosa cannot operate the washing machine. Her employer discovers her washing clothing by hand near the fancy swimming pool and tells her to stop: "I couldn't stand the thought of her . . . *scrubbing*."

The end of the film suggests the difficulty of separating the personal frustrations of the siblings from the economic system, from which there is "no exit." Enrique must choose between caring for his sister (who becomes very sick) and working in a good job. In the end he loses both and must return to the seemingly endless cycle of waiting for a day job at the local pickup stop for illegal immigrant labor. Even exploitative contract work with a labor gang would seem superior to this dead end.

Most viewers find the scenes in rural Guatemala so vivid that its horrors seem like hallucinations or a nightmare. Indeed Gregory Nava uses the "magic realism" of dreams and nightmares to great effect: we see Enrique attacked by a Guatemalan soldier in a foggy Tijuana street before we realize it is simply a nightmare. But Tijuana's shantytown is so ugly that it seems the siblings have simply run from one hell to another. Los Angeles does give them a piece of the Dream—the TV sets, flush toilets, and electricity their old copies of *Good Housekeeping* promised them when they were still in Guatemala. But the Migra is ever-present, waiting to snatch "el Norte" away from them. Not many films handle such moments in depth or even with feeling; perhaps Tony Richardson's "The Border" (1982) comes close, but that film is essentially from the point of view of a police officer, however sympathetic he may be.

See also: ["The Border"].

Availability: Easy.

Further reading: Canby, Vincent. "'El Norte': A Fine Movie Fueled by Injustice." *New York Times*, 22 Jan. 1984, II.17. "One of the most boldly original and satirical social-political statements ever to be found in a film about the United States as a land of power as well as opportunity."

Maslin, Janet. "A Better Life." *New York Times*, 11 Jan. 1984, C15. Maslin calls the film "a remarkable accomplishment," with "solid, sympathetic performances by unknown actors and a visual style of astonishing vibrancy."

Note: I follow the style of most video guides, which alphabetize this film under "E," however linguistically incorrect (since "el" means "the") that may seem.

⌒⌒
Fallen Champ: The Untold Story of Mike Tyson

A working-class hero in big trouble

1993, 93 mins., TVM, unrated, but PG
Director: Barbara Kopple
Scripted documentary by Barbara Kopple

PRINCIPAL FIGURES
Mike Tyson, boxing champion
Cus D'Amato, Tyson's first manager

Camille Ewald, D'Amato's companion and Tyson's surrogate mother

Teddy Atlas, first trainer, fired

Kevin Rooney, later trainer, also fired

Don King, manager and promoter

Robin Givens, actress and Tyson's ex-wife

Desiree Washington, Miss Black America contestant

Louis Farrakhan, leader of the Nation of Islam (Black Muslims)

Alan Dershowitz, Tyson's appeals lawyer

Joyce Carol Oates, novelist

After Barbara Kopple's two major Academy Award–winning union documentaries, "Harlan County U.S.A." and "American Dream," it seemed a bit odd for her to take on this network project, just a year after Tyson was sentenced to six years for the rape of a Miss Black America contestant from Rhode Island during the competition in Indianapolis in 1991. (Tyson was released in 1995.) But Kopple is dealing with a very popular working-class hero here, a powerful boxer who had a troubled (reform school) past but rose, under the tutelage of a white "family"—his manager, his German-born companion, and trainer—to become one of the youngest sports heroes to suffer—or take advantage of, depending on your viewpoint—the adoration of legions of female fans (the "groupies" who should have known better, sneers Alan Dershowitz, Tyson's appeal lawyer, at one point in the film).

Kopple exposes a sensitive, immature, cocky, virtually impossible youth who becomes used to literally grabbing every woman who pays any attention to him (and some who don't). Numerous interviews address the nature of the expression "no" in sexually charged situations.

Although this is not exclusively a documentary about boxing, Kopple includes enough footage of battles in the ring and the tough working-class environment to prepare the viewer for the explosively powerful and dangerous Tyson. At one point in the film he explains his philosophy of boxing as aiming for the opponent's nose so he can try "to punch the bone into his brain."

Some fascinating footage assembled by Kopple includes Tyson—who flies pigeons—as a clone of the Terry Malloy character in "On the Waterfront." We also see Robin Givens making it clear that she and her mother were "taking over" Tyson's life, Louis Farrakhan mimicking and mocking Desiree Washington's "come-on" to Tyson, and the Miss Black America competition with the victim-to-be as a giggly teenager in the presence of the mighty celebrity. This is a unusual film, mixing news from the date rape debate and the traditionally male and violent world of boxing.

Kopple has received more widespread support than any comparable filmmaker, much less any filmmaker dealing with labor-related topics. We should remember, for example, that Michael Moore's "Roger & Me," one of the most successful feature-length documentaries of our era, did not even receive an Academy Award nomination. Although Mike Tyson as a subject may seem a little off Kopple's beat, she gives her usual committed attention to the portrayal of the fighter and his troubled career.

The relationship between African-Americans as gladiators of a blood sport and the enormous economic structure of professional sports in American culture seems almost on trial in this film. Kopple's timing with regard to addressing current social topics of importance and her knack for uncovering the complexity of the human drama she films are obvious. Will her film about the twenty-fifth anniversary Woodstock concert mark the beginning of the end of her interest in making films with a working-class focus?

See also: "American Dream"; "Harlan County U.S.A."; "On the Waterfront."
Availability: Selected collections.
Further reading: Berkow, Ira. "Tyson Changes, But Not Enough." *New York Times*, 14 June
    1994, B12. An update on the denial of Tyson's parole (because he would not admit his guilt).
Feaster, Felicia. "Fallen Champ." *Film Quarterly* 47 (Winter 1993–94): 45–47. A critical review,
    arguing (with some difficulty) that Kopple "just contributes to [Tyson's] myth-making
    without truly questioning it."
Garrison, J. Gregory, and Randy Roberts. *Heavy Justice: The State of Indiana vs Michael G.
    Tyson.* Reading: Addison-Wesley, 1994. Coauthored by the special prosecutor of the case,
    who "had not lost a jury trial in twenty years."
Oates, Joyce Carol. *On Boxing.* Garden City, N.Y.: Doubleday, 1987. A celebrated novelist,
    short-story writer, and boxing fan attempts to understand the supermasculine world of
    boxing.
Sandomir, Richard. "A Poet of the Proletariat Finds an Unlikely Subject." *New York Times*, 7
    Feb. 1993, II.28. A discussion of the film and of Kopple's career.

༄

Fast Food Women

No fries, no frills, no benefits

1992, 28 mins., unrated, but suitable for all
    ages
Director: Anne Lewis Johnson
Unscripted documentary
PRINCIPAL FIGURES
Marion Clark, co-owner and manager,
    Druthers, Whitesburg, Kentucky
Sereda Collier, cook, Druthers

Nellie Kincer, cook, Druthers
Angie Hogg, kitchen staff, Druthers
Mike Super, human resources manager,
    Druthers, Inc.
Marcella Fields, crew chief, Pizza Hut
Barbara Garson, author
Zelpha Adams, crew chief, McDonalds
Pam Banks, former waitress, Pizza Hut

The "fast-food women" interviewed in this brief but excellent film are mostly older women who are the sole support of their families in small Eastern Kentucky coal towns. They are resigned to their fates as low-paid "backup" workers for their men, who may never get back their well-paying jobs in the coal mines. The women speak sincerely and with remarkable good humor of the hard work, the low pay, and the

Angie Hogg, part of the Druthers kitchen staff and one of the principal figures in "Fast Food Women." Courtesy Appalshop Films.

sense that they are serving an indefinite sentence. A few hold out for the moment when their husbands will go back to work. "Then I'm out of here," says one.

The myth that fast-food workers are teens picking up sneaker money dies hard, especially among corporate executives. Mike Super, Druthers' human resources manager, says the teenagers who work at Druthers don't need "frills": "Susie is sixteen years old. Her father works in the coal mine. . . . Susie doesn't need benefits."

Susie, as Johnson's gentle but probing camerwork reveals, is really forty-eight years old and has been working for Druthers for years. In fact, Johnson got the idea for her film as she was sitting in her Appalshop media lab, across the street from the Whitesburg, Kentucky, Druthers, and noticed how many older women worked there.

On the surface, the most insincere moments occur during interviews with two of the top managers of the Druthers chain, headquartered in Louisville. Clearly, these two managers have never thought—until the moment of the filming—about the implications of the corporate philosophy taught in their equivalent of McDonalds 101. When asked whether the restaurant workers need to be creative, one Druthers exec says, "We are not looking for creativity as much, . . ." whereupon his thought is finished by his colleague: "as looking for somebody that would be more content with following procedures and practices and getting their sense of achievement from an area other than being creative about it."

Barbara Garson, who has written extensively on the effects of repetitive work, appears in the film as its only "expert." She comments on the decision-making process in such companies as McDonalds, in which people "think creatively about making the other people's jobs uncreative." She analyzes the process by which "the person at the end [cooking the food or serving the public] doesn't have to think at all."

Johnson was the associate director of Kopple's "Harlan County U.S.A." and directed the award-winning Appalshop documentaries "On Our Own Land," about strip mining, and "Chemical Valley," about a toxic waste spill near Charleston, West Virginia. Her other Appalshop documentaries, "Roving Pickets, 1961–1965" and "Mine Wars on Blackberry Creek," are part of her historical survey of the specific struggles of eastern Kentucky miners. Footage from her film on the Pittston strike ("Justice in the Coalfields") was included in Kopple's "Out of Darkness," a history and contemporary account of coal miners.

Certainly "Fast Food Women" goes a long way in "responding" to criticism that Appalshop's regional folksiness "invents" an unreal Appalachia: while certainly about Kentucky, "Fast Food Women" also is a political statement about fast-food restaurants everywhere and the exploitation of part-time labor nationally and internationally.

See also: "Out of Darkness."

Availability: Selected collections; Appalshop; ILR Media.

Further reading: Beeching, Veronica, and Tessa Perkins. *A Matter of Hours: Women, Part-Time Work, and the Labor Market.* Minneapolis: University of Minnesota Press, 1987. "Part-time work is overwhelmingly women's work"—as of the mid-1980s, 90 percent of these jobs in Britain were held by women.

Gaines, Jane M. "Appalshop Documentaries: Inventing and Preserving Appalachia." *Jump Cut* 34 (1985): 53–63. A history of Appalshop and a survey of its films; suggests some problems with its somewhat purist "folk" approach to the region.

Garson, Barbara. *The Electronic Sweatshop: How Computers Are Transforming the Office of the Future into the Factory of the Past.* New York: Simon and Schuster, 1988. The title says it all; includes a chapter on McDonald's "fast food women" (and men).

Howe, Louise Kapp. *Pink Collar Workers: Inside the World of Women's Work.* New York: Putnam, 1977. Documents the ongoing devaluation of women's clerical and restaurant work.

Leidner, Robin. *Fast Food, Fast Talk: Service Work and the Routinization of Everyday Life.* Berkeley: University of California Press, 1993. The clash of personal autonomy and corporate culture.

Noble, Barbara Presley. "While the Men Wait at Home." *New York Times,* 9 Aug. 1992, II.23. A review of the film with a profile of filmmaker Johnson.

Paules, Greta Foff. *Dishing It Out: Power and Resistance in a New Jersey Restaurant*. Philadelphia: Temple University Press, 1991. This participant-observation report explains how the "rationalization of service" (teaching workers not to think) is developing in standard family restaurants.

∾
Final Offer

Roger, Bob White, & Me

1985, 78 mins., unrated, but suitable for all ages	Roger Smith, CEO, General Motors (GM)
Director: Sturla Gunnarsson	Rod Andrew, chief negotiator, GM of Canada
Scripted documentary by "codirector" Robert Collison	Owen Bieber, president, UAW
PRINCIPAL FIGURES	Fred Morris, foreman
Bob White, president, United Auto Workers (UAW) of Canada	Danny Johnson, assembly-line worker
	Brian Blakeney, group leader

Take the uncomic Roger Smith (chair of General Motors) out of the satiric masterpiece "Roger & Me" and place him in a Canadian variation of Barbara Kopple's controversial "American Dream" and you have this film, a potential Canadian Nightmare. This National Film Board of Canada documentary charts the 1984 contract negotiations between the Canadian section of the UAW and General Motors. The leader of the Canadians is Bob White, an independent and popular figure who soon finds himself caught between Roger Smith of General Motors and Owen Bieber, president of the UAW international union.

Both Smith and Bieber want White to accept an "American" contract, pushed by GM during a flush season, the heart of which is a profit-sharing scheme: workers get bonuses in good years; they take wage cuts in bad. The Canadians have been used to a steady 3 percent hourly wage increase for many years and simply do not trust GM. Bieber, however, wants the Canadians to sign the contract, and, more to the point, he wants White to accept and go along with union "discipline." Encouraged by the Canadian workers' rising militancy and their independent tradition, White digs in and begins to walk a dangerous line, negotiating separately with both the GM leadership in Canada and Bieber himself.

The film begins with a close-up, intimate portrait of workers on the line and their immediate supervisors, demonstrating in concrete terms why the tension has been rising. Unlike Kopple's film, which moves back and forth between rank-and-file workers and the union leadership, Sturla Gunnarsson's camera soon leaves the assembly line and concentrates on the negotiating team, making only occasional forays out of the hotel, where the negotiators are holed up for months at a time.

Perhaps Minnesotans don't curse as much as their Canadian brothers, but "Final

Offer" has more "f-words" than autoworkers. At one point, when White's team is on the verge of saving its guaranteed annual hourly wage increase *if* they can call it something else, White suggests it be called the CFI, in which C and I stand for "Canadian" and "Increase."

White knows at the end of the negotiations that he is initiating a divorce: "We are talking about the end of the international." He knows that when you try to fight Owen Bieber and Roger Smith at the same time, you have set yourself up for a big fall. But White's charismatic style and careful maneuvering lead his workers to retain their traditonal hourly increase: Roger Smith, who at first seemed to be relying on the fact that Bieber would withdraw a strike authorization given to the Canadians, apparently backs down. Like the struggle between P-9 and the United Food and Commercial Workers documented in "American Dream," the casualty—if there is one—is the principle of international solidarity.

The film presents White as its hero, despite his occasional roughness. It correctly anticipates his becoming the leader of an independent union, the Canadian Auto Workers, although it does not name the organization. Besides, who can resist a man who, after incredibly strenuous but victorious negotiations, says, "Gotta go call my mother"?

See also: "American Dream"; "Roger & Me."
Availability: Selected collections; California Newsreel.

F.I.S.T.

Looks like Rocky, but still another Hoffa

1978, 145 mins., PG	Senator Andrew Madison = Rod Steiger
Director: Norman Jewison	Max Graham = Peter Boyle
Screenplay: Joe Eszterhas and Sylvester	Anna Zerinkas = Melinda Dillon
Stallone	Abe Belkin = David Huffman
CAST:	Babe Milano = Tony Lo Bianco
Johnny Kovak = Sylvester Stallone	Vince Doyle = Kevin Conway

Sylvester Stallone films do not usually generate moderate reactions: most viewers either run to or *from* the box office. "F.I.S.T." should have been an exception: the story is solid—basically another version of the story of Hoffa's Teamsters—and one of the key issues (Mob control of the unions) is virtually guaranteed to have cinematic flourishes. And Joe Eszterhas and Stallone's script comes very close to Hoffa's own vision of his career (see "Hoffa: The True Story"): that is, the union has to be in contact with Mob forces; otherwise, management will start using them first.

The acronym for this fictitious union stands for the Federated Interstate Truckers, but of course it refers to the "muscle" behind the fist as well. As a thinly disguised version of Jimmy Hoffa's career in the Teamsters, the film argues that Big Labor is by its nature prone to violence, simply because it cannot police itself. None of the establishment policing methods are much better, however, in that a crusading senator—perhaps a satiric portrait of Senator John L. McLellan of the so-called Rackets Committee (Senate Select Committee on Improper Activities in the Labor or Management Field)—is clearly up to self-aggrandizement as he probes the union's weaknesses.

This film is not my first choice for an encounter with Jimmy Hoffa's many fictional selves. It has some exciting moments, mostly when the union is outmaneuvered during some set-piece strikes characteristic of all Teamster epics. In Nicholson's and DeVito's "Hoffa," the camera is so far away from the struggle that it is sometimes impossible to see who is fighting whom. Here the budget is smaller and the camera is closer, but too often all we see to convey concern for the union is Stallone's blank face.

Norman Jewison has done some important films ("A Soldier's Story" and "In Country") and some musical epics ("Fiddler on the Roof" and "Jesus Christ Superstar"). This film suggests there is another Norman Jewison—a director who will let a weak script carry an even weaker star. The result is a film that makes yet another union look like it's run by the Godfather.

See also: "Hoffa"; "Hoffa: The True Story"; ["In Country"]; ["A Soldier's Story"].
Availability: Easy.
Further reading: Canby, Vincent. "F.I.S.T." *New York Times*, 26 April 1978, C15. Praises the cast and Hollywood's attempt not to "play it safe" with this topic.
——. "F.I.S.T. Delivers." *New York Times*, 14 May 1978, II.17. "A massive, sometimes clumsy and oversimplified but ultimately very moving melodrama."

∾

The Fountainhead

. . . with waters muddy with Rand's "philosophy"

1949, 113 mins., B & W, unrated, but suitable for all ages
Director: King Vidor
Screenplay: Ayn Rand, from her novel of the same title
CAST
Howard Roark = Gary Cooper

Dominique Francon Wynant = Patricia Neal
Gail Wynant = Raymond Massey
Ellsworth Toohey = Robert Douglas
Enright = Ray Collins
Peter Keating = Kent Smith

When the history of neofascist cultural twaddle in American culture is written, Ayn Rand's novel and King Vidor's adaptation will unfortunately occupy a lot of pages.

"Neofascist" because so many of the speeches in Rand's work pretend to celebrate the power of the individual but really applaud the willpower of a super-being. In this story, the will to prevail is embodied in the architect Roark (played by a barely breathing Cooper), who insists on building his own visions and society be damned.

"Twaddle" because Rand's novel and script call for characters who could only exist in a never-never land of capitalist utopia; for example, the newspaper owner and financier Wynant grew up in Hell's Kitchen in New York and then bought the whole neighborhood to build the world's largest skyscraper there. Or the newspaper columnist Ellsworth Toohey, who—although it looks like he couldn't organize a polo match—somehow controls the pressmen's union with the campaign slogan "I play the stock market of the spirit, and I sell short."

When Roark's rugged individualism in architecture goes out of style, he works as a laborer in a granite quarry, where Wynant's wife-to-be, played by a hyperventilating Patricia Neal, can admire his muscles as he handles a horizontal power drill. Eventually he has a comeback as an architect, working his way up from designing gas stations to designing a public housing project.

It is sad that director King Vidor made this film after making such populist films as "Our Daily Bread" and "The Citadel." By 1944, however, he had made "An American Romance" (another vision of a capitalist utopia) and joined the anticommunist, antilabor Motion Picture Alliance for the Preservation of American Ideals (see the "An American Romance" entry).

This film could be called "Our Daily Rand." Thank heavens Gary Cooper went on to make "High Noon" three years later. Nonetheless, it reveals a philosophy of capitalism that is still seductive in American culture. Look for a H. Ross Perot forerunner, Enright (played by Ray Collins), who used to be a coal miner but now is so rich he can do whatever he wants. And be aware that Ayn Rand wanted very badly to have world-famous architect Frank Lloyd Wright be considered—for publicity purposes—the role model for Roark in the book. Wright resisted but then objected to Cooper playing the role because the actor was more famous than he was. (In the meantime, Wright apparently read some Rand on negotiating, because he asked for 10 percent of the film's total budget to supply Cooper with architectural drawings; Hollywood said "no.")

There are workers in this film, but they are not in the foreground. Gary Cooper looks like he took lessons on how to drill. He may not have taken lessons on how to draw.

See also: "An American Romance"; "The Citadel"; "Gold Diggers of 1933"; "Our Daily Bread." *Availability:* Easy.

Further reading: Biskind, Peter. *Seeing Is Believing: How Hollywood Taught Us to Stop Worrying and Love the Fifties.* New York: Pantheon, 1983. Despite (or as a result of) the tongue in-cheek title, this is an excellent analysis of the film as a "Wagnerian soap opera for the radical right."

Branden, Nathaniel. *Who Is Ayn Rand?* New York: Random House, 1962. Explanations and defense of Rand's politicized philosophy by her biggest disciple.

Crowther, Bosley. "The Fountainhead." *New York Times*, 9 July 1949, 8. A devastating critique of this "high-priced twaddle" of a film.

Rand, Ayn. *The Fountainhead.* New York: NAL, 1943. Readers may conclude the filmmakers did the best they could.

ᔆ
Fury

Depression vigilantism

1936, 94 mins., B & W, unrated, but suitable
  for mature children
Director: Fritz Lang
Screenplay: Bartlett Cormack and Fritz Lang
CAST
Joe Wheeler = Spencer Tracy

Katherine Grant = Sylvia Sidney
District Attorney = Walter Abel
Kirby Dawson = Bruce Cabot
Sheriff = Edward Ellis
Bugs Meyers = Walter Brennan
Tom = George Walcott

Fritz Lang's film (his first American one) is about a lynching or, more precisely, a near-lynching, as an independent gas station owner-operator played by Spencer Tracy is mistakenly identified as the kidnapper of a young girl in a California town. The local crowd is incited to vigilante action by a traveling salesman and a visiting scab, who brags that he has just been strikebreaking where "we know how to take care of guys like this."

Lang based his scenario for the lynching on the Hart kidnapping case in San Jose, California, which occurred just three years before the film was made and in which two confessed kidnappers and murderers were brutally lynched by a crowd whose actions were publicly applauded by then-governor James "Sonny" Rolph. Lang took pains to emphasize official complicity in the lynching by having an adviser to the governor talk him out of sending the National Guard in to protect the jail.

The film uses newsreel footage of an attempted lynching that is strikingly similar to the videos that are becoming more and more a part of courtroom evidence in controversial trials today. Tracy and his brother only want to make a living from their modest gas station, but Lang's pessimistic view of the Depression suggests that hard work may not be enough. The finale in the courtroom is incredible but fascinating, as Tracy's character comes "back from the dead" to torment his accused murderers.

See also: "Metropolis"; "They Drive by Night."

Availability: Selected collections.

Further reading: Bergman, Andrew. *We're in the Money: Depression America and Its Films.* New York: New York University Press, 1971. Describes lynching films in the context of the Depression.

Cormack, Bartlett, and Fritz Lang. "Fury." In *Twenty Best Film Plays*, edited by John Gassner and Dudley Nichols. 1943. Reprint. New York: Garland, 1977. The screenplay.

The Garment Jungle

Dress shops owned by Murder, Inc.

1957, 88 mins., unrated
Director: Vincent Sherman
Screenplay: Harry Kleiner, from *Reader's Digest* articles by Lester Velie
CAST
Walter Mitchell = Lee J. Cobb
Alan Mitchell = Kerwin Mathews

Theresa = Gia Scala
Artie Ravidge = Richard Boone
Tulio Renata = Robert Loggia
Lee Hackett = Valerie French
Kovan = Joseph Wiseman
Tony = Harold J. Stone

Like its cinematic cousin, "On the Waterfront," this film originated in a series of investigative or "exposé" magazine articles written for the *Reader's Digest* by one of its "roving editors," Lester Velie. "The Garment Jungle" also opens with a murder, but it has three murders to Elia Kazan's two. Lee J. Cobb, who played the vicious union gangster in the earlier film, is here again, but this time he becomes a sympathetic character, and once it is clear that he no longer will pay protection money to thugs, he himself falls victim to them.

Cobb, as Walter Mitchell, owner of a nonunion garment-manufacturing plant, has been paying a "protector" $2,000 a week for fifteen years. (That was a lot of money in the 1950s!) When his son rebels against this and openly allies himself with an International Ladies' Garment Workers' Union organizer, Tulio, who is then murdered, father and son resolve their differences so quickly that it makes our heads spin.

The film has some pro-labor moments, which is surprising given the premises of Velie's articles. As Ken Margolies points out, organizer Tulio is "portrayed as respectable, reasonable, dedicated, intelligent, firm, and concerned with the wishes of the workers." What would happen to the workers if he were not on the scene is made quite clear when an old Jewish worker complains about a new piece rate: "Mr. Foreman, I don't want to make a big *tsimes* [fuss], but this garment takes too much time for the money." Her foreman replies: "Who don't like, pick up your check and get out of here."

When we realize that Hollywood released two films about the garment industry in 1957—this film and "The Pajama Game"—we cannot help wonder about this new emphasis. But "The Garment Jungle" opened in eighty-nine neighborhood theaters in New York City, and the producers certainly knew that the issues were hot.

It is curious but not surprising that "The Garment Jungle," which covers ground similar to "On the Waterfront," has never received one-tenth of the attention given to Kazan's film. Both films have Lee J. Cobb, of course, but Kazan had Marlon Brando and Eva Marie Saint, while Vincent Sherman had Kerwin Mathews and Gia Scala. (Who?!) None of these are household names, although in his day Sherman directed several decent films with top stars (Rita Hayworth and Glenn Ford, for example, in "Affair in Trinidad," their follow-up film to the classic "Gilda," five years before "The Garment Jungle"). But Kazan had the better script and a reputation for realistic drama, which guaranteed that Brando's "I could've been a contenda" speech would come to be associated with one of the most popular labor union films of all time, while Lee J. Cobb's girlfriend must point out—lamely but correctly—that "there's no love in the dress business."

Nevertheless, "The Garment Jungle" is worth a close(r) look: from its opening moments, when Cobb rips a new dress off one of his bored models and argues with his pro-union partner, who soon plunges to his death in a rigged elevator, to its use of documentary footage of union demonstrations and funerals, the film rarely lets up. And when is the last time you saw a union organizer in a film holding a baby at the union hall while his wife teaches the rank and file how to dance the mambo?

See also: "Edge of the City"; "On the Waterfront"; "The Pajama Game."
Availability: Selected collections.
Further reading: Margolies, Ken. "Silver Screen Tarnishes Unions." *Screen Actor*, 23 (1981): 43–52. Discusses the film in the context of a discussion of how unions are portrayed in several films.
Thompson, Harold. "The Garment Jungle." *New York Times*, 16 May 1957, 28. A positive reaction from a reviewer who wondered out loud why the police and other union officials never seem to show up during violent labor union films.
Velie, Lester. "Gangsters in the Dress Business." *Reader's Digest*, July 1955, 59–64. Surveys the dangers of union organizing in the Garment District in New York City.

Germinal

Depardieu underground

1994, 158 mins., French (with English subtitles), R
Director: Claude Berri
Screenplay: Claude Berri and Arlette Langmann, from Emile Zola's novel of the same title
CAST
Maheu = Gerard Depardieu
Maheude = Miou-Miou

Catherine = Judith Henry
Étienne Lantier = Renaud
Chaval = Jean-Roger Milo
M. Hennebeau = Jacques Dacqmine
Mme. Hennebeau = Anny Duperey
Deneulin = Bernard Fresson
Bonnemort = Jean Carmet
Souvarine = Laurant Terzieff

Claude Berri's strategy for adapting a substantial literary classic like *Germinal*—a text "thick" with sociological and historical detail—was to take the essence of each major scene and carefully reproduce it. Thus, Emile Zola's overall vision of a capitalist venture in which both worker and owner are trapped in a system they cannot change is intact in the film. Zola's socialist leanings come through because the primary focus of our sympathy is almost always with the miners and their suffering families, but the well-fed and pampered bourgeoisie have a few problems, too.

The leading character, Étienne Lantier, comes from a long line of troubled folk in Zola's novels (actually, he is introduced in the thirteenth of Zola's Rougon-Macquart series of twenty novels). Étienne is on the lam after a fight with a supervisor on his last job and thus is willing to take a job in what seem to be the murderous conditions of the Le Voreux mine.

Zola's purpose in his massive series was to examine the effects of heredity and environment on a single multigenerational family. In both the novel and the film, the effects of the mining environment almost always dominate Étienne's life. And so intense is Zola's exposé of the horrors of the mines that it is difficult to imagine any other possibility. Of course Étienne could quit and go elsewhere, and no doubt his somewhat sour personality contributes to his eventual rebelliousness, but these characteristics are hardly exclusively a function of his family. Given some of his notorious blood relatives in Zola's novels—several murderers, victims of suicides, and a famous prostitute, Nana—most commentators (see Tancock) find Étienne remarkably wholesome.

In both the novel and the film, Étienne boards with the Maheu family and becomes intimately involved with their struggles. Maheu is a gang leader (not a foreman, as some reviewers thought) who is responsible for the production and therefore the income of a handful of miners, including one of his own daughters. We follow this family through a cycle of back-breaking labor, personal scandals, and eventual collapse as Maheu is killed by the military squad guarding the mine during a strike.

The film re-creates the miners' life and work in remarkable detail. Berri shot the film in the old mining villages of northern France, specifically the Wallers-Arenberg mine, where there was a mining museum and which enabled him to recruit five hundred extras from among the retired coal miners of the region (where Zola himself had witnessed a strike in 1884).

The film ends with an impossible melodramatic moment underground: Étienne fighting another worker named Chaval for Catherine, Maheu's daughter. They have all been imprisoned as a result of the terrorist bombing of one of the mine shafts by the Russian anarchist Souvarine, who has just been moved to do the inevitable since the capitalists won't keep the already-weakened shafts repaired and the union is powerless to compel them to do so. (See "The Stars Look Down" for a similar plot development, although a Russian anarchist was not likely to be found in a Welsh coal field.) Zola's detailed rendition of the death of Chaval—spilling "brains and blood"—may have more in keeping with an Oliver Stone production than a Berri production, where the camera is remarkably discreet.

Several reviewers felt that Berri's adaptation of Zola was "over the top"—too extreme, too overwrought. But Zola was already way over the top himself: Maheu baring his chest before the troops and asking to be stuck with a bayonet, Chaval leering grotesquely, a woman gleefully castrating the shopkeeper Maigret after he's dead. All of these "exaggerations" are in the novel and if anything Berri tones Zola down a bit—the woman uses a knife rather than ripping Maigret's privates off by hand! This is a rich rendition of a rich novel.

Zola's crusade in this novel was to enhance the life of miners and reduce the abuses by the owners, but he never flinched from exposing the problems on both sides. The ultimate catastrophe that begins the ending of both the novel and the film—the flooding of the mines by exploding the shaft sunk past "sunken" underground lakes—is, after all, the result of the anarchist Souvarine's bombs. Souvarine is tolerated by the miners because they seem to like the anarchist's feistiness, but it is clear in both the novel and the film that he is not a man to be trusted by anybody. In the novel we learn that he is a Russian emigré; in the film we are not told his origins, but Berri selected an actor—and made him up—to resemble Lenin!

The film is dedicated to Berri's father, a politically conscious worker who always voted for the Communist Party. Publicity for the film also emphasized the working-class roots of the two principal stars: Depardieu's father, who was a metalworker, and Miou-Miou's mother, who sold vegetables in a market.

Because mining is the occupation most referred to in this guide, it is perhaps appropriate to note that "Germinal" is probably the most ambitious of all the films in its realistic depiction of mining conditions and the politics of both capitalism and labor organizing. Its status as a subtitled foreign film may keep it from as wide an audience as it should receive perhaps, which is unfortunate.

Leonard Tancock's introduction to his translation of the novel argues that Zola's indictment of the French mining situation was already out-of-date when the novel was published in 1885: the worst abuses of children and women in the mines, for example, had already been remedied. But as a vision of an underground hell, Zola's and now Berri's vision can hardly be faulted.

Zola's funeral cortege in Paris in 1902 was accompanied by coal miners who shouted "Germinal! Germinal!" during the procession. This film makes that spirited sendoff understandable.

See also: "Kamaradschaft"; "The Stars Look Down."
Availability: Easy.
Further reading: Lane, Anthony. "The Shaft." *New Yorker*, 14 March 1994, 90–91. A patronizing review of the film, with some valid criticisms.
Maslin, Janet. "From Claude Berri, a Zola Classic." *New York Times*, 11 March 1994, C1, C14. The film "may be hobbled by obviousness, but it remains a formidable accomplishment."
Perrot, Michelle. *Workers on Strike: France, 1871–1890.* Translated by Chris Turner. New Haven, Conn.: Yale University Press, 1987. A cultural history of strikes, with relevance to Zola.
Riding, Alan. "Does 'Germinal' Speak across a Century?" *New York Times*, 6 March 1994, VIII.31. An overview of the production, its attempt at historical accuracy, and the director.
Traugott, Mark, ed. and trans. *The French Worker: Autobiographies from the Early Industrial Era.* Berkeley: University of California Press, 1993. Seven revealing memoirs of nineteenth-century workers in France (although no miners).
Zola, Emile. *Germinal.* Translated by Leonard Tancock. 1885. Reprint. New York: Penguin, 1956. Includes an excellent brief introduction by the translator.

❧
Gold Diggers of 1933

"We're in the money!"

1933, 96 mins., B & W, unrated, but suitable for all ages	Polly Parker = Ruby Keeler
Director: Mervyn LeRoy	Brad Roberts = Dick Powell
Screenplay: Erwin Gelsey and James Seymour, from Avery Hopwood's play of the same title	Fay Fortune = Ginger Rogers
	Faneuill H. Peabody = Guy Kibbee
	Trixie Lorraine = Aline MacMahon
CAST	J. Lawrence Bradford = Warren William
Carol = Joan Blondell	Barney Hopkins = Ned Sparks

"Gold Diggers of 1933" has the reputation for being fluff—but what beautiful fluff!—because it employed the greatest mass-dance choreographer of all time, Busby Berkeley. But if you have never seen it or remember only the fluff, it deserves another look, for it captures the economic contradictions of the Great Depression in a way rivaled only by Preston Sturges's comedies. The "gold diggers" are of course the chorus girls who want to make it—not by successfully hoofing it in a big Broadway show but by marrying rich guys!

Stanley Solomon characterizes the film as one in which "money looms as an obsession, poverty as an ever-present threat," but Arthur Hove emphasizes that the moral of the story is that "chorus girls really do have hearts of gold." And while we remember the "gals" costumed as gold coins and dancing a capitalist jig, we forget that the film ends with images of unemployed veterans who have been forced to walk the breadlines. Sound familiar? Styles of filmmaking change, of course, but some problems never go away.

Homeless World War I vets were in the news as part of the threatening Bonus Army, which had marched on Washington in 1932 to demand a wartime "bonus." Joan Blondell's rendition of her "forgotten man" begins like a wail for a missing lover ("Ever since the world began, / A woman's got to have a man"), but the film's powerful imagery of the homeless vets almost shakes the fluff right out of the film.

Although the film is like a Shakespearian comedy—lovers separated, lovers misidentified, lovers reunited and married—several moments reminded the audience of the troubled world of the Depression outside the theater. Almost immediately, one of the unemployed chorus girls serves up their breakfast after casually stealing a quart of milk from a neighbor. The astonishing choreography of Busby Berkeley presents more than fifty chorus girls each playing a neon-light-outlined violin who in turn form one enormous violin, but he also presents a startling final tableau of marching soldiers in a dark parody of a rainbow while homeless vets gather in the foreground. We see shot after shot of the homeless until there is a spectacular marching sequence with men in uniform.

The "gold diggers" reappeared in 1935 and 1937 with new directors but perhaps a little less pizazz; Busby Berkeley himself directed "Gold Diggers of 1935," which featured the Oscar-winning song "Lullaby of Broadway." But most of the sharp economic analysis (if that's not too strong a phrase) had by then gone even farther downtown. By 1934, Warner Brothers had secured injunctions against rival companies trying to cash in on the "gold digger" concept: it was simply worth too much for them to share the wealth. The only coins Warner Brothers ever gave away were the chocolate and aluminum advertising tokens used to promote the opening of the 1933 hit.

See also: "Sullivan's Travels"; "Fury."
Availability: Selected collections.

Further reading: Bergman, Andrew. *We're in the Money: Depression America and Its Films.* New York: New York University Press, 1971. An excellent film history with a section on the "Gold Diggers" films.

Hall, Mordaunt. "The Screen." *New York Times,* 8 June 1933, 22. Applauds everything about the first "Gold Diggers" film, singling out "The Forgotten Man" number for special praise.

Hove, Arthur, ed. *Gold Diggers of 1933.* Madison: University of Wisconsin Press, 1980. The screenplay and extended commentary on the film.

Sennwald, Andre. "Gold Diggers of 1935." *New York Times,* 15 March 1935, 25. With jokes about an "all-Eskimo cast" doing Shakespeare, it becomes clear than the series is no longer about the unemployed.

Solomon, Stanley. *Beyond Formula: American Film Genres.* New York: Harcourt, Brace, 1976. A short but excellent analysis of the film.

❧ The Golden Cage: A Story of California's Farmworkers

On the road again . . . and again

1989, 29 mins., unrated, but suitable for all ages	Larry Galper, grape grower
Director: Susan Ferris	Daniel Haley, Western Growers Association
Scripted documentary	Enrique Reynosa, former migrant farm worker
PRINCIPAL FIGURES	Jesu Barajas, former migrant farm worker
Cesar Chavez, United Farm Workers of America (UFW) organizer	Lydia Villareal, attorney
Huberto Gomez, UFW organizer	Dr. Marion Moses, UFW physician
	B. Haakedael, U.S. border patrol agent

This film briefly reviews the origins of the United Farm Workers in the terrible conditions of these workers in the early 1960s, covering similar ground as Edward R. Murrow's classic "Harvest of Shame": the lack of drinking water and toilets and their exclusion from coverage under the National Labor Relations Act.

The film raises several issues sometimes ignored in discussions of migrant farm labor. Despite the recent amnesty and the new laws that mandate employers to obtain proof of citizenship or permission to work, illegal aliens respond to the pressure from growers to hire anybody to do the work, as more and more Americans, both by birth and naturalization, leave the fields for easier employment. The illegals are literally driven to extremes: some are shown living in cardboard-lined miniature dirt caves, while one family takes up residence in the bucket of a giant abandoned construction vehicle.

The persistent dangers of the workers lives are nowhere more graphically illustrated than in the dangers of pesticides: one worker, exposed while pregnant, gives birth to an armless but otherwise perfectly normal child.

A migrant worker in "The Golden Cage."
Courtesy Filmakers Library.

See also: "El Norte"; "The Grapes of Wrath"; "Harvest of Shame"; "Our Land Too."

Availability: Selected collections; ILR Media.

Further reading: Levy, Jacques E. *Cesar Chavez: Autobiography of La Causa.* New York: Norton, 1975. An early biography.

Meister, Dick, and Anne Loftis. *A Long Time Coming: The Struggle to Unionize America's Farm Workers.* New York: Macmillan, 1977. A very thorough history that covers the period from the mid-nineteenth century through the organizing efforts of Chavez's UFW in the 1970s.

The Grapes of Wrath

The Depression classic

1940, 129 mins., B & W, unrated, but
    suitable for all ages
Director: John Ford
Screenplay: Nunnally Johnson, from John
    Steinbeck's novel of the same title
CAST
Tom Joad = Henry Fonda
Ma Joad = Jane Darwell
Pa Joad = Russell Simpson
Casey = John Carradine
Muley Graves = John Qualen
Granpa = Charley Grapewin

Granma = Zeffie Tilbury
Al = O. Z. Whitehead
Rosasharn = Dorris Bowden
Connie = Eddie Quillan
Uncle John = Frank Darien
Noah = Frank Sully
Winfield = Darryl Hickman
Ruth = Shirley Mills
Government Caretaker = Grant Mitchell
Wilkie = Charles D. Brown
Davis = John Arledge

Although John Ford has long been identified with Westerns with such macho cowboys as John Wayne, all four of his Academy Awards were for films in other genres, and two of the four are included in this guide, "How Green Was My Valley" and "The Grapes of Wrath." Despite Ford's reputation as a bit of a crusty conservative, his films about workers were fairly progressive. In taking on John Steinbeck's novel, he was certainly adapting a well-known writer who had been sympathetic with (but not uncritical of) radical interests in California for almost a decade.

Steinbeck's experiences with migrant laborers, "red" organizers, and vigilante committees in California come through in his novels *In Dubious Battle* (optioned by documentary filmmaker Pare Lorentz but never filmed) and of course in this classic. This is the novel that should have ensured that Steinbeck would win a Nobel Prize, but its radical critique of American society took a little time to reach its current classic status.

Very few people do not know at least one version of this story of the migration of the Joad family. Forced out of their homestead, joined by their son, who has just left

Okies in "The Grapes of Wrath" read one of the many announcements of jobs in California.

a penitentiary for serving a sentence for manslaughter, they head west to California, the promised land, on a rickety truck packed with their possessions. The visual images of the Depression, in still photography and film, memorialize their trek and the voyages of many others who were forced by economic scarcity to confront an unknown future.

The Joads' drama is hardly over when they get close to California. There are still cruel twists ahead for them. In the film, the concluding sequence, featuring a repressive migrant camp with gun-toting violent guards, is brilliantly contrasted (in a New Deal twist) with a federally controlled camp, whose caretaker bears a remarkable resemblance to FDR himself!

The film's ending—a conversation between Tom Joad and his mother before he leaves the family again—is an example of pure Hollywood populism: the people will persevere, preferably by themselves but certainly with the help of the Democratic Party if necessary. (Tom Joad doesn't say *all* of that, of course, but he wants to.) The ending of Steinbeck's novel is more ambiguous and to a certain extent more daring. As Joseph R. Millichap points out, the film takes Ma Joad's speech from an earlier chapter when they depart their first "Hooverville" and moves it to the end of the film, after the dancing to the tune of "Red River Valley," a typically Ford nostalgic moment (a symbol "of an almost mystical harmony," concludes Millichap). The film sends Tom away in a striking composition similar to his arrival at the beginning, but in the novel the family struggles on to a cotton farm where conditions are terrible. Certainly the final scene in which Rosasharn shares her milk-swollen breasts with a dying old man would not have been filmable then (or now), although Steinbeck apparently believed it to be an appropriate life-affirming coda.

Steinbeck's complexity is a little hard to catch the first time through. Certainly the film doesn't do any aspects of his overall vision justice—either the frustrations of the contest between "red" organizers and bread-and-butter unionists in *In Dubious Battle* or the struggle between "bad" capitalists and New Deal capitalists in *The Grapes of Wrath*.

See also: "Fury."

Availability: Easy.

Further reading: Lorentz, Pare. *FDR's Moviemaker*. Las Vegas: University of Nevada Press, 1992. Contributes a sense of the narrow band between documentary and feature film during the FDR period and discusses Lorentz's plans to film *In Dubious Battle*.

Margolies, Ken. "Silver Screen Tarnishes Unions." *Screen Actor* (Summer 1981): 43–52. Singles out Ford's film for special praise, in the context of a discussion of other labor films.

Millichap, Joseph R. *Steinbeck and Film*. New York: Ungar, 1983. An authoritative discussion of Steinbeck's career and excellent comparisons between novel and film: "John Ford's 'The Grapes of Wrath' is a beautiful, moving, and intelligent film, though not the great novel John Steinbeck wrote."

Steinbeck, John. *In Dubious Battle*. 1935. Reprint. New York: Bantam, 1961. Steinbeck dramatizes the tension between communist and (bread-and-butter) trade union organizing among California's agricultural workers.

——. *Working Days: The Journal of the Grapes of Wrath, 1938–1941*. Edited by Robert DeMott. New York: Viking, 1989. Steinbeck's revealing musings about his work, with excellent annotations that situate the novel in contemporary affairs.

Stott, William. *Documentary Expression and Thirties America*. New York: Oxford University Press, 1973. An excellent survey of the documentary impulse in films, still photography, and literature.

∾
Gung Ho

Japanese calisthentics for the UAW

1986, 111 mins., PG-13
Director: Ron Howard
Screenplay: Lowell Ganz and Babaloo
   Mandell

CAST
Hunt Stevenson = Michael Keaton
Kazihiro = Gedde Watanabe
Audrey = Mimi Rogers

Hunt Stevenson (Michael Keaton) with a Japanese manager from Assan America and an American worker in "Gung Ho."

Buster = George Wendt   Willie = John Turturro
Sakamoto = Soh Yamamura   Saito = Sab Shimono
Junior = Jihmi Kennedy   Paul = Clint Howard
Googie = Rick Overton   Heather = Michelle Johnson

Although the United States and Japan have harbored mutual obsessions and suspicions (especially about the surprise attack on Pearl Harbor and the atomic attacks on Hiroshima and Nagasaki) for four decades, only two recent major films besides this one ("Iron Maze" and "Come See the Paradise") deal with related economic issues or workers. Indeed, the title of this film is the same as that of a classic anti-Japanese World War II film, in which actor Randolph Scott and others tear up the enemy viciously. Americans, it is true, had already appropriated the Japanese phrase "gung ho," often without much consciousness of its origins.

In this film, Michael Keaton plays an auto union shop steward named Hunt Stevenson who confidently journeys to Japan to offer Assan Motors, a corporate giant there, the opportunity to buy out his local defunct auto plant. The fact that he comes from Hadleyburg—as in Twain's "The Man Who Corrupted Hadleyburg"—should have warned the Japanese or us that the satire in this film would be extremely broad.

His cultural miscommunications and blunderings amuse his Japanese investors enough that they send one of their losers—a disgraced manager—to take charge of their new American branch. Most of the slapstick humor in the film involves the cultural clashes that occur between the Japanese managers and the American workers. Stevenson makes a pact with the devil and keeps it from his membership: if they turn out fifteen thousand cars in one month, he will guarantee their jobs and their old comfortable wages. Not knowing about Stevenson's quota deal, the workers believe that all they have to do is try a little harder and they will be rewarded.

In the end, the film shows us that Americans work as hard as their Japanese counterparts, even if a lot of American cars are defective. Most viewers find this film very funny, even if none of the solutions to the problems of the American auto industry is amusing or even likely to work. Stevenson's local meets once in a while, but basically he is always in charge.

See also: "Come See the Paradise"; "Iron Maze"; "Rising Son."
Availability: Easy.
Further reading: Canby, Vincent. "Banzai Detroit." *New York Times*, 14 March 1986, C8. Canby finds the satire too light.
Kamata, Satoshi. *Japan in the Passing Lane: An Insider's Account of Life in a Japanese Auto Factory.* Translated by Tatsuru Akimoto. New York: Pantheon, 1982. A critical account of a journalist's six-month job in Japan; the last chapter is called "The Dark Side of Toyota."
O'Brien, Tim. *The Screening of America: Movies and Values from "Rocky" to "Rain Man."* New York: Continuum, 1990. Discusses the film in the context of other 1980s films about workers and business ("Tucker," "Working Girl," and "Wall Street").
Note: The World War II film with almost the same title, "Gung Ho!" is most emphatically not about workers.

∿

Half Slave, Half Free

". . . Nothing else is known about him."

1984, 113 mins., TVM, unrated, but suitable for mature children
Director: Gordon Parks, Sr.
Screenplay: Lou Potts and Samm-Art Williams, from Solomon Northup's autobiography, *Twelve Years a Slave*
CAST
Solomon Northup = Avery Brooks
Anne Northup = Petronia Paley
Henry Northup = Michael Tolan
Jenny = Rhetta Greene
Eliza = Janet League
Ford = Mason Adams
Bass = Kent Broadhurst
Epps = John Saxon
Mrs. Epps = Lee Bryant
Tibeats = J. C. Quinn
Noah = Joe Seneca
Birch = Ralph Pace
Merril Brown = Royce Willman
Bram Hamilton = Thomas Campbell

Solomon Northup lived for twelve years what must have been a common nightmare to free black men and women everywhere in pre–Civil War America: as a slave *again* or, in his case, for the first time, stripped of the status of a "free person of color," as they were then known. Northup was a fiddler and a carpenter in Saratoga Springs, New York. In his autobiography he recalls his somewhat naive acceptance of a job in 1841 as a musician in a traveling circus run by two doubtful entrepreneurs, Hamilton and Brown, who convince him that having papers indicating his status as a free man would protect him in slave territory, that is, in Washington, D.C. Northup accompanies a pathetic set of circus acts to Washington, where he is shanghaied into slavery, most likely through connivance by his new and very smooth employers. He is then literally beaten into slavery by a particularly nasty trader named Birch, who specializes in kidnappings.

The film version of Northup's autobiography makes Hamilton and Brown active and immediate agents in his enslavement. They drug him at the beginning of his trip from New York, and he ends up in the slave owners' pen in D.C. No circus interlude for him.

This costume drama was clearly made on a relatively low budget, and too often most of the extras and some of the principal characters look like the static performers in a historical theme park. (Their costumes are much too clean.) But the film's portrayal of free black men and women as workers as well as slaves makes it an unusual survey of labor in the mid-1800s. And although the film does not do complete justice to the complexity of Northup's literary rendition of the various jobs both free and slave men and women held in the last decades of American slavery, it certainly helps to highlight slavery as an economic institution. Its board of consultants and labor historians (including Eric Foner, Eugene Genovese, Herbert Gutman, Benjamin Quarles, Willie Lee Rose, and Kenneth Stampp) suggests a commitment to accuracy rare in films about southern history.

Northup's story covers some of the same ground as the salacious and sadistic "Mandingo" (1975), in which interracial sex becomes the only labor on a plantation. In Parks's version of this especially "peculiar institution," interracial sex (never graphically depicted) has economic implications. On the ship that brings Northup from a Washington, D.C., slave pen to New Orleans, he encounters the light-skinned Eliza, who has been the mistress of a Virginia planter. Unfortunately, she and her master's biracial child have been sold away from the homestead by jealous family members (her white "half" sister in Northup's narrative but a wife in the film). Another young woman, Jenny, purchased in the same "drove" as Northup, falls in love with him in the film but becomes the open mistress of Epps, the last of Northup's slave masters, before he is finally freed by his namesake, the white Henry Northup, whose family had owned Solomon Northup's father.

In the film Northup's considerable talents as a worker become both his protection and a threat to his survival. Because he simply knows so much more than any "hereditary" slave, he stands out: he can build a bed and household furniture, as well as a raft to float timber downstream. But his intelligence, refined manners, and good speech make him a threat to "white trash" like Tibeats, who sees him as a challenge to white supremacy.

The film strengthens Northup's view, never made explicit in his narrative, that while a single black person remains a slave, no one can be free. At the time of publication (1853), Northup's book fueled the abolitionists' fires that Harriet Beecher Stowe's novel *Uncle Tom's Cabin* (1851–52) had helped to spread. Gordon Parks's film explores the more philosophical implications of Northup's gruesome adventure: the act of free work (and his music as a fiddler) in a sense creates the idea of a free man. Thus, two acts of destruction—a fellow slave takes an ax to Northup's bed, and his master Epps smashes his fiddle—both dramatize the need of the racist system to destroy the freedom of creative work.

To carry out this vision, Parks has to shy away from some of the unpleasantness in which Northup felt compelled to participate. In the film Northup only pretends to whip Jenny at one point, but in the book he at first whips her namesake (Patsey) as she is tied hands and feet to four stakes in the ground. Northup delivers almost thirty-five lashes to Patsey's naked body before he finally refuses to continue. Perhaps as a concession to the subgenre of made-for-TV films, Parks suggests that Northup did have a relationship with Jenny and so could hardly whip her almost to death.

The end titles inform us that the New York State trial of the kidnappers (Brown and Hamilton) was inconclusive and that the slave trader Birch was acquitted in a Washington, D.C., trial because Northup as a black man could not testify. Although his book was a best-seller, Northup (like the black packinghouse workers in "The Killing Floor") has been lost to history: "Nothing else is known about him or where and when he died," reads the film's end title.

"Half Free, Half Slave" joins Parks's other successful film, "The Learning Tree" (based on Parks's autobiography of his boyhood in Kansas), and Martin Ritt's "Sounder" as films that successfully examine the rural traditions of life and labor in African-American history.

See also: "The Killing Floor"; ["The Learning Tree"]; ["Mandingo"]; "Sounder."
Availability: Easy.
Further reading: Bennetts, Leslie. "TV Film by Parks Looks at Slavery." *New York Times*, 11 Feb. 1985, C18. Surveys Parks's career and his handling of Northup's story.
Corry, John. " 'Solomon Northrup's Odyssey,' Story of a Slave." *New York Times*, 13 Feb. 1985, C25. A review of the film, emphasizing its tendency to be informative about slavery but perhaps a little too "benign" in its criticism of the institution.
Davis, Charles T., and Henry Louis Gates, eds. *The Slave's Narrative.* New York: Oxford

University Press, 1985. A collection of essays on slave narratives, emphasizing the difficulty of accepting such narratives as Northup's as authentic voices since many were edited by white abolitionists.

Douglass, Frederick. *Narrative of the Life of Frederick Douglass, an American Slave.* 1845. Reprint. Doubleday, 1963. The American classic of slave narrative—Northup's journey in reverse, as it were—as Douglass escapes from Baltimore to New York in 1838.

Guerrero, Ed. *Framing Blackness: The African American Image in Film.* Philadelphia: Temple University Press, 1993. Although there is only a brief discussion of "Half Slave, Half Free" and relatively little about Parks's other films, Guerrero's book places the film in the context of other films about slavery.

Osofsky, Gilbert, ed. *Putting on Ole Massa: The Slave Narratives of Henry Bibb, William Wells Brown, and Solomon Northup.* New York: Harper & Row, 1969. The autobiographical source of the film, with two other slave narratives and a dated but helpful introduction by the editor.

Stowe, Harriet Beecher. *Key to Uncle Tom's Cabin.* 1853. Reprint. Port Washington, N.Y.: Kennikat, 1968. In her collection of documents supporting her view of slavery as a vicious institution, Stowe includes and relies on Northup's kidnapping case, "since it is a singular coincidence that this man was carried to . . . that same region where the scene of Uncle Tom's captivity was laid."

Note: "Half Slave, Half Free" was originally presented in two parts for PBS/American Playhouse: the first part, the subject of this entry, appears in some video guides as "Solomon Northrup's Legacy" (with an "r" in the second syllable of the hero's last name, as many of his contemporaries and ours spell it); "Half Slave, Half Free 2," not included in this book, appears in some video guides as "Charlotte Forten's Mission: Experiment in Freedom." This film, unrelated to part 1 except in overall theme, is also based on a true story (an educated free black woman from the North becomes a teacher on a Georgia sea island).

The Harder They Come

". . . the harder they fall, one and all."

1973, 98 mins., Jamaican (some English subtitles for Jamaican Creole dialect), R (but not really)
Director: Perry Henzell
Screenplay: Perry Henzell and Trevor D. Rhone
CAST
Ivanhoe ("Ivan") Martin = Jimmy Cliff

Elsa = Jane Barkley
Jose = Carl Bradshaw
Pedro = Ras Daniel Hartman
Preacher = Basil Keane
Hilton = Bobby Charlton
Detective = Winston Stona

The criminal career and subsequent folk-hero popularity (like that of Bonnie and Clyde) of Ivanhoe "Rhygin" Martin, the first of the great "ghetto gunmen" in Jamaican history, who shot his way into the news in 1948, is the basis of Jimmy Cliff's

Ivan (Jimmy Cliff) poses as a western gunfighter in "The Harder They Come."

portrayal in this film. Although "Rhygin" saw himself as a cowboy from "wild West" movies, his crimes and the other daring deeds committed in "his" name created a formidable and politicized urban crime wave.

Although many commentators argue that music, specifically the great tradition of Jamaican reggae, is the "star" of this film, it is nonetheless a compelling drama about the political and economic difficulties at the heart of this former British colony. The struggle to get a job in this country begins the drama for country boy Ivan, who goes to Kingston, a city of contrasts (affluent suburbanities and homeless garbage scroungers). At first he is simply willing to survive and works there for a preacher as a handyman. But he feels that he can make it as a singer, and he joins other hopefuls who are forced to audition at the auto gate of the home of the most important record producer and distributor in the city. Eventually, he does make a successful record, but he is tricked out of any significant income from it, and, in any case, he has already joined the "ganga" trade as a runner of dope from the countryside to the city.

The film argues persuasively that the music, the dope, and the police who control a potentially rebellious population are all related. As one character says, after Ivan's troubles with the law have forced the city to crack down on all illegal activities and many legal ones: "No hit parade. No ganga. Then law and order finished."

Ivan's tragedy is compounded by many forces: he thinks he should have more of the ganga profits for himself, he wants some income from his hit record, and he believes too fervently in the romantic heroes of the cinema. When he is forced to become a fugitive, he does become a folk hero, like the gun-toting heroes of his favorite films. (He sends the press his favorite pinup of himself in his gun-fighter pose.) All over the city, graffiti are written, celebrating his escape and exploits: "I was here but disappear" is scrawled on numerous walls. "I am everywhere" is even painted on the wall of the police compound. In the end his escape to "revolutionary" Cuba by boat is aborted. His hit song becomes his ironic epitaph: "The harder they come, the harder they fall, one and all."

But it's Ivan who falls, not those coming after him. His fantasy of fighting in a Western-style duel (he is imagining this cinematic flashback in the end) is impossible in the face of the heavily armed military who hunt him down.

Jimmy Cliff's portrayal of Ivan and Cliff's rendering of two other powerful songs on the soundtrack—"Many Rivers to Cross" and "You Can Get It If You Really Want"—have given the film cult status. Ivan's rise and fall are nonetheless both an economic tragedy and a personal choice: not all Jamaicans try to cross all the rivers between them and the evil, seducing city of Babylon.

See also: "Sugar Cane Alley."
Availability: Selected collections.
Further reading: Cham, Mbye, ed. *Ex-iles: Essays on Caribbean Cinema.* Trenton, N.J.: Africa World Press, 1992. Includes two essays on the film's origins and its context in Jamaican culture.

ᕽ
Harlan County U.S.A.

A never-ending struggle

1977, 103 mins., PG	PRINCIPAL FIGURES
Director: Barbara Kopple	Lois Scott, leader of women's group
Unscripted documentary	Basil Collins, company gun thug

Lawrence Jones, murdered miner
Tony Boyle, president, United Mine
  Workers of America (UMWA)
Jock Yablonski, challenger for Boyle's
  presidency

Florence Reese, composer of "Which Side
  Are You On?"
Norman Yarborough, president, Eastover
  Mining Company

"Harlan County U.S.A.," like Kopple's "American Dream," demonstrates her knack for finding appropriate and inevitably dramatic struggles in which she and her film crew can immerse themselves. In this instance they filmed an extended strike at the Brookside Mine of the Eastover Mining Company, a division of Duke Power. Unlike "American Dream," however, there's not much doubt when you watch "Harlan County U.S.A." "which side" she is on. According to Richard Skorman in *Off-Hollywood Movies* (New York: Harmony Books, 1989), her film was (at one time) required viewing of all master's degree candidates at the Harvard Business School (although this sounds like a piece of folklore to me).

"Harlan County U.S.A." competes with "Norma Rae" as the most "popular" labor film. The frustrations of the UMWA men when they seem to be losing their strike to court-ordered injunctions, scabs, police officers, and armed company thugs make this a very somber contrast even to "Norma Rae," in which the heroine at least seems to be on the winning team. But when the miners' wives and women-folk join the battle, taking it upon themselves to "woman" the picket lines and plot some strategy and tactics of their own, the mood of the film changes rapidly. (See "Salt of the Earth" for a similar decision on the women's part in New Mexico in the 1950s.)

But the women's decision to step in also brings problems. First and foremost, there is the question of violence, since at least one of the women (Lois Scott) makes it clear that she is going to pack her pistol just like many of the men. The women also have to deal with some internal tensions—accusations of stealing a man here and there—but for the most part Kopple captures the new-found heroism that both the men and the women (and even the film crew) share when they go off early in the morning to meet the scabs and their gun-toting thugs.

Kopple includes some early examples of the UMWA's use of a "corporate campaign" strategy when she follows a contingent of miners to Wall Street, where they do informational leafletting on Duke Power. Furthermore, she covers the murder of Yablonski, Tony Boyle's eventual downfall, and Miller's election as the new president of the union. Viewers who need a good catch-up lesson in the UMWA and mining history in general will do well to look at both "Harlan County U.S.A." and Kopple's related film, "Out of Darkness: The Mine Workers' Story."

This Academy Award–winning film is part of a long tradition of film documentary usually associated with left political or at least grass-roots movements. These documentaries have tended to be pro-working class, in part because the filmmakers often sympathized with their subjects and because not too many non-Hollywood filmmakers relate to the thrill of another corporate takeover or a particularly sweet Wall Street deal that will send a stockbroker off with a new Porsche. (And, of course, some of these Wall Street deals hinged on illegal insider trading.) Another reason for this orientation is that most of these documentaries were made during the Depression, when unemployment, union organizing, revolutionary rhetoric, and natural disasters dominated people's lives and representation in documentary films followed the photojournalistic style of the Depression.

The characteristics of Kopple's style will be obvious. She celebrates the spirit and courage of the miners and their families in the context of violence that seems never to end, in a class war that seems more appropriate to the 1930s than the 1970s. When a New York City policeman speaks to one of the picketers in the film, it seems to the policeman that the miner has stepped out of a time machine. Indeed he has. For in the Appalachian coalfields the present bleeds into the past—for many in Harlan County, 1970 *is* 1930. When Florence Reese, the composer of "Which Side Are You On?" stands up in front of a union convention in 1972 and sings her 1930s rallying song, past and present are almost indistinguishable.

See also: "Act of Vengeance"; "American Dream"; "Coalmining Women"; "Out of Darkness"; "Salt of the Earth."

Availability: Selected collections.

Further reading: Harris, Fred. "Burning Up People to Make Electricity." *Atlantic*, July 1974, 29–36. Senator Harris from Oklahoma led a blue-ribbon panel to investigate conditions in Harlan County.

Kleinhans, Chuck. "Interview with Barbara Kopple." *Jump Cut* 14 (1987): 4–6. Kopple explains her sympathies with the miners and her film strategies.

Klemesrud, Judy. "Coal Miners Started the Strike—Then Their Women Took Over." *New York Times*, 15 May 1974, 50. Background story on the women's group led by Lois Scott.

Rosenthal, Alan. *The Documentary Conscience.* Berkeley: University of California Press, 1980. Contains a detailed interview with director Kopple.

⌒ Harry Bridges: A Man and His Union

Workers of the docks, unite!

1992, 58 mins., unrated, but suitable for all ages
Director: Berry Minott
Scripted documentary by James Hamilton

PRINCIPAL FIGURES
Harry Bridges, founding president, International Longshoremen's and Warehousemen's Union (ILWU)

Harry Bridges and his pigeon in "Harry Bridges: A Man and His Union."
Courtesy the Cinema Guild, Inc.

James Landis, judge, 1940 deportation trial
Pat Tobin and Bill Bailey, retired
  · longshoremen
Tommy Trask, international vice president,
    Hawaii ILWU
Sidney Roger, former editor, ILWU
    newspaper

Wayne Horvitz, former vice president,
    Matso Navigation Company
Charles Larrowe, Bridges's "unauthorized"
    biographer
Studs Terkel, narrator

Harry Bridges, the long-standing president and radical voice of the West Coast longshoremen's union, appears at the beginning of this film in an interview late in his life, commenting on the "charge" that his union was always "left-wing." He quotes Marx—"workers of the world unite, you have nothing to lose but your chains"—and says, in the Australian accent of his youth, which is barely modified by his fifty years in the United States, "and that's as good as the day it was said."

His trials and tribulations with the U.S. government, which spent millions of dollars and many years trying to prove Bridges was a communist or "affiliated" with the Communist Party, make up almost half the story of his life. The other half goes a long way in explaining why the government pursued him so relentlessly: he was a tremendously successful radical leader of one of the most powerful unions in the country, and he helped to lead one of the rare but momentous events in labor history—the 1934 San Francisco General Strike.

The film does not hold back on some of the most controversial moments in Bridges's career—his positions in favor of automation (container shipping) and the "steady man" (the company would hire such a man on a continuing basis, thereby taking the process of his hiring away from the union hall), not to mention touches of paranoia in the end. (One would have thought that a film that documents forty years of government harassment and persecution would have gone a little more easy on a man who thought people were out to get him!)

The government could never deport or convict this charismatic leader. Move out of the way, mate!

Availability: Selected collections; Cinema Guild.
Further reading: Bruno, Robert. "Harry Bridges: A Man and His Union." *Cineaste* 21 (1995): 48–49. A very positive review, with some reservations about the film's handling of the end of Bridges's career.
Kimeldorf, Howard. *Reds or Rackets? The Making of Radical and Conservative Unions on the Waterfront.* Berkeley: University of California Press, 1988. A convincing survey of the differences in the labor histories of the East and West Coast longshoremen's unions.
Larrowe, Charles P. *Harry Bridges: The Rise and Fall of Radical Labor in the United States.* New York: Lawrence Hill, 1972. An unauthorized biography written without direct help by Bridges but with his union staff's cooperation (which Bridges did not discourage).
Ward, Estolu E. *Harry Bridges on Trial.* New York. Modern Age Books, 1940. An extensive account of Bridges's first deportation trial, which the author argues represented a "conspiracy" against the CIO and the radical labor movement.

Harvest of Shame

A classic of investigative journalism

1960, 60 mins., B & W, TV program
Director: Palmer Williams
Scripted documentary by producer David Lowe
PRINCIPAL FIGURES
Edward R. Murrow, correspondent
David Lowe, interviewer
James Mitchell, secretary of labor

Charles Schulman, president, American Farm Bureau
Rev. Michael Cassidy, minister to the migrant workers
Mrs. Dobie, migrant worker and mother of nine children
Charles Goodlett, chief of police, Belleglade, Florida

Correspondent Edward R. Murrow reports from a field to be farmed by migrant workers in "Harvest of Shame."

Irene King, bean picker
The Parson Family, migrant workers
The Roach Family, migrant workers
Norman Hall, migrant workers' crew leader
Joseph Woods, veteran and farmer
Howard Jones, farmer

Ed King, migrant workers' crew leader
Sen. Harrison Williams, chair, Committee on Migrant Labor
Howard Van Smith, reporter, *Miami News*
Julian Griggs, chaplain to migrant workers

CBS aired this documentary on prime time on the day after Thanksgiving 1960, making it one of the earliest (if not *the* earliest) documentaries about the horrible conditions of American migrant workers. Part of Edward R. Murrow's and Fred Friendly's justifiably famous TV series "CBS Reports," which appeared from the mid-1950s through the 1960s, it is among Murrow's best work. Its theme music was from Aaron Copland's "Appalachian Spring," specifically, the motif based on the Shaker hymn "Tis a gift to be simple, / Tis a gift to be free."

The documentary tells a story that is far different from that of the self-sufficient Shaker farmers of the nineteenth century. It is structured as a "journey" of typical farmworkers as they leave their "winter" shacks in Belleglade, Florida, and journey north to pick the crops of the "best-fed nation in the world." After a series of interviews with migrant workers, a rarely seen farm owner or two, and some public figures, Murrow follows the workers back to Florida.

At various stops in this journey, Murrow includes sequences of whole families working in the fields. His voice-over narrative concentrates on a heartbreaking set of statistics, while his crew's cameras offer details of constant privation. So many of his shots recall, certainly deliberately and explicitly, the journey of the Joad family in Steinbeck's *The Grapes of Wrath* that we should realize that the Murrow team was "following" director John Ford's fictional journey, only twenty years later.

Murrow's documentary begins with a startling sequence: a town square, Third World in appearance, where numerous black workers and families are milling about. Murrow says: "This scene is not taking place in the Congo. It has nothing to to with Johannesburg or Capetown. It is not Nyasaland [Malawi] or Nigeria. This is Florida. These are citizens of the United States, 1960. This is a shape-up for migrant workers." Murrow also quotes a farmer: "We used to own our slaves. Now we just rent them."

A mark of Murrow's and David Lowe's style is the extended comparison: the legally sanctioned but miserable conditions of the laborers are not as good as those of the fruit and other produce they pick (they must be kept fresh), cattle (they must have fresh water), or thoroughbred horses at a racetrack (they have more living space).

One of the last interviews is with Julian Griggs, a chaplain to the migrants. He looks like the prototype for the Poverty Program workers or the activists in the Student Nonviolent Coordinating Committee who will follow Murrow's wake in the 1960s. Griggs asks, "Is it possible to have love without justice?" He recommends not charity but the elimination of poverty as the one goal worth pursuing. With a precision that he would have relished, Murrow's documentary appeared in 1960 at the beginning of a decade that promised but did not always deliver love and justice to the farmworkers of America.

Murrow's closing speech just before his signature sign-off was unusual fare for TV watchers: "The people you have seen have the strength to harvest your fruit and vegetables. They do not have the strength to influence legislation. Maybe we do. Good night, and good luck."

A sad footnote to the documentary and Murrow's career came after Murrow joined John F. Kennedy's New Frontier as head of the U.S. Information Agency. The British Broadcasting Corporation (BBC) had purchased "Harvest of Shame" and planned to run it. Florida politicians leaned on Kennedy's press secretary, Pierre Salinger, who in turn asked Murrow to call his contacts in the BBC to ask that the show, which was so embarrassing to the United States—and therefore potentially very useful for the Soviet propaganda machine—be withheld. Accounts differ about how enthusiastic Murrow would have been to do this, but enough of the story leaked that the man who broadcast from London such stirring and heartfelt radio reports as his description of the dead and dying at Buchenwald during World War II was felt to have compromised his legendary integrity. A CBS producer recalled that it was "sort of like God had stubbed his toe." Although Murrow tried to resign, Kennedy wouldn't let him, and the show was broadcast as scheduled.

Murrow's views were invariably liberal and almost always progressive, however. He was a rare and major public opponent of McCarthyism as early as 1954, when he broadcast in his news series ("See It Now") "The Case against Milo Raulovich, A0589839" (about an officer the McCarthyites tried to force out of the Air Force reserves) as well as another major program that focused on McCarthy's transparent lies. A. M. Sperber reported that someone, before "Harvest of Shame," had asked Murrow why he was so pro-union. He replied: "Because I hoed corn in a blazing sun." He might have also added: because I worked with the Wobblies in the lumber camps of the Northwest. Both experiences had long-term effects on his attitudes toward the working class.

Murrow's documentary was the standard by which later commentators measured their investigations. Seven years later, Mort Silverstein's documentary "What Harvest for the Reaper?" appeared on National Educational Television. The filmmakers visited a Long Island camp where workers were recruited from Arkansas: "I was struck," Silverstein concluded, "by the fact that in spite of the furor over ["Harvest of Shame"], so little had changed in the intervening years" (Rosenthal).

In 1990, TV's "Frontline" paid a thirty-year anniversary visit to the same Florida city Murrow had visited. "New Harvest, Old Shame" (directed by Hector Galan) intercuts Murrow's footage with contemporary shots: unfortunately, the story is the same, except Haitians have gradually replaced African-Americans at the bottom of the migrant ladder. "For migrant farm workers," the documentary states, "time has stood still."

See also: "The Golden Cage"; ["New Harvest, Old Shame"]; "The Grapes of Wrath"; "Our Land Too."

Availability: Selected collections; Ambrose Video (videocassette no. 4 of "Good Night and Good Luck: The Edward R. Murrow Television Collection").

Further reading: Emmet, Herman LeRoy. *Fruit Tramps: A Family of Migrant Farmworkers.* Albuquerque: University of New Mexico Press, 1989. A striking photographic album whose 1980s images eerily recall the great Depression and Dust Bowl photographers.

Meister, Dick, and Anne Loftis. *A Long Time Coming: The Struggle to Unionize America's Farm Workers.* New York: Macmillan, 1977. A very thorough history that covers the period from the mid-nineteenth century through the organizing efforts of Chavez's UFW in the 1970s.

Persico, Joseph E. *Edward R. Murrow: An American Original.* New York: McGraw-Hill, 1988. A balanced biography, including the transcripts of two of Murrow's famous radio broadcasts.

Rosenthal, Alan. *The New Documentary in Action.* Berkeley: University of California Press, 1971. Includes a chapter titled "What Harvest for the Reaper?"

Sonneman, Toby F., and Rick Steigmeyer. *Fruit Fields in My Blood: Oakie Migrants in the West.* Moscow: University of Idaho Press, 1982. The authors, students who became migrant workers (for fifteen years) and organizers (Migrant Workers of America), document this recurring theme: "We're a part of feeding the people who have this contempt for us."

Sperber, A. M. *Edward R. Murrow: His Life and Times.* New York. Freundlich, 1986. A good survey of Murrow's career, including the BBC incident.

∾

Hester Street

"For what purpose are you bringing this woman in?"

1975, 92 mins., B & W, PG
Director: Joan Micklin Silver
Screenplay: Joan Micklin Silver, from
   Abraham Cahan's novel *Yekl*
CAST
Jake = Steven Keats
Gitl = Carol Kane
Bernstein = Mel Howard

Mamie = Dorrie Kavanaugh
Mrs. Kavarsky = Doris Roberts
Joe Peltner = Stephen Strimpell
Fanny = Lauren Frost
Joey = Paul Freedman
Rabbi = Zvee Scooler
Rabbi's Wife = Eda Reiss Merin

"Hester Street" provides the dramatic background so sorely missed in a film such as "The Triangle Factory Fire Scandal," that is, how immigrants adapted—or struggled against adapting—in their new homes and jobs on New York's Lower East Side. Jake has preceded his wife from Russia to New York, where he takes a tailoring job, finds a girlfriend, and sets out to become an American. When Gitl, his wife, finally arrives, he realizes that she is so . . . foreign.

At the immigration interview, an officer (with a leer) asks Jake, "For what purpose are you bringing this woman in?" His reply, "For the purpose she's my wife," turns out to be, on his part, a falsehood, since he clearly doesn't want her anymore. She continues to wear the dresses, follow the customs, and use the language of the Old Country as they resume housekeeping with their child and a lodger, Bernstein, a former rabbinical student. This student, now a tailor, is constantly writing commentaries on the Talmud, except when he's staring at Gitl.

Jake and Gitl cannot become Americans together. But separately, yes. Along the way the work conditions of immigrants are dramatized, sometimes with great irony: when Bernstein can't get the hang of his job at a tailoring shop, the owner says, "The peddler becomes the boss and the Yeshiva student sits by the sewing machine. Some country."

"Some country" is, several reviewers complained, too artfully composed with peddlers' barrows and clothing racks. Take a few carts out here and there and you (unfortunately) have space for all the dancers in "Newsies" (which takes place, in theory, just three years later, in 1899). And without Carol Kane's convincing acting and the tailors hard at work, we might have been stuck with another "Yentl" (directed by and for Barbra Streisand) before its time.

Yekl was published in 1896 with the subtitle "A Tale of the New York Ghetto." Abraham Cahan's work had been promoted by mainstream writer William Dean Howells, who praised Cahan as a "new star of realism." Cahan was a socialist who began his career writing a column, "The Proletarian Preacher," a mixture of Old Country folklore amd Marxist ideas, for the Yiddish newspaper of the United Hebrew Trades organization of workers. He published his most successful novel, *The Rise of David Levinsky*, in 1917: in this story the immigrant worker leaves the ranks of his fellow immigrants to become a dress manufacturer. Cahan was a forerunner of the social realist writers of the Depression. "Hester Street" is perhaps a too-sanitized introduction to his work.

See also: "The Triangle Factory Fire Scandal"; "The Inheritance"; "Newsies."
Availability: Easy.
Further reading: Eder, Richard. "Hester Street." *New York Times*, 20 Oct. 1975, 44. For this
reviewer, the film is a "mostly unconditionally happy achievement."
Goodman, Walter. "'Hester Street'—Overpraised and Overdone." *New York Times*, 19 Oct.
1975, II.15. A grouchy reviewer, who accuses the other reviewers who liked the film of being
soft on Jewish women filmmakers!
Howe, Irving. *The World of Our Fathers*. New York: Harcourt, Brace, 1976. A detailed recreation of the Jewish immigrant world.
Miller, Gabriel. *Screening the Novel*. New York: Ungar, 1980. Includes a chapter with an extended discussion of both the film and the source novel.

Hoffa

The One Big Teamster

1992, 110 mins., R (for bad language)	Bobby Ciaro = Danny DeVito
Director: Danny DeVito	Billy Flynn = Robert Prosky
Screenplay: David Mamet	Carol D'Allesandro = Armand Assante
CAST	Frank Fitzsimmons = J. T. Walsh
Jimmy Hoffa = Jack Nicholson	Robert Kennedy = Kevin Anderson

"Hoffa" was the third in an ambitious series of Hollywood revisionist epics about the 1960s that attempted to do for organized labor what Oliver Stone's "JFK" did for the Kennedy assassination and Spike Lee's "Malcolm X" did for the history of black militancy. All three share the virtue (or the vice!) of focusing on a controversial figure whose biography (or at least some of its major facts) remains uncertain. All three films were greeted with mixed critical and popular receptions, primarily because they could not get the "facts" right.

But when history deals a complicated hand and then kills off the players one by one, it is hard to believe *everything* all the remaining card sharks have to say. The Kennedys are a marking point for the other two films: Malcolm's fall from Muslim grace accelerated when he said of Kennedy's assassination that it was a case of the "chickens coming home to roost," while Hoffa was hounded unmercifully by the Kennedys in what he regarded as a "class war" against him and his fellow unionists.

Probably Hoffa's most important contribution to the labor movement, his National Master Freight Agreement of 1964, which resulted in uniform wages and benefits across the country, is unfortunately not considered as important in this film as the visual spectacle—telephoto shots, especially—of clashing armies of workers and thugs. (Or are they workers and scabs? It's impossible to tell.) Danny DeVito's and David Mamet's sympathies are clearly with Hoffa, however: "He did what he had to do," the ad campaign says, and what he had to do, according to the film, was cozy up with some mobsters and ruthlessly fight the aristocratic Kennedys.

In a London interview (Grant), DeVito spelled out his interpretation of Hoffa: "Yes, he was involved with gangsters. Yes, he was a true American hero. Yes, he borrowed from the union pension fund and loaned money to mobsters. . . . He was good with his fists but better with his tongue. There was never a negotiator like him."

The end of Hoffa's career is so well known that DeVito sails through it after borrowing one dramatic sequence from Sam Peckinpah's "Convoy": as Hoffa is hustled off to prison, his numerous rank-and-file supporters line the road to the prison with their big rigs and give him a salute of their mighty horns.

The frame story for the film is not daring cinematically, but it is valuable in emphasizing the mystery of Hoffa's disappearance from history's stage. We begin and end with—and cut back to a number of times—Hoffa and his long-standing lieutenant, played by DeVito, waiting forever for Hoffa's mob contact to show up. The film—and perhaps real life itself—makes it reasonably clear how risky this idea of a meeting was, since Hoffa said he would "do what he had to do" to get back the presidency he believed was stolen by Frank Fitzsimmons in collusion with the Nixon administration.

To remind us of one of the real villains of the piece, Hoffa is reading Bobby Kennedy's *The Enemy Within* as he passes the time in his car. Hoffa and Ciaro are assassinated and then taken away, car and all, inside—heavy irony here—a long-haul truck. Hoffa's car surfaced later. Hoffa never did.

See also: "Blood Feud"; "F.I.S.T."; "Hoffa: The True Story"; "Teamster Boss: The Jackie Presser Story."

Availability: Easy.

Further reading: Dowell, Pat. "What Happened to 'Hoffa'?" *In These Times*, 11 Jan. 1993, 30–31. The film "framed Hoffa as the latest Hollywood cliché, as another American dreamer gone astray . . . and . . . depicted his rise and fall without a context to give it meaning."

Franco, Joseph, and Richard Hammer. *Hoffa's Man.* Englewood Cliffs, N.J.: Prentice-Hall, 1987. A good trashy read, this inside-the-world-of-hoodlums book nonetheless gives one of Hoffa's boys a chance to tell some of the Hoffa legends.

Grant, Steve. "Jimmy Riddle." *Time Out*, 10–17 March 1993, 20–22. An interview with DeVito in London about his views on Hoffa.

Hoffa, Jimmy. *Hoffa: The Real Story.* New York: Stein and Day, 1972. Hoffa's opinions, "as told to" Oscar Fraley.

Kennedy, Robert F. *The Enemy Within.* New York: Harper and Row, 1960. The "enemy without" is communism, but the "enemy within" is Hoffa, according to the chief counsel of the Senate Select Committee on Improper Activities in the Labor or Management Field.

Raskin, A. H. "Was Jimmy Hoffa a Hood? Or Was He Robin Hood?" *New York Times*, 20 Dec. 1992, IV.18. A survey of the film's portrayal of Hoffa's career.

Sloan, Arthur. *Hoffa.* Cambridge: MIT Press, 1992. The definitive biography to date.

༄

Hoffa: The True Story

Pretty close?

1992, 50 mins., TVM, unrated, but suitable for all ages
Director: Meg M. Kruizenga
Scripted documentary by Alan Goldberg
PRINCIPAL FIGURES
James Riddle Hoffa, leader of the Teamsters
James P. Hoffa, his son
Barbara Ann Crater, his daughter
Charles "Chucky" O'Brien, his "foster" son
John F. Kennedy, senator and president
Robert F. Kennedy, Senate committee attorney and attorney general
Frank Fitzsimmons, Hoffa's successor as president of the Teamsters
Arthur Sloan, Hoffa's biographer

The ganging up of the two Kennedys on Hoffa is not a pretty sight, and it is at the center of this TV (Arts and Entertainment Network) documentary released on video: at one point both Jack and Bobby are sitting next to each other at the McClellan Committee's head table taking turns having a go at Hoffa for his cunning unresponsiveness: "I never took the Fifth," he would later brag.

It is clear that Hoffa saw virtually everything as a class issue, between the working class he represented and the upper class who had to answer to no one. When, for example, he was told in 1960 that Jack Kennedy had strongly urged him to stay out of the election campaign, the film Hoffa replies: "Only an arrogant millionaire playboy who does not understand the Constitution of the United States could make such a statement."

Besides the Kennedys as (almost) villains, this documentary, composed of an impressive collection of archival, news, and "home-movie" footage, points the finger at Mob figures and Hoffa's own "foster" son, Chuckie O'Brien (never officially adopted), as the culprits in his disappearance and murder. The Teamsters are discussed in a mostly positive way. This film is therefore a must-see to balance some of the more hysterical anti-Hoffa sentiment in American popular culture.

Hoffa was a special target of the Kennedys, who assigned twenty lawyers to investigate him; Hoffa was also a special target of the media, who gave him more coverage than they do most presidents of the AFL-CIO. He was almost always cast in early TV news shows as the heavy. CBS's 1959 documentary "Hoffa and the Teamsters" was hailed by *Variety* (the Hollywood trade paper) as "a justifiable blow at a rotten phase of the labor movement." *Variety*'s reaction to ABC's "Close-up" feature on Hoffa in 1974 (after his release from prison) emphasized the left-wing socialist leanings of one of Hoffa's Minneapolis mentors. The Arts and Entertainment documentary is valuable precisely because so many of these early programs—ignoring the issues of balance for the moment—are simply not available for viewing.

Hollywood, in the form of Budd Schulberg, author of the screenplay for "On the Waterfront," also went after Hoffa. Bobby Kennedy personally selected Schulberg to make a film of Kennedy's anti-Hoffa book, *The Enemy Within*. Schulberg took on the project, hoping "to write not merely a sequel to 'Waterfront' but a significant extension of that film on a national scale" (Sheridan). Suffice it to say, Schulberg reported that Hoffa's allies and hoodlum friends threatened the Hollywood producers, until they surrendered and told Schulberg that the project was shelved "indefinitely."

Hoffa's contacts with organized crime have remained one of the major unresolved issues in an assessment of his career. One of his last interviews—in April 1975, just six months before he disappeared—was recorded at Cornell University's School of Industrial and Labor Relations. Hoffa analyzed a typical Teamster local's situation thus: besides the employer, such a local had other "forces" lined up against it; these forces had to be "neutralized" or the employer would employ them as "strikebreakers or supplying muscle." It is clear from the context that Hoffa means the Mafia and other organized crime outfits, but he says he doesn't use such language: the former is a "notorious tagged, titled organization," and the other is a "so-called other element." (Are these the Mafia and other rival "organized crime" outfits? So it would seem, but Hoffa refuses to identify them as such.) The Teamsters had to fight these "forces," but eventually they would make peace with them: "Neither one would get into each other's business . . . but we would help each other." Hoffa saw such groups in a political context, not as a moral or criminal issue: "If they had political trouble . . . we'd help them, and vice versa." This interview therefore offers a remarkably candid look at Hoffa's involvement in organized crime, a subject—needless to say—he was notoriously touchy about.

The A & E documentary, perhaps appropriately, treats Hoffa's connection with organized crime in a much more balanced way than most Hollywood feature films. It may come as close to Hoffa's own vision as we are likely to get.

See also: "Blood Feud"; "F.I.S.T."; "Hoffa"; "Teamster Boss: The Jackie Presser Story."
Availability: Easy.
Further reading: Hoffa, Jimmy. *Hoffa: The Real Story*. New York: Stein and Day, 1972. Hoffa's opinions, "as told to" Oscar Fraley.
Jacobs, Paul. *The State of the Unions*. New York: Atheneum, 1963. Essays on Hoffa in the late 1950s and early 1960s—a convincing view of Hoffa "in process," working out public and private deals.
Moldea, Dan E. *The Hoffa Wars: The Rise and Fall of Jimmy Hoffa*. New York: Grosset and Dunlap, 1978. Rev. ed., 1993. A popular survey by the dean of Hoffa conspiracy theorists (Hoffa conspired to kill President Kennedy).
Sheridan, Walter. *The Fall and Rise of Jimmy Hoffa*. New York: Saturday Review Press, 1972. Bobby Kennedy's investigative assistant offers "a chronology of corruption"; its real claim to fame is the introduction by director Budd Schulberg.
Sloan, Arthur. *Hoffa*. Cambridge: MIT Press, 1992. The definitive biography to date.
Variety. "Hoffa and the Teamsters," 1 July 1959, and "ABC News Closeup: Hoffa," 30 Nov. 1974. A sample of reviews of other documentaries (none available on videocassette).

How Green Was My Valley

Brigadoon for coal miners

1941, 118 mins., B & W, unrated, but suitable for all ages
Director: John Ford
Screenplay: Philip Dunne, from Richard Llewellyn's novel of the same title
CAST
Mr. Morgan = Donald Crisp
Mr. Gruffydd = Walter Pidgeon
Huw = Roddy McDowall
Angharad = Maureen O'Hara
Bronwen = Anna Lee
Ianto = John Loder
Mrs. Morgan = Sara Allgood
Cyfartha = Barry Fitzgerald
Ivor = Patric Knowles
Mr. Jonas = Morton Lowry
Mr. Parry = Arthur Shields
Ceinwen = Ann Todd
Dr. Richards = Frederick Worlock
Davy = Richard Fraser
Gwilym = Evan S. Evans
Owen = James Monks
Evans = Lionel Pape
Singing Welsh Miners = Chorus of the Welsh Presbyterian Church of Los Angeles

Director John Ford accepted the vision of Richard Llewellyn's best-seller of the somewhat sentimental but captivating portrait of a relatively well off South Wales mining family at the end of the nineteenth century. Family and community struggle over a number of issues, especially the decision to form a miners union (name not specified). The Morgans live well because they have five incomes from the mine (the father's and the four sons'), but gradually the mine owners cut wages until the sons (all good union men) disagree with their father over the need for a union, since he favors the old way of "speaking to the boss." Look for the startling speech on a snowy hill during a union meeting by Mrs. Morgan, who threatens to kill any miner who messes with her husband.

Numerous subplots involve the youngest son's delicate health and bookishness, Angharad's love life, and the stifling religion of the local "chapel." Winner of five Academy Awards, this production helped Americans appreciate the eternally folksy British, ahem, Welsh, who usually break into folk songs as they walk home from a hard day's work. Believe it or not, Barry Fitzgerald, Hollywood's favorite *Irish* drunk, plays a Welshman who loves to drink! Such was the nature of multiculturalism in a 1940s Academy Award winner.

John Ford had finished "The Grapes of Wrath" the year before he made this film: both films celebrate family values in communities under attack by the forces of capitalism (agribusiness in "Grapes"). Ford's instinctive radicalism—the sons are clearly right to resist their father's stubborn acceptance of the paternalistic mine tradition—is constantly at war with his nostalgia—the desire to look back to when cooperation (and fathers) ruled the community.

The frame story opens with Huw as a man of sixty packing to leave the Valley, which is framed by "stacks, cranes, and towering slag heap"; this shot dissolves into an edenic view, only lightly scarred by a "small slag heap," with a colliery and a chapel, as Philip Dunne's screenplay closely follows the narrator of Llewellyn's novel.

The more politically charged material in the novel and the first script about workers seizing control of the mines was dropped in subsequent revisions because Darryl F. Zanuck, the head of the Twentieth Century-Fox studio, said that he'd be "damned . . . to go around making the employer class the out-and-out villains in this day and age" (Walsh).

See also: "The Corn Is Green"; "The Grapes of Wrath"; "The Stars Look Down."
Availability: Selected collections.
Further reading: Crowther, Bosley. "How Green Was My Valley." *New York Times*, 29 Oct. 1941, 27. Crowther calls the film "a stunning masterpiece."
Dunne, Philip. "How Green Was My Valley." In *Twenty Best Film Plays*, edited by John Gassner and Dudley Nichols. 1943. Reprint. New York: Garland, 1977. The screenplay.
Walsh, Francis R. "The Films We Never Saw: American Movies View Organized Labor, 1934–1954." *Labor History* 27 (1986): 564–80. An excellent discussion of the reduction in the story's militancy during script development.

∾
I'm All Right Jack

"Not to worry," the British say.

1959, 104 mins., B & W, unrated, but
   suitable for mature children
Director: John Boulting
Screenplay: Frank Harvey, John Boulting,
   and Alan Hackney, from Hackney's novel
   Private Life
CAST
Fred Kite = Peter Sellers

Stanley Windrush = Ian Carmichael
Major Hitchcock = Terry-Thomas
Aunt Dolly = Margaret Rutherford
Cox = Richard Attenborough
Bertram Tracepurcel = Dennis Price
Malcolm Muggeridge as himself

Since the British are reputed to be more obsessively class-conscious than Americans, this satire on both unions and management was understandably extremely popular in Great Britain when it was released. It had a strong following in the United States as well. Some of its humor remains on target, although the struggle for a factory owner's Oxford-educated nephew to become "one of the lads" on the shop floor seems a little unconvincing and forced. "Work to rule" is one of the satiric targets, as well as the British shop steward's worshipful attitude toward the Soviet Union, and there is no doubt that unions more than management suffer the more embarrassing jokes.

British comic Ian Carmichael plays Stanley Windrush, a lovable upper-class twit who, having graduated from Oxford, figures to get a job as a manager of a factory where he has family connections. He ends up on the workplace floor and is astonished to see that no British union man actually does any work. Despite boarding at union leader Fred Kite's apartment, Stanley soon makes it clear that he has no intentions of accepting the union's lackadaisical attitudes. (British audiences would have already been familiar with his type, as he and a number of other characters from this film had already appeared in an earlier film, "Private's Progress," in 1956, the product of the same director, screenwriter, and novelist. Stanley, in the earlier film, had failed as an officer and had to go into the army as a private.)

After achieving the dubious status of a national hero because he refuses to give in to the union, Stanley ends up on a national TV talk show hosted by the then-popular professional curmudgeon and social critic Malcolm Muggeridge. Stanley denounces both unions and employers—by now he is even more cynical—when Muggeridge admonishes him to "stick to the facts." In response, Stanley throws up a satchel of cash given to him by his family as a bribe, saying that bank notes are the only "facts." He causes a riot in the studio as participants and the studio audience alike run amok

Shop steward Fred Kite (Peter Sellers) strikes a mock-heroic pose in "I'm All Right Jack."
Courtesy British Film Institute Stills, Posters, and Designs

after the bills. The soundtrack song sums up the English character quaintly being satirized here: "Wherever you look, it's blow you, Jack, I'm all right."

Stanley's refusal to go along with the union system brings him to the ultimate utopian escape—a nudist colony where the only facts are naked and friendly. At this point we are a long way from industrial strife. The Sunnyglade Nudist Camp is a comic but farcical alternative to the smoky factories Stanley at first thought he was born to manage.

See also: "The Man in the White Suit."
Availability: Selected collections.
Further reading: Hackney, Alan. *I'm All Right Jack.* New York: Norton, 1959. The source novel as it was published in the United States.
Hill, John. *Sex, Class, and Realism: British Cinema, 1956–1963.* London: British Film Institute, 1986. A very thorough survey of Boulting's film and related British films of the period.

~
The Inheritance

"Golden America, half dream, half nightmare"

1964, 55 mins., B & W, unrated, but suitable
for all ages
Director: Harold Mayer
Scripted documentary
PRINCIPAL VOICES:
Robert Ryan, narrator
Franklin D. Roosevelt, president

Jane Addams, leader of Hull House social
welfare movement
John L. Lewis, president, United Mine
Workers of America
Folksingers: Millard Lampell, Pete Seeger,
Tom Paxton, Judy Collins, Barry
Kornfeld, John R. Winn, and Carlo
Totolo

"The Inheritance" is one of the early workhorses of labor history documentaries: not flashy, a little slow, but able to go great distances with good staying power. It surveys the history of numerous immigrant groups as they created multicultural unions at the turn of the century. Since the film was sponsored by the Amalgamated Clothing Workers of America (ACWA), its focus is the garment workers during the first thirty years of the union's struggle to become the chief democratic voice of the exploited ethnic Americans who made up the vast majority of its membership.

Unlike the more specialized and often more radical labor history documentaries that followed it more than a decade later, "The Inheritance" relies on a combination of labor and "standard" history to tell its stories: thus, a viewer fresh to this film will certainly learn about some of the essential elements of twentieth-century labor history—sweatshops, slum housing, child labor, the Bonus Army, the CIO, the Flint Sit-Down Strike of 1937, the Republic Steel Massacre of 1937, and labor's involvement in the civil rights movement. To set these important moments in historical context, the film relies on some canned footage about the Roaring Twenties, the Depression, and World War II.

Other perhaps less famous moments specific to the labor history of the garment workers also come through loud and clear: the murder of Chicago garment worker Charles Lazinska by a clothing factory foreman during a 1910 strike; the murder of Ida Brayman, a seventeen-year-old garment worker during a 1913 Rochester, New York, strike; and the pioneering benefits of the ACWA (low-rent co-op housing, a members' bank, unemployment insurance), which were the models for some of the New Deal's legislation.

The ACWA was founded by 75 percent of the delegates who walked out of a United Garment Workers convention in Nashville in 1914 because they regarded it as "fixed" against their interests. Unfortunately, only a little of this history is included in the film. Instead, the filmmakers concentrate on the "feel" of being part of the immigrant workforce—through stills, songs, and archival footage—until a composite picture of a union, a labor movement, and a people dedicated to social justice emerges. Millard Lampell's "Pass It On" was written for and is sung in the film, underscoring the theme that "freedom is a hard-won thing."

"The Inheritance" was released during the civil rights era in the fiftieth-anniversary year of the ACWA, and the film concludes with the sit-in movement in the South and the March on Washington. Regrettably, African-Americans are not sufficiently represented in this film until it deals with the 1960s. Individual blacks are in the crowds, but the special exclusions, difficulties, and arrangements of the American labor movement and its African-American brothers and sisters are scant throughout most of this documentary.

See also: "Hester Street"; "Norma Rae"; "The Triangle Factory Fire Scandal."
Availability: Selected collections; AFL-CIO.
Further reading: Doherty, Jonathan L. *Women at Work: 153 Photographs by Lewis W. Hine.* New
   York: Dover, 1981. An excellent collection of vintage photographs of women in the "needle
   trades" in both the North and South.

ᔑ
Inside Detroit

In need of retooling

1956, 82 mins., B & W, unrated, but suitable   Gus Linden = Pat O'Brien
   for all ages   Joni Calvin = Tina Carver
Director: Fred F. Sears   Barbara Linden = Margaret Field
Screenplay: Robert E. Kent and James B.   Gregg Linden = Mark Damon
   Gordon   Narrator = John Cameron Swayze
CAST
Blair Vickers = Dennis O'Keefe

Documentary-like frame stories were a popular device for serious Hollywood problem films in the 1950s. Nunnally Johnson's "The Three Faces of Eve," for example, has an introduction narrated by none other than Alistair Cooke, who pontificates briefly on matters psychological.

Another veteran TV broadcaster, John Cameron Swayze, takes his turn in "Inside Detroit," in which he introduces the story of a gangster's attempt to take over a United Auto Workers (UAW) local. After a bomb hits the local's headquarters, President Vickers (Dennis O'Keefe as a "good-guy" player) begins to pursue gangster Gus Linden (Pat O'Brien, usually a "good-guy" player himself). Fortunately for the future of the UAW, Vickers romances the gangster's daughter and puts his "moll" into neutral.

This unlikely plot comes from the melodramatic film-noir tradition, which features—as it does in many much better films such as "On the Waterfront"—dark streets, speeding cars, repentent bad guys, and sensitive leads, all filmed with numerous odd angles, shadows, and other cinematic techniques that are used to suggest a world that is out of joint.

See also: "On the Waterfront"; "The Garment Jungle."
Availability: Not currently available.
Further reading: "Inside Detroit." *New York Times*, 28 Jan. 1956, 10. Finds the film "low on gas."

Intolerance

Griffith tries a comeback.

1916, 178 mins., B & W, silent (although original version was tinted and accompanied by an orchestra)
Director: D. W. Griffith
Screenplay: D. W. Griffith
CAST OF "THE MODERN STORY"
The Boy = Robert Harron
The Dear One (a.k.a. The Girl) = Mae Marsh
The Girl's Father = Fred Turner
Strike Leader = Monte Blue
The Musketeer of the Slums = Walter Long
A Friendless One = Miriam Cooper

The Kindly Policeman = Tom Wilson
The Governor = Ralph Lewis
Chief Detective = Edward Dillon
Judge of the Court = Lloyd Ingraham
Warden = W. H. Brown
Society Charity Worker = Mary Alden
Jenkins, the Industrial Magnate = Sam de Grasse
Mary T. Jenkins, His Sister = Vera Lewis
The Mother of Us All (a.k.a. The Woman Who Rocks the Cradle) = Lillian Gish

Only silent film buffs as a rule enjoy the entire epic of "Intolerance," but one of the four stories—"The Modern Story"—begins with a restaging of a strike that is quite convincing, although Griffith seems to lose interest in the strike as a secondary plot—boy meets girl, boy gets in big trouble, girl helps boy—takes over. This story, originally titled "The Mother and the Law," was the germ of the entire epic.

The Industrial Magnate cuts wages so he can make public displays of charity with the money he has "saved." His workers rebel and strike, but the struggle is vicious and eventually the Boy and the Girl—brought together by the killing of her worker father—leave the town, marry, and live in the big city, where domestic tragedy overtakes them. He is condemned to die for a murder he did not commit, and their baby is taken away by meddling charity ladies. Of all the four stories of "Intolerance," only this one has a happy ending, as the Girl sets in motion a pardon and a rescue, providing Griffith with one of his signature cross-cutting sequences (gallows being readied, the Girl rushing toward prison with the pardon, back to the gallows, and so on).

Before making "Intolerance," Griffith had adapted an already atrociously racist novel—*The Clansman* by Thomas Dixon—and turned it in "The Birth of a Nation" into a celebration of the "birth of the Klan." Griffith said afterward that he didn't know the gun was loaded in "The Birth of a Nation": translated from southern paternalistic speech, what he meant was that excesses were committed on both sides—Klan and Radical Reconstructionists. Without carpetbaggers, black self-defense leagues, and Thaddeus Stevens (the radical abolitionist and reconstructionist from Pennsylvania), the South might have just been defeated at war's end—not defeated *and* angry. When "The Birth of a Nation" captured the hearts of racists and fence-sitters with its inflammatory antifreedom message, the gentle heart of the showman (so he said) was shocked. The racism of the film is, by virtually any standard then and now, nonetheless virulent.

Griffith turned at this point to a story he thought would make his liberal critics in the North appreciate him: he would bash the Rockefeller types and their violent repression of trade unionists. The result was "The Modern Story," one of four examples of "intolerance" through the ages. (The other three are the crucifixion, the massacre of the Huguenots, and the betrayal of Babylon.)

To connect these four stories as they unfolded in alternating sequences, Griffith filmed transitional shots of Lillian Gish playing the Mother of Us All rocking a cradle, bringing to life Walt Whitman's ode "Out of the Cradle Endlessly Rocking." The "modern" example of intolerance is in effect "explained" by the massive flashbacks and intercuttings of the three "ancient" stories. Intolerance is thus seen as a social construct of virtually all cultures at all times. If Griffith felt his views on the glorious days of slavery were being treated *intolerantly*, it may be a sad truth that his relatively progressive film "Intolerance" was made for a strange reason.

See also: "A Corner in Wheat"; "Strike."
Availability: Selected collections.
Further reading: Pratt, George C. *Spellbound in Darkness*. New York: New York Graphic Society, 1973. A history of silent film, with contemporary reviews of Griffith's films.
Stern, Seymour. "D. W. Griffith's 'Intolerance.'" In *The Essential Cinema*, edited by P. Adams Sitney, 1–54. New York: Anthology Film Archives, 1975. A detailed (almost exclusively cinematic) analysis of the film.
Note: Versions of varying length may be available for rental.

ᑌ
Iron Maze

A Japanese Disneyland in the Rust Belt

1991, 102 mins., R (accurate because of
   scenes of disturbing sex and violence)
Director: Hiroaki Yoshida
Screenplay: Tim Metcalf, from Ryunosuke
   Akutagawa's short story "In a Grove"

CAST
Barry Mikowski = Jeff Fahey
Chris Sugita = Bridget Fonda
Junichi Sugita = Hiroaki Murakami
Jack Ruhle = J. T. Walsh
Mikey = Gabriel Damon

A handsome Japanese developer and his stunning American wife come to the depressing, dying town of Corinth, near Pittsburgh. The workers hope he is going to reopen the steel mill; instead, he wants to create a Disneyland with rides (in scoop cranes?!) in this industrial setting. A triangle forms with this couple and Barry, an ex-steelworker who is working as a hotel bellhop. The title refers to the fact that the film is both a remake of the Japanese classic "Rashomon" and a contemporary story of western Pennsylvania's Rust Belt.

Imitating the complicated maze of possibilities in "Rashomon," the woman in "Iron Maze" (1) may have been raped by Barry, (2) may have been his willing sexual partner, or (3) may have tried to kill her husband. Despite this art film premise, some of the anger and frustration typical of workers in collapsed steeltown economies come through reasonably well in this odd but intriguing film.

The Japanese filmmakers who made "Iron Maze" may not have understood all the details of plant closings, but Bridget Fonda is convincing as Chris, the spoiled but reckless working-class girl made good, even if she bears a startling resemblance to the animated heroine Naomi in Yoshida's previous underground classic, "Twilight of the Cockroaches," the story of a species "war" between humans and a tribe of house roaches.

Ultimately, Chris goes back to the small-town bar from whence she came, while Barry and Sugita jokingly toss skipping stones at the construction equipment that seems to be converting the plant into a Japanese theme park. Before "Rising Son" and "Rising Sun" had been made, it was rare for a Hollywood film to confront the issue of Japanese economic competition. The ending of "Iron Maze" has the goofy impossibility of Yoshida's "Twilight of the Cockroaches," and he certainly doesn't know how to solve the problems of the Rust Belt. Then again, not many people do.

See also: "Rising Son."
Availability: Easy.
Further reading: Akutagawa, Ryunosuke. "In a Grove." *Rashomon and Other Stories.* Trans-

lated by Takashi Kojima. New York: Liverright, 1952. The stories from which "Iron Maze" and the original Japanese film "Rashomon" are adapted.

Canby, Vincent. "Iron Maze." *New York Times*, 1 Nov. 1991, C13. "Leading entry in the looniest movie of the year sweepstakes."

"Iron Maze." *Sight and Sound* (Dec. 1991): 42. A short and generally negative review.

∿
Joe

A worker-management alliance against . . . hippies!

1970, 107 mins., R	Mary Lou Curran = K. Callan
Director: John G. Avildsen	William Compton = Dennis Patrick
Screenplay: Norman Wexler	Joan Compton = Audrey Caire
CAST	Melissa Compton = Susan Sarandon
Joe Curran = Peter Boyle	Frank Russo = Patrick McDermott

Visiting "Joe" after all these years is definitely a trip to early Archie Bunker-land. Joe works hard, hates hippies and African-Americans (they are moving in down the block), drinks beer and burps a lot, and has a wife who is obsessed with TV soap opera intrigue. Actually, dinkbat Edith is a lot more progressive than Mrs. Joe. The totally improbable plot has Joe forming an alliance with an advertising executive who is in a rage because his daughter (Susan Sarandon in her first film role) has run off with some dope-smoking (and dealing) hippies. The father beats her hippie boyfriend to death and escapes detection, but Joe instinctively finds him out and the two form an unholy alliance, with tragic consequences. The film was surprisingly successful, tapping into popular resentment about Vietnam veterans being ignored and the thrill of seeing a genuine hippie orgy.

John Avildsen's broad strokes create a character who is almost unwatchable today. Perhaps *The Quotations of Worker Joe* might have had a chance at bestsellerdom when the film was first released: "Forty-two percent of all liberals are queer," Joe announces at the bar when he first meets advertising exec William Compton. Later he notes that hippies don't respect Easter Sunday: "The day Christ rose they're all screwing."

Joe works hard. Everybody believes that, although only rarely is he seen actually working—grinding a rod or two at some unspecified factory. He has sprung from a screenwriter's anti–hard hat imagination, although some of the construction workers in the early 1970s who rallied behind Nixon's Vietnam War policy might do for the reality.

See also: "Bloodbrothers."
Availability: Easy.

Further reading: Canby, Vincent. "Playing on Our Prejudices." *New York Times*, 2 Aug. 1970, II.1. "One of the most outrageously, most wastefully manic-depressive movies ever made, a movie so convincingly schizoid that it has prompted paeans of praise from socially-conscious critics on both the left and the right."

Hamill, Pete. "The Revolt of the White Lower-Middle Class." In *The White Majority: Between Poverty and Affluence*, edited by Louise Kapp Howe, 10–22. New York: Random House, 1970. A classic analysis of white working "Joes," some of whom resent African-Americans so much that they are more than ready to act out this film's fantasies of revenge.

Thompson, Howard. "Joe." *New York Times*, 16 July 1970, 40. The film has "a devastating, original idea" but "cynically slopes into a melodramatic, surface fiasco," with Peter Boyle as "a poor dangerous slob come to life."

Joe Hill

" 'I never died,' says he."

1971, 114 mins., Swedish (with English subtitles), unrated, but suitable for mature children	Cathy = Cathy Smith
	Paul = Hasse Persson
	David = David Moritz
Director: Bo Widerberg	Richard = Richard Weber
Screenplay: Bo Widerberg	Ed Rowen = Joe Miller
CAST	George = Robert Faeder
Joe Hill = Thommy Berggren	Elizabeth Gurley Flynn = Wendy Geier
Lucia = Anja Schmidt	The Tenor = Franco Molinari
Raven a.k.a. "The Fox" = Kelvin Malave	The Sister of Mercey = Liska March
Blackie = Evert Andersson	

Joe Hill was born Joel Hagglund. A Swedish immigrant, he became Joseph Hillstrom as he worked his way across North America from 1901 until his execution in 1915. He was a worker and an organizer for the International Workers of the World (IWW), but he was most known as a union songwriter and a singer: "There is one thing that is necessary in order to hold the old members and to get the would-be members interested in the class struggle and that is entertainment" (letter, 29 Nov. 1914).

And entertain he did, writing some of the most popular union songs of the twentieth century: "Casey Jones—The Union Scab" virtually changed a folk hero into a folk scab; "The Preacher and the Slave" (stealing the melody from a Salvation Army song) warned of "pie in the sky" from Salvation Army soup kitchens; "The Rebel Girl" celebrated organizer Elizabeth Gurley Flynn and other IWW women; and "There Is Power in a Union" became an unofficial anthem of all unions.

His success in spreading the word may have made him a target for the Salt Lake City police, who arrested him in 1914 for killing a grocery store owner and his son. Joe did have a gunshot wound, but he said he received it during a lovers' quarrel; furthermore, he could not produce a witness for his alibi because it would be embarrassing for "her." After a trial with dubious evidence, he was shot by a firing squad on 19 November 1915.

The thirty thousand mourners at his Chicago funeral began a process of turning Hill into one of the greatest labor heroes of the century. His belief that a song "learned by heart and repeated over and over" is so much more effective than a "pamphlet, no matter how good . . . never read more than once" helped secure his status as a legend. His wish to have his ashes scattered in every continent and all the states of the union (except Utah) and the part of his Last Will and Testament to IWW leader Big Bill Haywood—"Don't waste any time mourning—organize!"— have made him a symbol of labor union dedication.

Director Bo Widerberg and actor Thommy Berggren are widely known as two of the talents who inflicted "Elvira Madigan," a romantic tearjerker, on filmgoers in 1967. Certainly the two films Widerberg directed after "Elvira"—"Joe Hill" and "Adalen 31"—helped counter the idea that his touch was pure Swedish "Love Story." There are love scenes in "Joe Hill," but the overwhelming impression a viewer comes away with is of Hill's dedication and his feeling of being at home with the itinerant workers and riffraff of the IWW.

The film surveys a remarkable amount of Hill's life and his trial for murder, inventing perhaps only the dialogue nobody could ever know to match the organization Hill gave his life for. When he meets his first organizer for the IWW, for example, the man tells Hill: "The selfish unions are just out to help themselves. Did you ever see a Mexican or Indian with a union card?"

Since Widerberg is clearly sympathetic to Joe Hill as a hero, it may not be surprising that he doesn't include the few pieces of information that have convinced writers such as Wallace Stegner that Hill *was* guilty of murder. (Otto Applequist, Joe's roommate—and for Stegner a partner in crime—disappeared the night of the murders.)

And as much as critic Joan Mellen admires the film, she faults Widerberg for occasional misinterpretations of Hill's beloved IWW. The film ends, for example, with IWW leaders divvying up Hill's ashes (as per his request) to send them to every state. Their task is interrupted by music from a dance in a neighboring room. We then see the IWW men dancing their hearts out with younger lassies. Widerberg's camera brings us back to an abandoned table with Joe's ashes. The scene is pure fiction and certainly unfair to the IWW. And Joe's Last Will and Testament comes on the soundtrack as Joan Baez is singing "The Ballad of Joe Hill" ("I dreamed I saw Joe Hill last night . . ."), and so the cynical abandonment of Joe's ashes for a good time seems especially cruel.

See also: "Adalen 31"; "The Wobblies."

Availability: Not currently available.

Further reading: Bjorkman, Stig. *Film in Sweden: The New Directors.* London: Tantivy Press, 1977. Reviews Widerberg's career.

Dos Passos, John. *1919* and *Midcentury.* New York: Modern Library, 1937. Joe Hill appears in these two novels of the *USA* trilogy as an American icon and foil to the run-of-the-mill capitalist heavies and other labor leaders.

Foner, Philip. *The Case of Joe Hill.* New York: International, 1965. Argues that Hill was the victim of a frame-up because he was a Wobbly.

——, ed. *The Letters of Joe Hill.* New York: Oak Publications, 1965. An important collection of letters.

Hampton, Wayne. *Guerrilla Minstrels: John Lennon, Joe Hill, Woody Guthrie, Bob Dylan.* Knoxville: University of Tennessee Press, 1986. Discusses the reality and the myths associated with these radicalized folksingers.

"Hillstrom Is Shot, Denying His Guilt." *New York Times,* 20 Nov. 1915, 4. A detailed account of Hill's execution, including a last-ditch battle in his cell and his own "Fire!" command to his executioners.

Mellen, Joan. "'Sacco and Vanzetti' and 'Joe Hill.'" *Film Quarterly* 25 (Spring 1972): 48–53. A critical review; Mellen overwhelmingly likes Widerberg's film, but she faults his version of the Wobblies.

Stegner, Wallace. *Joe Hill* (a.k.a. *The Preacher and the Slave*). New York: Doubleday, 1950. Stegner's "biographical novel" offers Hill as riffraff—a "yegg" (burglar or safecracker)—as well as a Wobbly who *did* commit the murders for which he was executed.

Thompson, Fred, and the IWW. "Letter and Statement." *New Republic,* 9 Feb. and 13 Nov. 1948. Objections to Stegner's novel.

Note: The film is also known as "The Ballad of Joe Hill."

Kamaradschaft

Solidarity across the border

1931, 93 mins., German and French (with English subtitles), B & W, unrated, but suitable for mature children
Director: G. W. Pabst
Screenplay: Karl Otten, Ladislaus Vajda, and Peter Martin Lampel
CAST
Wittkopp, the German Miner = Ernst Busch
Frau Wittkopp = Elisabeth Wendt
Kasper = Alexander Granach
Wilderer = Fritz Kampers
Kaplan = Gustav Puettjer
Jean, the French miner = Georges Charlia
Francoise = Andree Ducret
Emile = Daniel Mandaille
The Grandfather = Alex Bernard
George = Pierre Louis

"Kamaradschaft" celebrates the solidarity that emerges between French and German miners on the border of their two countries when a mining disaster in a

French workers struggle with the police in "Kamaradschaft."
Courtesy British Film Institute Stills, Posters, and Designs.

French town breaks down mutual distrust and rivalries. The title could be translated as "comradeship" or even by the French borrowed word "camaraderie." The dialogue in the film was originally in both German and French to suggest the unity of the miners' struggles, but the current videocassette is subtitled. The film is dedicated to "The Miners of the World," specifically the more than twelve hundred miners killed by mine gas in the French mine at Courrieres ("Courbiere" in the film) in 1906.

G. W. Pabst changed the setting to a mine at Lorraine on the French border in 1919; underground, the mine is segregated by country because a wall has been erected like the border aboveground. Actual mining towns on both sides of the border were used for location shooting, although the convincing underground scenes were filmed on carefully constructed studio sets in Berlin.

The film opens with a symbolic visual overture: a German boy and a French boy are happily playing marbles. German miners nearby apply at the border for work but are turned back by the French. The little boys begin to argue. Pabst then cuts to an interior shot of the German section of the mine, from which a fire on the French side can clearly be seen. The film then alternates between social scenes (a French beer hall) and personal life (the family of Jean, a French miner) and an explosion, which spreads the fire throughout the mine.

On the German side of the border, the German miners debate helping the French. Wittkopp begins the discussion by asking if the French have rescue equipment. One of his mates says: "Who cares? They are richer than we are." But Wittkopp leads a rescue party, which is greeted by the French with amazement: "Les Allemagnes! Ce n'est pas possible!" ["The Germans! It's impossible!"]. Three miners who had earlier been treated in an unfriendly way at a French dance hall, open up another rescue route by tearing down the fence erected as part of the Treaty of Versailles frontier.

All of these impressive cooperative gestures are temporarily shattered by a brilliant and terrifyingly classic scene: a dazed French miner sees and hears a German man in a gas mask approaching him and hallucinates, thinking the approaching figure is a German soldier. Pabst intercuts shots of a battle from World War I as the French miner attacks his rescuer.

Nonetheless, the daring rescue and cooperation seem to be pointing toward a future of international cooperation. A Frenchman says: "It is because we are *all* miners that you have saved us. . . . We have only two common enemies—GAS and WAR!" The epilogue, showing a new iron fence underground separating the two sections of the mine, provides the ironic reversal of the new "kamaradschaft."

Pabst filmed this cynical epilogue, which was offered in the German release of the film but eliminated when it was booed in Berlin when the film was first played but retained it in the French version; the 1932 American premiere and the current videocassette offer the (cynical) German version. An additional terrible irony of the miners' solidarity is that less than a decade after the film's release, the old hatreds boiled over in a new fascist war between the French and the Germans.

Director Pabst had an unusual if not opportunistic career. "Kamaradschaft" followed a similar antiwar film, "Westfront 1918" (1930), which ends with dying French and German soldiers trying to reconcile. In 1933, when the Nazis came to power, he emigrated to Hollywood and then later returned to France. Later he said he was "trapped" in Austria when the war broke out. Nevertheless, Joseph Goebbels welcomed him back to the German film industry, for which he made several films. With the defeat of Nazism, Pabst began making anti-Nazi films through the 1950s.

See also: "Germinal"; "Matewan"; "The Stars Look Down"; "Strike."
Availability: Selected collections.
Further reading: Atwell, Lee. *G. W. Pabst.* New York: Twayne, 1977. A good survey of the
   director's career and achievements.

Hall, Mordaunt. "The Screen." *New York Times*, 9 Nov. 1932, 28. This and "On the Berlin Screen" were very positive contemporary American reviews.

Kracauer, Siegfried. *From Caligari to Hitler*. Princeton, N.J.: Princeton University Press, 1947. Places Pabst's career in the context of "a psychological history of the German film," emphasizing its authoritarian (Nazi-like) tendencies.

"On the Berlin Screen." *New York Times*, 27 Dec. 1931, VIII.7.

Killer of Sheep

Killer of dreams

1977, 84 mins., B & W, unrated	Stan's Wife = Kaycee Moore
Director: Charles Burnett	Bracy = Charles Bracy
Screenplay: Charles Burnett	Stan's Daughter = Angela Burnett
CAST	Eugene = Eugene Cherry
Stan = Henry Gayle Sanders	Stan's Son = Jack Drummon

Like Julie Dash ("Daughters of the Dust"), Charles Burnett is part of a new generation of black filmmakers who graduated from the film school at the University of California at Los Angeles and entered the business as independent "producer"-directors, with "producer" in quotation marks because these directors were more likely to apply to foundations for money than to obtain it from investors.

Burnett's "Killer of Sheep" was financed by grants and his personal income. It has none of the high production values or very clear soundtrack of a major film, but its topic and Burnett's angle of vision were sufficiently fresh to gain it a small but enthusiastic following, given its relatively limited exposure.

The title refers to the main character's job in a slaughterhouse. Ironically, an insomniac, Stan cannot even count what he kills every day! Although his job is frustrating and he feels degraded, he tries to provide his wife and children with stability and financial security. But his insomnia and job conspire to make him feel helpless and withdrawn, even from a wife who clearly loves him.

When two friends call on Stan to try to get him to join them in a contract killing, one of the men urges him on: "Look! What has Stan got? He don't even have a decent pair of pants." But Stan believes that since he makes donations to the Salvation Army, "he can't . . . be poor."

The film is filled with images of the working poor and their frustrating lives—their cars have flats, or, as in one now-classic scene, Stan and his friend buy a used motor and lug it onto the bed of a pickup truck, only to have it fall off when they drive away.

Stan and his friends are constantly searching for people who owe them money, or for part-time chores to earn money, or are stealing money, winning it on horse

Stan (Henry Gayle Sanders), the title character in "Killer of Sheep."
Courtesy Third World Newsreel.

races, or shooting craps. There is a lot of meanness in Stan's world—beatings, children fighting, a crippled girl who is pregnant—all intercut with shots of sheep in crowded pens eventually being led to the killing floor by Judas goats.

The professional look and mainstream cast of Burnett's other (major) film, "To Sleep with Anger," perhaps compliment the somewhat more successful working-class Los Angeles family in that film. But Stan's life is decidedly low budget, and he sleeps only with frustration.

See also: "The Killing Floor"; "To Sleep with Anger."
Availability: Selected collections; Third World Newsreel.
Further reading: Klotman, Phyllis Rauch, ed. *Screenplays of the African American Experience.* Bloomington: Indiana University Press, 1991. Includes Burnett's screenplay for "Killer of Sheep" and a brief bio of the filmmaker.

∾

The Killing Floor

. . . of both man and beast

1984, 117 mins., TVM, PG
Director: William Duke
Screenplay: Leslie Lee
CAST
Frank Custer = Damien Leake
Thomas Joshua = Ernest Rayford
Austin "Heavy" Williams = Moses Gunn
Robert Bedford = Wally Taylor
Joshua = Ernest Rayford

Harry Brenn = Dennis Farna
Dan Michora = Miklos Simon
Bill Bremer = Clarence Felder
Judge Alechuler = Nathan Davis
John Kikulski = Henryk Derewenda
John Fitzpatrick = James O'Reilly
Eliza (The Letter Writer) = Mary Alice
Mattie Custer = Alfre Woodard

Leslie Lee's screenplay for "The Killing Floor" was based on a story idea by Elsa Rassbach, one of the founders of the "Nova" series on PBS, who envisioned "The Killing Floor" as a pilot for a proposed series of ten films about the history of the American worker. Unfortunately, the series was never made. Rassbach charged the Corporation for Public Broadcasting with having a case of nerves—of being afraid of the corporate sponsors who do not like labor relations films.

The second and third films surveyed nineteenth-century labor history: one was to be on the origins of industrial labor in the Lowell, Massachusetts, textile mills, while the other would focus on the Homestead, Pennsylvania, steel lockout. (Rassbach says she is still going to make these films.)

Instead of a series, however, we have to date only this portrayal of a dark and relatively little-known episode in the history of labor and race relations. William Duke, who later did the remake of "Raisin in the Sun," directed this excellent TV movie.

At the outbreak of World War I, two young African-Americans leave the South, in what has become known as the Great Inland Migration, for jobs, they hope, in Chicago. Because of the war, blacks are being hired in the traditionally Eastern European immigrant job market—the Chicago stockyards. Frank survives because he learns his trade with a knife on "the killing floor," but his friend Thomas is racially harassed so much that he joins the army. The union—the Amalgamated Meatcutters and Butcher Workmen of North America—was attempting a mass recruitment of all workers, regardless of race. At one glorious moment, at a union hall meeting, speeches are delivered in English and Polish as Frank and others are urged to join the union.

Other African-Americans in the shop, most notably "Heavy" Williams and his sidekick Joe, are more suspicious of the union and argue for all-black unity in the sea of untrustworthy white faces. "Heavy" is also clearly a front man for the bosses, however, and at one point clearly instigates a riot by throwing a brick at a union speaker. A series of complicated episodes in union-management negotiations, including an important lockout that tests most of the African-Americans in their resolve to remain a part of the union, are clearly dramatized in the film. Management wants to break the union and determines that fomenting racial tension is the best way.

The Big Five meatpackers reached an agreement in 1918 with the federal government that for the duration of the war the union would gain limited recognition (with no binding contract, however), and, in return, the companies would give the union a no-strike guarantee. A federal judge would referee whatever contentious issues might arise.

Unfortunately for the union, a notorious episode in Chicago history occurred in July 1919: a black youth, swimming in Lake Michigan, crossed the imaginary line (39th Street "extended" eastward into the water) that separated "colored" from "white" bathing areas. Although eyewitness testimony differed, it seems in retrospect to matter little: the African-Americans believed that the young man had been stoned and subsequently drowned, while the police did not arrest anyone. The Chicago Race Riot of 1919 was under way.

Since Frank and the other black workers had to cross a white "zone" (Canaryville) filled with Irish gangs to get to their jobs, the "race rioting" and union integration soon became incompatible. In fact, blacks and whites on both sides were ambushed by rioters and killed. A Lithuanian (Polish in the film) section of the town was set on fire; again, eyewitness testimony varied, but several historians agree that whites in blackface carried out the deed.

This incredible but terrible historical moment is dramatized carefully and convincingly in the film. The filmmakers' decision to use the actual names of the union recruits and officers as well as documentary footage and historical titles, go a long way in establishing the film's objectivity. (All the newsreel footage of the Chicago Riot, with one or two exceptions, is authentic.) In the end, when it seems that no more conflicts can possibly arise, Frank decides to cross his own union's picket line and go back to work. He has already had to face the double humiliation of ducking bullets from white rioters and receiving charity from the meatpacking plant, courtesy of his nemesis, "Heavy" Williams.

The militia, sent out to escort Frank and the black workers into the meatpacking plant to scab, suddenly leave the area (clearly obeying a signal from one of the Big Five packing company bosses), and confront the white union members at the company gates. When the white union members refuse to attack the black workers, the white workers leave singing "Solidarity Forever," a tribute to their own discipline. But the black workers go to work.

Inside his now-familiar lockerroom, Frank keeps his union button hidden, but some hope is held out in the form of a young black worker who accepts Frank's closing speech that warns the blacks about the company reducing them to another form of slaves. The closing credits include end titles that trace the subsequent career of the union activists and officials in the film. Ironically, as these end titles make clear, the Frank Custers and the "Heavy" Williamses literally disappeared into unrecorded history, since they were never officially part of the record once their interviews with the Chicago Commission on Race Relations were completed in the early 1920s. The end titles also indicate that the United Food and Commercial Workers (UFCW) is the inheritor of the union tradition chronicled in the film.

See also: "Killer of Sheep"; "Matewan."

Availability: Easy.

Further reading: Asher, Robert. "Union Nativism and the Immigrant Response." *Labor History* (Summer 1982): 325–48. Places the Chicago struggle in the context of similar union organizing of (or refusal to organize) immigrants.

Barrett, James R. *Work and Community in the Jungle: Class, Race, and Ethnicity.* Urbana: University of Illinois Press, 1987. Good analyses of the forces that motivated such men as Frank Custer and "Heavy" Williams.

Brody, David. *The Butcher Workmen: A Study in Unionization.* Cambridge: Harvard University Press, 1964. A history of the Chicago unions, including material on some of the film's real-life characters.

Chicago Commission on Race Relations. *The Negro in Chicago: A Study of Race Relations and a Race Riot.* 1922. Reprint. New York: Arno Press, 1968. An incredibly detailed account by the official investigating commission.

Cohn, Lawrence. "Duke's Killing Floor, amid Brouhaha, to Be Released." *Variety,* 24 Feb. 1992, 40. On the failure to develop the pilot film into a series.

Grossman, James R. *Land of Hope: Chicago, Black Southerners, and the Great Migration.* Chicago: University of Chicago Press, 1989. An authoritative study of the main issues.

Klawans, Stuart. "Films." *Nation,* 30 March 1992, 425–28. Reviews the film and surveys Rassbach's controversy with the Corporation for Public Broadcasting.

O'Connor, John J. "'Killing Floor,' American Workers." *New York Times,* 10 April 1984, III.22. One of the few reviews, and it is very positive.

Sandburg, Carl. *The Chicago Race Riots, July, 1919.* 1919. Reprint. New York: Harcourt, Brace, 1969. News articles with an excellent brief overview by the young poet.

Sinclair, Upton. *The Jungle.* 1905. Reprint. New York: NAL, 1960. The first major fictional exposé of Chicago's meatpacking industry.

Tuttle, William M. *Race Riot: Chicago in the Red Summer of 1919.* New York: Atheneum, 1970. Best overall account of the riot by the "historical consultant" to the film.

Last Exit to Brooklyn

A film with something to offend everyone

1989, 102 mins., German (but in English), R
  (and here this rating should be carefully
  heeded)
Director: Uli Edel
Screenplay: Desmond Nakano, from Hubert
  Selby, Jr.'s novel of the same title
CAST
Harry Black = Stephen Lang

Tralala = Jennifer Jason Leigh
Big Joe = Burt Young
Boyce = Jerry Orbach
Vinnie = Peter Dobson
Regina = Zette
Donna = Ricki Lake
Georgette = Alexis Arquette

When a German director adapts the maverick and uncouth semi-underground American novel "Last Exit to Brooklyn," the film is bound to be one of the strangest in this guide, perhaps even stranger than "Boxcar Bertha" with which it is linked as an exploitation film in the Thematic Index. The central action of the film, a 1952 strike out of the cinematic Teamster tradition, has much in common with films such as "F.I.S.T." and "Hoffa" with its violent action and very little nuts-and-bolts organizing.

The tough life in the Brooklyn factories and streets is vividly re-created here, with more than a few touches of the grotesque characters from Hubert Selby's novel: in short, it presents a world-view that would disturb many viewers. The shop steward and strike captain of the fictional Federated Metal Workers Union local falls in love with a man and neglects his strike duties; Tralala, a hooker (played with an over-the-top trashy style by Jennifer Jason Leigh) is gang-raped. Eventually, the union president has to come in and straighten out the mess, and he kicks the pathetic shop steward out of the strike office. Not a very pretty sight. And not a film to inspire confidence in any union, or human beings, for that matter.

See also: "Boxcar Bertha."
Availability: Easy.
Further reading: Canby, Vincent. "Last Exit to Brooklyn." *New York Times*, 2 May 1990, C15.
  Although viewers may find it hard to believe, Canby wrote that the film "never appears to exploit its sensational subject matter."
Selby, Hubert, Jr. *Last Exit to Brooklyn*. New York: Grove, 1964. No one can argue that the film is any more or less exploitative than the novel by an ex-sailor who believes in street talk.

༙

The Life and Times of Rosie the Riveter

War of the Rosies

1980, 60 mins., C and B & W, unrated, but   Gladys Belcher
   suitable for all ages   Lyn Childs
Director: Connie Field   Lola Weixel
Semiscripted documentary   Margaret Wright
PRINCIPAL ROSIES
Wanita Allen

This film tracks five women who left traditional roles and jobs in the 1940s to become part of the army of millions of women who worked in factories while "the men were at war." Combining archival black-and-white footage, old photographs of the women, and contemporary interviews (most of them on the locations of the women's early working lives), Connie Field offers us a captivating (and ultimately bittersweet) portrait of women who not only rose to the occasion but exulted in it: the money was good; for the most part, they liked their challenging jobs; and they experienced an independence denied to them before the war and unavailable to them afterward.

Before the war, the five women had other jobs: two as domestics (the two black women, Wright and Allen), one as a farmworker (Belcher), and two as housewives (Weixel and Childs); after the war, they returned to the same or similar jobs. In between, they riveted and fabricated planes and ships.

Director Field has a great eye for the telling propaganda film or newsreel. At the beginning of the war, American women were told they could operate a lathe just like the juice extractors in their kitchens. Their femininity would be intact: "They come out from work looking like business girls on vacation," reports one cheery voice-over as we see women streaming out of the factory gates. The soundtrack of contemporary songs backs up the visual messages: not only do we have the then-famous "Rosie the Riveter," but also "Minnie's in the money. . . . She's a welder," and "If you want your country free, don't be an absentee!"

When the war was over, the government propaganda machine went into reverse: the women's "postwar plans" had to include going home and giving up their jobs to returning vets. One authoritative documentary voice from the 1940s announces, "The family was founded on the father as patriarch and breadwinner, and the mother as cook, housekeeper, and nurse to the children." The working women, the story went, were also leaving children at home "without adequate supervision or restraint"; one public service ad with a crying baby makes it clear: it's "your baby" or "your job."

Ultimately, gender politics prevailed: Field has unearthed a wonderful clip of Dr. Marynia F. Farnham, coauthor of *Modern Woman: The Lost Sex*, in which the author attributes the postwar anxiety the men felt to the fact that "their wives have become rivals."

Field's film was part of the wave of 1970s documentaries that reexamined women and labor history from a feminist point of view. Despite Hollywood's attempt to cash in on this revisionist history (Goldie Hawn in "Swing Shift," for example), Field's documentary remains remarkably fresh and convincing. Perhaps more on how the women interacted with organized labor would have provided some important background; for this, however, the viewer will have to look at "Union Maids."

Lola Weixel, formerly of Kaufsky's Welding Shop in New York City, almost steals the film from the other Rosies with her humor. "We were really a smart-looking group of ladies," she reminisces, but in the end "we gave up everything" to raise babies. In the companion book (see Frank, Ziebarth, and Field), Lola's testimony ends with the difficulties of a woman in the union environment of this era, but her film testimony has her wistfully (and only a little angrily) commenting about her work as a welder: "All I really wanted was to make a very beautiful ornamental gate." She still thinks about it to this day whenever she passes such a gate: "Was that so much to want?"

In both the film and the companion book, the women emphasize the sense of patriarchal betrayal the owner of the small welding shop in Brooklyn felt when they began to organize: "We were no longer 'his girls.'" In both, the union's struggle with a lockout is emphasized, and in both the double trouble of being a *woman* worker becomes increasingly apparent: while Lola and the women of her family worked nights to keep everyone fed and her crowded apartment clean, her brother-in-law, who worked at the Brooklyn Navy Yard, would lie on the couch and listen to jazz records.

See also: "Swing Shift"; "Union Maids."

Availability: Selected collections.

Further reading: Frank, Miriam, Marilyn Ziebarth, and Connie Field. *Life and Times of Rosie the Riveter: The Story of Three Million Working Women during World War II.* Emeryville, Calif.: Clarity Educational Productions, 1982. An essential companion book to the film, tracing and expanding on the role of the women Field interviewed.

Galerstein, Carolyn. "Hollywood's Rosie the Riveter." *Jump Cut* 32 (1987). 20–24. An excellent survey of films *other* than "Swing Shift" made about "Rosie" (unfortunately, none is currently available on videocassette).

Goldfarb, Lyn. *Separate and Unequal: Discrimination against Women Workers after World War II.* Union of Radical Political Economists, 1976. Detailed critique of UAW policies.

Honey, Maureen. *Creating Rosie the Riveter: Class, Gender, and Propaganda during World War*

II. Amherst: University of Massachusetts Press, 1984. Excellent analysis of how the media made and remade images of women workers.

Kessler-Harris, Alice. "Rosie the Riveter: Who Was She?" *Labor History* 24 (1983): 249–53. Questions the director's choice of these Rosies as representative of "women in the pre-war labor force"—"they were lucky; perhaps they were special; but they were not typical."

Lundberg, Ferdinand, and Marynia F. Farnham. *Modern Women: The Lost Sex*. New York: Harper, 1947. Freudian advice from Dr. Farnham to Rosie and her sisters—stay home, raise babies, and be happy.

Tobias, Sheila, and Lisa Anderson. *What Really Happened to Rosie the Riveter—Demobilization and the Female Labor Force, 1944–47*. New York: Pantheon, 1977. Especially good on examining the role of the UAW.

Zheutlin, Barbara, ed. "The Art and Politics of the Documentary: A Symposium." *Cineaste* 11.3 (1981): 12–21. Field explains her strategy for the film: "not scripted," but "carefully planned before shooting," including extensive interviews with the five Rosies before shooting.

Note: Also known as "Rosie the Riveter."

ᘉ
Look Back in Anger

Look back in amazement.

1958, 99 mins., British, B & W, unrated, but suitable for mature children	Alison Porter = Mary Ure
	Helena Charles = Claire Bloom
Director: Tony Richardson	Cliff Lewis = Gary Raymond
Screenplay: Nigel Kneale and John Osborne, from the latter's play of the same title	Inspector Hurst = Donald Pleasence
	Colonel Redfern = Glen Byam Shaw
CAST	Mrs. Tanner = Dame Edith Evans
Jimmy Porter = Richard Burton	Kapoor = S. P. Kapoor

We look back with some amazement on the idea that Jimmy Porter, a British market-stall worker, played by Richard Burton, would have been seen in the 1950s as a rebellious character instead of the complaining, unpleasantly violent, and horny—the British would say "randy"—character he now appears to be. His rebellion seems to be mainly against his upper-middle-class wife and her colonial-administrator father, both of whom he constantly berates for not being working class (although he himself moved closer to his wife's class by attending university).

At the same time, he defends an Indian stall worker against racist pressure to abandon his pitch, and he seems to represent an almost trade union solidarity of the stall workers against an obnoxious city inspector (played brilliantly by Donald Pleasence). At one point, the film he and his wife's best friend see at the movies is about British colonial troops massacring the local natives. And, speaking of his wife's best friend, his love affairs are by turns tender and cruel, extremes that may sum up the film's message about British working-class (nonunionized) life in the 1950s.

As a hit of the London stage in 1956, John Osborne's play helped to bring a generation of working-class playwrights to center stage. Osborne belongs to the rising working-class generation of British writers who were nicknamed the "Angry Young Men" after their class-obsessed upstart heroes. That no women were angry, and British trade union militancy never a part of their movement, which was also close to that of "kitchen sink" realism, should not keep curious viewers away from this intimate and compelling look at one version of survival in the 1950s.

Publicity for the play emphasized Jimmy Porter's sexy charm: "You are asked to believe that two women love this volcano of ceaseless, sputtering venom [and] you believe it. . . . The truth about this conscienceless sadist is that he is absolutely alive." Jimmy Porter wasn't the only dazzler in this period: numerous angry young men appeared in novels and films at the end of the 1950s and 1960s, most of them centered on a working-class bloke who was head up against the class system and in love (or in lust) with a middle-class woman: "Room at the Top" (1959) and "This Sporting Life" (1963) are two of the best, of which the former emphasizes the value of class mobility for its hero, while the latter—about a rugby player who keeps his day job at a factory—touches on a scandal or two involving workers compensation.

It is reasonably clear in retrospect that the "anger" in Osborne's play and the other films and novels of the 1950s was mainly class resentment in a society traditionally committed to keeping working-class people in their place. Occasionally, as in Jimmy Porter's struggle against Inspector Hurst (*not* a trace of which is in the original play), the anger becomes more politicized, but too often so much of the struggle ends up being like that of male deer at rutting time.

See also: ["Room at the Top"]; ["This Sporting Life"].

Availability: Selected collections.

Further reading: Braine, John. *Room at the Top.* London: Eyre and Spottiswood, 1957. The first "angry young man" novel.

Crowther, Bosley. "Look Back in Anger." *New York Times,* 16 Sept. 1959, 45. More cynical than other reviewers about this so-called angry young man, which Crowther considers "a conventional weakling, a routine crybaby."

Hill, John. *Sex, Class, and Realism: British Cinema, 1956–1963.* London: British Film Institute, 1986. Sets the film in the context of numerous other important working-class films of this period.

Mortimer, John. "The Angry Young Man Who Stayed That Way." *New York Times,* 8 Jan. 1995: II.5. A fellow playwright reviews Osborne's career on the occasion of his death.

Storey, David. *This Sporting Life.* New York: Penguin, 1963. A sharp look at working-class rugby culture.

Note: There are two other versions of the play available on videocassette in selected collections. Lindsay Anderson directed Malcolm McDowell and Lisa Barnes as Jimmy and Alison Porter in 1980, while a Thames Television production, directed by David Jones (from the stage production directed in turn by Judi Dench) and starring Kenneth Branagh and Emma Thompson as the Porters, appeared in 1989. Although both have very strong casts, neither has the audacity and rebellious potential of the original. Both of them follow the original stageplay more slavishly than Richardson's film, thus eliminating the subplot with the Indian stall worker, for example, and retaining Jimmy Porter's very literate references to such writers as Emily Bronte. (Do "Angry Young Men" read *Wuthering Heights*? Richard Burton's Jimmy Porter didn't.) Both seem more like filmed plays (which they are) than cinematic adaptations of a play. Those viewers familiar with British television—especially the productions of Masterpiece Theatre—will find these closer to that standard than the rough-and-tumble world of the original Jimmy Porter of the 1950s.

∾
Mac

Building houses the Italian-American way

1993, 118 mins., R (for language only)
Director: John Turturro
Screenplay: John Turturro and Brandon
  Cole
CAST
Mac Vitelli = John Turturro
Vico Vitelli = Michael Badalucco

Bruno Vitelli = Carl Capotorto
Alice = Katherine Borowitz
Nat = John Amos
Polowski = Olek Krupa
Oona = Ellen Barkin
Papa = Joe Paparone

As a portrait of an Italian-American immigrant carpenter and his three sons in Queens in the 1950s, this is John Turturro's film all the way: it's a tribute to his own father, nicknamed Mac in the film, which was written, directed, and stars Turturro. Mac represents the ethnic blue-collar craftsman who at first tries to make it as a skilled worker for an independent contractor building private houses.

When that arrangement falls apart, Mac and his brothers form a construction business of their own. The tensions and triumphs of this self-obsessed family provide us with a comic but convincing version of Italian-American working-class life (featured in the old days in "Marty" and more recently in "Moonstruck" and "Wait until Spring, Bandini'). To my untrained eye, the brothers, especially Mac, seem to spend an incredible amount of time having temper tantrums and knocking down the studs and scaffolding of the houses that they (or their stand-ins) built off-screen.

The film concerns the passion of these craftsmen to do a job well and how difficult it is to sustain that passion in capitalist America. The construction businesses in this

Mac (John Turturro) helps an injured worker in "Mac."

film are small—a mega-enterprise like Levittown is mentioned only briefly—and so the real competition for Turturro's Vitelli Brothers is another (Eastern European) immigrant's small business. There is also disharmony among the brothers themselves, however, since Mac's younger brothers simply cannot stand the incredible appetite for work Mac exhibits.

Unionism among construction workers is mentioned only briefly, when Mac demands one of his workers redo a cement floor because of the flotsam and jetsam that the worker has sloppily left in the soup (pants, a boot, and a toilet seat). The worker refuses, threatening to get his "union rep" to back him up. Mac prevails here, as he does so often in his quest to make it as an independent contractor. But the film criticizes his unyielding personality: quoting his father (who has the best scene when he pops up from the dead at his own funeral to attack the workmanship of his coffin), Mac says there are only two ways to do a job—"the right way and my way," and "both ways are the same." (Papa's remark parodies a scene in "The Caine Mutiny" when Captain Queeg maintains that there are *four* ways: the right way, the wrong way, the Navy way, and *his* way.)

There's an amusing subplot with Ellen Barkin as a Jewish beatnik model and poet who fascinates and is in turn fascinated by two of the three brothers. Perhaps inevitably (given this culture), women are subsidiary but interesting, and how Mac finds one as good as his mamma (always heard but never seen) is amusing. But it's craft, not a happy union, that ultimately matters.

See also: "Marty"; ["Moonstruck"]; "Riff-Raff"; ["Wait until Spring, Bandini"].
Availability: Easy.
Further reading: Canby, Vincent. "Pride and Craftsmanship in a Blue-Collar Family." *New York Times*, 19 Feb. 1993, C17. Compares the film—"a very good movie with a mind"—to Ken Loach's British film about construction, "Riff-Raff."

Macario

Never make a deal with a man in black.

1960, 91 mins., B & W, Mexican (in Spanish; subtitled in English), unrated, but suitable for all ages
Director: Robert Gavaldon
Screenplay: Robert Gavaldon and Emilio Caballido, from B. Traven's short story of the same title

CAST
Macario = Ignacio Lopez Torres
Macario's wife = Pina Pellicer
Death = Enrique Lucero
A Charro or Cowboy (the Devil) = Jose Galvez
A Hermit (the Lord) = Jose Luis Jimenez
Don Ramiro = Mario Alberto Rodriquez

"Macario" combines realism and fantasy in a form now popularly known in literary circles as Latin American "magic realism": Macario, a poor hard-working woodcutter, is always hungry and is barely able to supply his wife and five children with any sustenance. In desperation, he steals a turkey and goes off alone to enjoy his feast in the woods. There he meets three strangers who want him to share his turkey with them: a Charro (the Devil), a white-haired figure (the Lord), and a scrawny man in a dark cloak. Using bad logic, Macario decides that the third stranger only wants a gesture of kindness from him: the others are making, he thinks, both lower (diabolical) and higher (divine) demands.

Macario offers the third stranger some turkey, and to thank him, the stranger brings forth a miraculous spring of water from which Macario fills his gourd. Hereafter Macario can cure anyone with the water if Death—for that is who the third stranger is—stands by the inflicted's feet. Once Death moves to the head, Macario's magic will not work. Macario, of course, is the only character who can "see" Death.

Soon peasant Catholics and then grand families patronize Macario, who saves (and earns money from) virtually everyone who comes to see him. And on the rare occasion when he fails to cure someone, he insists that his fee be returned to the deceased's family. Macario likes his new life—we see a shot of an evening meal with a turkey for every member of his family!—until the Inquisition suspects him of practicing witchcraft and Death reveals that he drives a very hard bargain.

Scenes of the Mexican holiday, the Day of the Dead, and the underground candle-lit world of the souls entrusted to Death were brilliantly photographed by Gabriel Figueroa, the cinematographer who apprenticed to Gregg Toland ("The Grapes of Wrath"; "Citizen Kane") and became a virtual collaborator with Spain's greatest director, Luis Buñuel. The scenes of rural poverty and contrasting town affluence and productive labor (a bakery) are also nicely done. Filmed in 1960, "Macario" shows a not-so-ancient Mexico of hard lives, official power, and magic.

"Macario" is only the second of B. Traven's visions of anarchistic and "proletarian" life in Mexico in the 1920s that is available on videocassette: the first was the very successful "The Treasure of the Sierra Madre," with Humphrey Bogart as the prickly gold prospector in a band of ne'er-do-wells. "Macario," like all of Traven's work, celebrates the rural Indian culture of Mexico. Traven's other works, such as *The White Rose* (1929), about the takeover of land for oil drilling, are more sharply critical of American capitalist incursions into Mexico; *The Cotton-Pickers* (1926)—originally titled *The Wobbly*—celebrates the IWW's itinerant riffraff and successful strikes by Mexican workers.

After "Macario," Robert Gavaldon completed two other Traven films, although neither was released in the United States: "White Rose" ("Rosa Blanca"), made in 1961, was not even released in Mexico for more than a decade, making it (according to Chon Noriega and Steven Ricci), "one of the most noted cases of censorship in Mexico," and "Days of Autumn" ("Dias de Ontono"), made the following year, about women workers in a bakery shop.

Neither "Macario" nor "The Treasure of Sierra Madre" develops Traven's more radical side, since "B. Traven" was actually the pen name of Ret Marut, a German anarchist and revolutionary who fled the "Soviet" uprising in Bavaria in 1918 to take up residence in Mexico as a writer.

It is a small miracle that "Macario" is available in such chains as Blockbuster because it is not even listed in such popular video guides as Leonard Maltin's. With the exception of "Salt of the Earth," which received negative publicity when its Mexican star, Rosaura Revueltas, was deported because of the redbaiting of the film, and, more recently, with the popularity of the art theater hit "Like Water for Chocolate," Mexican cinema and its substantial filmmaking tradition have been virtually inaccessible to those in Mexico's nearest North American neighbor.

See also: "Salt of the Earth"; ["The Treasure of the Sierra Madre"].
Availability: Selected collections.
Further reading: Berg, Charles Ramirez. *Cinema of Solitude: A Critical Study of Mexican Film, 1967–1983.* Austin: University of Texas Press, 1992. Includes a chapter on films like "Macario" about the "unassimilated Indians," different because of their skin color, geography, language, customs, and social status.
Crowther, Bosley. "The Screen: 'Macario.'" *New York Times,* 28 Sept. 1961: 48. A positive review of a film "rich in human revelations and vivid pictorial qualities."
Guthke, Karl S. *B. Traven.* Translated by Robert C. Spruns. Brooklyn: Lawrence Hill Books, 1991. An excellent biography; places Traven's films in the context of his mysterious career.
Noriega, Chon A., and Steven Ricci, eds. *The Mexican Cinema Project.* Los Angeles: University of California Film and Television Archive, 1994. This excellent collection of essays on (and a mini-guide to) Mexican cinema covers all of the films by Gavaldon that are cited in this entry.
Traven, B. *The Cotton-Pickers.* New York: Lawrence Hill Books, 1956. The odd jobs of a wandering Wobbly.
——. *The Night Visitor and Other Stories.* New York: Hill and Wang, 1966. Besides "Macario," this volume includes the neglected comic classic "The Assembly Line," a short story of Indian handicraft versus American capitalism.
——. *The White Rose.* Westport, Conn.: Lawrence Hill, 1979. The destruction of a small farmer.
White, Armand. "Figueroa in a Landscape." *Film Comment,* Jan.–Feb. 1992, 60–63. A picture essay on the cinematographer.
Zogbaum, Heidi. *B. Traven: A Vision of Mexico.* Wilmington, Del.: Scholarly Resources, 1992. Traces the political views of his novels in the context of Mexican labor history.

The Man in the White Suit

. . . is a labor-management problem.

1951, 84 mins., British, B & W, unrated, but suitable for all ages
Director: Alexander Mackendrick
Screenplay: Roger Macdougall, John Dighton, and Alexander Mackendrick, from Mackendrick's play of the same title

CAST
Sidney Stratton = Alec Guinness
Daphne Birnley = Joan Greenwood
Alan Birley = Cecil Parker
Michael Corland = Michael Gough
Sir John Kierlaw = Ernest Thesiger

Workers are skeptical about the claims of the Man (Alec Guinness) in the White Suit. Courtesy British Film Institute Stills, Posters, and Designs.

Cranford = Howard Crawford
Bertha = Vida Hope
Frank = Patrick Doonan
Harry = Duncan Lamont

Wilkins = Harold Goodwin
Hill = Colin Gordon
Miss Johnson = Joan Harben
Roberts = Roddy Hughes

When Sidney, a lowly dishwasher at a textile mill who secretly works on his own experiments, invents a new miracle fabric, his dreams of becoming a research chemist finally seem to be coming true. His fabric will create clothing that will never wear out or become dirty. The mill owner's daughter—for reasons of her own—supports his research, but eventually the implications of his invention strike horror in both management and labor. If clothes never need to be replaced, textile mill managers and workers will soon be unnecessary.

In a fit of capitalist pique, one company decides to monopolize Sidney's invention. But the collective industrial geniuses point out that eventually there will be no profits for anyone. Both managers and trade union leaders want him stopped, by any means necessary. Sidney becomes a hunted man. In a classic scene of Ealing

Studio comedy, Sidney is chased up and down the streets at night, literally glowing white in his radioactive-fiber suit, his only supporter a waifish girl who tries to misdirect his pursuers, who consist of both managers and trade unionists. When he is finally cornered, to their great delight and his mortification, Sidney's white suit gradually disintegrates, leaving him standing in his shirt and boxer shorts: it turns out his miracle fabric has only a very short life.

Although Sidney is virtually silent, somewhere along the way he admits that as a misunderstood Cambridge first-class graduate he has always been a maverick worker and never been appreciated. When we see him in the end, he is clearly ready to go incognito at another factory, where he will disrupt the orderly compromise there that labor and management have so far maintained.

The film ends with the sweet (to Sidney) music of the bubbling flasks of his favorite experiment. In an Ealing Studio comedy like this, a plot is never resolved but simply waited out. Unlike the case in most traditional comedies, Sidney apparently must also lose both his girlfriends—the fellow trade unionist Bertha and the industrialist's daughter, Daphne: the ways of class conciliation are never smooth in an Ealing Studio film either.

See also: "I'm All Right Jack."
Availability: Easy.
Further reading: Crowther, Bosley. "Man in the White Suit." *New York Times*, 1 April 1952, 35.
   A "deft and sardonic little satire on the workings of modern industry."
Stead, Peter. *Film and the Working Class.* London: Routledge, 1989. Includes a discussion of the
   Ealing comedies.

∿

Man of Marble

Feet of clay

1977, 160 mins., Polish (with English subtitles), unrated, but suitable for mature children	Michalek = Piotr Cleslak
	Film editor = Wieslaw Wojcik
	Television man = Boguslaw Sobczuk
Director: Andrzej Wajda	Cameraman = Leonard Zajaczkowski
Screenplay: Alexander Scibor-Rylski	Sound engineer = Jacek Domanski
CAST	Agnieszka's father = Zdzislaw Kozien
Agnieszka Hulewicz = Krystyna Janda	Museum employee = Irena Laskowska
Mateusz Birkut = Jerzy Radziwilowicz	Bar owner = Wieslaw Drzewicz
Hanka Tomczyk = Krystyna Zachwatowicz	Colonel = Kazimierz Kaczor
Witek = Michel Tarkowski	Secretary = Ewa Zietek

Andrzej Wajda's film dissects a particular type of communist hero of the Stalin era in the Soviet Union and its Eastern European satellites: the "stakhanovite" or

Champion bricklayer Mateusz (Jerzy Radziwilowicz) at work in "Man of Marble."
Courtesy British Film Institute Stills, Posters, and Designs.

superhero worker, the man who in his selfless drive to establish a communist utopia worked harder and longer than everyone else for the collective good. Money, vacations, fame—none of these mattered. The Soviet model was Stakhanov, the working stiff as overachieving superstar. Wajda's film is about a Polish bricklayer, Mateusz Birkut, who, selected for his already considerable accomplishments as a good worker and his boyish good looks, becomes (relatively briefly) a national hero when he strives to break a record and lay thirty thousand bricks in one eight-hour shift.

The form of the film is similar to that of Orson Welles's classic "Citizen Kane": we learn of Mateusz's life, heroic rise, and tragic fall through films within films, secret archival footage, and interviews—with flashbacks—with his friends, loved ones, and "guardian angels" (those who spied on him). The frame story for the film is the quest by Agnieszka, a film student, to make a film about Mateusz for her graduate diploma. She uses her ambition, her sneakiness, and her attractiveness (she is a tall blonde who towers over most of her subjects in part because she wears enormous platform sandals under her bell bottoms), to get her interviewees to tell "the truth" about Mateusz. The truth, however, is very elusive, although by film's end it is clear that Mateusz was a victim of communist overachieving, cheating, and bureaucratic evil.

Wajda, Poland's greatest living filmmaker, intercuts the contemporary story of Agnieszka's quest and Mateusz's story by creating an entire set of fictional short films. Thus, Agnieszka first screens inflated state-sponsored films about Mateusz, with titles such as "Birth of a City" and "Architects of Happiness," which survey Mateusz's super skills and how they were put to service building a new workers' city and steel plant in the "socialist" city of Nowa Huta. She then interviews the celebrated filmmaker of these puff pieces, who gives his own (in flashbacks) version of the time he spent filming Mateusz in the 1950s. The technique—repeated in Wajda's film with other characters and other film footage—results in a remarkable series of multiple viewpoints on the same characters and their actions.

Mateusz's honeymoon with the socialist state comes to a crashing halt one sunny day when he is out at a new site "teaching" the local workers how to overachieve and work themselves to death for the common good. He is with his trusted friend and assistant, Witek. The two employ a team approach to laying bricks, which is Mateusz's special contribution to socialism. Thus, Mateusz and his four assistants lay bricks incredibly quickly: two men prepare the cement base, two others place the bricks, and Mateusz makes the final alignment. As yet another bricklaying feat is about to be staged, Mateusz is handed a burning-hot brick, which injures his hands horribly. The government spy suspects Witek, who says he's innocent because he was wearing gloves and did not know the brick was booby-trapped.

In continuing scenes of chilling communist justice, Witek literally disappears from a room at the Public Security Office to which he has been summoned and later reappears in a kangaroo court, where Mateusz is supposed to testify against him. We never know if he is really guilty, but Wajda's point is that it doesn't make any difference: the State is simply looking for scapegoats. Mateusz first and then Witek recant their testimony in front of newsreel cameras, but that footage is repressed and only comes to light years later when Agnieszka is making her film.

Wajda's satiric approach is relentless. Witek, it turns out, becomes rehabilitated after staying in prison and becomes the director of a major steel plant. Mateusz is convicted of leading a group of "imperialist spies" called the "Gypsy Band": in fact, Mateusz hires a gypsy band of musicians to accompany him when he throws a brick through the Public Safety window. *His* hands, however, remain gloved the rest of his life because of the burns.

By the time Wajda was completing his film, the Solidarity movement had been launched from the Gdansk shipyards, with Lech Walesa as one of its leaders. In her search for Mateusz—he has literally disappeared since his release from prison in 1956, the year of the Khrushchev "thaw"—she finds his son at the shipyards. At first, he will have nothing to do with her. One quest is ended, however, when he curtly tells her that his father is dead. This section of the film was censored by the Polish authorities in 1977 when the film was finished: in the current videocassette release, Gdansk is just a name—there is no organized activity portrayed—and a graveside scene specifying where Mateusz was killed—at the 1970 Gdansk workers' protests—is omitted. (Wajda includes this information in his sequel, "Man of Iron.")

Like his heroine Angieszka, Wajda's film becomes compromised: she is kept from finishing her film by officials at the TV station since the essential footage she needs (and has seen) is no longer available to her. She does make a comeback, however, in Wajda's sequel.

Wajda rarely overburdens his strong political subject matter. Our first glimpse of Mateusz is actually of a literal "man of marble," a socialist-realist statue of him as a greater-than-life-size worker with a determined jaw and a serious set of muscles. Using this statue as the first step into Mateusz's life, Wajda has challenged a glorified view of art in this remarkable deconstruction of the concept of a socialist hero. A resolute modern artist, he loves the self-reflexiveness of the medium: at one point the "man of marble" statue is presented as a sharp contrast to the "degeneracy" of western art, represented by Henry Moore's abstract figures that have holes in their torsos.

A viewer who needs a crash course in Polish history from World War II to the relatively recent past could rent this film and its sequel, "Man of Iron" (1980), which traces our filmmaker Agnieszka's relationship with Mateusz's son, who works at the Lenin Shipyard in Gdansk, the founding home of the Solidarity movement; add Agnieszka Holland's "To Kill a Priest" (1992), which dramatizes the very strong Catholic side of the Polish resistance to communism, and some of the most important factors in Polish political and economic life will have been covered. (Holland, now a successful filmmaker in exile, was Wajda's assistant for several years and is a possible source of his heroine's name—if not her radical persistence—in "Man of Marble.")

See also: ["Man of Iron"]; "To Kill a Priest."

Availability: Selected collections.

Further reading: Canby, Vincent. "Man of Marble." *New York Times*, 17 March 1979, 10. A positive review of this "big, fascinating, risky film that testifies not only to Mr. Wajda's remarkable vision, but also to the vitality of contemporary Polish life."

Goodwyn, Lawrence. *Breaking the Barrier: The Rise of Solidarity*. New York: Oxford University Press, 1991. A very thorough history of the Solidarity movement.

Moszcz, Gustaw. "Frozen Assets: Interviews on Polish Cinema." *Sight and Sound* 50 (Spring 1981): 86–91. Filmmakers, including actress Janda, discuss their participation in Solidarity and that movement's effect on the Polish film industry.

Paul, David W., ed. *Politics, Art, and Commitment in the Eastern European Cinema*. New York: St. Martins, 1983. A detailed survey of the film and of Wajda's career.

Marty

"What do you want to do, Marty?"

1955, 91 mins., B & W, unrated, but suitable
for all ages
Director: Delbert Mann
Screenplay: Paddy Chayefsky, from his TV
play of the same title
CAST
Marty = Ernest Borgnine

Clara = Betsy Blair
Marty's Mamma (Mrs. Pilletti) = Esther
Minciotti
Catherine = Augusta Ciolli
Angie = Joe Mantell

Famous for the question above that Marty's bored—and boring—friend Angie asks, this film features a Bronx Italian-American butcher, played wonderfully by Ernest Borgnine, who wants to find "a nice girl to marry," avoid his boring friends at the bar, and perhaps—hard for him to admit—stop listening to his mother. Part of the 1950s ethnic working-class cycle of films, "Marty" also acts out the American myth of "making it on your own," that is, by breaking out of the working class by having one's "own little business." Marty has to decide whether to buy out his boss and own the butcher shop himself. Whether it's a union shop or not is never made an issue in the film. The threat of supermarkets eating up the small shops, the breakup of the extended ethnic family, and the difficulties two shy people have while falling in love are just some of the dilemmas Marty faces. His new girlfriend is trying to break free of some family ties as well. Despite some 1950s creakiness in the characterizations, most viewers who are not made entirely of gristle like this film.

Originally a television play, "Marty" became Delbert Mann's first feature film and a classic of 1950s working-stiff social realism. When Marty tells Clara, an equally lonely heart he meets at the Stardust Dance Hall one Saturday night, that she is "not really as much of a dog" as she thinks she is, we are supposed to see that this is the highest compliment a working stiff like Marty can muster.

Marty's mother seems pure Italian-American working class; Marty is a little less so. Chayefsky (as some critics have been saying for some time) confirmed recently in Shaun Considine's biography that he always used autobiographical materials in his TV and film work, but because of an implicit ban on Jewish subjects, he was forced to use other (European) ethnic families to tell his stories. If this is true, he became the expert on the Universal Ethnic in New York City in the 1950s, because so much of his work captured the dilemmas and aspirations—in social realist style—of these working-class people.

Against stiff competition, "Marty" was the first American film to take the top award at the international film festival at Cannes. Such an award, and the positive reviews that greeted the newly energized American release of "Marty," virtually guaranteed Chayefsky a continuing string of hits, which lasted through "Network," the satire on his own original medium, TV.

When another one of his TV plays from the 1950s ("The Mother") was remade in 1994, the leading character was an Irish woman who tries to get her old job back in the garment district. Although there were certainly Irish-Americans working in the needle trades, Chayefsky had a Jewish working woman foremost in his mind—his own mother!

See also: "The Catered Affair"; "Mac."
Availability: Easy.
Further reading: Considine, Shaun. *The Life and Work of Paddy Chayefsky.* New York: Random House, 1994. An excellent survey of Chayefsky's career, emphasizing his innovative TV and film portrayals of working-class ethnic characters (and his autobiographical scripts).
Crowther, Bosley. "Marty." *New York Times,* 12 April 1955, 25. A positive review that empha-sizes the film's portrayal of the "socially awkward folkways of the great urban middle [sic] class."
O'Connor, John J. "Nostalgia for Drama of TV Past." *New York Times,* 24 Oct. 1994, B3. An interpretation of Chayefsky's "ethnic" maneuvers.

Matewan

One Big Union in one small town

1987, 130 mins., PG-13	Griggs = Gordon Clapp
Director: John Sayles	Hickey = Kevin Tighe
Screenplay: John Sayles	C. E. Lively = Bob Gunton
CAST	Mayor Testerman = Josh Mostel
Joe Kenehan = Chris Cooper	Bridey Mae = Nancy Mette
Elma = Mary McDonnell	Rosaria = Maggie Renzi
Few Clothes = James Earl Jones	Fausto = Joe Grifasi
Danny = Will Oldham	Hillard Jenkins = Jace Alexander
Sid Hatfield = David Strathairn	Mrs. Elkins = Jo Henderson
Sephus = Ken Jenkins	The Singer = Hazel Dickens

John Sayles's deservedly popular film combines two genres or types of films. We have at the center the miners' struggle, culminating in a western shootout in the center of town, but this is also a traditional Appalachian story in which an old man as a voice-over narrator barely distinguishes between past and present.

The film's plot sticks reasonably close to an actual incident in Mingo County,

West Virginia, at the eastern Kentucky border, after World War I, when the United Mine Workers organized at a coal mine protected by Baldwin-Felts agents. The central character, Joe, is a pacifist union organizer; he is also an ex-Wobbly or IWW man (Wobblies were sometimes pacifists, it is true, but they were not always so nonviolent). The initial unfriendly reception Joe receives in the town (except from one young miner, Danny), Sheriff Sid Hatfield's siding with the miners against the Baldwin-Felts private police force, informers' plots against Joe and the strike, and the need for an alliance among white, black, and Italian immigrant miners are portrayed with verve and conviction.

Joe has to hold together a fragile unity of Appalachian whites, African-Americans, and Italian immigrants, two-thirds of whom have been brought to the West Virginia hills to scab. The suspicions of the locals are not surprising: they need to survive in a company town, are being harassed by company cops, and are almost destroyed by a company spy in their own local.

The film is unified by Danny, a young miner in the midst of the struggle, and by his voice-over as an older miner looking back on the events that brought the union to his valley. The Matewan Massacre was followed by the Battle of Blair Mountain (also known as the Miners' March on Logan), when thousands of miners, many of them World War I veterans, marched to Logan County in sometimes loosely, some-times quite sharply organized formations, to protest against the Logan County authorities who, many miners believed, let the informer C. E. Lively and the others get away with the murder of Sheriff Sid Hatfield. They were met by an army of deputies and the U.S. Army as well, including bomber planes. But that's another story, on film as rare archival clips only in Barbara Kopple's documentary "Out of Darkness." It was omitted from Sayles's film for obvious reasons, although the intensity of the reaction in support of and against Sid was also omitted: he was not simply just a good-guy sheriff as the film has it; he also actively supported and helped lead the union organizing.

The music for the film provides a unity among the different ethnic groups. African-American blues, Italian mandolin music and other songs (the communist song of the "red flag," "Avanti Populo"), and traditional Appalachian a capella tunes provide the same fragile unity as the miners' struggle. Hazel Dickens, a contemporary mountain singer, opens the film with "Fire in the Hole," a song celebrating the miners' resistance; later she sings "The Gathering Storm" at a funeral for a friend of Danny's who was viciously murdered by Baldwin-Felts agents. Her final song, "Beautiful Hills of Galilee," is a traditional ballad she had already recorded.

Sayles, a generally political writer and director, wrote some excellent short stories and a novel, *Union Dues* (which has a few pieces of the "Matewan" screenplay embedded in it), before he began to write and direct films. His film "Brother from Another Planet" (1981) portrayed working-class Harlemites sympathetic to an escaped alien slave who looked like them. A more recent film, "City of Hope" (1991), is an ambitious dramatic survey of the ethnic and racial tensions of urban life.

"Matewan" is certainly Sayles's best film and perhaps one of the best features about labor history in years. Well researched and scripted, it reminds us what so many other labor films sometimes have lacked—a literate and artistic script; for example, when Sid rejects a notice from Baldwin-Felts to evict a mining family, he tells the agents: "I know Mr. Felts. I wouldn't piss on him if his heart was on fire."

See also: ["Brother from Another Planet"]; ["City of Hope"]; "Harlan County U.S.A."; "Out of Darkness."

Availability: Easy.

Further reading: Jones, Virgil Carrington. *The Hatfields and the McCoys.* Chapel Hill: University of North Carolina Press, 1948. A good, popular account of the West Virginia incident.

Savage, Lon. *Thunder in the Mountains.* Pittsburgh: University of Pittsburgh Press, 1990. The story line Sayles generally follows in "Matewan."

Sayles, John. *Thinking in Pictures: The Making of the Movie "Matewan."* Boston: Houghton Mifflin, 1987. An excellent background study about film in general and "Matewan" in particular.

Waller, Altina L. *Feud: Hatfields, McCoys, and Social Change in Appalachia, 1860–1900.* Chapel Hill: University of North Carolina Press, 1988. A definitive background study of the "Matewan Massacre."

Metropolis

"The City of Dreadful Night"—Thompson

[I] 1926, 120 or 94 or 90 mins., B & W, unrated, but suitable for mature children

[II] 1984, 87 mins., B & W and color tinted, unrated, but suitable for mature children

Directors: (I) Fritz Lang and (II) Fritz Lang and Giorgio Moroder (as editor)

Screenplays: (I) Fritz Lang and Thea von Harbou, from the latter's novel of the same title, (II) with additions by Giorgio Moroder

CAST (for both versions)

Maria and the Robot = Brigitte Helm

John Frederson (the Master of Metropolis) = Alfred Abel

Freder = Gustav Froelich

Rotwang = Rudolf Klein-Rogge

Slim = Fritz Rasp

Josaphat = Theodor Loos

No. 11811 = Erwin Biswanger

Foreman = Heinrich George

In 1984, Giorgio Moroder, the successful pop composer of film scores (such as the score for "Flashdance," for which he won an Oscar the year before), created a new version of Fritz Lang's classic futuristic film of the clash between labor and capital. Moroder tinted the film and added his own score plus new songs (by such recording stars as Pat Benatar, Adam Ant, and Freddie Mercury of the group Queen); as a result of extensive archival research, he also reconstituted missing scenes by adding rediscovered footage and stills. He even re-created a key prop (a statue of Freder's mother). He argued that all his efforts were an attempt to get closer to Lang's original vision, which was (and still is) in circulation in different lengths with different sequences. (Calling Moroder codirector of the second version would be a stretch, but viewers will at least see my point.)

In both versions—Moroder's and any of the different-length "silents," such as the ninty-minute film with Rosa Rio's musical accompaniment—the power of Lang's vision of workers oppressed by mighty machines comes through. Moroder's may strike us as being an MTV version of a classic, but there is no doubt that his tinting and reassembled sequences add a glow and pulse that are hard to overlook. In this sense Moroder has achieved on a much more modest scale what he set out to do: to imitate "Napoleon," the 1927 tinted, triple-image, long-lost silent masterpiece by Abel Gance, restored and rereleased by Kevin Brownlow in 1981 with a new score by Carmine Coppola.

The plots of both versions of Lang's film are essentially the same: Freder, at first the carefree son of the Master of Metropolis, learns from the angelic Maria the sufferings of the working-class people who create the wealth of the city. His father, ever watchful for signs of revolt among his workers, spies on an underground meeting of the workers in which Maria offers the startling suggestion that there can never be happiness in Metropolis unless the heart mediates between the hands (the workers) and the mind (the capitalists). She suggests that if they just hang on, a great mediator (a messiah?!) will come. The Master hatches a plot in which Rotwang, a mad scientist type (and his former rival for Freder's mother's love!), invents a robot *who is given Maria's features* and who is sent to lead the workers in an ill-fated revolt. If they follow her—and she is so sexy they cannot resist—they will destroy the machines and flood the working-class districts where their children live.

Although this plot has some interest (even if on the surface it is quite absurd), it is the individual shots and sequences of labor that hold the eye. At one point, for example, Freder takes the place of a worker who is manipulating the hands of what looks like a giant clock—each time a bulb on the periphery flashes, the worker must move the "hand" to it. Freder realizes to his horror that he must do this for a ten-hour shift.

Pauline Kael, perhaps unfortunately, made Lang's (pre-Moroder) versions of his film into an object of camp, to be viewed as interesting bad art (especially the hero's knickerbockers and Maria-Robot's lascivious wink), but she also praised some of the visual successes of the film, such as the way "human beings are used architecturally" and the Tower of Babel sequence. If she had commented on Moroder's version, she might have been impressed with the upper-class "Olympics," set in a surrealistic stadium, or the impresssively decadent Yoshivara (Temple of Sin) sequences.

Critics have taken Moroder to task for "interfering" with Lang's vision. But Lang's

"Metropolis" is essentially all special effects, odd-angled buildings, and choreographed crowd scenes. Moroder has simply accentuated Lang's pseudo-Marxist film of class struggle, really a successful imitation of H. G. Wells's *The Time Machine* (with the laboring class belowground and the leisured class above). Hitler and Goebbels, Lang always reminded interviewers, loved the film too and wanted Lang to work for the Nazis. They too had a class struggle in mind but not the heart Lang aimed for.

Ten years after "Metropolis," Lang was making his first American film, "Fury" (1936), the story of the attempted lynching of a garage owner. In between, he made the startling German film "M" (1931), the story of the hunt for a child murderer. Lang was rarely predictable and usually daring. Moroder has helped make his vision a little bit more accessible.

See also: "Fury."

Availability (both versions): Easy.

Further reading: Insdorf, Annette. "A Silent Classic Gets Some 80's Music." *New York Times*, 5 Aug. 1984, II. 15, 20. An extensive discussion of Moroder's version.

Jensen, Paul M. *The Cinema of Fritz Lang*. New York: Barnes, 1969. Discusses the original production, changes that were made, and its critical reception in Europe and the United States.

Kael, Pauline. *Kiss Kiss Bang Bang*. New York: Atlantic Monthly Press, 1968. "One of the last examples of the imaginative—but often monstrous—grandeur of the Golden Period of the German film."

Kracauer, Sigfried. *From Caligari to Hitler*. Princeton, N.J.: Princeton University Press, 1947. An outrageous but intriguing interpretation of Lang's version of the film as a concession to authoritarian tendencies in the collective German mind.

Maslin, Janet. "Hey, Don't Forget the Audience." *New York Times*, 19 Aug. 1984, II.15. Very negative review of Morodor's version, mainly because his music becomes "both tiresome and irrelevant."

Note: In Blockbuster stores, the 1926 version is labeled "silent," while the 1984 version is labeled "revised."

The Milagro Beanfield War

More "magic realism"

1988, 117 mins., R (no way; suitable for all ages)
Director: Robert Redford
Screenplay: David Ward and John Treadwell Nichols from Nichols's novel of the same title

CAST
Ruby Archeleta = Sonia Braga
Amarante Cordova = Carlos Riquelme
Coyote Angel = Robert Carricart
Kyril Montana = Christopher Walken
Sheriff Bernabe = Rubén Blades

Ladd Devine = Richard Bradford   Herbie Platt = Daniel Stern
Charlie Bloom = John Heard   The Governor = E. Emmet Walsh
Joe Mondragon = Chick Vennera   Flossie Devine = Melanie Griffith

A deservedly popular film about a Mexican-American community in New Mexico that stands up to and defeats a land and recreation scheme, "The Milagro Beanfield War" is a very pleasant mixture of fantasy and reality with lots of great jokes and sight gags. The only explanation for the R rating for this family film is that the Hollywood ratings board has been captured by the same land development moguls who are the people's enemies in the film. Sonia Braga's name on the cast list may have triggered this response, since her previous film appearances have been steamy: here she wears only a marginally revealing outfit or two as she banters with the ex-lefty from the 1960s (John Heard) who runs the local newspaper.

Most of the townspeople are apathetic about their gradual displacement by golf courses for the wealthy, but a few know such schemes are not going to help them. Braga's Ruby wants the community to fight, but her inspirational speech comes down to this: at least our poverty has been *our own* poverty, not the result of land development. As dubious as this might be for political analysis, we must remember that this is a comedy, and the forces of right are triumphant because the People (with a capital P) tell better jokes than the rich folk. Plus the People have luck, angels, and efficient saints to pray to.

Amarante, played by Carlos Riquelme and assisted by his pet watch-pig, more or less steals the film from a remarkably strong cast. When he is asked by a visiting sociologist, played as a goofy good-hearted soul by Daniel Stern, if he talks to angels, Amarante replies, "Of course, they're the only ones who have time to talk."

The initial hero of the piece is Chick Vennera's Joe, who, frustrated by his jobless-ness, kicks open an irrigation gate that waters his small farm. When he decides to grow beans there (in effect reestablishing ancient but confused water rights), he comes into armed conflict with the land development company and its lackeys; the Milagro Beanfield War is on!

Most of the battles are, however, comic. When the U.S. Forest Service impounds Joe's cow for illegal munching, three ancient local men make it clear that if the rangers don't surrender Joe's cow, they'll shoot the "huevos" off the rangers. After they capitulate, one of the rangers announces, "I think we showed them that the Forest Service can be flexible."

Filmed in lovely and dusty detail in Truchas, New Mexico, the film is a tribute to a 1960s radical's fantasy of an armed People—they have guns and are willing to use them to scare the Establishment, but fortunately no one gets killed.

See also: "Macario."
Availability: Easy.

Further reading: Canby, Vincent. "Riparian Rights and Wrongs." *New York Times*, 18 March 1988, C17. A negative review: "Not Mr. Redford's finest hour."

Nichols, John Treadwell. *The Milagro Beanfield War*. New York: Holt, 1974. The film captures some of the same absurdities as this source novel.

Miles of Smiles, Years of Struggle: The Untold Story of the Black Pullman Porter

Black working-class mobility

1982, 58 mins., unrated, but suitable for all ages
Directors: Jack Santino and Paul R. Wagner
Scripted documentary by Jack Santino
PRINCIPAL FIGURES
A. Philip Randolph, founder, Brotherhood of Sleeping Car Porters (BSCP)

E. D. Nixon, former porter
C. L. Dellums, founding officer, BSCP
Rosina Coruthers Tucker, former president, BSCP's Ladies Auxiliary

By the 1920s, the Pullman Company employed more black workers than any other company in the United States. But too often these jobs furthered black stereotypes, especially that of the "happy" servant, thereby continuing the slavery tradition of the "happy" slave. Not surprisingly, the Pullman logo was a round, fairly abstract black face. But when jobs were scarce in general and racist hiring policies were in effect in many major corporations, Pullman's jobs were also very good jobs for African-Americans. We see footage from a Paul Robeson classic, "The Emperor Jones" (1933), in which Robeson as a newly hired Pullman porter—local man made good—is given a dramatic farewell from his church. The farewell was necessary, for the porters would be away from home for long periods of time, living in company hostels.

The filmmakers have assembled a small but important group of people associated with the original union drive. Rosina Tucker, one hundred years old, was a widow of a Pullman porter and an activist in the Ladies Auxilliary. C. L. Dellums is the only living member of the BSCP's original founding group.

Some of the other porters return to their old trains to show off their skills, such as getting the beds ready at night for their charges. Another veteran demonstrates how the segregated dining cars were set up, with a partition across the back of the car. The old men debate the issue of their servant status, a question they cannot totally resolve, in part because they clearly *were* servants and in part because they were proud of their jobs and their skills.

See also: ["The Emperor Jones"].
Availability: Selected collections; AFL-CIO; ILR Media.

Further reading: Harris, William. *Keeping the Faith: A. Philip Randolph, Milton P. Webster, and the Brotherhood of Sleeping Car Porters, 1925–1937.* Urbana: University of Illinois Press, 1977. The history of the union.

Levine, Lawrence. *Black Culture and Black Consciousness: Afro-American Folk Thought from Slavery to Freedom.* New York: Oxford University Press, 1977. Explores (in part) porters as middlemen between urban and rural lifestyles (e.g., bringing jazz records to the countryside!).

Mergen, Bernard. "The Pullman Porter: From 'George' to Brotherhood." *South Atlantic Quarterly* 73 (1974): 224–35. Examines the nickname and its implications.

Santino, Jack. *Miles of Smiles, Years of Struggle: Stories of Black Pullman Porters.* Urbana: University of Ilinois Press, 1989. Includes (and expands upon) the interviews in the film.

Terkel, Studs. *Hard Times.* New York: Pantheon, 1970. Another interview with porter E. D. Nixon, this one about the Montgomery, Alabama, 1955 bus boycott.

Modern Times

Never speed up a worker with a bowler hat!

1936, 89 mins., B & W, silent (for the most part), unrated, but suitable for all ages
Director: Charlie Chaplin
Screenplay: Charlie Chaplin
CAST
The Little Tramp = Charlie Chaplin
A Gamin = Paulette Goddard
A Cafe Proprietor = Henry Bergman
A Mechanic = Chester Conklin
The Burglars = Stanley Sandford, Hank Mann, Louis Natheux
President of a Steel Corporation = Allen Garcia

This is probably the last great "silent" film, despite a few moments when unusual bits of sound—Charlie singing what the *New York Times* reviewer called "some jabberwocky . . . to the tune of a Spanish fandango"—seem to leap from this comic/slapstick exploration of the world of factories under the command of the New Efficiency, a 1930s expression, of course, for the classic speedup. But Charlie has a hard time being sped up, and his most famous sequence is one in which the Little Tramp becomes the world's unlikeliest assembly-line worker and is fed into—and ground by—the massive gears of a giant factory machine.

The film has a startlingly modern look to this day: the factory boss communicates with his speedup foremen by "video" screens (that is, when he's not doing jigsaw puzzles or reading comics). Charlie's attempt to turn two nuts on parts riding an ever-faster conveyor belt soon becomes a sequence with wonderful visual puns (the buttons on a woman's outfit, for example, resemble those on Charlie's assigned task and his arms "automatically" want to twist them).

When the New Efficiency brings in a "feeding machine" for workers to keep them from having lunch breaks, Charlie (abused by this ridiculous machine) cracks. Chaplin's reputation for being a lefty was probably aided by this capitalist satire, although it is in the end a very gentle satire, like the Little Tramp himself. When Charlie accidentally leads a demo with a red flag from a construction vehicle, the satire is distinctly his.

The Little Tramp manages to reverse some of his earlier indignities by the end of the film: after his release from prison, he becomes a helper to a maintenance man who is himself caught in the gears of a monster machine. This time, Charlie, combining his lessons from earlier disasters, feeds the trapped man carefully through a funnel in his mouth.

In the end, however, Charlie takes to the open road with the gamin and, like so many of his unemployed countrymen during the Depression, becomes the Little Tramp outdoors again, one of the best loved of all the cinematic riffraff.

See also: "Gold Diggers of 1933."
Availability: Easy.
Further reading: Nugent, Frank S. "The Screen." *New York Times*, 6 Feb. 1936, 23. Sums up
   Charlie's career and the tension between his leftist politics and his comic self.
Von Wiegand, Charmion. "Little Charlie, What Now?" In *New Theatre and Film: 1934 to 1937*,
   edited by Herbert Kline, 245–54. New York: Harcourt, Brace, 1985. A contemporary (1936)
   political (left) interpretation.

ᘓ
The Molly Maguires

"See you in hell."—James McKenna/McParlan

1970, 123 mins., PG	CAST
Director: Martin Ritt	Jack Kehoe = Sean Connery
Screenplay: Walter Bernstein, adapted (but uncredited) from Arthur H. Lewis's *Lament for the Molly Maguires*	James McKenna/McParlan = Richard Harris
	Mary Raines = Samantha Eggar
	Captain = Frank Finlay

Although the Molly Maguires have now become virtual legends, no one can say with authority if they even existed or—if they existed—whether they were a self-conscious organization of Irish-American miners. Director Martin Ritt accepted one traditional interpretation of the Mollies and dramatized it in this film: the Pennsylvania Mollies were a secret cell or cadre of terroristic dynamiters who used the Ancient Order of Hibernians, an Irish benevolent society, as a cover; individuals became Mollies because they were frustrated by the failure of the strikes led by their

Pinkerton spy James McKenna (Richard Harris) walks through town with Mary Raines (Samantha Eggar) in "The Molly Maguires."

union (the Workingmen's Benevolent Association) and decided to blow up the mining companies instead.

To make a film about one of the most controversial episodes in American labor history was a daring move on Ritt's part. Like "Matewan," which John Sayles said was in part about whether Joe the union organizer could get justice for the miners without using a gun, any discussion of the Mollies raises the question of company and union violence.

Ritt's film in effect rejects an alternative view of the Mollies, first set out way back in 1932 by Anthony Bimba, that they were primarily trade union organizers, secret as a means of self-protection, who were framed and executed for deeds that they did not commit or that were committed by the mining companies and their agents. In Ritt's film, they are "guilty as hell," despite the presence of James McKenna/ McParlan (played by Richard Harris), a Pinkerton agent in their midst. The agent testified at the trials of the men hanged for their crimes as Mollies, as he does in the film. Bimba and others believed that the agent made up most of his testimony, but Ritt portrays him as a compassionate man who sometimes tried to talk his new friends out of some dangerous deeds. In the end, however, both the real-life and fictional agent betrayed twenty men, who were hanged in 1877.

Ritt builds on McKenna's friendship with Mary, the housekeeper at his lodgings, hinted at in Arthur H. Lewis's book (the uncredited source for the film), and turns this into a somewhat stereotypical romance. The film ends with an extremely un-likely jail cell confrontation when McKenna/McParlan visits Black Jack Kehoe. McParlan praises Jack for not taking the miners' lot passively: "You made your sound. You used your powder." But Jack resists the spy's flattery and attacks him. "No punishment short of hell will set you free," Jack tells him. "See you in hell," the rising Pinkerton star replies. In a chilling final shot, McParlan strides toward the camera as the gallows has a practice "drop" with dummies in the background. It repeats one of the opening shots of the film, when Jack walks toward the camera as the mines explode behind him: from terrorism to the gallows is the film's message.

Because the film comes from a respected pro-labor director and because so much of it seems authoritative, it is important to realize that its historical accuracy is open to question. New research on the Mollies raises three distinct but related interpreta-tions of their role in labor history.

First, the region of the Mollies, east-central Pennsylvania, had a contentious political history even outside the mines: men later named as Mollies, specifically Black Jack Kehoe (played in the film by Sean Connery), had been active during the Civil War as draft resistors. (This background information is never offered in the film.) The most active resistors, organized or not, were called Buckshots as well as Mollies; thus, various terms for "troublemaker" had already been established. Active trade unionism was often equated with draft resistance, although the draft resistors tended more often to be farmers, who were Democrats and therefore not of Lincoln's Republican Party, rather than miners. It may be that local draft officials (called "provost marshalls") used the army to get rid of union trouble-makers by drafting them. Kehoe was accused of killing one of these provost marshalls. In this view the Mollies were simply any men standing in the way of two major Republican Party goals—winning the war and extending the centralization of capitalism.

Second, mid-nineteenth-century Americans joined fraternal and secret organizations in extraordinary numbers. Everyone talked about the Irish Mollies, but the Welsh Protestant miners supposedly had the more rarely mentioned "Modocs" (who may have been company agents as well; see Boyer and Morais below). The Knights of Labor, founded in 1869, the major forerunner of American unionism, was such a secret fraternal organization. Other organizations founded during this period included the Know-Nothings (the anti-immigration party) in 1849, the Copperheads (anti-Republican or pro-southern groups) in 1861, the Ku Klux Klan in 1866, and the Grangers in 1866, for farmers. Many labor unions used the same mumbo jumbo of fraternal rituals for their organizations.

Third, the attack on the Mollies by McKenna and the Pinkertons was part of the nationwide reaction to the union and working-class struggles that were occurring all over America in 1877. The Mollies were executed at the height of the militancy among railroad workers, for example. The *New York Times*, in an editorial of 3 May 1877, complained about a prolonged strike by iron foundry workers in upstate New York and suggested that "it is possible that there is in our State a field for the exercise of a little Pennsylvania justice."

The man who hired McKenna, Allan Pinkerton, published what is basically a novel about the Mollies, *The Mollie Maguires and the Detectives* (1877), replete with bar scenes and Irish weddings. His more substantial *Strikers, Communists, Tramps, and Detectives* (1878) covered the great strike wave of 1877, emphasizing the involvement of secret organizations such as trade unions and the Mollies and especially calling attention to the communist and internationalist ideas of Karl Marx and the French Commune of 1871. Here is a sample of the high level of Pinkerton's analysis: "An organization, called the Knights of Labor, has recently attracted some attention in the coal regions of Pennsylvania. It is probably an amalgamation of the Mollie Maguires and the Commune [the Paris Commune!]. In the vicinity of Scranton and Wilkes-Barre two-thirds of the workingmen belong to it."

The "Mollies" may therefore have been the convenient label of individuals caught in an extraordinary mixture of fraternal, national, and political trends. But whether they were real or legendary or filmed characters, the Mollies always met the same end—hanging after a kangaroo court. The film does not emphasize these bizarrely unfair proceedings, such as Franklin B. Gowen, president of the railroad, dressed in his U.S. officer's uniform, helping with the prosecution. Nor does it mention (given its time frame, not surprisingly) that McParlan's next major assignment was to arrange the perjured testimony that almost got Wobbly Big Bill Haywood executed for the 1902 bombing involving Idaho's ex-governor Frank Steunenberg.

Ritt went on to direct such politically progressive films as "Sounder," a 1972 drama about a black sharecropper's family during the Depression, and "Norma Rae," the 1979 film about textile organizing. Ritt also directed a less famous drama about waterfront workers in 1957 called "Edge of the City" (currently unavailable in any format). He was blacklisted during the McCarthy era but got even with his 1976 film, "The Front" (starring Woody Allen).

See also: "Edge of the City"; ["The Front"]; "Matewan"; "Norma Rae"; "Sounder."
Availability: Easy.
Further reading: Aurand, Howard W. *From the Molly Maguires to the United Mine Workers.* Philadelphia: Temple University Press, 1971. A good general history.
Aurand, Howard W., and William Gudelunas. "The Mythical Qualities of Molly Maguire." *Pennsylvania History* 49 (1982): 91–105. Argues that the Molly Maguire episode has "the potential . . . to lend credence to any interpretive position."
Bimba, Anthony. *The Molly Maguires.* 1932. Reprint. New York: International, 1970. A well-researched left/communist interpretation.
Boyer, Richard O., and Herbert M. Morais. *Labor's Untold Story.* 1965. Reprint. New York: United Electrical, Radio, and Machine Workers of America, 1976. Includes a substantial section on the Mollies.
Broehl, Wayne G. *The Molly Maguires.* Cambridge: Harvard University Press, 1964. A solid history that assumes the Mollies were an "ancient order" within the Hibernians.
Carnes, Mark C. *Secret Ritual and Manhood in Victorian America.* New Haven: Yale University Press, 1989. Background on secret societies, including the Knights of Labor.
Dorson, Richard M. *America in Legend.* New York: Pantheon, 1973. Includes a chapter on the legends (folklore) of the Mollies, some persisting to this day.
Goldfarb, Lyn, and Anatoli Ilyashov. "Working Class Hero: An Interview with Martin Ritt." *Cineaste* 18.4 (1991): 20–23. Ritt on his approach to the Mollies and his other films.
Lewis, Arthur H. *Lament for the Molly Maguires.* New York: Harcourt, Brace, 1964. Despite the title, this source novel for the film more or less accepts the Mollies' guilt uncritically.
"The Mollie Maguires." *New York Times,* 23 Dec. 1875, 2. The Catholic Church announces that "Mollie Maguires, Hibernians, Buckshots or whatever else they may choose to call themselves . . . are excommunicated."
Palladino, Grace. *Another Civil War: Labor, Capital, and the State in the Anthracite Regions of Pennsylvania, 1840–68.* Urbana: University of Illinois Press, 1990. The political context of the Mollies.
Pinkerton, Allan. *Strikers, Communists, Tramps, and Detectives.* 1878. Reprint. New York: Arno Press, 1969. The boss of the private police offers his theories and practical advice.

ᘓ
Moving Mountains

"Women hold up half the sky."—Chinese proverb

1981, 30 mins., unrated, but suitable for all
   ages
Director: Laura Sky
Documentary

PRINCIPAL FIGURES:
Dave Carroll, president, Local 7884, United
   Steelworkers of America (USWA)
Local members = Ina Hees, Brenda
   Forrister, Lon Dansberg, Anna Bonnell

"Moving Mountains" makes a good nonfictional companion to "Wildrose": both are stories of women who rig explosives in open-pit coal mines or drive trucks five times the size of the workers' shuttle bus. When one woman in this documentary is interviewed beside her truck, the wheel is more than twice her height. The work of open-pit hauling is dangerous, the women emphasize: their loads are incredibly heavy, and the roads in British Columbia, where the film was shot, can be slippery.

The documentary was produced by the United Steelworkers to showcase one local's fight to include women in traditionally male-only jobs. Eventually, the local had to take legal steps to force the mines to hire women. The women, interviewed here as they do their work, explain how the men reacted to their being hired and why they like working in these jobs. The local union president also comments on his role in supporting the women's cause. At the time of the filming, this local of 1,121 workers in Elkford, British Columbia, had 80 women working in the mines.

See also: "Wildrose."
Availability: Selected collections; AFL-CIO (16 mm); ILR Media (3/4 inch video).

ᘓ
Never Steal Anything Small

. . . especially this videocassette.

1959, 94 mins., unrated, but suitable for all
   ages
Director: Charles Lederer
Screenplay: Maxwell Anderson, from his
   and Rouben Mamoulian's play *The
   Devil's Hornpipe*

CAST
Jake MacIllaney = James Cagney
Linda Cabot = Shirley Jones
Dan Cabot = Roger Smith
Winnipeg = Cara Williams
Words Cannon = Royal Dano
Pinelli = Nehemiah Persoff

Today this would be called a "high-concept" film in Hollywood: James Cagney as a crooked waterfront union leader who will do anything to become president of his local—including sing a few of the terrible songs that make this film (almost) a musical. Cagney, with a number of deceptions most city cats could spot a mile off, does win his election and spends the rest of the film trying to make some money and steal his naive lawyer's pretty wife. As long as you "never steal anything small," he sings, you can get away with it: steal small and you end up in jail. This backhanded compliment to white-collar crime does not, however, carry the day for Cagney's fighting Irishman, because the film has a few peculiar moral lessons to draw before it mercifully closes.

This film must have been predicated on the success of "The Pajama Game," another high-concept musical that was extremely popular just two years before and that took up the issue of labor-management relations in a similarly jaunty way. Both films were throwbacks to the old union comedy model of the 1940s, typified by "The Devil and Miss Jones," in which genuine grievances are resolved in a fantasyland projection of bosses who turn out to have hearts of gold and are really, well, just human.

Why use the docks? Certainly the gritty success of "On the Waterfront" just five years earlier should have caused Hollywood's wheels to grind a bit more slowly in producing a comedy about labor violence. But "Never Steal Anything Small" had also been a successful Broadway play and Cagney always seemed to satisfy his legions of fans, so a film that opens with a comic scene with an iron lung must have been appealing, even though the 1950s was the decade of polio.

Why the iron lung? Jake needs money to throw a party where he'll fix his election as president of the local. The money comes from a loan shark whom Jake shakes down, then dopes and stuffs in the iron lung. When the loan shark wakes up, Jake hustles him off to Yuma, Arizona, to recuperate. Equally dubious is the high-class madam Jake hires to turn his lawyer's head while he enjoys the company of the lawyer's wife. Winnipeg (the madam) requires a stiff payment: "I'm sorry, I want a Ferrari," she sings at a car dealer's showroom.

All of this would be so much Hollywood kitsch and beyond retrieval if it did not also contain large dollops of strange anti- and pro-union messages. Although Shirley Jones, with a bare-midriff outfit, sings "I haven't got a thing to wear," she also tells Jake that she doesn't want her husband to be his lawyer because she has researched his strike violence, bribery, and prison sentences. Jake's defense is that in a vicious world unions have to be "fighting fire with fire." In fact, he adds confidently, if he weren't in charge, "the union would be in the hands of crooks even bigger than me." Later, when Jake begins to make a positive impression on her, she responds, "Considering you're a crook and a horror, you're a pretty nice guy." After narrowly escaping an acid attack—à la the notorious blinding of labor columnist

Victor Riesel in 1956—Jake begins to think of himself as the little guy's candidate to unseat the big Mafia types running the international. Here he delves into labor history, making a speech about "outstanding men" like Gompers, Lewis, Dubinsky, Meany, and Reuther. How does he compare with them? "They're 100 percent and I'm only 15 percent."

Even that estimate seems high until the film contrives to make Jake into a rebel. Jake's local is ruled with a Mafia fist by Mr. Pinelli of the United Stevedores—and "he doesn't like wildcat strikes." Although Jake has framed his own lawyer for a theft of cargo Jake personally rescued (Cagney in a wet suit!) from the prepolluted Hudson, Jake eventually takes the rap because he realizes that his defense—that he really stole the money "for the men"—will help him in his election bid against Mr. Pinelli. Even when you hear something silly about this film, it is still hard not to watch it to see if your expectations come true. They will.

See also: "The Devil and Miss Jones"; "On the Waterfront"; "The Pajama Game."
Availability: Selected collections.
Further reading: Weiler, A. H. "Never Steal Anything Small." *New York Times*, 12 Feb. 1959, 23.
     An overly enthusiastic review.

ꙮ
Newsies

No newsies are good newsies?

1992, 125 mins., PG	Les Jacobs = Luke Edwards
Director: Kenny Ortega	Bryan Denton = Bill Pullman
Screenplay: Bob Tzudiker and Noni White	Medda Larson = Ann-Margret
CAST	Joseph Pulitzer = Robert Duvall
Jack Kelly = Christian Bale	Racetrack = Max Casella
David Jacobs = David Moscow	Crutchy = Marty Belafsky

Connoisseurs of trash are always hunting for candidates for cult status—a film that is good because it is sooo bad. Move over "Bride of Frankenstein," welcome "Newsies." Since there are virtually no newsboys (at least in America) anymore, even in the suburbs, it must have seemed safe for Hollywood to make a film about how they became unionized. Safely removed in time as well, the filmmakers' newsboys live in a never-never land of New York street talk: if a real street urchin sang about "mudder, dautter, fadder" (from newsboy Jack's song "So That's What a Family Is"), no newsboy would ever have been safe. But even contemporary news accounts captured these accents—"Dere's t'ree t'ousand of us, and we'll win sure"—so maybe people really did "tawk" that way.

This exercise in historical kitsch about the once numerous youthful riffraff who roamed every big city in America only touches on the real problems these youngsters faced. An early muckraking piece by William Hart (from *Everybody's Magazine* in 1908) exposed the unpretty side of the daily grind of selling the news on street corners (plus other things some of the night boys sold, like drugs). The newsies in this film are, of course, too old, too clean, too well fed, and too happy to be real. Even the one quaintly called "Crutchy" gets along fine. And there are even singing nuns in the streets!

Disney, alas, is about pretty, and the newsboys (there are no newsgirls, but fortunately there are sisters of newsboys) in this film have a well-fed wholesomeness that usually works for Disneyland. Since there has been an occasional uproar about violence and strange moral lessons in Disney films (from "Bambi" to "The Lion King") in the past, it should have occurred to Disney execs when "Newsies" was (mis)conceived that it is not wholesomeness that captures attention and word of mouth but the Dark Side.

The only Dark Side in "Newsies" consists of newspaper magnates Joseph Pulitzer (the *New York World*) and William Randolph Hearst (the *Journal*), who are interested in money and yellow journalism ("Nude Corpse on Rails Not Connected with Trolley Strike"), respectively. The strike portrayed here was actually a selective strike, which the film does not make clear: only boys who sold the *World* and *Journal* struck, and in fact a few adult women who sold the two scab papers were permitted to carry on as well. ("We ain't fightin' women," one of the newsboys told a *New York Times* reporter, who tipped him a dime for his chivalry.)

One can only imagine Disney executives screening "Dirty Dancing"—the last successful job for choreographer and director Kenny Ortega—and deciding that without any of the sexy gals in "Dirty Dancing," they could have a great children's dance film that could rival "Oliver!" or "Annie." Instead of the 1950s cultural rebelliousness of "Dirty Dancing," "Newsies" subverts the revolutionary rhetoric of the 1960s. At one point, in an unconscious parody of Black Panther and SDS Weatherman slogan mongers, the newsies sing, "Arise and Seize the Day." When the newsies really get ticked off, they sing, "Nothing can break us/No can make us give up our rights."

Having been somewhat unfair to this film, I should say that Disney does not pull many punches when it comes to the trolleymen's strike of 1899, the model for the newsies' organizing drive. The trolleymen fight back against the police escorts of the scab drivers, burn the trollies, and generally carry on fairly violently. Labor militancy in the summer of 1899 in New York City was quite extensive, as a reporter for the *New York Times*—not a scab newspaper that year—explained: "The strike fever, after extending from the street car employees and freight handlers on the railroad piers to the newsboys, has now spread to the telegraph messenger boys" (22 July 1899). The newsboys were able to win their strike in part because they numbered three thousand in Manhattan alone and in part because their militancy—beating up scab newsboys and ripping up their newspapers—usually went unchecked since the police were called away to trolley strike duty. For the most part, the police should have been happy that children had their own strike to pursue, since some ten-year-olds had been helping the trolleymen by throwing bricks at scab-driven cars.

The film makes only partial use of this militancy, although the union lessons strike home. One of the newsies says of his father, who has lost his job after being injured at a factory: "He's got no union to protect him." The newsboys had a simple demand: the wholesale cost of each newspaper had to remain at a half-cent per copy. (They sold them for a penny.) It is perhaps a pity that this film was thrown away on a fascinating moment in labor history. An investment in some time looking at back issues of the *New York Times* might be time better spent than renting this movie, even if the film does have one other thing right: there really was a newsboy named "Racetrack" who was in charge of (unsuccessful) negotiations with the chief of police for parade rights. The chief said "no" to this leader of the real Newsboys' Union, who clearly didn't always get what it wanted.

Eventually, Governor Teddy Roosevelt comes down on the side of the boys, conveniently enough, just when they are about to launch a citywide "child labor" strike, called by what looks like a junior version of the Wobblies—One Big Union of children from the garment sweatshops, the stables, and, of course, the Messenger Boys, who, in the final demonstration, lead the masses of child laborers against Pulitzer's newspaper citadel. It is (almost) enough to make the hardest heart soften. Since this guide lists so few films especially for children, "Newsies" may be helpful in raising some potential young militants.

Availability: Easy.

Further reading: Burroughs, Harry. *Boys in Men's Shoes: A World of Working Children.* New York: Macmillan, 1944. An immigrant arrives in Boston in 1903, rises from newsboy to lawyer, and establishes a foundation to provide welfare and career services for other "newsies."

Hart, William. "De Kid Wot Works at Night." In *Popular Writing in America*, edited by Donald McQuade and Robert Atwan, 257–63. 5th ed. New York: Oxford University Press, 1993. Despite the jokey title, Hart's 1908 article about the exploitation of "newsies" led to child labor reform in Chicago.

Maslin, Janet. "They Sing, They Dance, They Go on Strike." *New York Times,* 8 April 1992, C17. A heartless attack on the film's virtues.

New York Times. "Newsboys Go on Strike," 21 July 1899, 2; "The Strike of the Newsboys," 22 July 1899, 4; "Newsboys Act and Talk," 25 July 1899, 3. Sample articles on the newsboys' strike.

New York Times. "Strikers [Trolleymen] Return to Work," 21 July 1899, 2; "Messenger Boys May Strike," 22 July 1899, 4; "The Messenger Boys Strike," 25 July 1899, 3. Sample articles on the other strikes.

∽
9 to 5

No "business as usual"

1980, 110 mins., PG
Director: Colin Higgins
Screenplay: Colin Higgins and Patricia
  Resnick
CAST
Judy Bernly = Jane Fonda

Doralee Rhodes = Dolly Parton
Violet Newstead = Lily Tomlin
Franklin Hart Jr. = Dabney Coleman
Tinsworthy = Sterling Hayden
Roz = Elizabeth Wilson

Despite their widely differing acting styles and character types, the three female leads of "9 to 5" seem to mesh amazingly well as they play out a fantasy of revenge on a loutish sexist boss. The film takes advantage of Dolly Parton's film debut by having her sing the title song, a hit with a life of its own ("You're just a step on the boss man's ladder"). And any film that uses her legendary figure to trap her lecherous boss has a lot of nerve.

Although some of the film will seem out-of-date—the women's pot party (on *one* joint) goes on forever—other jokes still seem to work: Violet mistaking rat poison for her boss's coffee creamer, for example, or Judy Bernly confessing to her ex-husband that she has been playing "M and M" games while her boss has been kidnapped (her husband doesn't know that) and bound in a leather and chain outfit.

The political heart of the film, however, is the rebellion against the petty and grand exploitation of the women office workers. Especially sharp is Violet, the efficient and creative administrative assistant who trains the new men and watches in frustration as they get promoted over her.

The women's revenge is sweet, and they make a number of economic points as well. After they kidnap their boss, they simply take over the department in his name: they get to institute equal pay for equal work and flex time, set up a day-care center, and create a humane office environment. Not only are these changes good for them, but they turn out to be good for business.

The film's realistic side is briefly interrupted by its broad comedy and by several fantasy sequences based on film and other popular culture traditions. All three women get to dream about what they would do with their boss: Dolly Parton dreams of hog-tying him, Jane Fonda dreams of leading the office workers on a safari against him, and Lily Tomlin offs him as Snow White as cute Disney animals cheer.

There's more than a sitcom to this film, but inevitably it is the one-liners that remain memorable: "I killed the boss," Violet says at one point, "Do you think they're not going to fire me for that?!" Or Doralee when she tires of her boss's manhandling: "I've got a gun in my purse. I'm going to change you from a rooster to a hen with one shot."

Despite the occasional satire against corporate defensiveness—we hear of the company's need to "clamp down on any sign of unionization"—the film provides only dream solutions to real problems. Nonetheless, the popularity of the film certainly indicated that for a fair number of viewers that was at least something. It wasn't enough for the *Times* reviewer, however. He thought the film ignored "the energy crisis, inflation, recession, job shortages, the disappointing sales of the Chrysler 'K,' urban blight, and the price of gold" (Canby). Does every film about labor have to solve *all* the problems of capitalism?

See also: "Business as Usual."
Availability: Easy.
Further reading: Bravo, Ellen, and Ellen Cassedy. *The 9 to 5 Guide to Combatting Sexual Harassment.* New York: Wiley, 1992. A popular and informative handbook with revealing analyses and strategies for change.
Canby, Vincent. "Revolt of the Women." *New York Times*, 19 Dec. 1980, C20. A little snippy about the film's "waving of the flag of feminism."
Farley, Lyn. *Sexual Shakedown: The Sexual Harasssment of Women on the Job.* New York: McGraw Hill, 1978. An early but thorough report.
Garson, Barbara. *All the Live-Long Day: The Meaning and Demeaning of Routine Work.* 2d ed. New York: Penguin, 1994. Interviews and commentary on many different kinds of jobs, including office work.
Howe, Louise Kapp. *Pink Collar Workers: Inside the World of Women's Work.* New York: Putnam, 1977. À la Studs Terkel, interviews and commentary on office workers and other "traditional low-paying female occupations."

∿
1900

Italian workers and bosses at the millennium

1977, 311 mins. (1991 release) or 243 mins. (1977 release), Italian-French-American (in English), NC-17 (basically an R, although there is a disturbing murder of a child)
Director: Bernardo Bertolucci
Screenplay: Franco Arcalli, Giuseppe Bertolucci, and Bernardo Bertolucci
CAST
Alfredo Berlingheri = Robert De Niro

Anita = Stefania Sandrelli
Ada = Dominique Sanda
Olmo Dalco = Gerard Depardieu
Leo Dalco = Sterling Hayden
Attilo = Donald Sutherland
Berlingheri Senior = Burt Lancaster
Regina = Laura Betti
Signora Pioppi = Alida Valli

The women's blockade in "1900."
Courtesy British Film Institute Stills, Posters, and Designs.

The opening credits of "1900" show a famous Italian painting of a militant march of striking workers—Pelizzo Volpedo's "Fourth Estate" (on exhibit in Milan's Metropolitan Gallery of Modern Art). In this "freeze-frame," determined workers stride toward the viewer, while a woman with a baby is seen ambiguously gesturing toward her husband: Does she want him to stop? To fight on? This painting, simultaneously labor-related and very personal, sets the visual and emotional tone of Bernardo Bertolucci's masterpiece to come.

When an American film depicts the relationship between political or working-class movements and communism, the American communists are usually portrayed as dangerous criminals, inhuman zombies, slaves of Soviet Russia, and sometimes all three. In a European film like "1900," however, communists are portrayed as just another political force in the demographic mix.

The film begins with a dramatization of the peasant and landowning classes on one estate in 1900. The rise of fascism in the 1920s and the surrender of the old landowning class to Mussolini's vision spells hard times for the workers, who only begin to return to some strength with the communist-led Resistance during World War II.

But these political issues are primarily the backdrop for an engrossing story of numerous individuals and the lives of three sets of "parallel" couples: the padrone (landowner) Berlingheri and his decadent wife, Ada; the revolutionary couple Olmo and Anita; and the fascists Attilo and Regina. More narrowly, the film follows the fate of two men born on the same day at the turning of the millennium: the padrone Alfredo and his virtual serf Olmo. They begin as an odd couple of friends, then gradually become separated by class and politics as the film moves through three major "acts" or periods: pre-World War I, the fascist era of the 1920s and 1930s, and the hours following the overthrow of fascism in 1945. The narrative structure is actually a little more complicated and visually stunning: the film opens and ends with a frame story—Olmo's and Anita's daughter and the peasant women attacking the fleeing fascists at the end of the war—before beginning the narrative proper in 1900.

Outstanding character portrayals dominate the film's historical scope: Donald Sutherland as the viciously corrupt fascist Attilo, Stefania Sandrelli as the charismatic leader of the women's movement, and Gerard Depardieu as the stolid and handsome hero of the Resistance movement. Their lives criss-cross during these catastrophic years. The international cast, almost all of whom speak English well (there are no subtitles needed, as the few non-English-speaking actors' voices are dubbed), help any non-Italian understand why one-third of Italian voters continued to cast their ballots for the communists (under a new name now) fifty years after the war ended.

Some of the Marxist politics behind Bertolucci's vision need some explaining for viewers new to his films. A recurring red flag–bedecked train, for example, carries evacuated children away from their starving villages during a strike: in itself, it recalls the evacuation of the children during the IWW-led strike of mill workers in Lawrence, Massachusetts (the "Bread and Roses" strike of 1912). But the train reappears at the end of the film in a dreamlike sequence, signifying the Marxist maxim that "revolution is the locomotive of history." In a similar way, a shot of a burrowing mole during this sequence is a visual pun or in joke for a quotation (famous among European Marxists like Bertolucci) from Marx's *Eighteenth Brumaire of Louis Bonaparte* when Europe "speaks" to Revolution, "Well-grubbed, old mole!"

These bits of Marxist insider comments should not convince the viewer to avoid this film as too difficult or intellectual. It is a visual and emotional roller-coaster and more than worth the rental price. Its director, cast, award-winning composer (Enrico Morricone), and cinematographer (Vittorio Storaro) all joined in an ambitious attempt to present half a century of working-class history in Italy.

See also: "Bitter Rice"; "The Organizer."

Availability: Selected collections.

Further reading: Bondanella, Peter. *Italian Cinema from Neorealism to the Present.* 2d ed. New York: Ungar, 1989. Sets Bertolucci's films in their Italian political context.

"Red Flags and American Dollars." *Cineaste* 7.4 (1977): 2–9, 50. Interviews with Bertolucci, in which he discusses his (and his films') politics extensively.

Norma Rae

Pure union

1979, 113 mins., PG
Director: Martin Ritt
Screenplay: Irving Ravetch and Harriet
   Frank, Jr.
CAST
Norma Rae = Sally Field

Reuben Marshasky = Ron Leibman
Sonny = Beau Bridges
Vernon = Pat Hingle
Leona = Barbara Baxley

Martin Ritt's film version of Crystal Lee's life sticks remarkably close to the story of how her personality developed and the incidents that led to her union activism. The seemingly impossible relationship between Norma and Reuben parallels Crystal's with Eli Zivkovitch, who, while not a New Yorker like Reuben, nonetheless had to make do in Roanoke Rapids, the North Carolina cotton mill town that was the preserve of J. P. Stevens & Company. Many of Reuben's struggles in the film were also Eli's, as the Amalgamated Clothing and Textile Workers Union strove to gain a presence in a company that was traditionally very hostile to unions. The importance of meeting in black churches, of an integrated labor movement, of Crystal's private and domestic demons are all captured here.

The film dramatizes the frustrations and difficulties of Norma's life and family in a mill-dominated town where everybody knows your business. Norma, her mom, and her dad all work at the (fictional) O. P. Henry Textile Mill: her mom is losing her hearing, while her dad—in a horrifying sequence—literally keels over after Norma (temporarily promoted to a timing supervisor) has clocked him working at a slower-than-permitted rate. Norma is constantly involved with men who are up to no good (for her), but eventually she finds her calling in the union as Reuben recruits her to help organize for a certifying election. Her troubles become just as numerous, of course, but different in kind: the company tries to split the workers along racial lines, her new husband doesn't like her staying out all the time, and, in a now-classic scene after she is fired and stands up on a machine with her hand-lettered "union" sign, she is hauled off to jail.

Norma Rae (Sally Field) gets thrown out of the textile mill where she works when she becomes a union organizer.

The union wins the election by a close margin—427 to 373—and the film ends wistfully: the never-to-be romance between Reuben and Norma has changed to a friendship, and Reuben's organizing job takes him on the road again.

One of the most popular pro-union films of our era, "Norma Rae" never makes the organizing drive look too easy. It balances the eventual selflessness of Norma with the stubborn nature of her father, who mistrusts the union. It also confronts with some honesty the mixture of personal and altruistic motives that an organizing drive sometimes satisfies: Norma Rae *needs* this union, not only to help protect her job but to maintain her self-respect.

Availability: Easy.

Further reading: Canby, Vincent. "Unionism in the South." *New York Times*, 2 March 1979, C10. "Sally Field's 'Norma Rae' Is a Triumph," *New York Times*, 11 March 1979, II.19. Two rave reviews of the film and of Field's acting.

Conway, Mimi. *Rise Gonna Rise: A Portrait of Southern Textile Workers.* New York: Anchor, 1979. Oral histories of workers, à la Studs Terkel, concentrating on those in union struggles with J. P. Stevens.

Goldfarb, Lyn, and Anatoli Ilyashov. "Working Class Hero: An Interview with Martin Ritt."

Cineaste 18.4 (1991): 20–23. Ritt on "Norma Rae"—"I was trying to make a labor film with teeth."

Leifermann, Henry P. *Crystal Lee: A Woman of Inheritance.* New York: Macmillan, 1975. A nonfiction book that recounts many of the incidents that are in the film.

Wolf, Jackie. "Filmmakers Take on J. P. Stevens." *Jump Cut* 22 (1980): 8, 24, 37. A review of documentary films (unfortunately not available on videocassette) about Crystal Lee and organizing J. P. Stevens.

Northern Lights

Pure prairie mischief

1979, 90 mins., B & W, unrated, but suitable for all ages
Directors: John Hanson and Rob Nilsson
Screenplay: John Hanson and Rob Nilsson
CAST
Ray Sorenson = Robert Behling
John Sorenson = Joe Spano
Uncle Thor = Thorbjorn Rue

Sven = Nick Eldridge
Inga Olsness = Susan Lynch
Murphy = Harold Aleshire
Forsythe = Gary Hanisch
Henrik Sorenson = Ray Ness
Howard = Jon Ness
Henry Martinson as himself

This independent feature dramatizes the plight of Norwegian-American farmers in North Dakota during the period of World War I. The personal story of an engaged couple (Ray and Inga) becomes part of the larger social and economic struggle that their people must wage to survive. Ray reluctantly at first and then more enthusiastically agrees to help organize for the Nonpartisan League. Its politics are more than a little obscure in the film, but it is crystal clear what the farmers are up against, according to Ray: "[Low] grain prices, short weights, dockage fees, phoney grading [of their crops], land speculation, mortgage fees." Although it is hard to imagine anyone not supporting a group with these causes as its focus, the film dramatizes the individualist philosophy that has brought so many of these sturdy, hard workers to this point in time: "The small farmer is better off by himself," one old farmer tells Ray.

The use of grainy black-and-white footage gives this film a nostalgic look, making it seem as if we are looking at a grandparent's musty photo album of the "old country." Ray's father dies at the foot of the wooden frame of an old scarecrow, an upright that looks more like a crucifix than a deterrent to birds. Banker Forsythe, who dispossesses Inga's family because of a failed mortgage, is snug in the only fur coat we see in this chilly countryside. The filmmakers are able to capture the threat and promise of a threshing crew rushing to get in a crop as the first blizzard arrives.

At some points, however, one is tempted to say, "It must be a Norwegian thing," for example, when we witness Uncle Thor telling an enthralling story of how he once heard "the grass grow." And at another point, a potential recruit to the League asks Ray to wrestle. If Ray wins, the man will join. When Ray is pinned, he has just enough energy to tell the man that he will be the loser in the long run.

Ray does succeed as an organizer but at some personal cost: he must delay his wedding to Inga, and they always live apart. Inga provides the viewpoint of women who always stay at home while their men search for extra work or make strides in politics: "The people you're fighting," Inga tells Ray, "won't give up. If we win we'll be fighting them off the rest of our lives. . . . If we lose, we'll have each other." But Ray tells us that "isn't enough." Some critics of the film found its portrayal of women incomplete: the League supported full suffrage for women, for example, and the League had women activists as well (see Markusen or the introduction to Morlan).

Eventually, Ray and his brother lose their farm: as League sympathizers, they cannot sell their wheat at a decent price. They rally behind the League candidate in the primary for governor, Lynn J. Frazer, who does carry enough of the rural districts to be a contender for governor. (The film's historical survey breaks off at this point; it doesn't cover the actual elections of 1916, which Frazer won.)

The film may be an acquired taste. A few speeches in Norwegian (subtitled in English) and a methodical pace based on the voice-over narrator's use of Ray's diary will not satisfy everyone's curiosity about this—perhaps unfortunately—out-of-the-way episode in labor history. The directors make a virtue out of their low budget by filming their characters in impressive close-ups. Divide County and its people make a good showing as well, as nonprofessionals join professionals in the cast. The film's topic *is* important, however, and its message will win over most viewers.

Ray's story is somewhat ingeniously framed by an introduction and conclusion by a surviving member of the Nonpartisan League, the ninety-four-year-old Henry Martinson, who is filmed looking at Ray's diary and typing *his* version of Ray's life—the version, presumably, we get in this film. As the film closes, we return to Martinson, whose voice-over strikes a note of optimism not always present earlier: "I'm an optimist. Good comes out of bad. Things are going to change. I'm sure of it. I got time. I can wait."

See also: "Wildrose."

Availability: Selected collections.

Further reading: Canby, Vincent. "A Look at Long Ago." *New York Times*, 26 Sept. 1979, C19. "When the film's focus is on labor history, remembered or recreated, it is extremely moving."

Garland, Hamlin. *Main-Travelled Roads.* New York: NAL, 1960. Classic short stories, published between 1891 and 1922, on the hard life of farmers in North Dakota and other midwestern settings.

Gaston, Herbert Earle. *The Nonpartisan League*. New York: Harcourt, Brace, 1920. An insider's view.

Markusen, Ann. "Who Were Your Grandmothers, John Hansen? A Review of 'Northern Lights.'" *Quest: A Feminist Quarterly* 5 (Summer 1980): 25–35. Argues that the film ignores the political role of women in the League.

Morlen, Robert L. *Political Prairie Fire: The Nonpartisan League, 1915–1922*. 1955. Reprint. Minneapolis: Minnesota Historical Society, 1985. An excellent history of the movement.

Russell, Charles Edward. *The Story of the Nonpartisan League: A Chapter in American Evolution*. New York: Harper, 1920. An early history of the movement.

Nothing But a Man

. . . but nothing less either

1964, 95 mins., B & W, unrated, but suitable for all ages	Driver = Martin Priest
Director: Michael Roemer	Frankie = Leonard Parker
Screenplay: Michael Roemer and Robert M. Young	Jocko = Yaphet Kotto
	Dawson = Stanley Greene
CAST	Effie = Helen Lounck
Duff Anderson = Ivan Dixon	Doris = Helene Arrindell
Josie Dawson = Abbey Lincoln	Pop = Milton Williams
Lee = Gloria Foster	Raddick = Melvin Stewart
Will = Julius Harris	Mrs. Dawson = Gertrude Jeanette

This remarkable independent film, virtually forgotten in the thirty years since it was a minor but solid hit at the 1964 Venice Film Festival, develops two stories, one private, one sociological: in the first, a young black man tries to come to terms with fatherhood—he has virtually abandoned his own son (at least he thinks he may be his son) to a friend of his former wife, while he has been cruelly dismissed by his own alcoholic father; in the second story, he moves from job to job, experiencing the discrimination and difficulty of holding regular employment in Alabama at the beginning of the civil rights era.

Both stories are closely connected: Duff's father's problem is at least exacerbated by an accident in a saw mill, which left him with a dangling, useless left arm. Duff has been reluctant to find his son because he is unsure of his paternity, while his stints as a railroad laborer on "section gangs" repairing tracks have sent him to locations where the men of the gang are holed up in abandoned railway car "hostels" for weeks at a time.

The minister's daughter (played by jazz singer Abbey Lincoln) in "Nothing But a Man."

When *Variety* reviewed the film, it noted that its chances of playing in the South were "problematical." This understatement reminds us that the film was made and released at the beginning of a heroic and violent era. Children had been killed in a church bombing in Birmingham, where the film is set. Duff's been a union man, but only on the railroad, he tells his white foreman who has heard (from a fellow black worker who snitched) that Duff believes that the men ought to "stick together." This is enough to get Duff into big trouble: in front of all of Duff's fellow workers, the foreman expects Duff to back down and say that they shouldn't stick together. When Duff refuses, he's out of the job and blacklisted. And he never tried to organize anything! He simply stopped being "a white man's nigger" and stopped saying "yassuh, boss" over and over.

Although there are a few bluesy and jazz club tunes and some spirituals (by The Gospel Stars)—all in their proper place, of course—the real hits of the film are from the Motown groups who dominate the soundtrack: Mary Wells, Martha and the Vandellas, The Miracles, Stevie Wonder, and The Marvelettes. (Duff's wife, played by jazz singer Abbey Lincoln, does not sing.)

By allowing Duff to cross a thin but significant class line—he's a laborer, but he falls for the educated schoolteacher daughter of a prominent black minister— Michael Roemer and Robert Young set up numerous dramatic opportunities to explore the tensions in a southern black community in the 1950s and 1960s. The white community clearly depends on Rev. Dawson to be an accommodationist of the old school: if the members of his community "behave," there will be jobs available for them. If one of them steps over the line—we hear there was a lynching just eight years before—it's back to the past again. When the minister sizes up Duff as liable to marry his daughter, it becomes clear within seconds that Duff will be found wanting. And, not surprisingly, Duff thinks the reverend is an Uncle Tom: his daughter tells Duff that her father knew who the lynchers were but said and did nothing about it.

The production values of this film are high, even though it's an independent. When Young (who wrote and photographed the film) shoots his reluctant hero in black cities in New Jersey (!), with the backdrop of obviously ordinary (and real) citizens going about their daily lives, the film, oddly enough, only gains in authenticity. Some early appearances of very fine actors grace the film as well: Yaphet Kotto as a crumpy coworker on the railroad team, the late Moses Gunn (who plays "Heavy" Williams in "The Killing Floor"), and the TV star Esther Rolle (Lena in the second version of "A Raisin in the Sun") as a church woman.

Ivan Dixon never made as big a name for himself in Hollywood as he did on television, but he did appear as Asagai, the Nigerian student, in the first film version of "A Raisin in the Sun," and the film he directed, "The Spook Who Sat by the Door," about a black CIA agent who organizes a guerrilla movement, continues to have some fans of its quirky plot.

Although Robert Young was credited with the screenwriting and cinematography of "Nothing But a Man," his work with director Roemer was consistent with his own directorial efforts during his quiet yet solid career. His documentary work, such as "The Eskimo: Fight for Life" (which won an Emmy in 1971), "Sit In" (an NBC "White Paper"), and "Cortile Cascino" (a suppressed "White Paper" about a Sicilian slum), preceded his successes in such full-length features as "Short Eyes" (a prison drama) and "The Ballad of Gregorio Cortez" (about a Chicano folk hero and "rebel").

Critic Donald Bogle has argued that some scenes in "Nothing But a Man," such as Duff's postwedding dinner party with his old work-mates, suffered because black filmmakers would have understood the men's behavior more clearly. But he concluded (as of 1988) that "no other American film has yet treated a black male/female relationship with as much sensitivity." High praise indeed.

See also: ["The Ballad of Gregorio Cortez"]; "A Raisin in the Sun."
Availability: Easy.
Further reading: Bogle, Donald. *Blacks in American Film and Television: An Encyclopedia.* New
    York: Garland, 1988. Includes entries on the film and on Dixon.
————. *Toms, Coons, Mulattoes, Mammies, and Bucks.* New York: Continuum, 1994. A brief
    but helpful discussion of the film in the context of other films of the 1960s about
    African-Americans.
Crowther, Bosley. "Nothing But a Man." *New York Times,* 21 Sept. 1964, 37, and *Variety,* 9 Sept.
    1964. Two of the rare—and very positive—reviews of the film; Crowther called it "an off-
    beat venture of which this country can be proud."
Peary, Gerald. "Robert M. Young's Ordinary People." *American Film,* July–Aug. 1982, 67–71.
    A thorough survey of the screenwriter's career, including films he directed.
"Venice Films." *Variety,* 2 Sept. 1964. "One of those rare films delivering an insight
    into Southern life and the place of the Negro without patronizing or using fake
    histrionics."

ॐ
On the Waterfront

A classic fight, but labor takes the dive

1954, 108 mins., B & W, unrated, but suitable
    for all ages
Director: Elia Kazan
Screenplay: Budd Schulberg, from Malcolm
    Johnson's *Crime on the Labor Front*
CAST
Terry Malloy = Marlon Brando

Edie Doyle = Eva Marie Saint
Father Barry = Karl Malden
Johnny Friendly = Lee. J. Cobb
Charley Malloy = Rod Steiger
"Kayo" Dugan = Pat Henning
Pop Doyle = John Hamilton

This is another film that popularized (eight Academy Awards!) a particularly unsavory stereotype of the American worker and trade unionism. Based on a series of newspaper articles (what we would call today investigative journalism) and a nonfiction book, entitled *Crime on the Labor Front*, written by newspaper reporter Malcolm Johnson, the film preceded—but was intimately related to—Budd Schulberg's novel *Waterfront*. Schulberg wrote his screenplay based on Johnson's book and his own research. He later turned the same material into a novel, which does not end as optimistically as the film.

The film's story is so familiar that it is probably necessary to give only a summary here. Marlon Brando, as Terry Malloy, unknowingly sets up one of the neighborhood boys, Joey Doyle, for a rooftop murder because Joey has been talking to the Crime Commission ("I only thought they was goin' to lean on him," Terry says later). Edie Doyle (Joey's sister), Father Barry, and Terry's conscience all work on him until the hold of the mob (including that of his own brother, Charley the Gent) has been loosened. But Johnny Friendly has Charley killed because he can no longer control Terry.

The scene in the back of the cab when Charley and Terry talk about Terry's lack of allegiance to mob boss Johnny Friendly has become one of the classic sequences in twentieth-century film. Terry realizes that Charley in a sense had already betrayed him by getting him to take a dive in the ring for the mob years before: "You don't understand! I could've had class. I could've been a contenda. I could have been somebody. Instead of a bum, which is what I am, let's face it. It was you, Charley." (This speech has had a life of its own in American popular culture. In 1980, for example, Robert De Niro did the punchy fighter Jake La Motta doing Terry in Martin Scorsese's "Raging Bull.")

After Charley's death, Terry agrees to testify against the mob. In the final scene, he is beaten by Johnny Friendly's gang but still manages to lead the men into the warehouse, despite Johnny Friendly's threats. In Schulberg's novel, Johnny Friendly is put in jail briefly but still runs the local. Terry disappears, only to turn up in a barrel of lime in a New Jersey swamp. Hollywood, it seems, needed its hero to get up from the count.

When Johnson, Schulberg, and Kazan worked on the material that became this film, the East Coast longshoremen were clearly not doing as well under the International Longshoremen's Association leadership as their West Coast brothers under the leadership of the controversial Harry Bridges. Most observers noted that the shape-up method—whereby the dock boss or foreman selected workers in the morning for that day—led to kickbacks, patronage, and gang control of the access to work; this key practice in turn led some local unions to engage in loan-sharking, to accept kickbacks from shipping companies, and to develop cozy relationships with management. Thugs became union officials and hiring bosses. When rank-and-file leaders developed, they were dealt with violently: one of the models for Terry Malloy (especially for the Terry of Schulberg's novel), Peter Panto, was found dead in a New Jersey lime pit two years after he began to campaign against mob control.

Into this volatile situation stepped several activist Catholic priests, especially Father John Corridan, the model for Father Barry in the film. Corridan, a veteran activist with the anticommunist Xavier Labor School in New York, campaigned against the "triple alliance of business, politics, and union racketeering" (see Raymond).

Obviously, the extent of corrupt or mob control of certain unions is an important and ongoing issue. But even assuming that mob control in the 1950s or now is a reality, why was Hollywood so attracted to this particular aspect of the labor movement?

Director Kazan had already used Brando successfully in "A Streetcar Named Desire" in 1951 and in "Viva Zapata!" in 1952. He was a natural choice for the slightly punchy but ultimately good-hearted Terry Malloy. His Method acting style was appropriate to the portrayal of another alienated proletarian: watching Brando, the audience could easily accept one of the Method's basic ideas—the actor has to believe that his "imagined" truth is as real as the "actual" truth.

Both Schulberg and Kazan were called the same name that Terry Malloy was in the film—stool pigeon—because both Schulberg and Kazan named names before the House Un-American Activities Committee. "On the Waterfront" may be seen as a long apology for testifying before a government committee, but it is certainly more than that.

See also: ["The Front"]; ["Raging Bull"]; ["A Streetcar Named Desire"]; "Viva Zapata!"; "Waterfront."

Availability: Easy.

Further reading: Basinger, Jeanine, John Frazer, and Joseph W. Reed, Jr., eds. *Working with Kazan.* Middletown, Conn.: Wesleyan University Press, 1973. A compilation of comments by numerous film pros who have worked with Kazan.

Bell, Daniel. *The End of Ideology: On the Exhaustion of Political Ideas in the Fifties.* New York: Free Press, 1962. Discusses corruption among the longshoremen in a classic chapter, "The Racket-Ridden Longshoremen: The Web of Economics and Politics."

Burks, Edward C. "'On the Waterfront' Returns to Hoboken." *New York Times,* 24 May 1973, 49. Still another model for Terry Malloy (Anthony de Vincenzo) returns to Hoboken with the filmmakers.

Georgakas, Dan. "The Screen Playwright as Author." *Cineaste* 11.4 (1982): 7–15, 39. An extensive interview with Schulberg.

Johnson, Malcolm. *Crime on the Labor Front.* New York: McGraw-Hill, 1950. Nonfiction, based on author's Pulitzer Prize–winning newspaper articles.

Kimeldorf, Howard. *Reds or Rackets? The Making of Radical and Conservative Unions on the Waterfront.* Berkeley: University of California Press, 1988. A convincing survey of the differences in the labor histories of the East and West Coast longshoremen.

McGrath, Tom. *This Coffin Has No Handles*. New York: Thunder's Mouth Press, 1988. A more political novel than "On the Waterfront," written in 1947 and with the same setting.

Miller, Arthur. *A View from the Bridge*. New York: Viking, 1955. A play about waterfront workers, one of whom also "rats" on his friends.

Neve, Brian. "The 1950s: The Case of Elia Kazan and 'On the Waterfront.'" In *Cinema, Politics, and Society in America*, edited by Phillip Davies and Brian Neve, 97–118. New York: St. Martin's Press, 1981. An excellent detailed article on the film.

Raymond, Allen. *Waterfront Priest*. New York: Holt, 1955. Includes extensive details about the model for Father Barry.

Sayre, Nora. *Running Time: Films of the Cold War*. New York: Dial, 1982. Contains a good chapter on the film in the context of McCarthyism and other "friendly" witnesses (like Schulberg) to the House Un-American Activities Committee.

Schulberg, Budd. "Joe Docks, Forgotten Man of the Waterfront." *New York Times Magazine*, 28 Dec. 1952, 3, 28–30. The first version of the film's material, a nonfiction piece emphasizing the ethnic makeup of the docks.

———. *On the Waterfront*. Carbondale: Southern Illinois University Press, 1980. Includes the screenplay and an afterword that explains how the film was produced; a less political version of this essay was published in the *New York Times Magazine*, 6 Jan. 1980, 28–35.

———. *Waterfront* 1955. Reprint. New York: Donald S. Fine, 1987. Schulberg wrote the screenplay before he wrote this novel: it emphasizes Irish-American culture and Catholicism more than the film does, but it essentially has the same plot.

∾
The Organizer

Struggling against the twelve-hour day

1963, 126 mins., Italian, unrated, but suitable for mature children	Martinetti = Bernard Blier
	Adele = Gabriella Giorgelli
Director: Mario Monicelli	Maestro Di Meo = Francois Perier
Screenplay: Furio Scarpelli and Mario Monicelli	Pautasso = Folco Lulli
	Cav. Baudet = Vittorio Sanipoli
CAST	Cenerone = Giuseppe Cadeo
Professor Sinigaglia = Marcello Mastroianni	Cesarina = Elvira Tonelli
Niobe = Annie Girardot	Porro = Giampiero Albertini
Raoul = Renato Salvatori	Bergamasco = Pippo Starnazza

Professor Sinigaglia is an organizer; he is also a socialist, wanted, poor but middle class, and a man who loves pastries but knows that hunger is often the more likely alternative. Very few actors could carry such a character, but Marcello Mastroianni, the star of Italian films for many years, convinced viewers that he was such a sincere though somewhat inept hero. Coming from a tradition of "commedia all'italiana" (emphasizing the comic side of social and political life) in the 1960s (see

Workers demonstrate in "The Organizer" over "Too Much Work and Too Little Bread."
Courtesy British Film Institute Stills, Posters, and Designs.

Bondanella), this film offers a tragicomic look at the tremendous difficulties Turin textile workers had in mounting a strike at the turn of the century.

Monicelli had made "The Big Deal on Madonna Street" (also with Mastroianni) in 1958, about criminal riffraff who are hopelessly inept. Applying his satiric style to a Turin strike was fairly daring, since Turin is known as Red Turin because of its leftist labor movement and its pre-Mussolini factory councils.

The professor arrives in Turin by train, and as he hops down from a free ride in a cab, in the background is a remarkable shot of the textile workers having a half-mean, half-silly snowball fight with one of the comic louts, Pautasso, who has been disciplined for being caught sounding the company's whistle during an abortive protest. The naïvete of the professor's followers is usually assumed by the filmmakers but not always in a patronizing manner. At one point, to push the people toward collective action, the professor even resorts to a parody of Marc Antony's funeral oration from Shakespeare's "Julius Caesar." Since the textile workers are about to end their strike, extreme irony is justified: "The majority are wise," the professor says of those who vote to go back to work. "They find their salary sufficient. . . . No one has actually *died* of starvation yet."

The film is filled with remarkable insights into the poverty of the workers. But none are as poor as the man they call "The Sicilian." (Others call him "the Ethiopian," "the Bedouin," or "the Arab," all terms expressing the casual racism of the North toward the South.) The workers assess him as being so poor that he is beneath their notice, and they let him scab.

Given the workers' conditions, anything they demand would be reasonable: at the opening of the film, they are working fourteen-hour days and have no accident insurance and no vacations. Although viewers want them to win, they clearly cannot. After all, the professor is only a schoolteacher with little more experience than they have, and the plant owners—the police and the army—have all the power.

Although the personality of the professor dominates virtually every scene he is in, we are always aware that the nastier world he longs to defeat is near by. After sneezing into the coffee cup of a new friend (a prostitute with a heart of gold), he explains his separation from his wife: "It's my fault. I've been leading a rather disorganized life." Later, this cheery hooker says that she heard that at some point in his disorganized life he wounded an official in Genoa during a demonstration. "Self-defense," he says with a sheepish grin.

See also: "Bitter Rice."
Availability: Selected collections.
Further reading: Bondanella, Peter. *Italian Cinema from Neorealism to the Present.* 2d. ed. New York: Ungar, 1992. A good survey of Italian films, including all of those in this guide.
Crowther, Bosley. "The Organizer." *New York Times,* 7 May 1964, 31. Crowther celebrates this "simple social drama," which "turns out to be engrossingly human, compassionate, and humorous."
Di Bernardo, Giovanna, et al. "Red Flags and American Dollars." *Cineaste* 7 (1977): 3–9, 50. Extensive interviews with the director, focusing on his politics.
Macdonald, Dwight. *On Movies.* Englewood Cliffs, N.J.: Prentice Hall, 1969. Contains a short but very appreciative review of the film, emphasizing the director's use of the anticlimax—deliberately undercutting the operatic style found in many Italian films.

◌ Our Daily Bread

Rural socialism with a few tears

1934, 74 mins., B & W, unrated, but suitable for mature children	CAST
Director: King Vidor	John Sims = Tom Keene
Screenplay: King Vidor and Elizabeth Hill, based on one or more uncredited *Reader's Digest* articles	Mary Sims = Karen Morley
	Chris = John Qualen
	Sally = Barbara Pepper
	Louie = Addison Richards

King Vidor's film suggests that creating socialist farming co-ops was the only way out for the unemployed in the early Depression years. Although there is a fairly unnecessary romantic subplot and even a blonde femme fatale, the heart of the film is the movement of numerous unemployed and underemployed workers (plumbers, carpenters, blacksmiths, and so on) out of the city and into the countryside, where they accept the unlikely leadership of city dweller John Sims. Many of the extras in the film were actual unemployed and other riffraff who were recruited from the streets of Los Angeles, giving the film an authentic look.

Vidor wanted to counterbalance Hollywood's "glamor cycle," but he could not get financing for the film until he borrowed the money on his own stock and real estate. This solution was inevitable, Vidor realized, when bankers he approached read the part of his script in which a bank sends out a sheriff to run a foreclosure sale on a home. Vidor wanted very badly to make the film, since he had witnessed the Hoovervilles "springing up all over," while milk trucks were spilling their milk to keep prices high.

The direct inspiration for the film was an article or two in the *Reader's Digest* that profiled cooperatives all over the country that were relying on barter, not money, to survive. The most likely article, Scott Simmon and Raymond Durgnat argue, was "An Agricultural Army," which emphasized the need to bring together "*unemployed men* and *unemployed acres*." Another possible but less likely source was an article that covered the same ground but questioned whether "city dwellers" could make a go of it in the countryside. Whatever the inspiration, Vidor managed to convince progressive Charlie Chaplin to sponsor the film and release it under his United Artists logo.

To achieve continuity with his earlier film, "The Crowd," which featured a couple on hard times, Vidor used that couple's names—John and Mary Sims—again: "The same people," Vidor said, "under different economic conditions. It was the 'average man' idea." The couple, and America by extension, could make a comeback if they went "co-op."

The co-op must withstand two major "external" attacks, the first simultaneously economic and political, the second natural. In the first case, the sheriff tries to sell the co-op's land at a public auction. The co-op members use a radical technique pioneered in North Dakota and Iowa and celebrated in Josephine Herbst's "proletarian" series of novels in the 1930s: the farmers control the bidding by keeping (by threats of force if necessary) anyone but themselves from bidding.

The second struggle is resolved in the final sequence of the film, as the men cut a long and complicated two-mile irrigation canal to bring water to their parched corn. It celebrates teamwork among labor, a concept rarely dramatized other than in the innovative Soviet films of the 1920s. Matching the editing rhythms of the film to the muscular rhythms of a gang of pick-and-shovel men provides a view of labor as heroic and re-created the style of such great Soviet films as Sergei Eisenstein's "Strike" and Vsevolod I. Pudovkin's "Mother."

Vidor also experimented with sound editing for the final sequence of the ditch cutting. He used a metronome on a tripod and a bass drum off-screen so that each shot of the men digging would have a controlled but gradually increasing rhythm. By adding an undercranked camera (making the final film action appear faster) and an inspiring musical score, he created an emotional celebration of pure labor.

The film develops a fairly strong set of internal political themes that mirror, Simmon and Durgnat argue, national political developments. At a political meeting three major viewpoints are argued: those of a self-important defender of democracy, a socialist (formerly an undertaker before joining the co-op), and an advocate (Chris, the only actual farmer) for a form of dictatorship—a "big boss" for a "big job." Perhaps inevitably, this debate is "resolved" only by work, the digging of the irrigation ditch, when all must pull together to save the crops.

Although the film did well at the box office, the variety of viewpoints on co-ops satisfied no particular political camp. Thus, the Los Angeles Hearst papers labeled it "pinko," whereas some of the Russian exhibitors found it too "capitalistic." Vidor's defense often came down to the film's source: how could it be un-American if its ideas originated in the *Reader's Digest*? In the end the League of Nations gave it an award "for its contribution to humanity," and the 1935 Soviet International Exposition of Film gave it a certificate of merit. (Vidor's interest in co-op ventures was part of an international trend; see the entry on "The Crime of Monsieur Lange.") The *New York Times* reviewer judged the film as many film historians now do, as "a brilliant declaration of faith in the importance of the cinema as a social instrument."

See also: "The Crime of Monsieur Lange"; ["The Crowd"]; "The Fountainhead"; ["Mother"]; "Strike."

Availability: Selected collections.

Further reading: Dowd, Nancy, and David Shepherd, eds. *King Vidor.* New York: Scarecrow Press, 1988. Material on the making of the film.

Herbst, Josephine. *The Executioner Waits.* New York: Harcourt, 1934. One of the "proletarian novels" of the 1930s, whose themes come close to those in Vidor's films.

Legge, Alexander, and Neil M. Clark. "Back to the Land?" *Reader's Digest*, 22 Nov. 1932, 45–47.

McDermott, Malcolm. "An Agricultural Arm." *Reader's Digest*, 21 June 1932, 95–97. Vidor never specified which article inspired the film, but this and the Legge and Clark are two likely candidates (according to Simmon and Durgnat).

Sennwald, Andre. "Our Daily Bread." *New York Times*, 3 Oct. 1934, 25. A rave review, including Vidor's placement in contemporary "socially-minded art."

Simmon, Scott, and Raymond Durgnat. *King Vidor, American.* Berkeley: University of California Press, 1988. A thorough analysis of the film and of Vidor's career.

Vidor, King. *A Tree Is a Tree.* New York: Harcourt, 1953. The director's autobiography, with his comments on the ideas behind his film.

∾ Our Land Too

Roll the SFTU on!

1988, 57 mins., unrated, but suitable for all ages
Director: Kudzu Productions
Scripted documentary
PRINCIPAL FIGURES:
Eddie Albert, narrator
John Kenneth Galbraith, Harvard economist

H. L. Mitchell, dry-cleaning store owner; later, secretary, Southern Tenant Farmers Union (STFU)
Clay East, manager, gas station
D. C. Clark, Arkansas sharecropper and union worker
George Stiff, organizer

The radical idea of having black and white sharecroppers in a single union origi-nated in 1934 at an organizing meeting near the small Arkansas town of Tyronza. The twenty original founders were black and white, an astounding fact in itself. They met to discuss how they might get their fair share of benefits as a result of the new Agricultural Adjustment Act. One old black sharecropper proposed that they re-main together in an integrated union: "We colored people can't organize without you, and you white folks can't organize without us." He argued for the unity neces-sary to resist the landlord, who "is always betwixt us, beatin' us and starvin' us and makin' us fight each other." After electing an integrated group of officers, they later recruited two known local "radicals," H. L. Mitchell and Clay East, from Tyronza. They were Norman Thomas socialists and eventually became secretary and presi-dent of the new union, which was to be open to all tenant farmers, sharecroppers, and day laborers.

The film makes a persuasive case for the Southern Tenant Farmers Union's pio-neer status in both labor and civil rights history since it was organized in Arkansas, a state not known for its hospitality to labor unions or to interracial organizations. The sharecroppers were, as John Kenneth Galbraith, one of the film's commentators emphasizes, only one step away from slavery. Even a film clip from the 1936 "March of Time" newsreels emphasizes "the economic bondage of Cotton in the South." Sharecropping was an ideal solution to the post–Civil War planters: they had no money to pay their freed slaves, and the slaves—as well as poor whites—of course had no jobs.

Eventually, the modern counterparts of the planters figured out how to take advantage of the New Deal: when the Agricultural Adjustment Act put the subsidy system into place, the farm owners kept the whole cash subsidy, although they were entitled to only half. The other half was to go to their sharecroppers, who in a sense were also supposed to be paid "for not working" under this system.

Rather than pay the sharecroppers, the farm owners threw them off the land to join the nation's ever-increasing numbers of homeless. The dangers faced by the curiously political and daring union highlighted in this film were therefore real. Norman Thomas, socialist candidate for president, often spoke at their meetings. A woman who worked for the Department of Agriculture to secure a share of the subsidies for the sharecroppers commented on some of the powers that be lined up against the sharecroppers: "Al Capone's men were pantywaists compared to the boys in Crittenden County [Arkansas]." Meetings were raided, organizers beaten, and union members and other leaders were arrested; the film also offers the too-familiar horror stories of lynching and other violence typical of the South in this era.

The close of the film emphasizes some of the political twists and turns of the union's history. In the late 1930s, it became part of the CIO and several members remember being pressured to join the Communist Party. One of the chief organizers, socialist H. L. Mitchell, would emphatically not join. Mitchell's loyalty was always with Norman Thomas, who became a kind of guardian angel to the union. The film appropriately emphasizes Thomas's patronage of the union but does not quote a famous message he broadcast over NBC: "There is a reign of terror in the cotton country of eastern Arkansas. It will end either in the establishment of complete and slavish submission to the vilest exploitation in America or in bloodshed, or in both. For the sake of peace, liberty, and common human decency, I appeal to you who listen to my voice to bring immediate pressure upon the Federal goverment to act" (quoted in Kester).

The film is appropriately bracketed by the music of Woody Guthrie—"This Land Is Your Land"—and by the folk song that the union pioneered and that became an anthem during the civil rights movement: "We Shall Not Be Moved." Another union classic, "Roll the Union On," was written by an STFU organizer, John Handcox, who recalls some of the southern hospitality that was manifested when he had to run from lynchers. His remarks are typical of the appreciation expressed by everyone in the film for the courage and legacy of this remarkable union.

See also: "The Golden Cage"; "The Grapes of Wrath."
Availability: Selected collections; AFL-CIO.
Further reading: Edid, Maralyn. *Farm Labor Organizing: Trends and Prospects.* Ithaca, N.Y.:
ILR Press, 1994. A history and survey of farmworkers unions.
Kester, Howard. *Revolt among the Sharecroppers.* 1936. Reprint. New York: Arno Press, 1969.
An early and enthusiastic history of the STFU.

~

Out of Darkness: The Mine Workers' Story

Into the light, dimly

1990, 100 mins., unrated, but suitable for all ages
Directors: Barbara Kopple and Bill Davis
Scripted documentary by Gene Carroll, John Duran, James Green
PRINCIPAL FIGURES (SELECTED):
Richard L. Trumka, president, United Mine Workers of America (UMWA)
Cecil E. Roberts, vice president, UMWA
John L. Lewis, president, UMWA, 1918–60
Mike Odom, president, Pittston Coal Group, Inc.
Tony Boyle, president, UMWA, 1963–72
Jock Yablonski, candidate for president, UMWA
Lane Kirkland, president, AFL-CIO
Arthur Miller, president, UMWA, 1972

Elizabeth Dole, secretary of labor
Sid Hatfield, sheriff of Matewan
Marty Hudson, Pittston strike coordinator
UMWA organizers: Mike Livoda, Don Barnett
Daughters of Mother Jones: Deborah Herd, Edna Sails
Ludlow Massacre survivors: Emma Zanatell, Alex Bisulco, Donald Mitchell, Steve Surisky
Retired miners: John Monroe Smith, Cory Lee Harris, Harry Whitaker, Frank Jackson, Joe Doers, Earl Stuckert, John Valdez, Jack and Shine Miller, Claude and Lawrence Amiacarella, Nimrod Workman

Barbara Kopple's and Bill Davis's strategy for this documentary was to present both a history of the United Mine Workers and a chronicle of the Pittston strike of 1990. The former is accomplished through the use of numerous interviews with retired miners and selections from archival and feature film history, while the latter is presented through interviews with current officials and activists and footage of the imaginatively contested Pittston strike.

In ways perhaps not intended by the filmmakers, the earlier struggles are highlighted by death, while the Pittston struggle celebrates collective action, labor solidarity, and community spirit. The history of the mineworkers is punctuated by fatal explosions, assassinations of miners and activists, and countless funerals after disasters in mine shafts. The retired miners tell—and the film demonstrates—the dirty, dangerous business miners involve themselves in until, too often, early and sudden death hits them belowground or slow terrible death from black lung disease takes them aboveground.

And if these horrors are not enough, miners and their families have too often been attacked by company thugs and even by the forces of law and order. The film includes extensive discussion and selected footage of the mining history of Eastern Kentucky and West Virginia, using two classics of labor history, John Sayles's "Matewan" and Kopple's "Harlan County U.S.A."

These classics are supplemented by footage from archival films about other historical incidents, especially the Ludlow Massacre of 1914. The still photos and archival footage are supplemented by tales from survivors of the massacre, who tell story after story of the murderous attacks on the family encampment in Colorado by the state militia.

The footage of the Pittston strike, by contrast, shows the contemporary UMWA using a range of traditional union maneuvers and new organizing strategies. The campaign proceeded on a number of fronts. Besides traditional roadside picketing, the UMWA orchestrated sit-ins at Pittston's headquarters by miners' wives and other women supporters, who nicknamed themselves the Daughters of Mother Jones in honor of the great leader of the miners. AFL-CIO president Lane Kirkland and nineteen other national union presidents were arrested in such a sit-in. And in a daring imitation of the great Flint Sit-Down Strike of 1937, UMWA members and supporters occupied Pittston's Moss 3 Preparation building. (Anne Lewis Johnson, who directed "Fast Food Women," contributed footage from her earlier Appalshop film, "Moss 3.")

The other footage assembled for this documentary is also impressive. Kopple and Davis excerpted numerous documentaries made by such regional film workshops as Appalshop of Whitesburg, Kentucky, especially for the Pittston strike sequences. Rarely seen footage of the March on Blair Mountain, for example, carefully documents this Logan County, West Virginia, incident of 1921. This follows footage of the "Matewan Massacre" of Baldwin-Felts agents and eventually the agency's retaliatory assasination of Sheriff Sid Hatfield. After an excerpt from Sayles's "Matewan," which dramatizes the killing of the Baldwin-Felts security police, Kopple and Davis footage shows Sid, the World War I vets of the minefields who organized the paramilitary march against the Logan Country sheriff they felt allowed Sid's murder, and the counterforce of federal troops and bomber planes (yes, bomber planes), including one flown by Charles Lindbergh.

This film, like Kopple's more recent documentaries, "American Dream" and "Fallen Champ: The Untold Story of Mike Tyson," solidifies her position as the premiere American filmmaker of working-class and union history.

See also: "Harlan County U.S.A."; "Matewan."
Availability: Selected collections.
Further reading: Aurand, Howard W. *From the Molly Maguires to the United Mine Workers.*
   Philadelphia: Temple University Press, 1971. A little dated, but a good general history.
Zieger, Robert H. *John L. Lewis, Labor Leader.* New York: Twayne, 1988. A biography of the
   famous founding president of the UMWA.

The Pajama Game

One size fits all.

1957, 101 mins., unrated, but suitable for all ages	Sid Sorokin = John Raitt
Directors: George Abbott and Stanley Donen	Gladys = Carol Haney
	Hines = Eddie Foy, Jr.
Screenplay: George Abbott and Richard Bissell, from the latter's novel *7 1/2 Cents*	Poopsie = Barbara Nichols
	Mae = Thelma Pelish
	Prez = Jack Straw
CAST	Hasler = Ralph Dunn
Babe Williams = Doris Day	Max = Owen Martin

Every once in a while a musical about labor unions comes along. Years pass, and audiences who view it later almost always ask, "Was this funny? Entertaining?" The 1930s had "Pins and Needles" (never filmed), the 1990s have "Newsies," and the 1950s—era of such great musicals as "On the Town" and "Singin' in the Rain"—had "Never Steal Anything Small" and "The Pajama Game."

If you were lucky enough to be a member of Local 343 of the Amalgamated Shirt and Pajama Workers of America and could have the fabulous picnic featured in this film, complete with choreographer Bob Fosse's great dance team, you might not have worried about the 7 1/2-cents-an-hour raise you didn't get for cutting pajama bottoms.

Stanley Donen's magic clearly worked with Gene Kelly in "On the Town" and "Singin' in the Rain," but for this labor-management adventure he must have left his lantern home. Leading man and new superintendant of the Sleeptite Pajama Factory, Sid Sorokin, played by John Raitt (Bonnie Raitt's father), is a stick with a lovely voice, although at one point he sings a duet with himself after he has recorded "Hey There, You with the Stars in Your Eyes" on his dictaphone (after giving a memo to his secretary: "The last six lots went over the estimate. Better check your product!"). Doris Day, in a remarkable ducktail hairdo, plays Babe Williams, chair of Sleeptite's grievance committee, who at first is at odds with her new boss, then falls in love with him, and then has a falling-out with him when the local threatens to strike for their 7 1/2-cent raise ("Everyone else in the city is getting it").

We know we are in a fantasy world almost immediately, despite the interior shots of the factory, which look genuine enough (although too clean and neat). The "girls" on the shop floor—a number of these union maids are working in high heels—sing a happy song of speedup ("Hurry up! Can't waste time!") with their supervisor. The speedup becomes comic, conveyed by fast-action filming. Later, they use a parody of their speedup song as a diversion to organize a slowdown.

When Babe realizes a strike is likely, she warns her boss, "That contract, lover, that's important." With his love life in the balance, not to mention his career (he confesses that he's just "a cutting room foreman who bluffed" himself into his new job), Sorokin has the incentive to find a way to come up with the 7 1/2-cent raise. How he does so is too complicated and silly to summarize here, although the bottom line is that *his* boss has been cooking the books and adding the 7 1/2 cents to the cost of the company's product for the last six months. Sorokin allows the boss to announce the settlement at a union rally as long as the union agrees not to ask for the 7 1/2 cents retroactively.

Since most of the union members are more interested in dancing and modeling pajamas, they easily accept the settlement, although a rousing trio of workers sing "Steam Heat," which most of us no doubt have long forgotten was a pro-union number. ("Come on, union, get hot!" is one of its lines.) Other famous tunes, such as "Hernando's Hideaway," are also in this film, but few of them have any union relevance. One of them almost mocks the 7 1/2-cent raise, up to the end the only bit of serious business in the film or so it seems. At the rally the grievance committee sings to its members, "I Figured It Out," the message of which is if they just wait five years their raise will get them a washing machine or a forty-inch TV set, ten years will get them a trip to France or a foreign car, and twenty years will enable Babe to buy the factory and have its former owner work for *her*. It is clear at this point that all the singing has gone to their heads, and the workers end up with a real "pajama party," at which Babe and Sid are happily married.

Richard Bissell's original novel was only marginally more complicated and certainly not any funnier. It doesn't end with Babe and Sid sharing a set of pajamas (as the film does), but they plan to take their honeymoon "through the steel mills in Gary, Indiana." So much for romance. Bissell's other books on his life as a deckhand on Mississippi tugboats, such as *A Stretch on the River* (New York: NAL, 1951) have a lot more grit, but they have never been filmed.

See also: "Never Steal Anything Small"; "Newsies."
Availability: Easy.
Further reading: Bissell, Richard. *7 1/2 Cents.* Boston: Little, Brown, 1953. Almost makes you wish for the complexity of the film!
Crowther, Bosley. "The Pajama Game." *New York Times,* 30 Aug. 1957, 12. A reviewer who likes the music but ignores the 7 1/2 cents.

∾
A Raisin in the Sun

"What happens to a dream deferred?"

[I] 1961, 128 mins., B & W, unrated, but suitable for all ages
Director: Daniel Petrie
Screenplay: Lorraine Hansberry, from her play of the same title
CAST
Walter Lee Younger = Sidney Poitier
Lena Younger = Claudia McNeil
Ruth Younger = Ruby Dee
Beneatha Younger = Diana Sands
Travis Younger = Stephen Perry
Joseph Asagai = Ivan Dixon
George Murchison = Louis Gossett
Mr. Lindner = John Fiedler
Bobo = Joel Fluellen
Willie Harris = Roy Glenn

[II] 1989, 171 mins., TVM
Director: Bill Duke
Filmed from the stage production directed by Harold Scott
CAST
Walter Lee Younger = Danny Glover
Lena Younger = Esther Rolle
Ruth Younger = Starletta DuPois
Beneatha Younger = Kim Yancey
Travis Younger = Kimble Joyner
Joseph Asagai = Lou Ferguson
George Murchison = Joseph V. C. Phillips
Mr. Lindner = John Fiedler
Bobo = Stephen Henderson
Mrs. Johnson = Helen Martin

The New York Critics Circle selected Lorraine Hansberry's "A Raisin in the Sun" as the Best American Play in 1958; it was also a major breakthrough for an African-American woman to have a major Broadway production. She took her title from a Langston Hughes poem in which the "dream deferred," if frustrated, may "explode."

The "dream" alluded to has an ironic edge in both film versions. Mrs. Younger's dream is to have a house and a garden—to escape her ghetto flat with a shared bathroom in the hallway. Her son's dream is to quit his job as a chauffeur and open a liquor store; in short, his is the recurring working-class dream of being self-employed. These dreams are not compatible, especially when sister Beneatha also needs money to go to medical school. The subsequent clash of these competing dreams propels the action forward toward a reconciliation. In the meantime, the films explore the role of the matriarch and the extended black family, the rise in consciousness of the African roots of black culture, abortion, the generation gap, and the integration ("assimilation") versus separatism debates of the 1950s.

Although early reviewers (for example, Bosley Crowther in the *New York Times*) assumed Daniel Petrie intended to emphasize the single room of the original script—and certainly accepted it as a way of emphasizing that "its drama takes place mainly in the hearts of its people"—we now know from the publication of Hansberry's original screenplay that she wanted her play to be even more "opened-up." The few scenes that do leave the Younger household—Walter as chauffeur,

Beneatha Younger (Diana Sands) is eager to show off her new African finery for boyfriend George Murchison (Louis Gossett) in the 1961 version of "A Raisin in the Sun."

Walter at the bar with his mother, the family's arrival at their new house—get the film outside, but in only small ways. (Ironically, the 1989 remake, although it stays closer to Hansberry's intentions for the Broadway staging, seems much more claustrophobic.)

The relationship between the hit theatrical play and the first film version is complicated. The play omitted a few key moments from Hansberry's script; Petrie's film followed that pattern, but it also added some scenes, to "open up" the play somewhat. In a sense, Petrie used the script almost more than the screenplay Hansberry had written, since about one-third of her screenplay does not show up in the final film. There are thus *three* literary texts, all with the same title: the 1959 script for the play, the 1988 script (which became the American Playhouse TV film "Raisin" [II] in this guide), and the 1961 "unfilmed original screenplay." (There was even a Tony Award–winning *musical* version in 1974, revived for road shows in recent years.) These matters are of some importance, because exactly *what* has been filmed (or not) reflects the images of African-American working-class people over the last three decades.

The American Playhouse TV production restores three scenes omitted from both the 1958 Broadway and the 1961 filmed versions of the play: young Travis chases a rat with his friends in the street, Beneatha sports an (early) "Afro," and the friendly Mrs. Johnson arrives with the news of the firebombing of the home of a black family who dared to move into a white neighborhood. (Numerous other scenes were also filmed in the first version, but they ended up on the cutting-room floor; see the 1992 edition of Hansberry's screenplay.)

The American Playhouse production therefore develops a fuller context for the visitor from the Park Improvement Association—played both times by John Fiedler—by emphasizing how dangerous it could be for blacks to move into a white neighborhood. And, of course, the rat scene emphasizes how dangerous it was for them to stay behind.

It is always difficult for the new version of a film to compete with the old, especially when the old is a classic with an outstanding cast. Esther Rolle seems too young for the role of the matriarch, while Danny Glover seems too old to be her son. Nevertheless, it may be worthwhile to look at the more recent version to see how a contemporary black director like Bill Duke interprets Hansberry's material. Duke's "Killing Floor" preceded this film, and that was clearly a fresh look at southern blacks migrating to take jobs in the North, an old story but one that is rarely told. Sidney Poitier's hold as the leading black actor of his generation will remain clearly secure, but we should note with some irony that although Poitier has been in five of the thirty most successful films directed by African-Americans, they are all crime caper films such as "Uptown Saturday Night."

The first filmed production of Hansberry's portrayal of black working-class life in Chicago reminds us that two great talents associated with it died young: the playwright, dead at the age of thirty-five (in 1965) and Diana Sands, who played the rebellious and early Afrocentric Beneatha, dead at the age of thirty-nine (in 1973).

See also: "To Sleep with Anger."

Availability: Easy.

Further reading: Bogle, Donald. *Toms, Coons, Mulattoes, Mammies, and Bucks: An Interpretive History of Blacks in American Film.* 2d ed. New York: Continuum, 1989. A thorough coverage of Poitier and the rest of the talented cast of the first version of "A Raisin in the Sun."

Cripps, Thomas. *Making Movies Black.* New York: Oxford University Press, 1993. Situates the film in the era of "Hollywood timidity and the resulting wish to launder the more strident aspects of black culture as a device for assuring broader appeal to whites."

Crowther, Bosley. "Raisin in the Sun." *New York Times,* 30 March 1961, 24. A very positive review of the first version, but he doubts the effectiveness of John Fielder's role as the white visitor.

Farber, Stephen. "New 'Raisin in the Sun.' for TV Restores Scenes." *New York Times,* 31 Aug. 1988, 18. Argues that this new version "should lay to rest once and for all the misconception that this is a play about a middle-class black family."

Goodman, Walter. " 'Raisin in the Sun' through '89 Eyes." *New York Times,* 1 Feb. 1989, C24. The new version "has lost some of [the original play's] urgency but none of its awkwardness."

Hansberry, Lorraine. *To Be Young, Gifted, and Black.* Englewood Cliffs, N.J.: Prentice Hall, 1969. "An informal autobiography" adapted as a play by Hansberry's husband, Robert Nemiroff.

———. *A Raisin in the Sun.* New York: NAL, 1988. This Signet paperback is the "most complete edition" (of the 1959 stage version), according to Robert Nemiroff, Hansberry's husband and literary executor, and includes his excellent introduction.

———. *A Raisin in the Sun,* ed. Robert Nemiroff. New York: Plume, 1992. The original screenplay, with a much longer and more "cinematic" (less indoorsy) vision than Petrie's film.

"Make New Sounds: Studs Terkel Interviews Lorraine Hansberry," *American Theatre,* Nov. 1984, 5–8, 41. A revealing 1959 interview with the author.

"Playwright," *New Yorker,* 9 May 1959, 33–35. Hansberry on her theatrical influences and other aspects of her life.

Reds

Love means never having to support Kerensky.

1981, 200 mins., PG	CAST
Director: Warren Beatty	John Reed = Warren Beatty
Screenplay: Warren Beatty, based on	Louise Bryant = Diane Keaton
(uncredited) *Romantic Revolutionary: A*	Eugene O'Neill = Jack Nicholson
Biography of John Reed by Robert	Emma Goldman = Maureen Stapleton
Rosenstone	Zhdanov = Jerzy Kosinski

With few exceptions, Warren Beatty is usually the subject of a Warren Beatty film, and "Reds" is no exception: this is really the story of Warren and Diane playing at being two radicals, Jack (Reed) and Louise (Bryant). It is "Love Story" with a Bolshevik twist, except this time the man gets to die. If it weren't for the fact that Jack Reed celebrated the Russian Revolution in a still-impressive firsthand account (*Ten Days That Shook the World*) and that he is the only American buried inside the walls of the Kremlin, we might not be paying much attention to this film.

Beatty traces Reed's brief but spectacular career as a journalist/activist, from his coverage of the Mexican Revolution riding with Pancho Villa, through Greenwich Village bohemian days, to his triumph—witnessing the Bolshevik Revolution of 1917. It should come as no surprise that Beatty's Reed makes a key speech at a gathering of workers during the revolution and is wildly applauded. The film does not touch, however, on Reed's fairly objective rendering of the contribution of Stalin's arch-enemy, Leon Trotsky, references to which were "disappeared" from later editions of *Ten Days That Shook the World.*

What raises this film above other Hollywood dramas about historical heroes is Beatty's (then) radical innovation: he intercuts interview clips with thirty-two "witnesses" who knew (or knew of) Jack Reed and/or Louise Bryant. The comments of these witnesses are sometimes brief, sometimes not. These interviews blow genuine life into the film almost every time they appear because their subjects' memories of the revolutionary days of their youth sixty-five years before are both witty and revealing. This approach, along with its multimillion dollar production values, gives the film a historical look and feel that Beatty's mannerisms do not always deserve.

Virtually every documentary film uses interview clips or "talking heads." "Reds," like Stewart Bird's and Deborah Shaffer's documentary "The Wobblies," makes the interviewees "witnesses," which elevates their status considerably. But the same problem persists in both films: even though the opening credits name all the witnesses, by the time you see them you cannot possibly remember who they all are. The only way to absorb some of the historical weight of "Reds" is to see it with a photocopy of the cheat sheet provided in the March 1982 issue of *American Film* magazine ("If Warren Won't Tell, We Will" is the article's subtitle).

But pure memory power aside, the issue is still historical validity. Some of these witnesses natter on, but several have potentially very important things to say about this fascinating period of history and John Reed's role in it, such as Dora Russell, a delegate to the Comintern in Moscow, and Will Weinstine, an early organizer of the American Communist Party, and Emmanuel Herbert, a student in Petrograd during the Bolshevik Revolution. They barely get going when the camera cuts away from them. Others have achieved fame in related areas, such as Congressman Hamilton Fish, a classmate of Reed's at Harvard; Roger Baldwin, the founder of the American Civil Liberties Union; and Arthur Mayer, a film historian and another classmate at Harvard. Unfortunately, their opinions and insights, however brilliant they may be, burn out too quickly each time. (They end up too close to Rob Reiner's parody of them in "When Harry Met Sally"—cute but insubstantial.) We are left with a multimillion dollar show of the mannerisms of two beautiful Hollywood people. Surely John Reed, not to mention history, deserves more.

In 1981, Paramount organized a special showing of "Reds" for a former anticommunist organizer from Hollywood—President Reagan. He liked the film but said, "I was hoping for a happy ending."

See also: "Strike"; ["Ten Days That Shook the World," a.k.a. "October"].
Availability: Easy.
Further reading: Culbert, David. "'Reds': Propaganda, Docudrama, and Hollywood." *Labor History* 24 (Winter 1983): 125–30. A balanced review, but calls it "one of the most creative films to come out of Hollywood in years."
Grindon, Leger. *Shadows on the Past.* Philadelphia: Temple University Press, 1994. Includes a

chapter on "Reds," in which he argues that Beatty's film is his reaction to the 1960s ideal of integrating the political and the personal.

Hicks, Granville. *John Reed: The Making of a Revolutionary*. New York: Macmillan, 1936: An early biography by a fellow radical of the 1930s.

Reed, John. *The Education of John Reed*. Edited by John Stuart. New York: International, 1955. A collection of essays, including ones on the Mexican Revolution and the Wobblies.

———. *Ten Days That Shook the World* (1919). The 1960 Vintage Books paperback has a very good introduction to Reed and the political maneuvering that altered his text; likewise A.J.P. Taylor's introduction to the 1981 Penguin paperback.

Rosenstone, Robert. *Romantic Revolutionary: A Biography of John Reed*. New York: Knopf, 1975. The source book for the film, which includes some legendary "witnesses" as well.

Thomson, David. "Red Time." *Film Comment*, Jan.–Feb. 1982, 11–16. Emphasizes the fictionalizing of Reed's life in the film.

von Wiegand, Charmion. "The Quest of Eugene O'Neill." In *New Theatre and Film, 1934–1937*, edited by Herbert Kline. New York: Harcourt, Brace, 1985. Discusses the career of the sometime-"proletarian" dramatist ("The Hairy Ape") who was John Reed's friend and Louise Bryant's lover.

"Who *Were* All Those Eyewitnesses in 'Reds'?" *American Film*, March 1982, 8. Identifies all the witnesses by name, picture, and historical role.

∾ Riff-Raff

Homeless workers building homes for other people

1991, 96 mins., British (some English subtitles for British dialect), R	Susan = Emer McCourt
	Shem = Jimmy Coleman
Director: Ken Loach	Mo = George Moss
Screenplay: Bill Jesse	Larry = Ricky Tomlinson
CAST	Kevin = David Finch
Stevie = Robert Carlyle	

This is one of several films that made a slang expression virtually a cinematic category. The somewhat old-fashioned-sounding word "riffraff," suggesting low-class street people, dates no earlier than sixteenth-century British English, but it has been popular for about a hundred years. It was a well-known Victorian concept: the lowest class in the scheme developed by the Victorian "sociologist" Charles Booth, for example, consisted of "occasional laborers, street sellers, loafers, criminals, and semi-criminals"; Marx called this class the "lumpenproletariat." (See "Strike" in this guide.) During the American Depression, the term was used to describe all sorts of people, from homeless migrants to street-wise laborers.

In this tragicomic film, the riffraff are homeless people hired to rehab a place that, of course, they could never afford to live in. But since they cannot afford to live

Stevie (Robert Carlyle) on break at the re-hab site in "Riff-Raff."
Courtesy British Film Institute Stills, Posters, and Designs.

anywhere, they efficiently and knowingly hook up an abandoned apartment as a "squat" for one of their number. They also strike out "at the rich" by burning down the very site they've been working on, because, Loach told an interviewer in 1994 (Smith), "they've got nothing to lose and it's a gut response."

Loach wanted to confront the effects of "the early Eighties and Thatcherism" in England, but he didn't want to create "a political lecture." His screenwriter had been working on a building site in Glasgow and their resultant conversations about the life—and liveliness—of the building site crews helped to create the "warmth and humor" of the film.

Besides dirty hard work and constant bickering over job assignments and money flimflams, the site is dominated by rats. When asked if the rats were metaphorical, Loach said they were but hoped the image wasn't too "pretentious." In fact, the screenwriter had given up his job at the Glasgow building site because rats had been eating his sandwiches.

When there is some on-the-job agitation about safety, Larry (played by a former plasterer and union activist) threatens to call in a Union of Construction and Technical Trades organizer. He is fired immediately.

Loach's film follows a minor but distinctive tradition of contemporary British films about construction sites, squatters, and related political matters: Jerzy Skomolinski's "Moonlighting," for example, about Polish workers "trapped" in London when martial law is imposed back home, and a gradually increasing flood of films satirizing Thatcherism in general, such as Mike Leigh's "High Hopes." Loach did one of the first docudramas about homelessness, "Cathy Comes Home," almost thirty years ago (unfortunately, it is not available on videocassette). In the interview in 1994 he emphasized that "his view of history" was that it was "a class struggle." But when people see his films, he added, he wants them to think that the situations they see need to be changed.

See also: ["Cathy Comes Home"]; ["High Hopes"]; ["Moonlighting"].

Availability: Selected collections.

Further reading: Canby, Vincent. "A Blue-Collar Comedy in English, Subtitled." *New York Times*, 12 Feb. 1993, C10. A positive review and background story about the actors and screenwriter.

Malcolm, Derek. "Straight Out of Britain: Tales of Working-Class Life." *New York Times*, 31 Jan. 1993, II.20. A survey of the director's career.

Smith, Gavin. "Sympathetic Images." *Film Comment*, March–April 1994, 58–67. Contains good background information on this film and others by Loach.

Note: There are two other interesting films with the same title, including a 1947 American film (not included in this guide) in which American and other expatriates become involved in the criminal exploitation of Panamanian oilfields. It ripped off the successful "Latin American" drama with Rita Hayworth, "Gilda," from the year before. The other film called "Riffraff" is the 1935 "social problem" film more about raffish characters than about riffraff.

∾
Riffraff

Not if they have steady jobs . . .

1935, 89 mins., unrated, but suitable for all ages	Hattie = Jean Harlow
	Lil = Una Merkel
Director: J. Walter Ruben	Jimmy = Mickey Rooney
Screenplay: Frances Marion, H. W. Haneman, and Anita Loos	Nick = Joseph Calleia
	Flytrap = Victor Kilian
CAST	Brains = J. Farrell MacDonald
Dutch = Spencer Tracy	Pops = Roger Imhoff

Despite the riffraff tag, almost everyone in this film is employed, either in the tuna fishing industry or in support jobs on the wharves (such as diners). They are not therefore "riffraff" at all but raffish characters in a Disneyland of Labor.

The plot is melodramatic and complicated, but Dutch plays a cocksure natural leader of the fishermen who—despite extensive mentoring by the union leader called Brains—keeps to himself and his girlfriends most of the time. Since one of his girlfriends is played by Jean Harlow, none of his friends and few of his viewers are surprised by this decision.

When some kind of agitators—it's never clear who they are, but we suspect they're some kind of Reds—try to push the men into a wildcat strike against the wishes of the union leadership, Dutch comes through and keeps things on an even keel. The somewhat farcical handling of these events turns decidedly nasty and the film becomes less about unions on the wharf and more about how working people during the Depression could easily become riffraff or even criminals.

Although the focus shifts away form the union, the film reminds us that with labor unrest and economic instability a part of so many people's lives during the mid-1930s, we should not be surprised that Hollywood, especially Warner Brothers, made more and more of these tough "guy and gal" pictures.

See also: "Fury"; "Harry Bridges"; "They Drive by Night."
Availability: Selected collections.
Further reading: Nugent, Frank. "Riffraff." *New York Times*, 13 Jan. 1936, 14. The reviewer finds Harlow's presence so unlikely in a labor film that he can't make any sense of what he has seen.

Peter, Roffman, and Jim Purdy. "The Worker and Hollywood." *Cineaste* 9.1 (1978): 8–13. Discusses the film in the context of other Depression "social problem" films and suggests the San Francisco General Strike of 1934 was a factor in the film's portrayal of the longshoremen.

∾
Rising Son

Falling father

1990, 92 mins., TVM, M, but really suitable
   for all ages
Director: John David Coles
Screenplay: Bill Phillips
CAST:
Gus Robins = Brian Dennehy
Martha Robins = Piper Laurie

Charley Robins = Matt Damon
Des Robins = Tate Donovan
Carol = Emily Langstreth
Meg Bradley = Jane Adams
Ed = Ving Rhames
Billy = Graham Beckel
Tommy = Richard Jenkins

Filmed at the Rayloc factory in Georgia, "Rising Son" is a drama about a long-term factory worker and then general production supervisor whose company collapses partly because of Japanese competition in the auto industry and partly because of the leveraged buyout fever of the Reagan years. The fictional Jillis Company in Travers, Pennsylvania, has been manufacturing starter motors for years, but the family-run company has been sold to a conglomerate whose owners don't care whether the company's subsidiaries manufacture motors or widgets.

Gus, played as a feisty and domineering family man by the ubiquitous Brian Dennehy (who must average five films a year), is a fictional cousin to Willy Loman in "Death of a Salesman." Like Loman, Gus has a lot of stories about his brilliant and successful sons, who turned out to be unsuccessful and mighty miserable. (And, like Loman, Gus tries being a salesman and is suicidal.) The title refers to the rebelliousness of Gus's second son and is also a pun on the flag and symbol of Japan—the "rising sun."

Although the material on Japan is not always central to the plot, it nonetheless forms an intriguing commentary on Gus's life: during a work stoppage, Gus makes a speech to his workers about Americans who have—compared with the Japanese—lost their work ethic; later he tells his son about a World War II incident in which he interfered when a Japanese soldier tried to commit an "honorable" suicide. Both speeches, one public and one private, point to the Japanese as Gus's personal demons. Further, he is at first hostile to the idea of relocating to a new Japanese-American factory, even when his union man from the old plant proudly demonstrates its robot efficiency.

TV producers often waste five or six hours of screen time on movies about Long Island tabloid scandals: "Rising Son" is a relatively short film that would have benefited from being longer. The integration of workers and management in such small-town activities as the volunteer fire department is a touch that many films ignore and that we could have had more of; such details bring to life the complexity of a company town.

The Falling Father (Brian Dennehy) and the Rising Son (Matt Damon) in a publicity still that emphasizes their emotional distance.

See also: ["Death of a Salesman"]; "Iron Maze."
Availability: Easy.
Further reading: Miller, Arthur. *Death of a Salesman* (1949). The tragedy Gus manages to avoid.
O'Connor, John J. "Pride in His Sons and His Country." *New York Times*, 23 July 1990, 16. A very positive review.
Note: This is not the same as Michael Crichton's "Rising Sun," which is also about a U.S.-Japanese economic "war" (and other things).

↶
Rocky

Raging beef

1976, 119 mins., PG
Director: John G. Avildsen
Screenplay: Sylvester Stallone
CAST
Rocky Balboa = Sylvester Stallone

Adrian = Talia Shire
Mickey = Burgess Meredith
Paulie = Burt Young
Apollo Creed = Carl Weathers

In each of the three class-conscious dramas John Avildsen directed in the 1970s (two of which are in this guide), the personality of an actor/star is the controlling influence. Peter Boyle in "Joe" is the epitome of the resentful, racist, hard-hat reactionary of the Nixon era, while Jack Lemmon in "Save the Tiger" (not in the guide) is the frumpy, put-upon but ultimately benign garment industry exec trying to cope with a society he no longer understands.

The third, Sylvester Stallone's Rocky, is class-conscious, too, but in a more diffuse way: he's on the bottom, and he wants up. Like another gentle working-class nonhero from a different era, Ernest Borgnine's Marty, Rocky is socially inept but yearns for love. Rocky is at the same time supposedly beyond class: he's an all-American hero who epitomizes the values of his bicentennial-year appearance: in America, all you have to do is want something bad enough, train hard, and you can get it.

On a slightly more disturbing level, Apollo Creed clearly seems to be a caricature of Mohammed Ali and the match with Rocky a parody of the Ali-Wepner fight (see Leab). Apollo is brash, uppity, and condescending to Rocky: he is the black nightmare of Pete Hamill's "white lower-middle class."

"Rocky" re-created South Philly as a cityscape of working-class comebacks, in the same way that John Badham's "Saturday Night Fever" elevated Bensonhurst in Brooklyn to the working-class hall of fame of ugly but interesting neighborhoods. The film's set pieces all contribute to Rocky's underdog status: running through South Philly and other locations to the film's theme music, for example, or his use of the side of beef in Paulie's meat locker as a punching bag.

Daniel Leab demonstrated that "Rocky" quickly moved into the pantheon of moneymakers that includes "Gone with the Wind," "The Sound of Music," and "Jaws," although none of these films had a working-class hero. And only "Jaws" came close to having four sequels, as "Rocky" did.

"Rocky" was a formula film that used the clichés of a number of B movies of the past, including such ethnic films as "Marty," from the 1950s. (Rocky, like Marty, is remarkably shy, despite his half-hearted employment as the muscle for a local loan shark.) "Rocky" won three Oscars and generated four sequels. There is no doubt that "Rocky" has always been a "contenda" and a champ at the box office. Who could count it out?

See also: "Joe"; "Marty"; ["Saturday Night Fever"]; ["Save the Tiger"].
Availability: Easy, too easy.
Further reading: Hamill, Pete. "The Revolt of the White Lower-Middle Class." In *The White Majority: Between Poverty and Affluence*, edited by Louise Kapp Howe. New York: Random House, 1970. Charts ethnic resentment against African-Americans.
Leab, Daniel J. "The Blue Collar Ethnic in Bicentennial America: 'Rocky.'" In *American History/American Film: Interpreting Hollywood Images*, edited by John E. O'Connor and Martin A. Jackson, 257–72. New York: Ungar, 1979. An excellent discussion of the film and its patriotic gore.

ᶜᵛ
Roger & Me

Roger Smith can run, but he can't hide.

1989, 87 mins., R (makes no sense!)
Director: Michael Moore
Scripted documentary
PRINCIPAL FIGURES:
Michael Moore, director
Roger Smith, chairman, General Motors
Fred Ross, deputy sheriff in charge of
    evictions

Rhoda Britton, the bunny lady
Pat Boone, entertainer
Kay Lani Rae Rafko, Miss Michigan (later
    Miss America)
Bob Eubanks, game show host
Ben Hamper, former autoworker; writer

Michael Moore's 1989 documentary about the closing of auto plants in Flint, Michigan, was a "first" for several reasons. It was the one of the first documentaries with a labor focus to gain an even wider national audience than Barbara Kopple's Academy Award–winning "Harlan County U.S.A." It was the first comic documentary in which the filmmaker, like Woody Allen, basically played himself as a naive jerk. It was also the first film to be denounced by both General Motors and the United Auto Workers for being unfair to them, with the result that both organizations mailed out the same critical film review by heavyweight film critic Pauline Kael of the *New Yorker* to counter the film's success. The UAW did not like how the film portrayed its friendly relationship with management or its inability to celebrate the great Flint sit-down strike. The film also aroused forty-five filmmakers to petition the Academy Awards nominating committee when the film was denied a nomination, possibly because of a conflict of interest with an official on the committee (who was the distributor for other nominated documentaries).

Why all this fuss? Roger Smith is a perfect comic villain—he's incredibly powerful and unattractive and represents a class of individuals so out of touch with the common person that it is embarrassing. Two of Moore's other subjects—deputy sheriff Fred Ross and bunny lady Rhoda Britton—are survivors. And, finally, we have Moore himself—a bumbling giant who just wants to talk to Roger Smith. So what's the big deal?

There are no heroes in this story besides Moore, who grins idiotically but benignly into his camera lens. Deputy Fred is an ex-autoworker, but he makes his living by evicting people who don't keep up on their apartment or house payments. The bunny lady attracted Moore's attention because of the sign outside her house: "Rabbits—Pets or Meat." Her breezy self-confidence as she kills and skins a rabbit in front of Moore's cameras clearly reflect yet another kind of survival skill.

Transforming the traditional documentary mix of archival footage, media footage, stills, interviews, and clips from feature films, Moore followed the successful strategy of "The Atomic Cafe" (1982), an equally satiric documentary about the obsession with The Bomb in the 1950s. He improved on the strategy of juxtaposing materials by using as unifying threads his comic pursuit of Roger Smith (Moore tries to crash GM's boardroom and one of Smith's exclusive clubs) and a campy affection for both the stalwarts of American popular culture (Miss Michigan) and its outsiders (Fred and Rhoda).

Moore's 1992 short film "Pets or Meat: The Return to Flint" (available on a cassette of three short films entitled "Two Mikes Don't Make a Wright") updates the earlier film. Fred Ross has branched out into auto repossessions and auction sales, Rhoda is raising other animals for meat (but saves a bunny for a snake), and Roger Smith's pension is in such danger that Moore thinks about sending him some money.

Moore's success in not meeting Roger Smith led to Moore's short-lived NBC show, "TV Nation" (1994), in which he continued his top-down satires of American capitalism by inviting the CEOs of American corporations to "do" the most rudimentary tasks associated with their industries: thus, the IBM CEO was asked to format a computer disk (he did not reply); only Ford's CEO—in a thumb-your-nose gesture at GM's Roger Smith?!—agreed to change the oil in his car, which he did in front of Moore's camera.

"Roger and Me" is a one-of-a-kind film. Though it comes close to being like the absurdist postmodern documentaries of Errol Morris ("Vernon, Florida," "Gates of Heaven," "The Thin Blue Line") and Diane Keaton ("Heaven"), its focus on the auto industry and corporate negligence, not to mention the presence of the filmmaker himself, makes it a must-see.

See also: ["Two Mikes Don't Make a Wright"].

Availability: Easy.

Further reading: Bernstein, Richard. "'Roger & Me': Documentary? Satire? Or Both?" *New York Times*, 1 Feb. 1990, B20: A review of the controversy surrounding the film.

Hamper, Ben. *Rivethead*. New York: Warner, 1991. The autobiography of a Flint autoworker and a bit-part star of the film.

Cohan, Carley, and Gary Crowdus. "Reflections on 'Roger & Me,' Michael Moore, and His Critics." *Cineaste* 17.4 (1990): 25–30. Another review of the controversy about the film.

Harkness, John. "Roger & Me." *Sight and Sound*, Spring 1990, 130–31. A British reviewer argues that Warner Brothers ("part of the largest entertainment conglomerate in the world") released the film because its critique of capitalism is ultimately "harmless."

Kael, Pauline. "Current Cinema." *New Yorker*, 8 Jan. 1990, 91–92. The negative review circulated by GM and UAW; the film "uses its leftism as a superior attitude. Members of the audience can laugh at ordinary working people and still feel they're taking a politically correct position."

Marchese, John. "American Scene." *Esquire*, Jan. 1993, 44–47. The continuing misadventures of filmmaker Moore on his first feature film project after "Roger & Me."

Salesman

Selling tickets to heaven

1969, 90 mins., B & W, unrated, but suitable for all ages

Directors: David and Albert Maysles

Documentary (with some semiscripted scenes)

PRINCIPAL FIGURES:

Paul Brennan, the Badger

Charles McDevit, the Gipper

James Baker, the Rabbit

Raymond Martos, the Bull

Ken Turner, sales manager, Mid-American Bible Company

The disturbing focus of this film is four salesmen who work for the Mid-American Bible Company selling illustrated bibles to poor and working-class Catholics. The film traces their successes and failures, but at what a price! Fifty dollars for a red or white simulated leather-bound bible, illustrated with the "Old Masters," is clearly a lot of money for the people these men badger and bully into buying these books "that no Catholic home should be without." Because most of the salesmen are so pathetic, it is difficult for us as viewers to decide whether we want them to make their sales or not. Do we want them to earn their commission, or do we hope that their potential customers will hold onto their one-dollar-a-week payment?

They are a curiously compulsive lot, these salesmen. They drive fairly expensive-looking convertibles, seem to believe that selling bibles is "about [doing] my Father's business," and get in a moderately high-stakes poker game after a company rally. The men get their collective feet in the door by introducing themselves with such remarks as, "I'm Mr. Brennan from the Church," or telling their customers that their bible is "recommended by Pope Paul" or "approved by the Monsignor." They ask their customers if they want to pay cash or go on the "Catholic honor plan" (weekly or monthly payments). They drop bits of inside gossip to win their customers' confidence. Do you know why, one asks, the pope's guards are Swiss? Answer: because the Swiss are taller than the Italians.

If this sounds too much like an Irish Catholic joke, it is because most of these salesmen tell Irish jokes endlessly and are constantly sucking up to their customers' ethnic pride (although Brennan the Badger at one point mistakes a Polish customer for an Italian). Their supervisor selects a territory for them to handle after "sizing up" the local priest to see if "there's a good church in the neighborhood," or, in a loose translation, whether the local parish will let them set up an exhibit of their wares in a church building to gain the aura of sanctity and endorsement.

Although the film has the reputation for being genuine cinema verité ("truthful cinema"), the Maysles brothers paid the salesmen one hundred dollars each and contributed toward the cost of the company's sales meeting; the Maysles had to accept the company's decision not to let them use footage of the four salesmen handing out calling cards at an early-Sunday-morning church service. How these matters affect the Maysles' documentary is left to the viewer's judgment, but certainly the filmmakers' attitude came through clearly in the ad campaign, which featured a robed Jesus carrying a salesman's sample case in each hand.

The film is of a piece with Arthur Miller's "Death of a Salesman," in which the falling sales and castle building create a combination most nonsalespeople find overwhelming. But selling is what capitalism is about, and the Maysles brothers clearly think this disturbing team of door-to-door salesmen say something about the American character. "Get it blessed" is one piece of advice their customers are given; one woman, a reluctant purchaser, says at another moment, "I just hope I get around to reading it."

See also: ["Death of Salesman"]; "'Rising Son."

Availability: Selected collections.

Further reading: Barsam, Richard Meran. *Nonfiction Film: A Critical History.* Bloomington: Indiana University Press, 1992. Sets the film in the context of contemporary documentaries.

Levin, G. Roy. *Documentary Explorations.* New York: Doubleday, 1971. Contains an interview with the filmmakers about "Salesman."

Miller, Arthur. *Death of a Salesman.* 1949. The classic American play on the subject.

Rosenthal, Alan. *The New Documentary in Action.* Berkeley: University of California Press, 1971. Another interview with the filmmakers: "[The bible company] thought it was bad that Paul, the star of the film, wasn't a very good salesman. But the other three were, so they were happy."

Salesman. New York: NAL, 1969. All of the scenes and dialogue in the film, as well an introduction by Harold Clurman and production notes by Howard Junker.

⌒

Salt of the Earth

A film ahead of its time

1953, 94 mins., B & W, unrated, but suitable for all ages
Director: Herbert Biberman
Screenplay: Michael Wilson
CAST
Ramon Quintero = Juan Chacon

Esperanza = Rosaura Revueltas
The Sheriff = Will Geer
Frank Barnes = Clinton Jencks
Ruth Barnes = Virginia Jencks
Luis Quintero = Frank Talevera

In 1951, the International Union of Mine, Mill, and Smelter Workers, known as "Mine-Mill," was expelled from the CIO because its officers would not sign anti- or noncommunist pledges. The same year, its local, 890, was involved in a long strike against Empire Zinc in Hanover, New Mexico, in part because Empire would not sign a contract other mining companies had agreed to. With an injunction to bar the miners from picketing, it looked like the strike was broken. But 890's Ladies Auxiliary decided that the injunction didn't apply to them and that the scabs—and their own men—had better watch out. Ultimately, as the women became more "public" figures, many of their men were forced not only to do "women's chores" but to understand why fresh water and sanitation were "union" demands too.

This has always been a controversial film. In the 1950s, it was the answer to the prayers of the McCarthyites and members of the House Un-American Activities Committee, who believed that the film industry was chockablock with communists who were secretly slipping anti-American and pro-Soviet messages into every film. When there was finally *one* film—this one—in which communists were fairly active participants, the anticommunist forces, including the AFL-CIO, went wild. Because of the difficulties placed in front of the filmmakers, the production quality of the film is mediocre. For example, the Mexican star, Rosaura Revueltas, was deported before shooting was over, so that a number of her shots (filmed in Mexico) show her against the sky with no other background.

Director Herbert Biberman, screenwriter Michael Wilson, producer Paul Jarrico, and actor Will Geer were all blacklisted by the time they made this film together. Jarrico had done the World War II pro-Soviet "Song of Russia" film; Wilson was an Academy Award–winning screenwriter; and Biberman had served six months in federal prison for refusing to cooperate with the House Un-American Activities

Committee after he was named as a communist by Budd Schulberg, who wrote the screenplay for "On the Waterfront."

Made and repressed in the 1950s, the film was shown sporadically: even the *New York Times* (15 March 1954) acknowledged the "sub rosa difficulties of the film's producers in getting a theatre in which to show" the film in New York. It was revived in 1965 and later in the 1960s and 1970s by both radical and feminist groups as an alternative to what was perceived to be conservative American trade unionism and male-dominated left/liberal politics. Biberman himself did not direct another film until "Slaves" in 1969. (See "Uncle Tom's Cabin" entry.)

The screenplay for "Salt of the Earth" was discussed with the local union members, who made suggestions. Local union activist Juan Chacon played Ramon, and many of the union members played themselves. Three other main roles—the sheriff, the Anglo union leader, and Esperanza—went to professional actors.

Deborah Silverton Rosenfelt quotes from two newspaper articles that appeared during production to demonstrate the pressure the filmmakers faced. The *Hollywood Reporter* stated that "Hollywood Reds are shooting a feature length anti-American racial issue propaganda movie." Victor Riesel, a syndicated labor columnist, asserted, "Not too far from the Los Alamos Atomic Proving Ground . . . Tovarisch [comrade] Paul Jarrico brought two carloads of Negroes into the mining town" for a scene of mob violence against them." (No such scene is in the film.) As a result of this negative publicity, virtually the entire network of Hollywood and American production facilities and distribution systems turned against the film and it was rarely shown in the 1950s. Although most prints and cassettes are reasonably clear, the fine production values we associate with Hollywood feature films were simply not attainable in this shoestring production.

Some viewers have been puzzled by what appears to be the almost documentary "look" of the film. This is because it was based on some of the radical ideas of Soviet filmmaker Sergei Eisenstein (and other Soviets) who believed in using nonprofessionals (i.e., real workers or peasants) wherever possible, for the sake of authenticity. In "Salt of the Earth," this meant that the professional acting troupe of five was supplemented by numerous people who were recruited locally.

See also: "Harlan County U.S.A."; ["Slaves"].

Availability: Selected collections.

Further reading: Biberman, Herbert. *Salt of the Earth.* Boston: Beacon, 1965. The director's history of the film, with Wilson's screenplay.

Cargill, Jack. "Empire and Opposition: The 'Salt of the Earth' Strike." In *Labor in New Mexico,* edited by Robert Kern, 183–267. Albuquerque: University of New Mexico Press, 1983. A thorough survey of the issues in the original strike.

Crowther, Bosley. "Salt of the Earth." *New York Times,* 15 March 1954, 20. The "real dramatic crux of the picture is the stern and bitter conflict within the membership of the union."

Kingsolver, Barbara. *Holding the Line: Women in the Great Arizona Mine Strike of 1983*. Ithaca, N.Y.: ILR Press, 1989. Reporter and novelist Kingsolver tells the story of a contemporary mining struggle in which the women played major roles.

Miller, Tom. "Salt of the Earth Revisited." *Cineaste* 13 (1984): 31–36. How the main figures in the strike and film have spent the thirty years since the filming.

Rosenfelt, Deborah Silverton. *Salt of the Earth*. New York: Feminist Press, 1978. A very detailed, excellent essay on the film, plus Wilson's screenplay.

∾
Silkwood

The mysterious death of a union activist

1983, 128 mins., R (not really)
Director: Mike Nichols
Screenplay: Nora Ephron and Alice Arlen
CAST
Karen Silkwood = Meryl Streep
Drew Stephens = Kurt Russell
Dolly Pelliker = Cher

Angela = Diana Scarwid
Winston = Craig T. Nelson
Morgan = Fred Ward
Paul Stone = Ron Silver
Earl Lapin = Charles Hallahan
Thelma Rice = Sudie Bond

Karen Silkwood, who was killed in a car crash at the age of twenty-eight, may have been the nation's first "nuclear martyr." She was a union activist for the Oil, Chemical, and Atomic Workers (OCAW) in a Kerr-McGee plutonium-processing plant in Utah. Her particular concern as an executive officer of the union local was health and safety issues; the company clearly regarded her as a troublemaker. Because of the nature of the work done at the plant—plutonium is made into pellets, then welded into the rods that become the integral part of breeder reactors—the danger of worker contamination is very high. The risks are also very high: even the smallest contamination can cause cancer.

Most of this background information is uncontested. The difficulty in understanding Silkwood's short and tragic life lies in determining what she knew about Kerr-McGee that could have been damaging to its reputation and who was responsible for her becoming contaminated—the company (in her opinion), because of its lax safety rules or because someone at the company contaminated her urine samples with plutonium, or she herself (the company's opinion), because she needed to embarrass the company and put the union in a stronger bargaining position.

As if these issues aren't complex enough, there is the matter of her lifestyle: she was a mercurial individual, given to decisions that were sometimes hard to defend (letting her ex-husband have custody of her three children), and in her last years she lived with a boyfriend and a woman, causing not a few people to gossip about her.

Karen Silkwood (Meryl Streep) with her "family"—Dolly (Cher) and Drew (Kurt Russell)—at the plutonium-processing plant where they work.

Much of the above is part of the record as represented by the very thorough researcher Richard Rashke, who wrote *The Killing of Karen Silkwood*. But then Mike Nichols came along, joined by a strong pair of Hollywood insiders as screenwriters. This group ended up emphasising—to an incredible degree—the relationships and love life of the three housemates. Silkwood and Drew are lovers (reasonable enough), and Dolly eventually brings home her own housemate, a beautician from a morgue (gallows humor about contaminated workers is inevitable).

The film also expands on the issue of Silkwood's continuing bouts of contamination (and that of one of her coworkers, Thelma), hinting that some of these incidents might have been the result of company sabotage (a hole in one of Silkwood's safety gloves, for example, triggered the hand monitor in her workroom, thereby putting her in the clutches of a cleanup crew who scrubbed her with metal brushes while hosing her down in the shower).

As for the major case of contamination, both Rashke's book and Nichols's film trace it to a spilled specimen bottle of urine that contaminated her hands, parts of her bathroom, and some sandwich material in her house. In the film, Silkwood believes that someone sabotaged her urine kit, even if she spilled it by accident.

In the film, Silkwood forms a romantic attachment with a national union officer who helps her out and shows her the scene in Washington when she goes to a hearing of the Atomic Energy Commission (AEC). Much of what she wants to tell the AEC members is important—that the company is lax about safety regulations, that the company dismantled and buried a "hot" (radioactive) truck—but the national union leadership clearly gets most excited when she mentions that she knows that negatives show the quality of the control welds have been doctored (i.e., made to look safe when they were not). This falsification could lead to a failure of a major breeder reactor à la "The China Syndrome." Can she get documentation to support this skulduggery? If she can, the *New York Times* would be very interested.

When her car crashed, Silkwood was on her way with the doctored negatives to a nighttime meeting with a *New York Times* reporter. No such documentation remained in her wrecked car, however. In the film, she sets off to work and plans to get the documentation for the meeting, although she has tried on several occasions before to "steal" the negatives and has not had any luck. Either she cannot find the right ones or they are simply not in the vast file folders in the room she has been assigned to with one other worker, a man who is more than a bit of a sleaze and whom she has seen, in the past, actually doctoring negatives. (In the film, he admits that is what he is doing.)

The film thus remains more open-ended than Rashke's book on the subject of Silkwood's mission. Nichols's direction of the scenes involving Silkwood's relationships is lackadaisical until the very end of the film, when Nichols's camera comes alive during what are visually torture or "assault" scenes of the metal-wire scrub and water hosing. The final sequence, however, delivers what Nichols's other films ("The Graduate" and "Catch-22," to name two of his best) have delivered in the past—a visually arresting sequence that merges image and idea. In what will be Silkwood's last trip, we see her staring apprehensively at her rearview mirror as the bright lights of a car come much too close. The very next shot shows her crashed vehicle, followed by a pan shot of the car being towed, seen from the point of view of her friends and union buddies inside a cafe. The next shot shows her gravestone, but the lively Silkwood is captured by the next slow-motion long take, which turns out to be a flashback of her last farewell to Drew as she drove off to grab the documentation she wanted to hand over to the *New York Times* reporter.

In real life, Silkwood's crusade was vindicated by a lawsuit, but Nichols's film touches on none of that. For him, she is a will-o-the-wisp, a passionate, headstrong woman who may have been right about the dangers of nuclear contamination—who really knows?—but who had a heck of a lot of interesting relationships. For most viewers, that will simply not satisfy their desire to know what really happened to Silkwood and what an industry, then or now, can be allowed to get away with.

Nichols does include important details on Silkwood's union career, including a decertification election in which she helps to maintain the union's contract (but just barely, by a vote of eighty to sixty-one), a couple of meetings of the local, and a few national meetings that take serously the importance of the union's monitoring its members' working conditions. The inevitable romance with the national union rep clearly fits Nichols's view of Silkwood's personality, however, and perhaps we shouldn't be too hard on him; after all, part of why Martin Ritt was so successful with "Norma Rae" was that he portrayed her as a woman who knocked about more than most. None of these union maids are as pure as the Wobbly ballad that celebrated their roles. Without these union issues and without some realistic characters (with flaws, that is), we may as well watch James Bridges's "China Syndrome," which has a similar death/attempted murder but which never raises any questions about trade union or worker safety issues on its way to concentrating on whether a whole state will disappear as a result of a nuclear plant meltdown.

Karen Silkwood's death helped ensure the passage of the Occupational Safety and Health Administration's "Right to Know" legislation: it was the final national victory for an activist who started locally.

See also: ["The China Syndrome"].
Availability: Easy.
Further reading: Canby, Vincent. "Accident or Murder?" *New York Times*, 14 Dec. 1983, C27. An overall very positive review, but "the muddle of fact, fiction, and speculation almost, though not quite, denies the artistry of all that's gone before."
Ephron, Nora. "The Tie That Binds." *Nation*, 6 April 1992, 453–55. The author of the screenplay discusses the difficulty of writing a film based on "fact."
Kael, Pauline. "Busybody," In *The State of the Art*. New York: Dutton, 1985. Criticizes the director's "passive advocacy" and worries about Streep's miscasting as Silkwood.
Rashke, Richard. *The Killing of Karen Silkwood*. Boston: Houghton Mifflin, 1981. The title makes it clear that the author believes Silkwood was murdered by those who were threatened by her disclosures.
Scott, Rachel. *Muscle and Blood*. New York: Dutton, 1974. Muckraking essays on related dangers faced by the OCAW, such as beryllium (used in atomic reactors) and chemical poisoning.

∿

Sit Down and Fight: Walter Reuther and the Rise of the Auto Workers Union

Of tactics and the man

1993, 60 mins., unrated, but suitable for all ages
Director: Charlotte Mitchell Zwerin
Scripted documentary by Charlotte Mitchell Zwerin

PRINCIPAL FIGURES :
Walter Reuther, president, United Automobile Workers (UAW), 1946–70

Victor Reuther, former assistant to the president, UAW

Homer Martin, first UAW president

Harry Bennett, personal director and head of the Service [Security] Department for Ford Motor Company

Richard Frankensteen, organizer, Automotive Industrial Workers Association; vice president, UAW

Christopher Alston, labor organizer, 1933–62

Leonard Woodcock, president emeritus, UAW

Gordon Bellaire, participant, Kelsey Hayes sit-down strike

John L. Lewis, president, United Mine Workers

Henry Kraus, founder, UAW newspaper

Kenneth Malone, participant, Flint sit-down strike

Douglas Fraser, president emeritus, UAW

Dorothy Kraus, organizer, Women's Activities, Flint sit-down strike

Shelton Tappes, international representative, UAW

This documentary combines the history of auto manufacturing in America with the story of its most famous union organizer. The film chronicles the atrocious working conditions of the 1920s and 1930s through the organizing drives of the CIO, the great sit-down strikes, and finally the recognition of the UAW as the principal bargaining agent with the Big Three automakers. Walter Reuther is an important part of this survey but not the only part. As the film makes clear, the history of organizing in auto and Reuther's personal history are popularly assumed to be inseparable, but there were more than a few moments of difficult courtship.

The film includes a Flint, Michigan, 1990 reunion of the sit-down workers and their militant right arm, the Women's Emergency Brigade. Their story makes up one of the most familiar and dramatic tales of the UAW's history, but the film's use of interviews counterpointed with remarkable archival footage manages to tell this story in fresh and convincing ways. Without the sit-down strikes, it is hard to imagine that the UAW would have emerged victorious. The film details the tactical maneuvers of the sit-down strikers, their steadfast discipline, and the dangers (security guards' clubs, police tear gas, National Guard machine guns) they faced.

The film develops Reuther's history with admiration but notes his ability to compromise and constantly move to the centrist position on ideological and theoretical questions. When it was clear that the first UAW president, Homer Martin, did not have the right stuff (he continued his earlier calling as an erratic preacher and eventually formed a rival union with Henry Ford as his ally), the importance of the Communist Party members within the CIO and Reuther's eventual handling of them became more and more important. Eventually, Reuther went his own way, but the Communists did not persevere as an independent force.

A revealing incident in the history of the UAW was the handling of black workers, then working the hardest jobs in the foundry. Henry Ford had tried to position himself as a friend to black Americans, cultivating the friendship of George Washington Carver, for example. When the UAW launched black organizers to try to bring the black workers into the union, security chief Harry Bennett ordered the black workers to attack the mainly white picketers. This last-ditch race riot strategy failed, and with the slogan "Fordism Is Racism," the UAW succeeded in bringing many of these black workers into the union.

The film recounts the career of Reuther and the UAW in the post–World War II period in more abbreviated fashion. Even Truman is quoted as opposing the Taft-Hartley Labor Act as "a shocking piece of legislation," but the film closes with Reuther forming close ties with JFK, LBJ, Martin Luther King, and Cesar Chavez of the United Farm Workers before his death in 1970.

See also: "Harry Bridges"; "With Babies and Banners."
Availability: Selected collections; ILR Media.
Further reading: Cormier, Frank, and William J. Eaton. *Reuther.* Englewood Cliffs, N.J.: Prentice-Hall, 1970. A massive but readable biography.
Pflug, Warner. *The UAW in Pictures.* Detroit: Wayne State University Press, 1971. A photographic history drawn from the Archives of Labor History and Urban Affairs at Wayne State University.
Reuther, Victor G. *The Brothers Reuther and the Story of the UAW.* Boston: Houghton Mifflin, 1976. A memoir by Reuther's brother.

Slim

The working stiff as an "aw shucks" hero

1937, 80 mins., B & W, unrated, but suitable for all ages	Red Blayd = Pat O'Brien
	Cally = Margaret Lindsay
Director: Ray Enright	Stumpy = Stuart Erwin
Screenplay: William Wister Haines, from his novel of the same title	Pop = J. Farrell MacDonald
	Wilcox = Joseph Sawyer
CAST	
Slim = Henry Fonda	

Henry Fonda plays Slim, an "aw shucks" farmboy who knows excitement when he sees it: being a high-wire lineman. His career, from apprenticeship to mastery, is, by turns, melodramatic and sentimental but usually engrossing. The era of the Tennessee Valley Authority and the drama of rural electrification are the necessary imaginative leaps to prepare for this film: linemen were dedicated public servants who took chances, and to a certain extent they still do. (Try fixing your outside electric line yourself in a storm.)

The nobility of labor is emphasized throughout. Our hero is even given a girlfriend who is a nurse to remind us that we're all public servants. Unfortunately, his girlfriend has been waiting for years for Red, Slim's mentor, to settle down. When it becomes clear that Slim has to choose between dangerous "construction" high-wire jobs and the safer "maintenance," stay-at-home work, he chooses danger over his nurse. (The same safe stay-at-home choice is offered to the Fabrini brothers in "They Drive by Night," but they eventually choose the less dangerous option.)

But life in some 1930s movies has a way of upsetting such decisions. Red and Slim are called out on an incredibly dangerous job—fixing "hot" high wires during a blizzard. Red is killed, and Slim is knocked out. But he straps on his utility belt and starts to climb the tower again. His nurse is at the base of the tower, cheering him on. Fade to black. We never learn for sure if Slim will settle down, but it certainly won't be for quite a while.

The *New York Times* reviewer was enthusiastic about the film's "groping" toward "the major truth that there is a nobility inherent in labor from which sparks may be struck and take lodging in the soul of even an ordinary little man." But don't ask him to be a "maintenance" man.

See also: "They Drive by Night."
Availability: 16 mm; Swank.
Further reading: Nugent, Frank S. "Slim." *New York Times*, 24 June 1937, 30. A very positive but balanced review.

∽

Sometimes a Great Notion

Libertarian nation

1971, 114 mins., PG	Viv = Lee Remick
Director: Paul Newman	Leeland = Michael Sarrazin
Screenplay: John Gay, from Ken Kesey's	Henry Stamper = Henry Fonda
novel of the same title	Joe Ben = Richard Jaeckel
CAST	
Hank Stamper = Paul Newman	

In two revealing scenes near the beginning of this film, the libertarian message of Ken Kesey's independent heroes comes through loud and clear. In one scene these *real* men, the Stampers, casually throw dynamite sticks at a fleeing union man in a rowboat who has had the nerve to ask them to join a strike against the local logging companies. In a related scene the Stampers are outside at night in pouring rain doing a little home repair when the national officer of the loggers union (never specified by name) pays a visit and asks them to join the strike. (They offer him a beer.) The officer spells out the situation for them: even though they have nothing to do with the union—they are a small family operation—if they keep their logs off the market, it will help the union teach the companies a lesson.

The Stamper patriarch and his son, played by Henry Fonda and Paul Newman, two stars who specialized in being working stiffs and tough guys for generations, don't believe in unions because they sap the independent spirit of the American working Man with a capital M. In the end, Newman's film is more committed to this spirit than to providing solutions to any old union business. This spirit does the logging—the men just fill in every once in a while! Needless to say, the Stampers are not convinced about the value of union solidarity.

Vincent Canby, the *New York Times* reviewer, recognized the germ of Kesey's philosophy in the novel behind this film as characteristic of the great "working stiff" films of the 1930s, such as "Slim," also with Henry Fonda. Such films are about "lives lived entirely in terms of rugged, essentially individualistic professionalism." As such, viewers will realize, the question of any collective tug on the conscience of a Stamper is unreasonable, at least on their terms. If a union gets its way just once, the elder Stamper in effect argues, then "goodbye freedom."

Kesey has always believed (with Janis Joplin) that "freedom's just a word for nothing left to lose / And it ain't nothin' if it ain't free." A hippie "rugged individualist" may seem a contradiction in terms, but Kesey's fictional creations (if not himself) seem to live the contradiction. The heroes of "One Flew over the Cuckoo's Nest," for example, may seem crazy, but they know who the real enemy is: The Combine, or, as "Sometimes a Great Notion" would have it, the "sons of bitches" who think they can push you around.

Kesey's impossibly sprawling novel could not be rendered easily in a two-hour movie. Its title comes from a Ledbetter-Lomax song, "Sometimes I Live in the Country," which concludes, "Sometimes I get a great notion/ To jump in the river . . . an' drown."

Hank Stamper's final gesture—he perches his severed arm with an upraised middle finger on top of a load of logs he is moving downstream by himself—is characteristic of the family's ungrammatical motto: "Never Give a Inch."

See also: ["One Flew over the Cuckoo's Nest"]; "Slim."
Availability: Easy.
Further reading: Canby, Vincent. "Sometimes a Great Notion." *New York Times*, 2 March 1972, 34. A mainly positive review of a film that he fears may not stay around long.
Kesey, Ken. *Sometimes a Great Notion.* New York: Viking, 1964. The film is fairly loosely adapted from the novel.
Note: This film was retitled for TV as "Never Give a Inch."

ᘐ
Sounder

Sons and daughters of the dust

1972, 105 mins., G
Director: Martin Ritt
Screenplay: Lonne Elder III, from William
   H. Armstrong's novel of the same title
CAST
Rebecca Morgan = Cicely Tyson

Nathan Lee Morgan = Paul Winfield
David Lee Morgan = Kevin Hooks
Mrs. Boatwright = Carmen Mathews
Ike = Taj Mahal
Sheriff Young = James Best
Camille Johnson = Janet MacLachan

This story of a rural black sharecropping family in 1933 is set (and was filmed) in rural Louisiana. By all Hollywood standards, it is a "small" film—barely a year in the life of the Morgan family—but we move from Nathan's arrest for stealing food, the rest of his family keeping up their end of the tough sharecropping "bargain," and young David's quest for his father (who is held at a prison labor camp about a day's walk away).

The reason the father steals from a white neighbor's smokehouse is that his family is hungry. Having failed to bring home a raccoon on a hunt, Nathan justifies his stealing to his wife: "I did what I had to do." His sentence seems severe—a year at hard labor—but the greatest pain is that suffered by his family. Quaint Louisiana parish rules exclude women from visiting the jail at any time, and men can visit only on Sundays and holidays. But visits soon matter little since the sheriff announces that another rule is that the family will not be told what labor camp Nathan has been sent to. In the meantime, the difficult job of tending to the farm is left to Rebecca and her three children.

When the only sympathetic white character—a woman for whom Rebecca does laundry—ignores the sheriff's threats to embarrass her in front of the whole community and tells the Morgans where Nathan is being held, David Lee goes off on a journey to visit his father. He never finds him, but he is taken in by a kindly black schoolteacher who raises the first sparks of black consciousness in the boy by telling him about Harriet Tubman and Crispus Attucks and reciting a passage from W.E.B. Du Bois.

This film will appeal to children as well as adults, although the original novel is now marketed primarily for "young readers." There are only two incidents of violence, both of which would be disturbing to children: in one, the family dog, Sounder, is shot in the face as he tries to catch up to his handcuffed master; in the other, David Lee receives a vicious swipe on his hand from a prison guard. In both instances, the wounds heal. The psychological violence—the casual racism of the 1930s South—is also painful to watch, but for the most part, the stoical Rebecca manages to get in a rejoinder or two: "That is some low-down job you got," she tells the sheriff at one point.

The details of the sharecroppers' poverty and frustrations are central to the film, so that actual farm labor is presented in a sketchy though convincing way. We also see the operation of a cane press with an endlessly circling mule as the driving force. (The same apparatus is used in a scene set in the 1850s in "Half Slave, Half Free.") The issue of labor is presented here primarily in human terms, however. Cicely Tyson's portrayal of the incredibly hard-working Rebecca was one of the breakthrough roles for black actresses, who too often had been relegated only to the position of being Shaft's latest "big score" in the wave of black exploitation movies of the 1970s. (Tyson followed this film with the even more challenging lead role in "The Autobiography of Miss Jane Pittman," which has a much wider historical and political sweep than "Sounder" but less immediate labor relevance.)

In the end, "Sounder" is a coming-of-age film: upon his father's return from prison, David Lee will leave the family farm and go to live with the schoolteacher he admires. His father warns him, "Don't get used to this place," and clearly he hopes that his son will break out of the sharecropping cycle. From what we have seen of sharecropping, David's decision seems like an easy one, but clearly the filmmakers' intention was also to show what he would be missing.

See also: ["The Autobiography of Miss Jane Pittman"]; "Daughters of the Dust"; "Our Land Too."

Availability: Easy.

Further reading: Canby, Vincent. "All But 'Super Fly' Fall Down." *New York Times*, 12 Nov. 1972, B1. Compares Ritt's film—not too favorably—with many of the twenty black (mostly "exploitation") films that opened in 1972.

Greenspun, Roger. "Sounder." *New York Times*, 25 Sept. 1972, 49. A mixed review that emphasizes the film's strong performances.

Holly, Ellen. "At Long Last, the Super Sound of 'Sounder.'" *New York Times*, 15 Oct. 1972, B15. A rave review: "It constantly discovers an excruciating beauty in the unremitting toil and materially barren lives of the working poor."

Kael, Pauline. *Reeling*. New York: Atlantic Monthly Press, 1976. Calls Tyson "the first great black heroine on the screen."

Thomas, Sam, ed. *Best American Screenplays*. New York: Crown, 1986. The screenplay with a brief bio of its author.

Note: "Part 2, Sounder" (1976), the sequel, with a completely different production team and cast, is not available on videocassette, and, according to Donald Bogle in *Blacks in American Films and TV* (New York: Garland, 1988), it is just as well.

∾
Spartacus

"One big union" of Roman slaves

1960, 184 mins. (1985 release) or 196 mins. (1991 release), unrated, but suitable for all despite studio's fears about one scene
Director: Stanley Kubrick
Screenplay: Dalton Trumbo, from Howard Fast's novel of the same title

CAST
Spartacus = Kirk Douglas
Varinia = Jean Simmons
Draba = Woody Strode

Gracchus = Charles Laughton
Batiatus = Peter Ustinov
Crassus = Laurence Olivier
Antoninus = Tony Curtis
Julius Caesar = John Gavin
Helena = Nina Foch
Crixus = John Ireland
Glabrus = John Dall
Slave and Roman armies = five thousand soldiers from the Army of Spain

The current (and therefore longer) videocassette version of this epic of the Roman slave revolt of the first century B.C. contains material that was edited out of the original videocassette release of the theatrical version (e.g., a gay pass that Laurence Olivier makes at one of his slaves, played by Curtis, in a Roman bathhouse), but both the original novel and the screenplay have had to survive the author's blacklisting in the McCarthy era. Fast had been an active American communist in the 1940s and early 1950s, and his novel seemed—at least to censors—to suggest the idea of a working-class "union" of all the slave workers, a sort of precommunist Internationale or Wobbly (IWW) "One Big Union." Some of the inspirational scenes in the film do retain this flavor—the gladiators, for example, have a natural solidarity as worker-fighters after they are freed, and once the gladiators organize an army of slaves who come from all the regions of the Roman empire, they form a self-governing economic unit with an elaborate division of labor.

This challenge to central authority from a "worker"-led army must have seemed dangerously close to Red Army propaganda. The FBI agents who tried to keep Howard Fast's book from being published didn't know the real origin of his interest in Spartacus: he was the hero of Rosa Luxemburg, the German socialist leader who was murdered by German reactionaries after World War I.

Despite the political implications—or perhaps because of them—the film remains an exciting story of the decadence of Roman aristocrats and the courage of those who supported them literally on their backs. From the gladiator training and revolt to the organization and eventual betrayal of the slave army, "Spartacus" is an exciting film of Roman decadence and dramatic battles. When we move into the sentimental romance between Spartacus and Lavinia and the cutesy campside joking among the ranks of the slave army, part of the screen will sag before your eyes.

But the disturbing conclusion—especially a deep-focus shot of seemingly endless crucified slaves, the visual spectacle of Rome's revenge against the rebels—will stay in most memories for a long time.

Fast's novel and Stanley Kubrick's subsequent film attempted to turn Spartacus into a noble warrior of oppressed peoples. This romantic view does not bear too much historical scrutiny, although Fast certainly used the facts—such as they were—and the legends to create a perfect gentleman—for a gladiator, anyway. The "real" Spartacus certainly led the last of the great Servile (Slave) Wars, which lasted from 135 to 71 B.C. For sixty-five years Roman armies were challenged and occasionally defeated by slaves. If Spartacus had left Italy at the head of an army, he might have won his freedom; most historians do not think it likely that he would have—as the film implies—succeeded in bringing down the Roman Empire as well.

Since this film is an epic, all classes of Roman society are represented and all manner of absurdities are pursued (Olivier's Crassus is in love with Spartacus's slave companion, Lavinia). Solidarity is really the principal working-class message of Old Lefty Fast: when Spartacus and the slaves are captured, many come foreward to protect him and say, "I am Spartacus." The noble Roman's reply: "Crucify all of them."

Availability: Easy.

Further reading: Bernstein, Richard. "'Spartacus': A Classic Restored." *New York Times*, 18
April 1991, C15, C18. A history of the film and its re-release.

Bradley, Keith R. *Slavery and Rebellion in the Roman World, 140 B.C.–70 B.C.* Bloomington:
Indiana University Press, 1989. A scholarly but readable analysis of the slave wars; a somewhat less wholesome Spartacus emerges.

Cooper, Duncan. "A Second Look: 'Spartacus.'" *Cineaste* 6.3 (1974): 30–31. Argues that Fast's
novel was not as "ultimately hopeless" as the film, which he sees as producer and star Kirk Douglas's clichéd reduction of the radical potential of the story.

Crowther, Bosley. "Spartacus." *New York Times*, 7 Oct. 1960, 28. An early, somewhat mocking
review of the "romantic fiffle-faddle and historical inaccuracy" of the film.

Fast, Howard. *Being Red.* Boston: Houghton Mifflin, 1990. An autobiography of the novel's
author, with an account of his interest in Spartacus's story.

Kellogg, E. "Spartacus to the Gladiators at Capua." In *Shoemaker's Best Selections, No 1.* 1873.
Reprint Freeport, N.Y.: Books for Libraries, 1970. Crowther complained that much of the "noble savage" speeches of Spartacus sound too much like the (fictitious) Victorian speeches people recited from volumes of uplifting texts like this one.

Maslin, Janet. "The Two Messages of 'Spartacus.'" *New York Times*, 26 April 1991, C6. She says
"Spartacus" has (1) a lot of "muscle-flexing kitsch," and (2) a powerful but ideological message about noble slaves.

Plutarch. "Crassus." *Parallel Lives* (c. 100–140 A.D.). Most likely one source of Fast's novel
(although other Roman historians such as Sallust and Appian also cover the revolt); includes the stories of the gladiatorial revolt, the initial defeat of the Roman armies, and the betrayal by the pirates.

∾
The Stars Look Down

. . . on miners in the dark.

1939, 110 mins., British, unrated, but
   suitable for all ages
Director: Carol Reed
Screenplay: A. J. Cronin, from his novel of
   the same title
CAST
David Fenwick = Michael Redgrave
Robert Fenwick = Edward Rigby

Martha Fenwick = Nancy Price
Jennie Sunley = Margaret Lockwood
Joe Gowlan = Emlyn Williams
Mr. Barras = Allan Jeayes
Mrs. Laura Millington = Linden Travers
Mr. Millington = Cecil Parker
Mr. Nugent, M.P. = Milton Rosmer

Just a year after A. J. Cronin's *Citadel* was adapted for film, Carol Reed adapted another one of Cronin's successful novels about British mining communities. "The Stars Look Down" is more resolutely a mining film, although, like its predecessor, the hero is an idealistic man whose life is dedicated to helping those he left behind in the mines. Reed simplified a very complex novel in terms of both the plot and British mining history, but by narrowing the focus to one main subplot—the safety of the Scupper Flats section of the Sleescale mines in Wales—we are prepared for the specific (and inevitable) disaster that is to occur but less knowledgable about the culture and conditions of the miners.

David Fenwick and his family are the central characters. His father, Robert, leads an extended wildcat strike against both the union (unnamed) and mine owner Barras because of the danger of flooding in the notorious Scupper Flats. Robert Fenwick maintains that there are plans that indicate that the wall separating the current shafts from the flooded ones are dangerously thin, but owner Barras denies the plans exist. (We know he is lying.) When the locals revolt against a particularly obnoxious butcher, Robert is arrested for looting the shop. (This scene is similar in all but the women's ferocity to a scene in "Germinal.") In the meantime, David wins a scholarship to university and raises the issue of the private ownership of the mines in debates. (Peter Stead has called this debate sequence, in which images of David's old mining buddies are superimposed over him as he speaks, "one of the most stunning and effective sequences in the history of British cinema.") He falls in love, however, and allows himself to be talked out of studying for his degree.

When Scupper Flats finally does get flooded, the shots of men running through the mines to escape the flood and the townspeople aboveground rushing through the streets when they hear the distress whistle are unnerving. David helps in the rescue, but he loses his father and brother. The novel is clearer on a moment at the end of the film when we know the elder Fenwick is going to die: he is writing something we don't see, which it turns out is a note about the owner's knowledge of the thin walls in Scupper Flats.

The look of the rescue sequences is remarkably similar to these in "Kamaradschaft," filmed just seven years earlier. The shots of the trapped miners drifting into death are horrifying. Reed's realistic and moral vision persisted, culminating in his classic black-and-white thriller "The Third Man." For "The Stars Look Down," he reassembled some of the cast (especially Michael Redgrave and Margaret Lockwood for David and Jenny) of Hitchcock's successful thriller of the year before, "The Lady Vanishes," although there are very few comic flourishes in his mining film.

Although the owner clearly comes into sharp disfavor in this film, a disturbing anti-union sequence occurs at the end, before Scupper Flats has blown, when David tries to convince the national union executive board to authorize a strike. After an impassioned speech, David's argument is punctured by a union member who mocks his concern as self-serving revenge for a personal problem. (His wife has run off with a man making a deal for Scupper Flats coal.) Not only do they reject David's proposal, but the next order of business they take up is a paint job for a local's headquarters. David will eventually be proved right and the union executive wrong, of course, but it is at a terrible cost.

See also: "The Citadel"; "Germinal"; "Kamaradschaft"; ["The Third Man"].
Availability: Selected collections.
Further reading: "The Stars Look Down." *New York Times*, 24 July 1941, 15. A very positive review—the film "says what it has to say with complete and undeviating honesty."
Stead, Peter. *Film and the Working Class.* London: Routledge, 1989. Sets the film in the context of other British mining films: the film "depicted the miner more fully than in any previous film."
Note: There is clearly a slightly different British version of this film in circulation, since an opening and closing voice-over (according to Peter Stead) stating, among other things, that the miners are "often without a spokesman," is missing in the version available in the United States.

∿
Steel

Ain't nothing higher than a skyscraper in Lexington, Kentucky.

1980, 99 mins., PG
Director: Steve Carver
Screenplay: Leigh Chapman

CAST
Mike Catton = Lee Majors
Pignose Moran = Art Carney

Lew Cassidy = George Kennedy
Cass Cassidy = Jennifer O'Neill
Eddie Cassidy = Harris Yulin
Harry = Redmond Gleason
Valentino = Terry Kiser
Dancer = Richard Lynch

Kid = Ben Marley
Lionel = Robert Mosley
Tank = Albert Salmi
Cherokee = Robert Tessler
Surfer = Hunter Von Laer

Although released commercially, this tale about the completion of a hotel sky-scraper in the face of foreclosure by corrupt bankers had "TV movie" written all over it. Like many TV movies, it even had a disease (or at least almost a disease): one of the top-flight hard hats, played by Lee Majors, once froze on the job zillions of feet in the air. Will he still be able to walk a girder thirty stories aboveground? The cast even includes a model, Jennifer O'Neill, who plays the hotel owner's daughter who vows to finish her father's building after he is killed in an accident. She put the *New York Times* reviewer in mind of a "fashion model who is being photographed against an industrial background" (in fact, she is).

Since this film is very rarely available anywhere, no one has to worry about its unrealistic portrayal of how skyscrapers get built. If it appears on a cable channel, a few things about it will satisfy, but much will seem awkward. The first ten minutes with George Kennedy playing a tough-talking roughneck of a builder are exciting: "Tall buildings give me a hard-on still," he tells his chauffeur, who is riding in the back seat while Big Lew drives recklessly to his final job. Black-and-white stills and archival 1930s footage of ironworkers heroically climbing higher and higher prepare us in the credits sequence for Big Lew climbing a girder himself, after he fires a worker for drinking beer on the job. There is an explosion and Big Lew falls from what was going to be the biggest building in the state (and since we're talking Kentucky here, thirty stories would just about do it).

The film goes down the elevator shaft from here. O'Neill is not convincing as the daughter of Big Lew who vows to get this building up. Nine floors have to be built in three weeks to stop the bank from transferring the building to Big Lew's loser of a brother, who runs a trucking business that specializes in substandard material that gets workers killed on the job.

The only way to top out Big Lew's building is to bring in Mike Catton, a legendary ironworker, as the site's "ramrod" (to push the job through) and his mystically powerful crew, made up of Cherokee (although it was the Mohawks who did most of the high ironwork on skyscrapers for many years), Valentino (an Italian-American lover-boy), Harry (a comic former IRA terrorist who has been working as an explosives man at a strip mine), and so on. These guys get to "break the rules": the (unnamed) ironworkers union local lets them sign on immediately and suspends virtually all safety rules so that the building goes up on time.

Since this is Kentucky, we get some obligatory visits to a bluegrass horse farm and to Rupp Arena, where the bad guys, such as Big Lew's brother, get to play hardball not basketball. When the men are actually bolting girders high in the sky, we finally do pay attention. The finale, in which helicopters are bringing in the final top steel pieces, has a stirring moment or two, especially when we get a shot of the men at the four corners of the unfinished tower waiting for their steel to come down from the sky.

This melodramatic film has the look of a bad TV cop show, although there are never any police officers in Lexington to prevent either the bad guys or the good guys from breaking as many laws as they wish. The spirit of the film harks back to the days of the heroic linemen of "Slim," when real men took risks to get the job done. How Lexington badly needed additional office space may not be the moral equivalent of rural electrification, but the risks the workers take are clear enough. At one point the bad brother bribes an official of the truckers union to set up a wildcat strike against the bad brother's company so he won't be able to deliver steel to the building he hopes eventually to take over. If that makes sense, then this film is worth seeing.

See also: "Bloodbrothers"; "Slim."
Availability: Selected collections.
Further reading: Buckley, Tom. "Film: Hard Hats in 'Steel.'" *New York Times*, 13 Dec. 1980, 55.
     A rare but mocking review.
Note: This film is also known as "Look Down and Die" and "Men of Steel."

Strike

. . . or rebel or both.

1924, 73 mins., B & W, Russian, silent, unrated, but suitable for mature children
Director: Sergei M. Eisenstein
Screenplay: Sergei M. Eisenstein
CAST
Organizer = A. Antonov
Worker = Mikhail Gomarov
Spy = Maxim Shtraukh
Foreman = Grigori Alexandrov
Lumpenproletariat = Judith Glizer, Boris Yurtzev, and other actors of the First Workers' Theater of the Proletkult Collective

This film is about a strike by factory workers in czarist Russia in 1912 who, as they develop their strategy and tactics, are constantly at the mercy of management spies. The workers have no union, but they have an organization and a printing press: "Workers Unite!" is the title of a typical leaflet, and it reminds us that in this period depicted by many Soviet filmmakers, shop-floor organizing and antigovernment rebellion were essentially one and the same.

The actual strike is touched off by the suicide of a worker who has been wrongly accused of stealing a tool. The workers walk out. Their demands for a reduction in hours and an increase in pay result in attacks by mounted policemen. The long strike forces families into hardship, as the management spies increase their ingenious tricks (at one point a camera disguised as a pocketwatch photographs a worker removing a management sign). The managers' desperation becomes obvious as they hire the King of the Underworld for an arson job. The ultimate in riffraff, portrayed almost literally as *lumpen* workers (the "lumpenproletariat" in Marxist terms), his gang hides out in disused underground wine vats. The plan is to burn the factory and blame it on the workers. Although this plot fails, the fire brigades turn their hoses on the workers, not the burning building! Eventually, the strike is forgotten as soldiers, in visually stunning shots, attack the revolutionary masses.

The pessimistic ending of "Strike" was to have led, as in a Marxist analysis, to the eventual victory of the Soviet Revolution in a follow-up film. Sergei Eisenstein had rejected—many critics pointed out—stars, heroes, and plot, in favor of an experimental approach to filmmaking by using images of striking workers to demonstrate the necessity for revolution: silent film titles whirling and dissolving into parts of machines, point-of-view shots from the perspective of the miniature spy camera, and the final close-up shot of open staring eyes are all typical of Eisenstein's inventiveness. The acting has an exaggerated clownlike quality throughout, but the "montage"—the clashing of images to build meaning, as in shots of the throat of a bull being cut as the soldiers attack the crowd—still has the power to convey Eisenstein's revolutionary politics.

"Strike" may seem like a warm-up for Eisenstein's two somewhat more famous films: the 1924 "Potemkin," an epic about a mutiny on a ship against the oppressive officers, which contains one of the most famous sequences in all of film history (the "Odessa Steps" massacre of the citizens who support the ship's rebellion), and the 1928 "October" (also known as "Ten Days That Shook the World"), based in part on a book of "instant history" by the American John Reed (played by Warren Beatty in "Reds").

Nevertheless, "Strike" has some spectacular moments as well: the homeless riffraff emerging from their underground pipe homes in response to the call of the King of the Underworld is the most remarkable image in a film filled with dramatic images. Although Eisenstein is certainly the greatest of Soviet filmmakers and a world-class film artist, he eventually ran into trouble with a world-class censor, Stalin himself.

"Strike," as Eisenstein's first major film, shares with other "constructivist" avant-garde Soviet art of the 1920s a celebration of machinery and industrial design. Eisenstein's theater group was known for its innovative use of actual settings: Eisenstein staged a play, "Gas Masks," for example, at the Moscow Gas Works. It was perhaps inevitable that his first film, a year later, would be filmed on location and, in Eisenstein's words, by "superimposing images of man onto images of buildings—all an attempt to interrelate man and his milieu in a single complicated display" (*Film Form*). The opening shots of the film, belching smokestacks arranged diagonally, or later when the workers are seen with their arms folded to indicate their refusal to work as the enormous flywheel of the machinery comes to a gradual stop, convey the motion and power of the industrial scene. In Eisenstein's Marxist dialectic, the struggle is between laboring men and fat capitalists, not between workers and machinery. The latter may benefit the workers or be the instrument of their enslavement.

See also: ["October"]; ["Potemkin," also known as "Battleship Potemkin"]; "Reds."
Availability: Selected collections.
Further reading: Eisenstein, Sergei M. *The Complete Films of Eisenstein*. Translated by John Hetherington. New York: Dutton, 1974. Film summaries, with stills.
———. *Film Form and Film Sense*. Translated by Jay Leyda. New York: Harcourt, Brace, 1957. Sometimes overcomplicated, sometimes helpful discussions of early Soviet film technique. Includes discussions of "Strike" and Eisenstein's other films.
Lawder, Standish. "Eisenstein and Constructivism." In *The Essential Cinema*, edited by P. Adams Sitney, 58–87. New York: Anthology Film Archives, 1975. Detailed (almost exclusively cinematic) analysis of the film.
Leyda, Jay. *Kino: A History of Russian and Soviet Film*. New York: Collier, 1971. An analysis of "Strike" in the context of Eisenstein's career and the careers of other Soviet filmmakers.
Nichols, Bill. *Blurred Boundaries: Questions of Meaning in Contemporary Culture*. Bloomington: Indiana University Press, 1994. Offers an intriguing approach to the film as a variation of documentary filmmaking rather than as a feature film.
Swallow, Norman. *Eisenstein: A Documentary Portrait*. New York: Dutton, 1977. Recollections of Eisenstein by his contemporaries and collaborators.

ᐁ Sugar Cane Alley

A woman's version of a boy's coming of age

1983, 103 mins., French (with English subtitles), PG
Director: Euzhan Palcy
Screenplay: Euzhan Palcy, from Joseph Zobel's novel of the same title

CAST
José = Garry Cadenat
M'Man Tine = Darling Legitimus
Medouze = Douta Seck
Leopold = Laurent St. Cyr

The original French title, "Rue Cases Negres" (literally "Black Shack Alley"), captures the look of this unique film of life on sugar cane plantations on the Caribbean island of Martinique in the 1930s. Given that few films depict black labor, either slave or free, Euzhan Palcy's film makes a daring attempt to link African-Caribbean slavery and later virtual serfdom in the character of Medouze, an ancient working man who is a mentor to José, Palcy's young hero. "Sugar Cane Alley" concentrates on the two educations José receives: his white Western French education, which his grandmother is working so hard to support, and the education he receives from Medouze, who is wise in black history and the culture of the island.

Medouze explains their serfdom as a serious error after slavery was ended: "We were free but our bellies were empty. Our master had become our boss. . . . The whites owned all the land." He knows that he can "never go back to Africa" because "he has no one left there." He will return to Africa "when he's buried," but he "can't take the boy along."

In the meantime, M'Man Tine is working hard to keep the boy in school and, more to the point, to keep him out of the fields so he can be trained in other ways: "Learning is the key that opens the second door to freedom," she says. Eventually, the boy performs well enough to get a partial and then a full scholarship to the big school in Fort-de-France. Two related events bring the film and José's early years to a close: M'Man Tine dies (he realizes that "she's gone back to Africa" like Medouze), and Leopold, José's biracial friend, is arrested for stealing a ledger to prove that the workers have been cheated in their cane quotas. Leopold is taken off by the police while the workers all sing a rebellious song.

Palcy's career as a Third World woman director making mainstream films is unique. Her original impulse was to film Alan Paton's *Cry the Beloved Country*, but she turned to Joseph Zobel's novel about the Martinique that she felt was her "daily reality." She was just seventeen when she decided to make the film. Before directing "Sugar Cane Alley," she had been responsible for the first television drama from a French overseas department (i.e., a former colony). She then went on to adapt André Brink's novel *A Dry White Season*, about apartheid in South Africa.

Palcy has somewhat daringly mixed issues of class and race. José needs the white authority's system to escape the working-class drudgery of his family and friends. How much Palcy believes that escaping to the lower-middle class is justified is not clear.

See also: "Daughters of the Dust"; ["A Dry White Season"].
Availability: Selected collections.
Further reading: Canby, Vincent. "Third World Truths." *New York Times*, 22 April 1984, II.17.
    A long appreciative review: "Euzhan Palcy is a new writer-director of exceptional abilities."
Cham, Mbye. ed. *Ex-iles: Essays on Caribbean Cinema*. Trenton, N.J.: Africa World Press, 1992.
    Includes a review of the film and an interview with the director.
McKenna, Kristin. "Tough, Passionate, Persuasive." *American Film*, Sept. 1989, 32–37. A pro-
    file of the filmmaker and her films.

Maslin, Janet. "Moving Up." *New York Times*, 6 April 1984, C24. A brief but positive review.

ᴄᴡ Sullivan's Travels

Hollywood goes hobo.

1941, 91 mins., B & W, unrated, but
  suitable for all ages
Director: Preston Sturges
Screenplay: Preston Sturges

CAST
John L. Sullivan = Joel McCrea
The Girl = Veronica Lake
Sullivan's Butler = Robert Greig
Sullivan's Valet = Eric Blore

This wonderful satire begins with a Depression-era political joke. The Sullivan of the title is a director who has just finished a film that is "an answer to the communists." What we see of this film—two men duking it out on the roof of a freight-train boxcar until they knock each other into a river—becomes hilarious when we pull back from the screen-within-a-screen to hear Sullivan announce to his producers that it is about Capital and Labor destroying themselves. The director says that a film is a "sociological and artistic medium." Yea, his producers add, but always "with a little sex in it."

Eventually, Sullivan decides that to make realistic films for the masses, he needs to join the riffraff, become a hobo, and cast aside his affluent Hollywood lifestyle. His butler and valet are suitably shocked and try to talk him out of it: "The poor," one of them says, "know all about poverty. Only the morbid or the rich would find it glamorous." But Sullivan goes off, exploring hobo jungles, Salvation Army kitchens, and life with the Depression homeless. (Their camps resemble, in many ways any homeless camp today.) His adventures are appropriately sociological, "with a little bit of sex in it." For example, the Girl (Veronica Lake) strips as often as the plot (and the 1940s Motion Picture Code) will allow her to, and she has no illusions about poverty either.

After Sullivan is knocked on the head, however, he actually becomes a hobo. Our Hollywood hero discovers at his lowest point, when he is held in a prison farm with a sadistic warden, that the poor want and need comedies, not Marxist newsreels.

Some of the messages of Preston Sturges's satire come through in unexpected ways. A black rural church welcomes the integrated chain gang of prisoners for a show of cartoons; the minister puts his congregation on notice: "We are all equal in the sight of the Lord." Sullivan has ended up on this chain gang, he thinks, because a railroad guard thought he was "just a bum." If Sullivan the director had smacked the guard, nothing would have come of it, but because Sullivan the bum did it, he gets a seven-year sentence. If you are perhaps a little tired of Frank Capra's sentimentality ("It's a Wonderful Life"), then it might be time to watch a Sturges film.

See also: "Black Fury"; "Gold Diggers of 1933"; "The Grapes of Wrath"
Availability: Easy.
Further reading: Bergman, Andrew. *We're in the Money: Depression America and Its Films.* New York: New York University Press, 1971. An excellent film history with a discussion of this film.

Swing Shift

Goldie the Riveter

1984, 100 mins., PG	Lucky Lockhart = Kurt Russell
Director: Jonathan Demme	Hazel Zanussi = Christine Lahti
Screenplay: "Rob Morton"	Jack Walsh = Ed Harris
CAST	Biscuits = Fred Ward
Kay Walsh = Goldie Hawn	

For the "real" "Swing Shift," we may have to wait in vain for the "director's cut"— the version of the film the producers won't release because they don't think it will be commercial—since the director whose name is on the film (but who wants it off) was apparently more or less secretly fired before the project was completed and no screenwriter would take credit on-screen for the film: hence, the generic "phoney" name of "Rob Morton" on the credits. (On "director's cuts": it took Ridley Scott almost ten years to get his cut of "Blade Runner" released; for Stanley Kubrick, more than thirty for "Spartacus.") We know that actress Goldie Hawn chased Jonathan Demme away. No one knows why for sure, but some commentators suggest that Demme's vision was too radical for her (see Vineberg).

"Swing Shift" is the story of a housewife-turned-Rosie the Riveter named Kay Walsh. Other than gender stereotypes, what could Demme and Hawn have been fighting about? Plenty, apparently. The level of the film is not always high. The sexy Hazel (played by Lahti in her first big success) is told by a coworker, "Isn't it amazing that someone with your looks is a riveter?!" Kay's comeback when she fights with her new boyfriend: "If I can build a goddamn airplane, I can get myself home!"

The film should be seen with the documentary "The Life and Times of Rosie the Riveter," which provides a reasonably complete story of the days when defense contractors and the government urged women to leave their homes and help their men win the war. By the end of the war, the propaganda machine went into reverse, and the women were supposed to say (prompted by newsreels), "I'm going to be busy—at home." "Swing Shift" dramatizes these dilemmas reasonably well, overlaying them with a triangle—Kay; her husband, Jack, now off in the navy; and her work-mate and new lover, Lucky (i.e., "lucky" enough to be 4-F).

A more interesting story of gender roles is lurking in this film—Kay's life with her husband is frilly, at home, doing her DUTY, while her life with Lucky is at clubs in sexy outfits, having FUN—but the film stops way short of asking any big questions such as "What do women want?" and maybe this is why Demme was sent packing. (Demme has suggested he wanted to make a film about women's friendships during the war, not about the men in their lives.)

Workplace life as portrayed here is more comic than real, although the teasing and sexual harassment of the women seems to be the genuine article. The workplace—an aircraft factory—is racially integrated, but so are some of the clubs the workers visit. Maybe.

See also: "The Life and Times of Rosie the Riveter."
Availability: Easy.
Further reading: Canby, Vincent. "A Wartime Romance." *New York Times*, 13 April 1984, C13. The film "bends" but does not "break" the "cliches of a kind of romantic fiction not too far removed from World War II movies about the homefront."
Kael, Pauline. "Smaller Than Life." *New Yorker*, 14 May 1984, 138–40. Argues that the film fails to convey "the sass and bounce of the women workers, earning good money for the first time" and does not "put across the feeling that's so rousing in documentaries about the period."
Kessler-Harris, Alice. "Rosie the Riveter Goes Hollywood." *Ms.*, July 1984, 46. Echoes Demme's belief that the film changed from an "exposé" to a "salute."
Maslin, Janet. "At the Movies." *New York Times*, 4 May 1984, C8. A brief survey of the production disputes.
Vineberg, Steve. "'Swing Shift': A Tale of Hollywood." *Sight and Sound*, Winter 1990/91, 8–13. A detailed comparison of Hawn's and Demme's versions of the problems, which concludes that Hawn's version is a "political emasculation" of Demme's.

Taylor Chain

Strong links, weak chain

[I] "A Story of a Union Local"	[II] "A Story of Collective Bargaining"
1980, 33 mins., B & W, unrated, but suitable for all ages	1984, 30 mins., unrated, but suitable for all ages
Directors: Jerry Blumenthal and Gordon Quinn	Directors: Jerry Blumenthal and Gordon Quinn
Scripted documentary.	Scripted documentary.

PRINCIPAL FIGURES IN "A Story of a Union Local"

Ted Pusty, electrician

Paul Martin, electrician and president, Local 4041, United Steelworkers of America (USWA)

John Bierman, USWA staff representative

Rose Davis, packer; secretary, Local 4041

PRINCIPAL FIGURES IN "A Story of Collective Bargaining"

Bob Grantz, welder

Carl Hildebrandt, repairman

Ted Pusty, electrician

Al Gonzalez, inspector; president, Local 4041, 1975–81

Howle Moore, president, Taylor Chain Company (TCC)

Henry Owczarzak, repairman

Winnie McCauley, shipper; president, Local 4041

Birdia Morris, inspector

Rose Davis, inspector; secretary, Local 4041

Leon Rysicki, plant superintendent

John Sobolewski, union negotiation team member

Wally Moneta, union negotiation team member

Steve Crist, TCC lawyer

Jerry Volkmann, TCC plant manager

These two documentaries about the Taylor Chain Company of Hammond, Indiana (part of the sprawling industrial belt from Chicago east to Gary, Indiana) should be seen together: they chart two crucial stages in the life and death of a company established in 1873 by the Taylor family, who retained ownership and management through four generations. And, perhaps even more acutely, they chart the struggles of a union local to hold on to its contract in the face of the widespread devastation of its industry.

The first documentary focuses on a strike in 1972 by Local 4041 of the United Steelworkers over its third contract since winning recognition in 1967; the second film focuses on the company itself, which went bankrupt and was finally sold in 1980 to a group of investors who tried to save the plant and enter into negotiations with Local 4041.

Both films take us inside the plant, for many years the leading midwestern supplier of chain for industry (shipping, logging, drilling, and steel mill operations) and home use (tire chains and other hardware items). Although the actual making of the chains is featured in both films in fascinating detail—the filmmakers have a knack for seeing those interlocking links as flexible tools in the creation of industrial power—the real issue in the films is decision making, at both the local level, as the negotiating team walks a wavy line between the demands of the rank and file and the international, and the bargaining table, as the team confronts management as both sides alternate between the hard and soft sell.

The first film concentrates almost exclusively on the leadership of the local and the rank and file. When the negotiations for the third contract stall, the men (98 percent of the workforce) and women go on strike. The times were changing even then, for shots inside the strike headquarters trailer show not only a lot of *Playmate* posters but also a couple of nude men. Rose Davis, secretary of the local and a

Steelworkers from USWA Local 4041 in "Taylor Chain: A Story of a Union Local."
Courtesy Kartemquin Educational Films.

stalwart of the union (she is still secretary nine years later in the second film), jokes about not knowing who would have put up the posters of the men.

With only five years of unionized presence at Taylor Chain, it wasn't clear even to the membership how far it could go in insisting on strong health and safety "language" in the contract. Eventually, the local meets to debate whether it can push the company on wages or on "language." We see the negotiating process only from the vantage point of the interaction of the rank and file and their leadership. The latter is clearly split, so that the representative of the international (Bierman) favors acceptance while some of the other members of the committee urge the members to vote down the contract proposal, which they do.

There is some revealing interview footage when the issue of standing to indicate one's vote is discussed. After the meeting, some of the members agree with Bierman that the procedure intimidates the membership. (The second film shows a similar vote being taken nine years later. This time it is a secret paper vote.) The film ends somewhat abruptly two weeks after this meeting with a ratified contract and the workers back at the plant.

The second film presents a somewhat more sophisticated view of the local as the company is on the edge of bankruptcy. Not only is the film in color, but the events are more carefully outlined and documented.

In 1980, the collapse of the company—only twelve workers were on the floor!—was temporarily staved off by new investors. The cost to the local of bringing the workforce up to a hundred, however, was a wage freeze and, a year later, a 10 percent wage cut and a layoff of 5 percent of the workforce. Nonetheless, the workers pitched in to help the company make it. Repairman Owczarzak, for example, solves a big surplus rod problem and converts potential waste into a moneymaker.

The heart of the second film is a face-to-face meeting between the negotiating team and management. The negotiating team tries to take a position of no concessions and even attempts to win back the 10 percent wage cut it accepted just the year before. With an offer that includes a progressive rate change (a 1 percent wage increase is to be restored each quarter), the contract is sent to the members, who ratify it. A year later, that contract is extended, but more layoffs cannot hold off what turns out to be the end: the company goes bankrupt.

The film's end titles summarize the sad tale of this Reagan-era disaster: in 1980, one hundred workers; in 1984, 37 percent had found other jobs, 15 percent had retired, but 48 percent were unemployed. The film does not analyze these data politically or even economically: it is mainly a document of the running down of a local's livelihood. And there are no Gekko-like investors from the world of "Wall Street." In fact, the representatives of management, with rare exception, look as worried as the rank and file.

Kartemquin Educational Films has provided an excellent study guide for both films. Besides helpful general background on Chicago-area industrial issues, the guide emphasizes that the management of Taylor Chain represented two contradictory trends in the late 1970s and 1980s. On the one hand, atypically, Taylor Chain was in the end managed by an engineer, Howie Moore, who became the president of the company; on the other hand, the company was barely keeping up with innovative and new machinery, part of the necessary profile to keep an American company competitive with companies in Japan or Europe. Other topics in the guide are important (Quality of Work Life programs, for example) but are never really part of either film's dramatic movement.

These films are testimonials to the human costs of plant closings, not to mention the eroding of collective bargaining traditions. They complement nicely John David Coles's fictional film "Rising Son," in which a small starter-motor factory goes under.

See also: "Rising Son"; "Wall Street."
Availability: Selected collections; New Day Films; I: AFL-CIO and ILR Media.
Further reading: Lesage, Julia. "Filming for the City: An Interview with the Kartemquin Collective." *Cineaste* 7.1 (1975): 26–30. A profile of the filmmakers who began making "socially committed" documentaries.

Lynd, Staughton. *The Fight against Shutdowns: Youngstown's Steel Mill Closing.* San Pedro, Calif.: Singlejack Books, 1982. Recounts the same situation a state or two away and how community groups worked with the USWA to prevent the shutdowns.

Taylor Chain: A Study Guide for Workers and Corporations in the 1980s. Chicago: Kartemquin Educational Films, 1984. A guide to the regional and national issues surrounding the changes in the industry.

Teague, Carol H. "Easing the Pain of Plant Closure: The Brown and Williamson Experience." *Management Review* (April 1981): 23–27. The story of a three-year gradual shutdown in which efforts were made to ease the pains for employees and minimize production problems.

Zheutlin, Barbara, ed. "The Art and Politics of the Documentary: A Symposium." *Cineaste* 11.3 (1981): 12–21. A number of filmmakers, including the Kartemquin group that made the "Taylor Chain" films, discuss their films and their ideas about documentaries.

Teachers

"Those who can't teach, teach gym."—Woody Allen

1984, 106 mins., R	Roger = Judd Hirsch
Director: Arthur Hiller	Eddie = Ralph Macchio
Screenplay: W. R. McKinney	Dr. Burke = Lee Grant
CAST	"Ditto" = Royal Dano
Alex Jurel = Nick Nolte	Horn = William Shallert
Lisa = JoBeth Williams	Herbert = Richard Mulligan

When virtually everybody's favorite sensitive actor, Judd Hirsch, plays a high school principal who sells out his friend by collaborating with the opportunistic leadership of his union and when the irrepressible William Shallert is the best (although a substitute) teacher because he is an escaped lunatic, we know we can be in only one place—the troubled, impossibly neat, urban American high school. Nick Nolte plays Hirsch's friend, a teacher whose favorite female student, Lisa (JoBeth Williams), now a lawyer, wants to embarrass her alma mater for graduating a student who cannot read.

Not surprisingly, Lisa falls for her old English teacher, although the road to true love is mined with a union obsessed with its minor perks while the house of education be damned and the troubled rebel (played with particularly repulsive cloyness by Ralph Macchio) is dangerously ignored.

This mixture of TV school sitcom and urban reality seems to attract imitations like bad school lunches. Its best moments convey the comic abuse of power these films and sitcoms have been dramatizing for years: one teacher nicknamed "Ditto" has his students so well drilled that for a whole day the students walk in, pick up their dittoed sheets to fill in, and walk out before anyone realizes that "Ditto" has gone to the great teacher's rest in the sky.

Meanwhile, an opportunity to dramatize a white-collar union in a very difficult setting has been missed. The frustrated teachers, the students who don't get taught, and the administrators who are hopelessly outgunned by the system are all here. When director Arthur Hiller targeted the absurdities of heath care in "The Hospital" in 1971, he seemed very avant-garde. But this film makes him look like he hasn't gotten out of detention since 1969, when Frederick Wiseman's documentary "High School"—perhaps too sober but certainly on target—was released.

See also: "The Corn Is Green"; ["High School"]; ["The Hospital"].
Availability: Easy.
Further reading: Maslin, Janet. "Lesson in Learning." *New York Times*, 5 Oct. 1984, C10.
   Appreciates the realistic look of the school but finds the film a bit clichéd.
Murphy, Marjorie. *Blackboard Unions: The AFT and the NEA, 1900–1950.* Ithaca, N.Y.: Cornell
   University Press, 1990. A readable history of the two largest teachers organizations.

∾
Teamster Boss: The Jackie Presser Story

Another full-court press on Hoffa

1992, 111 mins., TVM, unrated, but suitable for mature children	Bill Presser = Eli Wallach
	Carmen Presser = Maria Conchita Alonso
Director: Alastair Reid	Tom Noonan = Jeff Daniels
Screenplay: Abby Mann, from James Neff's nonfiction book, *Mobbed Up*	Alan Dorfman = Tony Lo Bianco
	Maisha Rockman = Robert Prosky
CAST	Tony Provenzano = Frank Pelligrino
Jackie Presser = Brian Dennehy	Fat Tony Salerno = Val Avery

If we ignore for the moment its confused (and confusing) politics and its often maligned production status ("It's a TV movie"), "Teamster Boss" is an intriguing film. An inept Jackie Presser, managing a bowling alley and lightly scamming a small Teamsters local, is catapulted into more prominent leadership roles by his father, Bill Presser, the second most powerful Teamster in the country. The elder Presser is dying, and he wants someone to carry on the family firm, which, in this case, is cheating Teamster members of their dues money. Brian Dennehy plays young Presser as a foolish man who gradually realizes that there are worse things in life than being a union cheat and some dubious better things: he becomes an informer for the FBI when he feels threatened by the same people who helped Hoffa disappear and hooks up with an FBI agent, Tom Noonan, whom he tells, "You use me; I use you."

The film credits Presser with an attack of conscience, especially after he finds a good woman (his fourth wife) and a terminal illness (lung cancer). Trying to maneuver against the likes of Fat Tony Salerno and Tony Provenzano, both formidably unpleasant guys with nasty reputations even inside the world of the Mob, Presser thinks he can rely on his government contacts to help purify the Teamsters. Although he fails, the film credits him with causing enough of a hassle with the Mob that the first "democratically" elected president, Ron Carey, has an even better chance of saving the Teamsters.

This was the first major post-Hoffa Teamsters movie that also attempted to interpret the Reaganite 1980s in terms of its secret relationships with organized labor. Ironically, very little of the Teamsters' daily life of working or even union organizing is shown: the emphasis is almost entirely on the behind-the-scenes maneuvering among Teamster leaders, the Mob (both Jewish and Italian branches), the FBI, the Justice Department, and Reagan himself. The most obvious Teamster militancy is played out in a Cleveland local when the members try to keep their old leader and Hoffa's friend Bill Presser from imposing Jackie, his son, as president. Then baseball bats come out and the stereotypical violent Teamster is shown fighting not cops or goons or scabs but his own leaders.

The film follows James Neff's interpretation of Presser in *Mobbed Up* as Daddy's "clown" prince who eventually tried to play the FBI and the Mob against each other to achieve some good ends for his membership. When he tries to outmaneuver the crown prince of Hollywood, Reagan himself, he fails miserably. Much is made of how difficult it is to lead the nation's largest and most persecuted union—if its president cooperates with the Mob, the Feds throw him in jail; if he doesn't cooperate, he ends up like Jimmy Hoffa.

Should we accept this story as history? It's hard to say; on the surface, some of the details ring true. Presser was apparently an FBI informer, he did try to wheel and deal as if Reagan's corrupt attorney general, Edwin Meese, would back him up (he didn't), and the Justice Department did force a major change in Teamster elections. The film is a better-than-average docudrama, in which real people (and sometimes actual footage) are edited into a primarily fictionalized story.

The film adds some bite to its tale when it includes shots of both Ronald Reagan and George Bush happily accepting the Teamsters' support for their presidential election campaigns. At one point a senator threatens Presser with a congressional investigation if the Teamsters do not help to bail out a savings and loan in trouble in his state. If only a third of this film is true, Presser and the Teamsters may yet wash a lot cleaner than most other Hollywood movies would indicate.

See also: "Blood Feud"; "F.I.S.T"; "Hoffa"; "Hoffa: The True Story."
Availability: Easy.
Further reading: La Botz, Dan. *Rank-and-File Rebellion: Teamsters for a Democratic Union.*

London: Verso, 1990. An inside history by one of the founders of the Teamsters for a Democratic Union, with detailed narratives and analysis of the Presser years.

Neff, James. *Mobbed Up*. Boston: Atlantic Monthly Press, 1989. A reasonably well-documented nonfiction source of the film.

O'Connor, John J. "Corruption, Love, and Murder, All from Real Life." *New York Times*, 11 Sept. 1992, C34. Reviewer finds the film "packs the wallop of a political caricature by George Grosz," the great German antifascist artist.

Sloan, Arthur. *Hoffa*. Cambridge: MIT Press, 1992. The definitive biography of Hoffa, with important material about Presser as well.

◡

They Drive by Night

Riff-Raft

1940, 93 mins., B & W, unrated, but suitable for all ages	Paul Fabrini = Humphrey Bogart
Director: Raoul Walsh	Cassie Hartley = Ann Sheridan
Screenplay: Jerry Wald and Richard Macauley, from A. I. Bezzerides's novel *The Long Haul*	Lana Carlsen = Ida Lupino
	Ed Carlsen = Alan Hale
	Pearl Fabrini = Gale Page
	Irish McGurn = Roscoe Karns
CAST	
Joe Fabrini = George Raft	

Warner Brothers' 1930s tradition of making films about "tough guys and gals" was continued in this saga of the Fabrini brothers, independent long-haul truckers who fight to remain owner-operators against all odds. When an accident causes one brother to lose an arm, they try to settle in to the easier job of working for a big trucking outfit. But it's not easy. The boss's wife has been trying to put the make on brother Joe for years, and he has always resisted. She goes bonkers, see, and kills her husband (the boss) so Joe can take over and be hers. When Joe resists yet again, she frames him for the killing but later breaks down at the trial. The two brothers take over the business and turn it into a progressive driver-friendly line.

Fortunately for Warner Brothers, this trucker fantasy had two tough-guy icons— Humphrey Bogart and George Raft—and two tough-gal pinups—Ann Sheridan and Ida Lupino. Otherwise, this film would have been even more unbelievable than it is. The *New York Times* reviewer was fair when he accepted some of the realism and some of the fantasy: the film was "sweaty with honest toil and very loose with suggestive repartee," as it starred "the cream of [Warner Brothers'] ungrammatical roughnecks, starting with George Raft and Humphrey Bogart, and their ace baggage, Ann Sheridan."

Although the film is often billed in video guides such as Leonard Maltin's as the story of tough "truck-driving brothers battling crooked bosses," this is not what the film is about. (There really are no "crooked bosses.") The brothers are tough enough: "We're tougher than any truck that ever come off an assembly line." But "they drive by night" to make it as independent owners, to be their own bosses. In short, this is a Depression story of working-class aspiration that never goes away: Ernest Borgnine continued the tradition in both his working-class films of the 1950s, "Marty" and "The Catered Affair," and John Turturro updated it a little in "Mac." In a strange way the film also argues that although it may be a great idea to be an owner-independent, most working stiffs have a greater need for a benevolent boss.

See also: "The Catered Affair"; "Mac"; "Marty."
Availability: Selected collections.
Further reading: Crowther, Bosley. "They Drive by Night." *New York Times*, 27 July 1940, 17. A
    brief but very positive review.
Sklar, Robert. *City Guys: Cagney, Bogart, and Garfield.* Princeton: Princeton University
    Press, 1992. A discussion of this film in the context of a relatively new working-class urban
    hero.

∿
They Shoot Horses, Don't They?

The Dance of Death at a Depression marathon

1969, 121 mins., M/PG	Sailor = Red Buttons
Director: Sydney Pollack	James = Bruce Dern
Screenplay: James Poe and Robert E.	Ruby = Bonnie Bedelia
Thompson, from Horace McCoy's novel	Turkey = Al Lewis
of the same title	Rollo = Michael Conrad
CAST	Cecil = Severn Darden
Goria = Jane Fonda	Joel = Robert Fields
Robert = Michael Sarrazin	Shirl = Alyyn Ann McLerie
Alice = Susannah York	Spectator = Lillian Gish
Rocky = Gig Young	

The dance marathon was a peculiar Depression scene: amateur dancers, exploited ruthlessly by promoters, drove themselves into a frenzy, with cash prizes and possible recruitment by talent scouts as the bait. The creation of a self-contained world, with racing competitions (track suits plus running shoes) designed to attract the crowds and have spectators and businesses "sponsor" a particular couple, is captured beautifully in this film. The marathon was a major crossroads of riffraff, especially unemployed actors and actresses desperate for any job, drifters and hookers, mobsters and stars. Horace McCoy's novel and Sydney Pollack's film emphasize the Los Angeles setting as itself a movie set, with "actors" (the dancers) and a "director" (Rocky, played by Gig Young).

The film touches on the depths of poverty, despair, and absurdity that marked these marathon-dancing years until the Roosevelt recovery. The world portrayed here is the urban world that is the flip side of the world dramatized in John Steinbeck's "The Grapes of Wrath." The film is faithful for the most part to the chilling vision of McCoy's 1935 novel, applauded in a quiet way by American critics but celebrated by the French as a pure example of American existentialism (the dancers choose to participate in an absurd ritual of anxiety and alienation that imitates life itself). McCoy and other writers who wrote of the numbing despair of the out-of-work millions portrayed a class that had none of the jaunty airs of the riffraff of some popular Hollywood films, since their suicidal impulses were hard to joke about.

Before making "They Shoot Horses," Jane Fonda had been celebrated by the French for her portrayal of a forty-first-century comic-book sex goddess (Barbarella), so her tough-as-nails Gloria (whom Vincent Canby called a "Typhoid Mary of existential despair") was a real performance for a change. Almost all the leads capture the fevered desire of the would-be actors and people on the bum to make it, if not in Hollywood at least in this crazy marathon. Only Michael Sarrazin seems off; he's sleepwalking in every scene, including those in which his character is not supposed to be sleepwalking (or, more precisely, sleep-dancing, a skill the contestants develop).

The spectacle of the marathon, for which paraphernalia were purposely built to increase speed and endurance (the men's belts have hooks for the women to hold on to), and the cheering fans who sponsored individual dancers by providing them with food and clothes clearly represents a crossroads of economics and the American entertainment industry. Alice, a beautiful wannabe, seems to have star quality, but the announcer (Gig Young) steals her nice dress because she looks "too nice." The fans, he says, want to see people below them fighting their way up. Alice was trying to leap right to the top, hoping to catch the eye of the directors—like Mervyn LeRoy, who had just released his hit, "Little Caesar," with Edward G. Robinson as a famous Depression hood.

The film has a somewhat involved narrative structure: we have flashbacks of Robert's youth when his horse had to be put down because of an accident and a frame story of Robert's arrest and death sentence for shooting Gloria. When a cop asks him why he did it, he replies, "They shoot horses, don't they?" When pressed further, he adds, "Because she asked me to." The cop's reply, "Obliging bastard, isn't he!?" sums up much of the irony of this film.

See also: "Fury"; "The Grapes of Wrath."
Availability: Easy.

Further reading: Calabria, Frank M. *Dance of the Sleep-Walkers: The Dance Marathon Fad.* Bowling Green, Ohio: Popular Culture Press, 1993. A popular history that will convince viewers that the horrors of the film were genuine.

Depression Writers: a few of the more despairing stories that match the mood of McCoy's novel and Pollack's film are Meridel LeSueur's "Women on the Breadlines" (1932), which captures the despair of homeless and out-of-work women of the 1930s; Tom Kromer's novel *Waiting for Nothing* (1935; reprint; Athens: University of Georgia Press, 1986), and Albert Maltz's "The Happiest Man in the World" (1938). The last two offer suicidal men who will do anything to survive; the Maltz and LeSueur stories are available in both editions of volume 2 of the *Heath Anthology of American Literature* (Lexington, Mass.: Heath, 1990, 1994).

McCoy, Horace. *They Shoot Horses, Don't They?* New York: Avon, 1966. This paperback editon of the novel has an afterword with a biographical sketch of McCoy.

Miller, Gabriel. *Screening the Novel.* New York: Ungar, 1980. Includes a chapter that compares McCoy's novel and the film.

ᖰ
35 Up

"Give me a child until he is 7 and I will show you the man."—Jesuit proverb

1991, 128 mins., British, B & W and color, unrated, but suitable for mature children	Andrew
	Charles
Director: Michael Apted	Nick
Unscripted documentary	Jackie
PRINCIPAL FIGURES	Lynn
Paul	Sue
Tony	Symon
Suzy	Neil
Bruce	Peter
John	

In 1964, Michael Apted began filming a group of fourteen British schoolchildren, of all classes and backgrounds, who were seven years old. The students were selected mainly because they interviewed well; that is, they were willing to talk openly about their lives and aspirations. On assignment for Grenada TV, he returned every seven years, at which time he released a filmed report that drew on both old and new footage (thus, the films are entitled "7 Up," "14 Up," "21 Up," and "28 Up"; only the latter is available in video). The result is a unique sociological and human document of change and aging, a longitudinal record of great interest. It must also be the only continuous film record of its kind.

Three of the participants dropped out of the project when they became adults, but the others either enjoyed or accepted the attention of the filmmaker. And even those who dropped out remain in Apted's vision, since each succeeding film draws on footage from the earlier films to show the development of the individuals. In fact, with a shooting ratio of 30:1, Apted in effect had almost sixty hours of "unused" footage after each round that he could draw on in creating his next film. The result is a living psychological "museum" or personal "databank" for each of his subjects from which Apted can make "withdrawals" every seven years.

"35 Up" focuses on all fourteen individuals, but the three who wished to drop out are treated more cursorily: Peter, a teacher who was very critical of British schools seven years earlier, is now preparing to enter law school; upper-class Charles, now a TV producer (and who knows better than to participate in a TV program?!); and Symon (the only black person in the group), who does not participate for reasons of his own.

Those who dropped out clearly have some negative feelings; reviewers have suggested that the recurring publicity may have unnerved them. Most poignant of all, however, is Neil, the happy son of two teachers at the age of seven but depressed at the age of twenty-eight and virtually a homeless drifter at the age of thirty-five. His only ties, to a rural village in the Shetland Islands, are marginal.

Three working-class friends—Jackie, Lynn, and Sue—continued to be a spunky, good-humored, and very mature trio. One of the publicity shots, characteristic of Apted's vision, positions the three friends at the age of thirty-five holding a similar portrait of the three friends at the age of twenty-eight holding still another of them at the age of twenty-one. This cinematic "mirroring" seems especially appropriate for the three women, who—despite the difficulties they may have had over the years—accept themselves, their lives, and their friendships with continued good humor. Their portraits are also evidence of their enthusiastic acceptance of Apted's project.

Similarly, Apted films several of his subjects watching a video of themselves when they were younger. But even more characteristic of Apted's style is his continuous cutting from present to past and back again, as Tony at the age of thirty-five, for example, talks about what has become of his life, giving way to Tony at ages seven and fourteen predicting what he will be when he grows up, and so forth. Sometimes Apted cuts back and forth with as many as fifteen clips at different ages.

If any sociological conclusions about class and labor can be drawn from Apted's series, it is simply that England's class system remains remarkably intact. Working-class Tony, who at the age of seven wants to be a jockey, achieves this goal briefly but becomes a cab driver (and remains one despite a stint as a pub owner). The self-consciously upper-class boys—John, Andrew, and Charles—have gone on to become upper-class adults. At the age of seven, John defended the English "public" (we would say "private") school system: "I don't think it's a bad idea to pay for school, because if we didn't, schools would be so nasty and crowded." John at the age of thirty-five is seen, with his wife, the daughter of an ambassador to Bulgaria, fund-raising for Bulgarian charities.

The exceptions are still worth noting: Neil's homelessness is in a class by itself, but

Nick, from a Yorkshire farming family, graduates from Oxford in physics and becomes a professor at the University of Wisconsin.

Although Apted makes it clear in interviews that the series has dominated his working life, he has nevertheless found time to make well-regarded feature films since he emigrated to Hollywood. "Coal Miner's Daughter," perhaps because of its subject matter, seems to be a remarkably *American* film for a British director to have undertaken. Since the release of "35 Up," Apted has also been a consultant and/or producer on both South African ("7 Up in South Africa," 1992) and Soviet ("Age 7 in the USSR," 1991) projects that are similar to his own.

See also: ["Age 7 in the USSR"]; "Coal Miner's Daughter"; ["7 Up in South Africa"]; ["28 Up"].
Availability: Selected collections.
Further reading: Apted, Michael. "Filming Life, He Found His Own." *New York Times*, 12 Jan. 1992, II.11, 17. Apted's own history of the project.
Canby, Vincent. "Onward, 'Up'-ward with Apted." *New York Times*, 16 Feb. 1992, II.13–14. A detailed review of "35 Up."

To Kill a Priest

... in Poland is a big (political) mistake.

1988, 117 mins., French (but in English), R, but suitable for mature children	Stefan = Ed Harris
Director: Agnieszka Holland	Josef = Peter Postlewaite
Screenplay: Agnieszka Holland and Jean-Yvres Pitoun	Helina = Cheri Lunghi
	Anna = Joanne Whalley
	Igor = Timothy Spall
CAST	Feliks = Tim Roth
Father Alek = Christopher Lambert	The Colonel = Joss Ackland

Having become available on videocassette somewhat belatedly here and having effectively been banned in Poland for years, Agnieszka Holland's portrayal of the brutal murder of Jerzy Popieluszko, a pro-Solidarity priest, has lost a little of its topical punch but none of its political horror. Holland, an exiled Polish filmmaker (known for "Europa Europa," the successful adaptation of the autobiography of a Jewish boy who passed for a Nazi) and a former assistant to Andrzej Wajda, has created a fictional context for the story of Popieluszko: she calls him Father Alex, adds a subplot about his relationship with a woman in Solidarity, and dramatizes his doubts about his calling as a priest.

The core of her story—a priest openly defies the communist government to preach about the virtues of Solidarity and is then murdered in 1984 in what seems to be an almost free-lance operation by a Polish secret policeman—is here intact.

Holland decided to dramatize the life of the secret policeman, played by Ed Harris, as well. The result is a film about a collision course between two fevered spirits, one religious and magnanimous, the other Stalinist and bigoted. Ed Harris's killer is both cold-blooded and ideological. In his practice speech for his show trial, he says that he is "a normal man" who would kill the priest again if it were necessary to "save" his country and his party: "The future is on our side," he concludes. His henchmen are played by Tim Roth and Timothy Spall, who, like so many in this excellent international cast, nonetheless seem to be having their lines spoken about three feet from their heads (most members of the cast are native English speakers, but the film still seems dubbed).

Her film was important, director Holland has argued, in making the somewhat skeptical—and ultimately antireligious—film communities of the West understand the incredible popular following of the Catholic Church in Poland and the importance of the church in the fight for politcal freedom there. Indeed, in the end, the film is a tribute to Catholic Poland's devotion to this priest whom they regard as a martyr to their faith: we see small wayside altars and pictures of the slain man in the traditional ways saints have been honored for centuries. Over the closing scene of a shrine to the priest, Joan Baez is singing her religious folk song, "Crimes of Cain."

Such a tribute to the priest was inevitable. His monthly Mass for the Motherland at St. Stanislaw Kostka Church in Warsaw drew thousands of worshippers in a form of political mass rally. Re-created in the film, the mise-en-scène or look of the mass supports Lawrence Goodwyn's analysis that the Polish church is "so self-consciously the repository of a specific nationhood and . . . links its saints so intimately to the nation's struggle for independence."

See also: ["Europa Europa"] "Man of Marble."

Availability: Selected collections.

Further reading: Goodwyn, Lawrence. *Breaking the Barrier: The Rise of Solidarity.* New York: Oxford University Press, 1991. A very thorough history of the Solidarity movement, with a section on Father Popieluszko's murder and its political implications.

Tagliabue, John. "One Dark Polish Undercurrent Stirs Another." *New York Times,* 15 Dec. 1988, C15. A review and discussion of the film's private premiere in Poland.

Walsh, Brendan. *Poland's Priest Martyr: Jerzy Popieluszko.* London: Catholic Truth Society, 1989. A pamphlet from a London organization that publishes information on Catholic saints and other religious issues; includes a clear and concise history of Solidarity and Popieluszko's life and murder.

⟨∾⟩
To Sleep with Anger

. . . and wake up with the devil

1990, 102 mins., PG
Director: Charles Burnett
Screenplay: Charles Burnett
CAST
Harry Mention = Danny Glover
Gideon = Paul Butler

Sonny = Devaughn Walter Nixon
Junior = Carl Lumbly
Suzie = Mary Alice
Pat = Vonetta McGee
Babe Brother = Richard Brooks
Hattie = Ethel Ayler

Charles Burnett's story of a working-class family in Los Angeles literally bedeviled by an old country friend come to visit sets one of its leading characters on fire in the opening credit sequence: Gideon, dressed to the nines, is sitting stiffly by a table; first the bowl of fruit on the table, then his shoes, and finally his chest all burst into flame. We assume that this is "only a dream," but after Gideon's futile search for his "Toby," or family good-luck charm, and the arrival of old friend Harry Mention, we realize that the devil is literally up to his old tricks again. The credit sequence is therefore virtually a set piece of African-American "magic realism," as Burnett uses Harry as the "trickster" figure from African-American folklore.

The film mixes the heartfelt drama of this extended family and its circle of friends and the mysterious ways of their visitor. When Gideon's grandson accidentally touches Harry with a broom, Gideon spits on it and throws salt over his shoulder; every time Gideon's pregnant daughter-in-law tries to shake Harry's hand, her baby kicks her violently.

Babe Brother resists the family's devotion to hard work. He sarcastically quotes his father's watchwords: "Idleness is sinfulness" and "Calluses and sweat are the mark of a man." Babe Brother wants to get rich quick and is therefore an easy mark for Harry, whose smooth talk reveals a man who has not worked since he was on the railroad gang with Gideon. But Gideon's wife is also frustrated with her husband: "When are you going to fix the roof?!" Burnett seems to be telling a fable here of African-American religion and work, two cornerstones of its working-class ethic.

There is even a nod to William Faulkner's novel *As I Lay Dying*, for, in the end, Harry lies dead in Suzie's kitchen for a day before the morgue sends a truck to pick him up. The family tiptoes around Harry as if he were a monument to a past they wish to forget. At one point they even leave for a picnic their neighbors have been considerate enough to lay on while they are waiting. Harry's power is truly gone when one of Gideon's friends stops in, points to Harry's body with a piece of chicken, and says, "Who is that?"

Harry Mention (Danny Glover) works on a charm in "To Sleep With Anger."

The *New York Times* reviewer (Canby) was impatient with many of the voodoo interpretations of Harry's life and argued that Harry simply represented an "angry and unreconstructed" southern black sharecropper who has been overtaken by the kinds of things Los Angeles folks worry about, such as the midwifery classes Suzie teaches to white and black couples who want to get "in touch with themselves." Maybe. In any case, Harry has a history, and part of that history is lynching (in which he may have played an unpleasant part), work gangs, and sharecropping. That these important subjects are mostly in the background is not to fault this unusual film, Burnett's first with a major budget, but to agree (at least symbolically) with Vincent Canby that there is a lot more story to be told about this family.

See also: "Daughters of the Dust"; "Killer of Sheep."
Availability: Easy.
Further reading: Bates, Karen Grigsby. "'They've Gotta Have Us': Hollywood's Black Directors." *New York Times Magazine,* 14 July 1991, 15–19, 38, 40, 44. Surveys the difficulties in marketing "To Sleep with Anger," as well as films by Spike Lee, Bill Duke, and other black directors.
Canby, Vincent. "To Sleep with Anger." *New York Times,* 5 Oct. 1990, C10. This reviewer found it "a very entertaining, complex film."
Klotman, Phyllis Rauch, ed. *Screenplays of the African American Experience.* Bloomington: Indiana University Press, 1991. Burnett's screenplay for "Killer of Sheep" and a brief biography of the filmmaker.

‌The Triangle Factory Fire Scandal

Perjury and profit, but not on the screen

1979, 100 mins., TVM
Director: Mel Stuart
Screenplay: Mel Brez and Ethel Brez
CAST
Morris Feldman = Tom Bosley
Lou Rubin = David Dukes
Florence = Tovah Feldshuh
Sonya Levin = Lauren Frost
Rose = Janet Margolin
Gina = Stacey Nelkin
Vinnie = Ted Wass

Connie = Stephanie Zimbalist
Bessie = Charlotte Rae
Mrs. Levin = Erica Yohn
Mr. Levin = Milton Selzer
Max Levin = Michael Mullins
Mr. Roselli = Jerome Guardino
Loretta = Valerie Landsburg
Mo Pincus = Larry Gelman
Frieda = Lin Shaye
Edith = Judith-Marie Bergan
Fire Chief = Bart Burns

On 25 March 1911, one of the worst factory fires in history killed 145 employees, mostly young women, in just twenty minutes. The Triangle factory fire was a disaster waiting to happen. It could have happened in any of the other buildings near Washington Square Park in Manhattan or on the Lower East Side where immigrant women (and young girls) made the fashionable and useful shirtwaist, a blouse that became virtually the uniform of the "new women" of the early years of the twentieth century. But it happened in the Asch Building, which, as a voice-of-God narrator tells us at the beginning of the film, was "considered fire-safe."

This disaster and the subsequent scandalous trial certainly deserved better treatment than this underdeveloped fictionalization of the bare bones of the drama. The filmmakers chose to concentrate on three "cute" young ladies and their beaux (or lack of them). Jewish and Italian immigrants are featured, and it seems that—with the exception of the very religious Jews—most of the Lower East Side residents spent their time dancing in the street while their men pitched their love at whatever shirtwaist walked by.

The real scandal of this film is that the "scandal" of the time is literally never mentioned: after the hideous fire, our heroines meet up again in their Easter Sunday finery and instruct the youngest, Gina, on how to smile at the dance they will attend that night. The Jewish factory supervisor, who miraculously escapes with his young daughter on his back on a ladder stretched over ten stories of air between two buildings, decides to visit the Easter parade. (Is this ecumenical visit likely?!) Life must go on. But the trial of the Triangle factory owners occupied the attention and fervor of New Yorkers for months, as a parade of witnesses testified how doors were routinely locked and all safety precautions ignored.

The Triangle Shirtwaist Factory Fire became the tragic symbol of a decade of union organizing among immigrant garment workers. In 1909, the "Uprising of the 20,000," a movement of mostly Italian and Eastern European Jewish workers, had spread from New York City to Chicago and Cleveland, pursuing the demands of the International Ladies' Garment Workers' Union (ILGWU). The movement culminated in a joint demonstration with women in the suffrage movement on 8 March 1909, at which demands were made for better working conditions, an end to child labor, and the right to vote. (The anniversary of this date became International Women's Day.)

Just two years later, more than three hundred thousand marched in the funeral parade for the dead Triangle Shirtwaist Factory women. During the memorial meeting, sponsored by the Ladies Waist and Dressmakers' Union (Local 29 of the ILGWU), speeches were delivered in Yiddish, Italian, and English (the latter by Morris Hillquit, a Socialist Party leader and the general counsel of the union).

The only hint of this activity in the film comes from Lou Rubin, one of the shop engineers (a general fixit man), who speaks glowingly of "Dubinsky" (the ILGWU organizer) and the union. At one point he directs the only collective action of the film: when one woman's production of sleeves falls off, he solicits the women around her to donate some of their piecework to make up her quota: this is the kind of thing, he hints, that will come from unionism. His girlfriend, Rose, who is not so sure of this union business, gets more interested in Dubinsky when another overzealous suitor of hers calls the labor leader "Mr. Buttinsky Dubinsky."

What the film does best is to stage a convincing portrayal of the fire and the difficulty of evacuating the hundreds of women who worked in these sweatshops. As the actual cause of the fire, the film offers a worn lighting connection that eventually caught fire and dropped a piece of burning debris on a bin of fabric. The camera follows the young women as they charge about the top three floors, desperately trying to find a way out. One woman slid down the elevator cable. Others tried to jump onto the life nets held by firemen below. (In real life no one succeeded in this maneuver because they were jumping from too great a height; in the film one Italian-American girl succeeds.) Other women threw themselves from open windows rather than face the fire. In one instance we see a somewhat mysterious man helping the girls take their fateful step out into the air before he disappears: in real life a similar figure took the final step himself as well.

Viewers of this film should read Leon Stein's narrative of the fire and its aftermath, if only to understand the citizens' rage at the owners, reflected in the editorial cartoons of the city's newspapers. Stein reprints several of these cartoons: the *New York Call* pictured the "Real Triangle"—"Rent/Profit/Interest"—while the *Evening Journal* titled its drawing of a woman dead on the sidewalk—"This Is One of a Hundred Murdered: Is Any One to Be Punished for This?"

The answer was "no." The owners were acquitted of negligence, they collected insurance money, and only a union survived to carry the fight—often successfully—for better legislation to protect future shirtwaist workers and their peers in the garment industry.

See also: "Hester Street"; "The Inheritance."

Availability: Selected collections.

Further reading: Crute, Sheree. "The Insurance Scandal behind the Triangle Shirtwaist Fire." *Ms.*, April 1983, 81–83. After computing the insurance profits for the owners, we read a reminiscence by one of the only survivors (a child worker) alive in 1982.

Glenn, Susan A. *Daughter of the Shetl.* Ithaca, N.Y.: Cornell University Press, 1990. An excellent survey of immigrant women workers, with sections on the 1909–10 strike, which included the Triangle Shirtwaist Company.

Malkiel, Theresa Serber. *The Diary of a Shirtwaist Worker.* Ithaca, N.Y.: ILR Press, 1990. A fictionalized diary of a 1909 New York striker.

New York Times. "Many Now Tell of Fire Traps," 29 March 1911, 3; "Triangle Survivors Slide Down [Elevator] Cables," 12 Oct. 1911, 4; "Triangle Witnesses Got Increased Pay," 22 Dec. 1911, 7; "Triangle Owners Acquitted by Jury," 28 Dec. 1911, 1. Sample journalism about the investigation and the trial.

Stein, Leon. *The Triangle Fire.* New York: Carroll and Graf, 1962. Thorough and readable, this is the only definitive narrative account.

∿

Tucker: The Man and His Dream

The Big Three automakers close ranks.

1988, 111 mins., PG
Director: Francis Ford Coppola
Screenplay: Arnold Schulman and David
  Seidler
CAST
Preston Tucker = Jeff Bridges
Abe = Martin Landau

Vera Tucker = Joan Allen
Eddie = Frederic Forrest
Junior = Christian Slater
Jimmy = Mako
Alex = Elias Koteas
Howard Hughes = Dean Stockwell
The Michigan Senator = Lloyd Bridges

Francis Ford Coppola's drive for authenticity and his natural eagerness for publicity probably caused this film more trouble than it could bear. What should have been an exposé of a sordid chapter in American capitalism, when the Big Three automakers colluded with a Michigan senator to keep the safe Tucker cars off the market by conspiring against a competitor, turned into a celebration of American innovation and a maverick soul: a man outside the mainstream fights the big guys and almost wins. He and a few of his mates (mostly engineers and white-collar types; not too many mechanics) manage to build fifty beauties bursting with extras. Although we are talking about the Tucker automobile, too often Coppola wanted people to hear instead "a Coppola film," a tribute to his battle with Big Hollywood.

The result is a fascinating excursion into entrepreneural capitalism in the postwar period, when factories in war production were retooled for civilian use. A survey of returning GIs revealed that what they wanted most was a *car*. Tucker, whose fast (117 mph) tanklike "combat car" and a patented new "power-operated" gun turret were attempts to revolutionize military vehicles, was in an ideal position to satisfy the GIs and carry out his experimental ideas in auto design. He managed to rent the largest demobilized factory in the United States, the Dodge B-29 airplane plant in Chicago. He sold dealerships, floated shares, raised about $28 million, and was ready to turn out prototypes based on his radical auto design, which included a rear engine, fuel injection, seat belts, a safety windshield, and turning headlights.

Coppola follows fairly closely Tucker's story as we know it from other accounts, although occasionally there are lapses into anachronistic foolishness: when Tucker bemoans the lack of support for his innovations, he complains that in the future we may be buying our radios from the very enemy (the Japanese) we just defeated in the war.

Although articles by Lester Velie in *Collier's* and *Reader's Digest* may not have been the direct cause of Tucker's indictment, his lawyers moved that Velie and the editors of both magazines be held in contempt for being "part of a conspiracy to

Entrepreneur Preston Tucker (Jeff Bridges) inspects his primitive assembly line in the film about his life.

cause the whole Tucker venture to fail at any cost." Tucker's motion was based on the huge number of auto ads from the Big Three that these two magazines ran routinely. (Velie also wrote the articles on which "The Garment Jungle" was based seven years later. Hmmm.) Tucker in both real life and Hollywood won an acquittal but lost the war. Like his innovative car, his motion to get even with Velie failed. Most of the fifty Tuckers he built are still road-worthy, and his safety innovations are now routine. Even if Coppola's film romanticizes the way cars could be put together by a handful of idealistic misfits, it is at least a tribute to a great inventor with more than a touch of the P. T. Barnum about him.

See also: "Sometimes a Great Notion."
Availability: Easy.
Further reading: Gross, John. "A Movie That Cannily Celebrates the American Businessman as a Hero." *New York Times*, 4 Sept. 1988, II.33. Pokes fun at Coppola's tendency to make a myth out of Tucker.
Kearney, Jill. "The Road Warrior." *American Film*, June, 1988, 21–27, 52–53. A detailed production history of the film.
New York Times. "Tucker Acquittal Asked by Counsel," 20 Jan. 1950, 40, and "Tucker and Aides Cleared of Fraud," 23 Jan. 1950, 1. News articles that detail the film's hard-to-believe but (mostly) true courtroom ending.
Pearson, Charles T. *The Indomitable Tin Goose: The True Story of Preston Tucker and His Car.* New York: Abelard-Schuman, 1960. An extensive positive account of Tucker's career by an auto magazine writer who worked on Tucker's public relations campaign.
Velie, Lester. "The Fantastic Story of the Tucker Car." *Collier's*, 25 June 1949, 13–15, 68–72. The smear article that prepared the way for Tucker's indictment.

Uncle Tom's Cabin

"Life among the lowly"—Harriet Beecher Stowe

1987, 120 mins., TVM, unrated, but suitable for all ages	Augustine St. Clare = Bruce Dern
	George Harris = Sam Jackson
Director: Stan Lathan	Ophelia = Kate Burton
Screenplay: John Gay, from Harriet Beecher Stowe's novel of the same title	Topsy = Endyia Kinney
	Cassy = Paula Kelly
CAST	Emmeline = Troy Beyer
Uncle Tom = Avery Brooks	Haley = Frank Converse
Eliza = Phylicia Rashad	Little Eva = Jenny Lewis
Simon Legree = Edward Woodward	

Very few novels can be credited with changing public opinion on such a massive scale as Harriet Beecher Stowe's novel about the evils of slavery. The novel began as a serial publication in a small abolitionist magazine in 1851; within a year the demand for the book was so great that the printer had three presses going twenty-four hours a day, three mills to supply the paper, and one hundred bookbinders to keep up the pace of production. Abraham Lincoln, ten years later, supposedly paid Stowe this supreme compliment: "So this is the little lady who made this big war." (Or "So you're the little woman who wrote the book that made this big war." Or . . . !)

Perhaps because of its incredible popularity when it was published and the subsequent passage of so many of its characters into popular culture, the book has never been made into a first-class film. Uncle Tom, the Christian slave who wants to turn the other cheek; Eliza, who makes a daring escape across the ice floes of the Ohio River to safety in free Ohio territory; Simon Legree, the vicious slave overseer; Little Eva, the saintly young white girl who befriends Tom—these are characters who most literate people know so well that they cannot distance themselves from them to judge their life anew on the screen.

The TV mini-series "Roots" has become the standard for representations of slavery since it was first broadcast in 1979. It was also, above all, a historical drama of human endurance, and its success as such may explain why relatively few films have been made about slavery as an institution of work. While emphasizing the economic basis of slavery—especially that slaves were virtually a unit of cash—Stowe also wanted to tell a story with strong legal and religious implications. The Fugitive Slave Act of 1850 made, she believed, the North complicit in the business of slaves, since it mandated the return of escaped slaves to their southern masters even if they should reach free soil in the North. Her novel ends with a warning of the Christian "day of judgment"—the moment of reckoning for a country that holds human souls as chattel.

Stowe was acutely aware of the economic implications of slavery not only for African-Americans but for southern whites. In her "Poor White Trash" chapter of *A Key to Uncle Tom's Cabin*, for example, she outlined, in remarkably modern language, one of the central premises of her novel: "The institution of slavery has accomplished the double feat, in America, not only of degrading and brutalizing her black working classes, but of producing, notwithstanding a fertile soil and abundant room, a poor white population as degraded and brutal as ever existed in any of the most crowded districts of Europe."

Nonetheless, there have been several recent film adaptations of Stowe's novel, two of which are currently available. The African-American director Stan Lathan had adapted James Baldwin's *Go Tell It on the Mountain* in 1984, three years before he turned to *Uncle Tom's Cabin*. With Avery Brooks as a stronger, even more virile Uncle Tom than popular folklore has associated with Stowe's saintly hero, Lathan did not have to apologize for promoting a despised stereotype in an admirable character. Lathan was helped, in another way, by casting Brooks, since he had received good notices for his portrayal of the kidnapped free man Solomon Northup in Gordon Parks, Sr.'s "Half Slave, Half Free" three years before.

Lathan confronted the difficulty of his project, namely, how to adapt a novel that had not been checked out of the library of a black university such as Jackson State in Mississippi for twenty years: "I liked the challenge this production presented: a black man's interpretation of a white woman's interpretation of black reality—a reverse of 'The Color Purple.'"

Tom's progress and decline in the film follow Stowe's prescription for misery. After Eliza's escape to Ohio (not filmed on ice floes because actress Phylicia Rashad was pregnant during the production), Tom is sold to the good but weak St. Clare, whose saintly daughter Eva is the subject of one of the author's sentimental death-bed scenes. (Tom's is the other.) Tom is sold in the film to the vicious slaveholder Simon Legree, whose name, as a synonym for cruelty, has also entered our language, like Tom's and Topsy's ("I spect I growed. Don't think nobody never made me"). It is Legree's beating death of Tom, meek and forgiving to the end, that created (in part) the idea that an "Uncle Tom" is a black person who gives in too easily to whites.

The other version of "Uncle Tom's Cabin" that is currently available is best avoided. It was made in 1970 by what appear to be German or Eastern European filmmakers (the dubbing is awful) who believed that there were Franciscan monasteries in the South to which escaped slaves could go for sanctuary. A concluding voice-over no doubt reflected the filmmakers' frustrations: "Only God fully understands the United States." Amen.

Another version (unavailable) of Stowe's novel was directed by Herbert J. Biberman, who had been blacklisted by Hollywood in 1954 when he did "Salt of the Earth" and was still blacklisted until he made "Slaves" in 1969. In "Slaves"—very loosely adapted from Stowe's material—Ossie Davis plays Luke, who is sold (like Uncle Tom) by a relatively kind master to save the remaining slaves on the farm. Unfortunately for Luke, he is bought by a Simon Legree type from Mississippi.

Biberman wanted a much stronger Tom than Stowe's: Luke and his master's black mistress, Cassy (played by Dionne Warwick in her screen debut), rebel rather than give in and suffer their faith like Christian martyrs. Although the screenwriters should have known better—black novelist John O'Killins and Biberman himself—the dialogue seems to come from the Planet of the Saps when the master says to mistress Cassy: "Disgust makes you look so womanly. It's like a prelude to some man-woman truth."

Stowe's novel was not an economic treatise, but her analysis of slavery went beyond some of the sentimental characters she created. Lathan's film version, at least in some measure, faces that economic issue.

See also: "Half Slave, Half Free."

Availability: Easy.

Further reading: Farber, Stephen. "Cable Service Dusts Off 'Uncle Tom's Cabin' for TV." *New York Times*, 13 June 1987, C50. Despite the incorrect remark that this is the first film of Stowe's novel "in 60 years," this is a favorable review of the production's attempt to retrieve the novel's original message.

Hedrick, Joan D. *Harriet Beecher Stowe: A Life.* New York: Oxford University Press, 1994. The most recent and definitive biography.

O'Connor, John J. "Uncle Tom's Cabin." *New York Times*, 12 June 1987, C30. Another favorable review of the film.

Stowe, Harriet Beecher. *Key to Uncle Tom's Cabin*. 1853. Reprint. Port Washington, N.Y.: Kennikat, 1968. A collection of documents and arguments supporting Stowe's view of slavery as a vicious institution.

———. *Uncle Tom's Cabin* (1851). The NAL Signet paperback has a dated but still helpful afterword about the novel.

Note: The film directed by Stan Lathan is identified by Blockbuster as "Uncle Tom's Cabin—1987—Phylicia Rashad." The other version, identified as "Uncle Tom's Cabin—1970—Herbert Lom," is the one to avoid, especially since the package promises that Eartha Kitt (who is *not* in the film) is in the cast. (Lom plays Simon Legree.)

Union Maids

"For it's great to fight for freedom
With a Rebel Girl."—Joe Hill

1976, 48 mins., unrated, but suitable for all ages
Directors: Julia Reichert, Jim Klein, and Miles Mogulesco
Scripted documentary, based on Alice and

Staughton Lynd's *Rank and File: Personal Histories by Working-Class Organizers*
PRINCIPAL UNION MAIDS
Stella Nowicki
Kate Hyndman
Sylvia Woods

The three "union maids" featured in this film had long and active careers as union organizers and proponents of radical change: from Alice and Staughton Lynd's source book, we learn that two of the three (Stella and Kate) were openly Reds, but in the film only Kate's communist affiliation is suggested ("Gary Woman Called Red," is one headline we see about her). (Kate, for reasons never directly explained in the book or the film, goes by another name in the Lynds' book: Christine Ellis.) Most of the women's reminiscences come from the 1930s, when Reds and other radicals formed a solid contingent in the organizing committees of the CIO. But almost all of the women's activity was on the grass-roots level: Kate, for example, helped organize among the unemployed in Chicago, concentrating on resisting evictions.

The pace of the film is leisurely, gradually gaining in intensity, as the filmmakers cut back and forth among the three women, interviewing them about their backgrounds, experiences, and opinions. Kate came to work in the Chicago stockyards from a farm in Michigan, where she said she knew that if she remained she would have been just a cook and servant to the men. Stella, whose father was a (Marcus) Garveyite, also worked in the Chicago stockyards. Sylvia, originally from New Orleans, helped organize black and white workers in a large commercial laundry in Chicago.

In almost every instance, the interviewers (who are, for the most part, disembodied voices off camera) lead their subjects to explain the sources of their radicalism. Kate, a veteran of numerous dangerous eviction protests, says: "I have no regrets. I feel there was a purpose in my life." Her brand of socialism tells her to "let the people decide." Stella believes that "we made a lot of changes." And Sylvia sees her continued radicalism in joining the "women's movement," although she has some impatience with those in the movement who cannot relate to *working* women.

"Union Maids" is one of the pioneering efforts in labor and women's history documentaries. It has a few creaky moments—a little too much nonlabor historical footage, for example—but it still packs an occasional visual punch, as in its footage of black laundry workers fighting policemen in Chicago. Using the interview style Studs Terkel perfected in *Working*, the Lynds created a very commendable book; as a visual development of the Lynds' book, the film rightly celebrates the special role and pluck of these "union maids."

See also: "With Babies and Banners."
Availability: Selected collections; ILR Media; New Day Films.
Further reading: Lynd, Alice, and Staughton Lynd. *Rank and File: Personal Histories by Working-Class Organizers.* Boston: Beacon, 1973. Includes oral histories by other organizers, plus more details on the lives of the women featured in the film.
Rosenthal, Alan. *The Documentary Conscience.* Berkeley: University of California Press, 1980. Contains a detailed interview with the filmmakers.

❧

The Valley of Decision

To invest or not to invest

1945, 111 mins., B & W, unrated, but suitable for all ages
Director: Tay Garnett
Screenplay: John Meehan and Sonya Levine, from Marcia Davenport's novel of the same title
CAST
Mary Rafferty = Greer Garson
Paul Scott = Gregory Peck
William Scott = Donald Crisp

Pat Rafferty = Lionel Barrymore
Jim Brennan = Preston Foster
Constance Scott = Marsha Hunt
Clarissa Scott = Gladys Cooper
McCready = Reginald Owen
William Scott, Jr. = Dan Duryea
Louise Kane = Jessica Tandy
Delia = Barbara Everest
Ted Scott = Marshall Thompson

If ever there was a "Gone with the Wind" of Pittsburgh steel, "The Valley of Decision" was it. Instead of antebellum plantations, we have the post–Civil War industrializing North. Perhaps thankfully, however, only the first section (approximately one-third) of Marcia Davenport's extremely popular novel, tracing seventy years of an iron and steel family dynasty, was filmed. Whether this was a practical or a political decision is unclear: the film handles only one major episode—a strike at the mill in 1877, the year of incredible labor unrest throughout the United States—and since it includes nothing after the 1870s, we are deprived, for example, of the filmmakers' version of the development of the CIO's Steel Organizing Committee (which Davenport somewhat lightly but positively describes at the end of her eight hundred–page novel).

By focusing on only one major labor-management conflict, the film conveniently finesses most of the novel's description of the class conflicts and the tremendous disparity of wealth between mill owner and workers (not to mention servants), and we end up not too many flights above a Cinderella story (a fact the *New York Times* reviewer noted with some disdain). In this instance, Cinderella is Mary Rafferty, played by Greer Garson as a remarkable Irish-American servant girl, whose good sense and moral stamina help to protect the English mill-owning family she serves.

Cinderella does, however, have a family of her own—a widowed sister (with a baby) and an angry father in a wheelchair, who holds Mary's master responsible for his crippled and useless legs. Although Lionel Barrymore plays Mary's father as a sputtering fountain of venom, there is at least some truth in what he says: it was inevitable that workers who were exhausted by twelve-hour shifts would be maimed in accidents. (Davenport's novel provides a rationale for the twelve-hour shifts both in the process of nineteenth-century iron-making and the wage structure that the men favored; since we are very rarely even near any workers or furnaces in the film, the viewer is never provided such information.)

At least the film is true to the melodrama that was Davenport's conception. Mary and Paul Scott, the owner's son, fall in love and try to broker a truce between the workers and the company. Jim Brennan, another one of Mary's beaus, is both an innovative worker (and even Paul's friend) and the union's spokesman. Both labor and management agree to meet on a bridge that connects the public path and company property. But tragedy strikes, and Mary's father—believing that the company has broken its word about importing scabs and thugs—shoots Mary's potential father-in-law, the family patriarch.

Contemporary viewers will see these characters on both sides of the class struggle as pitching more woo than iron. The film would have driven most sensitive people back to the novel, although Davenport would hardly have satisfied most of them. Davenport's William Scott is a mill owner of the old school: "Strike! . . . They'd never dare."

Davenport's career was at least as melodramatic as parts of her epic. In 1948, she was more or less engaged to Jan Masaryk, the foreign minister of the Edvard Benes government of Czechoslovakia, then under intense pressure from communists within and Stalinists without to enter the Soviet sphere of influence as a communist nation. Although it is likely, Davenport argues, that Masaryk would have tried to serve in the new communist state, he was murdered by hands unknown just a short time before he was to marry Davenport. The official story was that he committed suicide. Although Davenport kept her silence about this incident for thirty years, she did include a Czechoslovakian subplot in her novel: the "Hunkies" begin to replace the Irish-Americans as the most exploited class in the Pittsburgh area.

Davenport also revealed in her autobiography that much of her research for her novel was accomplished through her first husband's association as managing editor with *Fortune* magazine and by "constantly meeting industrialists and men of business big and small, whom he brought to our house." Despite her husband's contact with Philip Murray and other "labor statesmen of Big Steel," her interest—as the film captures—was usually focused on Big Investors.

The film ends with an impossible scenario that Davenport pursues for the last two-thirds of the novel: Mary and Paul cannot marry because of their class differences and the inconvenient fact that *her* father (brother in the novel) killed Paul's father, but they are obviously eternally in love. Paul throws his wife of convenience (played scathingly by Jessica Tandy in one of her earliest roles) out of his house and trots off with Mary into the remarkably unsmoky Pittsburgh sunset in a carriage for two. The End. But we are never told what could possibly happen next. And we certainly never find out if the union comes to stay in the Old Man's mill.

Once the decision was made to cast Greer Garson as Mary Rafferty, it was inevitable that Garson, who had already charmed her way through such one-woman triumphs as "Mrs. Miniver" (coping with World War II) and "Madame Curie" (coping with radioactivity), would straighten out the twists and turns of the difficult life of Davenport's original heroine.

See also: "The Molly Maguires."
Availability: Selected collections.
Further reading: Crowther, Bosley. "The Valley of Decision." *New York Times*, 4 May 1945, 23. "Miss Davenport's fine American saga is barely perceived in this film, produced most extravangantly by Metro. But there is here a full romantic show."
Davenport, Marcia. *Too Strong for Fantasy*. New York: Scribner's, 1967. Although she declares herself content with the "faithful and gripping representation of the third of the book which had been used," Davenport does not discuss in this autobiography the significant changes in the film adaptation of her best-selling novel.

∿
Viva Zapata!

Viva Anthony Quinn!

1952, 113 mins., unrated, but suitable for all
  ages
Director: Elia Kazan
Screenplay: John Steinbeck, from his (then-
  unpublished) biography "Zapata"
CAST
Emiliano Zapata = Marlon Brando

Josefa = Jean Peters
Euphemio = Anthony Quinn
Fernando = Joseph Wiseman
Pancho Villa = Alan Reed
Madero = Harold Gordon
Pablo = Lou Gilbert
Huerta = Frank Silvera

The state of Morales lies south of Mexico City; at the turn of the century, it had a rich and moderately diverse farming culture. As big landowners had success growing and selling sugar cane, the peasant farming villages were taken over, without regard to right or custom. When "Viva Zapata!" opens, such a moment has occurred, and the peasants are petitioning their president to intervene against the landowners. When the peasants try to verify their ancient property markers, they are attacked by federal troops. Only Zapata, his brother, and a growing band of rebel outlaws are willing to fight for the peasants.

John Steinbeck wrote the screenplay for "Viva Zapata!" from a biographical study he had done of the peasant revolutionary leader. Steinbeck had been a journalist in the 1930s in California, and he drew on that experience in his two great Depression novels, *In Dubious Battle* and *The Grapes of Wrath*. He had also written a successful film for Alfred Hitchcock, "Lifeboat," which at the very least may be described as an anti-Nazi drama with some unusual ethical twists.

The director of "Viva Zapata!" was Elia Kazan, who had been a radical in the 1930s and 1940s but named former associates as communists in front of the House Un-American Activities Committee during the McCarthy era. Before "Viva Zapata!" Kazan had directed several excellent films: "Pinky" in 1949, about a young black woman who passes for white; "Panic in the Streets" in 1950, about a pneumonic plague outbreak (similar to the one in India in 1994) and underworld crime in New Orleans (an underrated film); and an adaptation of Tennessee Williams's play "A Streetcar Named Desire" in 1952. After "Viva Zapata!" Kazan filmed "On the Waterfront," the controversial story of union gangsterism on the New Jersey docks. What characterizes Kazan's work in all these films is the nitty-gritty realism, the believable portrayal of working-class life, the touch of sensationalism, and certainly the political sensibility.

"Viva Zapata!" is in many ways a simple celebration and romanticized view of a great Mexican peasant revolutionary. Zapata and his primitive leadership are the heart of the film. His refusal to become dictator (or whatever you want to call it) and the portrayal of his adviser, Fernando, are the most controversial parts of the film, but even whether Zapata was the leader of the peasant revolt from 1909 to 1919 in one province against President Porfirio Díaz has occasionally been challenged. The addition of the fictitious character Fernando has made purely historical judgments of the film difficult if not unnecessary. Equally difficult to assess are the characters Eufemio, Zapata's brother, who betrays the revolution after he has become degenerate, and Pablo, Zapata's sidekick, who betrays him and is executed. The story of the Mexican Revolution is so complex that the Madero who was so weak in the film did not, in real life, support Zapata at first but conspired against him with General Huerta.

Kazan and Steinbeck were criticized for making Fernando too obviously a conniving communist organizer. He certainly does capture the unfeeling zombie or "Invasion of the Body Snatchers" pod look popular among actors portraying communists in the anticommunist films of the 1950s. Kazan and Steinbeck intended, Kazan said, not to create a communist but a person with "a communist mentality," an organizer who seeks power for its own sake. Zapata, as apolitical as he was, according to their interpretation, turns away from power because he knows that power corrupts. Interestingly, Steinbeck wanted to re-release the film in 1963 with "publicity about Cuba." Whether Castro and his brother were to be the Zapatas or whether Castro was going to be Fernando, Steinbeck did not say.

Steinbeck did extensive research on and interviews with Zapata and members of his movement. In a prescreenplay biographical study ("Zapata, the Little Tiger"), which is more than three hundred pages long, he presented a Zapata with more personal contradictions than the film's final hero. He discovered, for example, evidence that established that Zapata was married to Josepha, the character who was later transformed into a middle-class but obedient spouse played by Jean Peters. Steinbeck's interviews with Zapatistas who fought in the Mexican Revolution were conducted in 1945, twenty-six years after Zapata was assassinated.

See also: "The Grapes of Wrath"; "Macario"; ["Panic in the Streets"]; ["Pinky"].
Availability: Easy.
Further reading: Biskind, Peter, and Dan Georgakas. "'Viva Zapata!': Pro and Con." *Cineaste* 7.2 (1976): 10–17. The never-ending debate on the film's message—reactionary or revolutionary?
DePalma, Anthony. "In a Rebel Cry, Zapata Rides Again." *New York Times*, 27 Jan. 1994, A4. The ongoing legend inspires 1990s rebels.
Hobson, Laura Z. "Trade Winds." *Saturday Review*, 1 March 1952, 6. A survey of the controversy about the film.
Kazan, Elia. "Letters to the Editor." *Saturday Review*, 5 April 1952, 22; 24 May 1952, 25 and 28. Kazan replies (twice) to his critics.

Steinbeck, John. *Viva Zapata!* New York: Viking, 1975. The final screenplay, with an essay by Robert Morsberger.

——. *Zapata.* Edited by Robert Morsberger. New York: Penguin, 1993. For many years unpublished, this is Steinbeck's biography (with the first screenplay), researched in Mexico in the 1940s.

Vanderwood, Paul J. "An American Cold Warrior: 'Viva Zapata!'" In *American History/American Film: Interpreting Hollywood Images.* Edited by John E. O'Connor and Martin A. Jackson, 183–201. New York: Ungar, 1979. The film "wrestles in an entertaining and provocative way with the contradictions and conservatism of the rebellion."

Womack, John. *Zapata and the Mexican Revolution.* New York: Knopf, 1969. A good general biography.

ᐷ
Wall Street

"If you're not inside, you're outside."—Gordon Gekko

1987, 124 mins., R
Director: Oliver Stone
Screenplay: Oliver Stone and Stanley Weiser
CAST
Bud Fox = Charlie Sheen
Carl Fox = Martin Sheen

Gordon Gekko = Michael Douglas
Darian Taylor = Darryl Hannah
Lou Mannheim = Hal Holbrook
Sir Harry Wildman = Terence Stamp
Kate Gekko = Sean Young

Although the Ivan Boesky "insider trading" scandals of Wall Street and Eastern Airline's battle between Frank Lorenzo and the International Association of Machinists (IAM) in the 1980s would be two good reasons to watch Oliver Stone's version of the Reagan years, the real reason most people watch the film is to see the greedy antics of the leading trader, Gordon Gekko, played to perfection by Michael Douglas and named, appropriately, after a lizard (although the gecko is not as scary as it looks). Gekko, as one character says, received an "ethical bypass at birth." He clearly loves money, but the ruthless pursuit of money excites him even more. That Gekko is like an unstoppable male beast in rut is clearly Stone's metaphorical intention. Thus, the first time we see and hear Gekko, he is on the phone making a deal and tells his stand-in on the phone, "Raise the sperm count of the deal!" When he is asked to meet for a meal, he replies: "Lunch? You got to be kidding! Lunch is for women."

Douglas's performance as Gekko reaches a high point at the stockholders' meeting of the Geldar Paper Corporation, which Gekko is trying to raid. He makes his now-legendary "greed is good" speech at this meeting and attacks the thirty-three vice presidents on the dais as do-nothings with dubious job descriptions. Management, not Wall Street, he tells the stockholders, is the real enemy: "I am not a destroyer of companies. I am a liberator of them." That his lies seem to work for such a long time—he basically wants to hold on to a company only long enough to loot its cash assets and sell off anything that is left—is part of his attraction to other Wall Street hustlers.

The film takes its plot line from two key events of the 1980s: the struggle between Eastern Airlines and the IAM and, more resolutely, the "insider" trading scandals, typified by Ivan Boesky. In the film Gekko apprentice Bud uses insider information on Blue Star Airlines that he receives from his father, the head of the airline's maintenance union. Gekko deceives Bud into thinking that the airline will be allowed to survive. But Bud knows better and to save the company, he wages a secret war against Gekko by forming an alliance of the pilots and flight attendants organizations, his father's union, and one of Gekko's chief rivals. Instead of a "garage sale at Blue Star," the company survives (unlike Eastern Airlines, we might add).

"Wall Street" is a fable primarily because a potentially good guy realizes the error of his ways and uses a stock war between Wall Street velociraptors for a noble end. (Bud's parallel in real life, Boesky's apprentice crook, Martin Siegel, was also wired to trap others, but he had no altruistic goals.) Clearly Stone has a point here: the deals at the top can make or break the people on the bottom. Boesky did get caught; Gekko is captured on tape incriminating himself. But Eastern Airlines is long gone, and so are millions of dollars past accounting.

See also: "Collision Course"; "Working Girl."
Availability: Easy.
Further reading: Canby, Vincent. "Greed." *New York Times*, 11 Dec. 1987, C3. A mixed review that you have to love because he writes that Darryl Hannah "has the screen presence of a giant throw pillow."
Robinson, Jack E. *Freefall: The Needless Destruction of Eastern Air Lines and the Valiant Struggle to Save It*. New York: Harper Business, 1992. Discusses Lorenzo and the unions that squared off against him (the pilots, the flight attendants, and the machinists).
Stewart, James B. *Den of Thieves*. New York: Simon and Schuster, 1991. A detailed narrative account of Boesky and his fellow "inside trading" swindlers.

Waterfront

Struggles on the docks "down under"

1983, 294 mins., unrated, but suitable for all ages
Director: Chris Thomson
Screenplay: Mac Gudgeon.

CAST
Anna Chieri = Greta Scacchi
Maxey Woodbury = Jack Thompson
Laughing Les = Warren Mitchell

Maggie = Noni Hazelhurst
Sam Elliot = Ray Barrett
Ernie Donaldson = Chris Haywood
Davo = Jay Mannering
Vera Donaldson = Elin Jenkins
Paddy Ryan = Frank Gallacher
Sheila Ryan = Jan Friedl

Llan Williams = Mark Little
Snowy Williams = Tony Rickards
Karry Geahry = Ted Hepple
Giorgio = Joe Spano
Inspector Legge = Wynn Roberts
Premier Hogan = Bruce Mytes
Sir Wiliam McPherson = Tony Hawkins

Those seeking an Australian equivalent to "On the Waterfront" will probably be disappointed by this epic evocation of waterfront life in the port city of Melbourne in the 1930s. "Waterfront" tries to do so much more than the American film, but it doesn't always rise above operatic "Gone with the Wind" histrionics.

The centerpiece of the film is a long strike, led for the most part by the "wharfies," white union men who must walk a thin line between the suffering of the strikers and the rising collusion of management and the fascists. Complicating matters are a partly corrupt leadership who have gangster ties, the Italian immigrants willing to take scab jobs to survive in their new world, and the occasional communist activist who wants to set the course on a more political keel. Mix this with the story of a stunning Italian immigrant (Greta Scacchi) and a reluctant rank-and-file leader (Jack Thompson, who played the lawyer for soldiers being rail-roaded in the Australian film "Breaker Morant") and you have an Australian mini-series.

While the love affair between "Eye-talian" immigrant Anna and "wharfie" Maxey is inevitably soap operish, a significant subplot is the relationship of the Italian antifascist immigrants to their new home. Anna, whose husband and brother were murdered by Mussolini's thugs, and her father, Professor Chieri, keep up the revolutionary spirit as best they can. Anna sings the "Internationale" at a Matteotti Club meeting. (Italian Socialist Party leader Giacomo Matteotti was murdered by the fascists in 1924 when all opposition parties were banned.) It's all the more pressing, then, for Maxey to convince the Italians not to participate in management's scab labor scheme.

A rising national fascist movement, the White Guards, creates havoc for management, making it virtually impossible for the union to survive. But the left-wingers in the union can't convince Maxey that a revolution is possible: "Revolution in this country? You'd have to advertise in the sports pages!" But Maxey does learn some ancient wisdom of political organizing when Anna's father lends him Machiavelli for some serious study. Unfortunately, Maxey's union mentor has had some criminal ties, and all of these political and social forces prove too much for Maxey in the end and he is murdered. His new girlfriend has to leave as well, for the union's power has been effectively broken. Its allies in the Labor government, its own muscle, and its leadership are not enough to defeat the reactionary forces.

See also: "1900"; "On the Waterfront."

Availability: Selected collections.

Further reading: Murray, Scott. *Australian Film, 1978–1992.* New York: Oxford University Press, 1993. Reviews other films by the director but not "Waterfront."

Note: This is not listed in most standard video guides, probably because "Waterfront" was first screened in Australia as a TV mini-series; it is available in some Blockbusters.

We Dig Coal: A Portrait of Three Women

Mining can "seep in your soul."—Merle Travis

1982: 58 mins., unrated, but suitable for all ages

Directors: Thomas C. Goodwin, Dorothy McGhee, and Gerardine Wurzburg

Documentary

PRINCIPAL FIGURES

Marilyn McCusker, coal miner

Alan McCusker, her husband

Bernice Dombroski, coal miner

Mary Louise Carson, coal miner

Harry and Jane Koptchik, coal miner and his wife

Dorothy McGhee, interviewer (off-screen)

This film highlights three women who were hired as miners by the Rushton Mining Company of Pennsylvania in 1977. The film focuses especially on Marilyn McCusker, whose two-year effort and sex discrimination suit in a federal court finally brought her employment as a deep miner. McCusker worked just two years until she became the first (known) woman to die inside a deep mine; while installing roof bolts, a twenty-by-sixteen-by-three-foot piece of shale fell on her.

McCusker's life and death highlighted safety issues in the mines as well as the hidden history of women workers underground. Research has revealed (Franklin) that women worked in coal mines during World War II and in family-owned mines at other times. When women were finally hired as a result of McCusker's suit, they often found themselves in a new kind of bind: foremen assigned them to unpleasant and dangerous jobs, hoping they would quit or, failing that, would "prove" themselves—as women—to be prone to injuries.

This may in fact have been McCusker's fate, as some comments (not included in the film) from the Rushton Company safety director suggest: "She would have been ten steps away" (Serrin) from the roof slate that killed her if she had been a man, that is, an experienced male miner. In fact, the man she was working with did successfully run to safety.

Since Marilyn McCusker was not alive when the film was made, her husband tells a good deal of her story. Bernice Dombroski and Mary Louise Carson tell their own stories. When Carson's husband was diagnosed with emphysema and had to leave the mines, she left her relatively low-paying job in a sewing factory to "take his

Bernice Dombroski, one of the coalminers profiled in "We Dig Coal."
Courtesy the Cinema Guild, Inc.

place." Both women report much harassment—such as having rocks thrown at them underground—but both agree with Carson's remark that "the only way to get me out is to carry me out."

By the time this film was made, 3,000 women had become miners, compared with 150,000 men. The two other subjects of this documentary, Dombroski and Carson, were still working in the mines when the film was released. In 1977, 144 miners died underground: Marilyn McCusker was the only woman.

The film doesn't cover the subsequent legal problems of McCusker's survivors. After her death, McCusker's husband and son received survivors' benefits, despite a Pennsylvania state law that guaranteed benefits for widows but not widowers. (Rushton Mining agreed to pay the benefits on the eve of a scheduled workers' compensation hearing two months after she died.)

See also: "Coalmining Women"; "Moving Mountains"; "Wildrose."
Availability: Selected collections; Cinema Guild.
Further reading: Franklin, Ben A. "Women Who Work in Mines Assail Harassment and Unsafe

Conditions." *New York Times*, 11 Nov. 1979, 30. A report on the first UMWA conference on women miners.

O'Connor, John J. "TV Weekend." *New York Times*, 2 July 1982, C21. A brief but positive review of the film.

Serrin, William. "One Fight for Women's Rights: A Coal Miner's Life and Death." *New York Times*, 8 Nov. 1979, A1, A16. An extensive profile of Marilyn McCusker.

∽
Where the Green Ants Dream

. . . the ground glows.

1984, 99 mins., German-Australian (but in English), R (but not really)
Director: Werner Herzog
Screenplay: Werner Herzog and Bob Ellis
CAST
Lance Hackett = Bruce Spence
Miliritbi = Wandjuk Marika
Dayipu = Roy Marika
Cole = Ray Barrett
Baldwin Ferguson = Norman Kaye

Miss Strehlow = Colleen Clifford
Fletcher = Ralph Cotterill
Arnold = Nicolas Lathouris
Blackburn = Basil Clarke
Coulthard = Ray Marshall
Malila = Dhungula I. Marika
Watson = Gary Williams
Fitzsimmons = Tony Llewellyn-Jones
Daisy Barunga = Marraru Wunungmurra

Uranium deposits underground and a group of Aborigines aboveground occupy the same desolate Australian outback, in this case, a desert landscape pockmarked and mounded with test drillings. Radioactive energy and aboriginal cosmic force are somehow equated in this film, but similar things can be said about many if not all of the films of Werner Herzog, whose roots are German but who has become a world-traveling filmmaker. Something is always behind something else, but the director has chosen to make it difficult for us to find out what (as in real life, he would say).

Lest I sound too philistine, there are many Herzog fans, some of whom have seen his films (such as the Amazonian opera, "Fitzcarraldo") numerous times. There is the soul of a proletarian sympathizer in Herzog trying to get out: his "Heart of Glass" was an intimate, boring, and detailed look at a legendary glass factory. His short films—usually not readily available—combine his political interests and exotic tastes with remote and difficult subjects—the Nicaraguan Miskito Indians fighting against the Sandinistas or mountain climbers in Pakistan.

Herzog moved a little closer to mainstream narrative film here by offering a familiar story: a mining company that "owns" the minerals belowground confronts the locals who choose to resist the encroachment. It is a story still being played out in Eastern Kentucky coal fields and on Navajo tribal lands. The dialogue, in Australian English and translated Aborigine language(s), makes the drama seem a little more exotic to American ears, of course, but Herzog reduces some of this difficulty by casting as a sympathetic mining engineer the popular Australian actor Bruce Spence, who almost stole the "Road Warrior" films with his snakes and homemade helicopter.

The title of Herzog's film refers to the Aborigine belief that each of their clans has an animal or totemic ancestor closely identified with specific sites. That animal's song and message are essential for the well-being of the clan. Bruce Chatwin's *The Songlines* sums up this belief thus: "The song and the land are one." Breaking up the land, as the ATCO mining company does in the film by blowing test holes, therefore, actively destroys the "songlines." These songlines are, of course, invisible to the non-Aborigine eye, and only one visible record of them can exist—a sacred barklike cylinder with marks that represent the wandering of the clan's dreamtime ancestors. In a sense this is the clan's land deed, since it marks their territory, "owned" collectively.

Unfortunately for the Aborigines, no uninitiated person is allowed to view this sacred object. Thus, when the Aborigines go to court to prevent ATCO from mining their land, they are doubly defeated: first, they have to violate their own laws by allowing the judge to look at their object, and, second, he can neither "read" it nor understand it. Their only victory—and it clearly is a small one—is the conversion of the mining engineer to their cause.

See also: ["Heart of Glass"].

Availability: Selected collections.

Further reading: Canby, Vincent. "Film: Two Short Works by Herzog." *New York Times*, 3 April 1985, C23. Discusses Herzog's maverick politics and short films.

——. "A Stand Down Under." *New York Times*, 8 Feb. 1985, C8. A brief but helpful review.

Chatwin, Bruce. *The Songlines*. New York: Viking, 1987. Essential reading for Herzog's film, as it clarifies the belief system Herzog doesn't always explain.

Murray, Scott. *Australian Film, 1978–1992*. New York: Oxford University Press, 1993. A review of the film—"an overseas director has come to make a film Australians should have."

∾
The Whistle at Eaton Falls

It blows for us.

1951, 96 mins., unrated, but suitable for mature childen
Director: Robert Siodmak
Screenplay: Lemist Elder and Virginia Shaler
CAST
Brad Adams = Lloyd Bridges

Mrs. Doubleday = Dorothy Gish
Eddie Talbot = Charleton Carpenter
Al Webster = Murray Hamilton
Joe London = James Westerfield
Abby = Lenore Lonergan
Bill Street = Ernest Borgnine

The pitch of this film may seem somewhat askew since it combined the talents of Robert Siodmak, a director known for his dark gangster films (such as the 1949 film-noir classic "Criss Cross"), and Louis de Rochemont, a producer known for his documentaries (the famous "March of Time" newsreels, which accompanied double features throughout the 1930s and 1940s). We end up with a semidocumentary feature, shot on location in a New England mill town with real mill workers as extras and the possible but unlikely elevation of a union leader from the rank and file to the presidency of the old mill when its owner—one of the grand matriarchs of Hollywood (Dorothy Gish)—dies.

Brad Adams is the ex-union leader who is forced to lay off his old coworkers and friends, first by instituting part-time work and then by totally shutting down the plant. Both labor and management (ex-labor!) become too cranky to reconcile. When it seems that unending unemployment is the only option for the future, a miracle happens: a new gadget, to be manufactured on labor-saving machines, brings all the workers back on three round-the-clock shifts.

De Rochemont's choice of a topic was not unusual, for his "March of Time" newsreels never backed away from controversial topics. He had more recently taken on another American "problem" film, "Lost Boundaries," in which a light-skinned black doctor (played by Mel Ferrer) and his family are challenged in numerous ways as they try to "pass" in a small New Hampshire town. Robert Siodmak was an odder choice, perhaps, for the film-noir director knew more about how to frame an innocent man ("Phantom Lady" in 1944) than how to portray the unemployed. The *New York Times* reviewer, Bosley Crowther, was fair: "It is no reflection upon [de Rochemont's] good intentions or his social integrity to observe that this overheated discourse on the relations of labor and management leaves much to be desired."

In another (perhaps more speculative) sense, de Rochemont's production of "The Whistle at Eaton Falls" was a harbinger of the cinematic link that would be made between semidocumentary realism and gangster-associated unionism. De Rochemont had already produced two successful spy films at the end of the 1940s ("The House on 92nd Street" and "13 Rue Madeleine"), both "based on the files of the F.B.I." Hollywood did not have to reach very far when it came time to make such films as "The Garment Jungle" and "On the Waterfront" in the 1950s. Both of these films also show aspects of the distinctive film-noir style, evident in such startling touches in "On the Waterfront" as the shot of the dead body of Terry Malloy's brother (Charley the Gent) suspended from a longshoreman's hook in a shadowy alley.

See also: "The Garment Jungle"; "On the Waterfront."
Availability: Not currently available.
Further reading: Crowther, Bosley. "'Whistle at Eaton Falls' Depicts Management-Labor Problems." *New York Times*, 11 Oct. 1951, 49. A contemporary review.

Elson, Robert T. *Time, Inc.: The Intimate History of a Publishing Empire, 1923–1941.* New York: Atheneum, 1968. Includes a survey of de Rochemont's "March of Time" series for the Luce news empire.

~

Who Killed Vincent Chin?

The killing of the American dream

1989, 82 mins., unrated, but suitable for all ages
Director: Christine Choy and Renee Tajima
Scripted documentary
PRINCIPAL FIGURES
Vincent Chin, Chinese-American engineer
Lily Chin, his mother
Helen Zia, leader of American Citizens for Justice
Ron Ebens, unemployed Chrysler Motors superintendent
Nita Ebens, former autoworker; Ebens's wife
Rich Wagner, Ebens's friend
Michael Nitz, unemployed Chrysler Motors worker (Ebens's stepson)
Frank Eamon, attorney for Ebens
Michael Gardenhire and Morris Cotton, Highland Park police officers
Racine Colwell, Fancy Pants Club waitress
Starlene, Fancy Pants Club dancer
Charles Kaufman, Wayne County circuit judge

Vincent Chin, a twenty-seven-year-old Chinese-American man, was celebrating his "bachelor party" at a Detroit bar on 19 June 1982 when Ron Ebens, a foreman from Chrysler Motors, and his stepson, Michael Nitz, apparently mistook Chin for a Japanese or Japanese-American. Ebens made some ethnic slurs, and a fight broke out. The fight continued outside the bar, but Chin and his friends escaped to a nearby McDonalds, where Ebens and Nitz caught up with them and beat Chin to death with a baseball bat. A series of trials followed, in which Detroit Asian-Americans, led by Chin's mother, fought to vindicate her son's death.

Ebens and Nitz plea-bargained and had their charge reduced from murder to manslaughter. They were sentenced to serve fifteen years in jail, but the sentence was suspended and they were given three years on probation and fined $3,780, certainly a lenient sentence by any standards. The sentence was so lenient, in fact, that the men spent only one night in jail (the night of their arrest), although Ebens complained bitterly about that.

The indignation of the Asian-American community led to the creation of the organization American Citizens for Justice, which pressured the Justice Department to indict the two men for federal civil rights violations. In June 1984, a jury of the U.S. district court in Detroit acquitted Nitz but sentenced Ebens to twenty-five years in jail. Ebens appealed, and in a new trial in Cincinnati, Ohio, in 1987, he was acquitted. The film offers a regional interpretation for his acquittal: jurors in a conservative city like Cincinnati knew nothing of the auto industry in Detroit or had any experience with hostility to Asian-Americans.

The filmmakers (in PBS "Point of View" interviews, which are part of the Indiana University videocassette release) suggest that their intention was to present numerous points of view as Akira Kurosawa did in the Japanese classic fiction film "Rashomon," in which the principal characters and an eyewitness narrate conflicting versions of a crime. Most viewers will find, however, that the filmmakers "believe" some of their "witnesses" more than others. Ebens, who admits to beating Chin to death but believes it "could happen to anyone," denies that he ever said these fighting words to Chin as they sat opposite each other at the topless dance club: "It's because of you little mother——s that we're out of work!" (Racine Colwell, a waitress at the club, testified he did.)

Vincent Chin's tragedy is therefore seen as part of the gradual collapse of some elements of the Michigan auto industry, under heavy and successful competition from Japanese car companies. The filmmakers portray a city under siege—a hunger emergency was declared in 1982 by the mayor—and a region looking for scapegoats: shots of foreign-car sledge-hammer bashes at malls suggest a rising surge of anger and violence in the community. The filmmakers also suggest that the clash of white blue-collar workers and those they perceived to be "stealing" their jobs is compounded because some Americans have "difficulty" distinguishing one hyphenated Asian-American from another.

Before the first civil rights trial in March 1984, Jesse Jackson spoke to American Citizens for Justice: "Perhaps it would have been a fairer trial if all the politicians, all the corporate executives, the union leaders, and the journalists who have told the American people to 'blame it on the Japanese' had stood trial with those two autoworkers" (Wei). Jackson often mentioned the Chin case in his presidential campaign speeches that year, but, perhaps unfortunately, the film includes only a short clip of Jackson comparing Chin's death with the martyrdom of Martin Luther King and Jesus Christ.

The film contains a few awkward moments. It is never clear how two armed police officers could have been eyewitnesses to Chin's extended beating and killing without intervening. We hear from—very briefly and then never again—an unidentified African-American man who says he was hired by Ebens and Nitz (for twenty bucks) to help them find Chin after the fight at the club. How these incidents affected the jurors' decisions in the various trials is never documented. Further, some footage of Chol Soo Lee, a Korean-American convicted of a crime he did not commit (and the subject of the film "True Believer") is shown but never explained.

Ultimately, this is a film that is less about trials than about changes in political and/or social consciousness (or in the case of Ebens and Nitz, a refusal to admit any consciousness). The final words of the film are reserved for Lily Chin, Vincent

Chin's distraught mother, who gave up her self-effacing role as a traditional Chinese woman to help American Citizens for Justice: "I want justice for my son." (Some measure of justice came in a cash settlement of her wrongful death suit against Ebens, but this development is not covered in the film.)

The film has won numerous awards, including Best Documentary at the Hawaii International Film Festival in 1988, and it received an Academy Award nomination in the same category the next year.

See also: "Come See the Paradise."

Availability: Selected collections; Filmakers Library; Indiana University.

Further reading: "Ex-Auto Worker Guilty in Slaying." *New York Times*, 29 June 1984, A10. A survey of the case after the civil rights conviction.

Leong, Russell, ed. *Moving the Image: Independent Asian Pacific American Media Arts.* Los Angeles: UCLA Asian American Studies Center, 1991. An overview of Asian-American films, including "Who Killed Vincent Chin?"

Nichols, Bill. *Blurred Boundaries: Questions of Meaning in Contemporary Culture.* Bloomington: Indiana University Press, 1994. Argues that the film is "the most important political documentary of the 1980s."

"$1.5 Million in Wrongful Death." *New York Times*, 1 Aug. 1987, 32. Ebens agrees to make lifetime monthly payments to Chin's estate.

Wei, William. *The Asian American Movement.* Philadelphia: Temple University Press, 1993. Sets the Chin case in the context of Asian-American political movements.

Wilkerson, Isabel. "For Asian-Americans, Acquittal in Rights Case Arouses Outrage and Fear." *New York Times*, 6 May 1987, A20. A survey of the case after the final trial.

❧
Wildrose

Struggling to grow in a pit

1985, 95 mins., unrated, but suitable for mature children	Rick Ogaard = Tom Bower
	Pavich = Jim Cada
Director: John Hanson	Karen = Cinda Jackson
Screenplay: John Hanson and Eugene Corr	Ricotti = Dan Nemaniack
CAST	Katri Sippola = Lydia Olsen
June Lorich = Lisa Eichhorn	Nolan = Ernest Tomatz

One of the only reviewers of this film about a strip mine worker in the Mesabi Range in Minnesota complained that the film is "tongue-tied" in its attempts to tell the dramatic story of June, who is, we assume, the "wildrose" of the title. But it is the character June herself who is tongue-tied: she speaks so little we are sometimes afraid she has not been given the same script as the rest of the actors. She is virtually screen center for the entire film, so this is a serious problem. It has to be one of the most underwritten roles in the history of feature films.

Her story is dramatic enough: she drives one of those mammoth open-pit dump trucks (also seen being driven by women in "Moving Mountains") until she gets bumped down to pit laborer because of layoffs and matters of seniority. Trying to do a "man's" job gets her taunted by men in her "pit rat" crew. In the meantime, she has to put up with a drunken lout of an ex-husband.

Although her union is never identified, we see the local debating issues such as cost-of-living allowances, seniority, and Occupational Safety and Health Administration regulations. One of her union brothers recites a speech she has heard too often (including from her own mother), that the local unemployment problem would go away if women were no longer hired.

Into this life of quiet desperation, a fellow pit rat falls for her and she (less enthusiastically) for him. His dream is to be an owner-operator of his own commercial fishing boat on Lake Superior. Part of the drama of the film is anticipating her decision regarding what we know will be his eventual offer to give up the dirty mining business and join him in pursuing his dream. This offer, surprisingly, gets her verbal motor going for a change. Don't attack my job, she insists.

John Hanson's direction of "Wildrose" has a lot in common with his direction of his earlier black-and-white feature, "Northern Lights." He has a genuine feel for rural working-class people, their rituals (a big family fish fry), their behavior (June finds it difficult to "stand up" to her ex-husband), and their opinions (when June does speak). But some of these scenes, shot with a mixture of professional and nonprofessional actors, have the look of overcompetent home movies and often lack a point other than that they are showing "real people."

Perhaps characteristic of this film, which seems so promising, is the log cabin June is building. It is a spare-time project, and she's hewing, notching, and setting the logs single-handedly. She seems to be making good progress, and the task shows her independent spirit, enables her to spend a lot more time on screen without talking, and helps us to measure and appreciate her physical strength as well. But we never see her finish the cabin!

See also: "Moving Mountains"; "Northern Lights"; "We Dig Coal."
Availability: Selected collections.
Further reading: Maslin, Janet. "Breaking Ground." *New York Times,* 5 April 1985, C4. A brief but positive review.

⌒ᴗ
The Willmar 8

Eight women against one bank

1981: 55 mins., unrated, but suitable for all
  ages
Director: Lee Grant
Unscripted documentary
PRINCIPAL FIGURES
Sandi Treml, cashier
Shirley Solyntjes, bookkeeper
Terri Novotny, bookkeeper

Glennis Andresen, teller
Sylvia Erickson, teller
Doris Boshart, head bookkeeper
Jane Harguth, head operator
Irene Wallin, head teller
Leo Pirsch, president, Citizens National
  Bank

On 16 December 1977, eight women, employees of the Citizens National Bank of Willmar, Minnesota, began the first bank strike in the state's history. The members of the self-styled Willmar Bank Employees Association, Local 1, struck because they were asked to train one too many men to be managers. When the women refused to train one more, the bank president told them, "We're not all equal, you know." For one and a half years through two Minnesota winters, the women (and occasionally a few labor and National Organization of Women allies) walked a picket line in front of the bank. Ultimately, they brought their case to the National Labor Relations Board (NLRB) and asked for back pay and reinstatement (since other women had been given their jobs).

Lee Grant, an actress and director, came to the Minnesota town (population: 14,000) midway through the strike. Previously, Willmar had been known as the American city with the highest rate of coffee consumption and one of the largest turkey-processing plants in the region. With a few exceptions, she was met by a "wall of silence": the Willmar 8 had apparently committed an unpardonable sin. Almost no one in Willmar, except one poker club (composed mostly of upper-middle class women with friends among the bank's executives and families) would speak openly to Grant and her camera crew. The card players ranged from noncommittal and defensive to near-hostile: their overriding message was that the bank women should just leave well enough alone. Only the Unitarian Church would invite the Willmar 8 to a service to explain their situation. (Oddly enough, the bank president's son was a Minnesota AFL-CIO official who supported their strike.)

The Willmar 8 became close friends despite their differences in age, religious beliefs, and interests. One of the women admitted that she didn't want to strike and would not do it again, but she remained a faithful picketer throughout the strike. Another woman, head bookkeeper Doris Boshart, was hired back but demoted; the other women accepted her decision to go back, and Doris picketed with them every day during her lunch break.

Toward the end of the strike, with their strike fund exhausted, the women learned that the bank's growth rate had been seriously affected by its unfair labor practices and that the bank had been sold. The NLRB ruling on 23 March 1979 was unfavorable, however. The Board ruled that the bank had committed unfair labor practices but that they were not the reason for the strike. The women ended their strike, but first they posed for a final portrait for Grant on the sidewalk where they had spent so many cold days: each close-up shows loss but not defeat. Six months after the strike, only Boshart remained a bank employee; of the others, one became a student, two were unemployed, and the rest were working in jobs ranging from bookkeeper for Kmart to nurse's aide.

The film opens with a remarkable verse from a Wobbly song:

> The banks are made of marble
> With a guard at every door,
> The vaults are stuffed with silver
> That the people sweated for.

It closes with a song by Peter Yarrow (of Peter, Paul, and Mary), "Like a Rose." We also hear such pop tunes as "Take This Job and Shove It" and such union classics as "I'm Sticking to the Union."

A Rochester, Minnesota, local of the United Automobile Workers (pre-AFL-CIO merger) sent money and support in the form of marchers, but there are more than a few hints that the state AFL-CIO may not have given the women as much support as it could have. It may be a weakness of the film that it does not explore some of these important issues. Perhaps because the women did not win, Lee Grant seems to put more of her faith in legal and government action: her end titles emphasize the legal battles women in banking have won since the Willmar 8 went down to defeat, and she ends with the announcement that in 1978 the Department of Labor targeted the banking industry for equal employment enforcement.

See also: "9 to 5"; "Working Girl."

Availability: Selected collections; AFL-CIO.

Further reading: James, Judith. "The Long March of 'The Willmar 8.'" *Ms.* Sept. 1978, 19. A sample of the publicity in the feminist press that actively supported the strikers.

Kellett, Suzy. "In Trouble." *People*, 27 Nov. 1978, 107+. A sample of the fairly positive national publicity for the strikers.

Note: Grant also made the (unfortunately titled) TV movie "A Matter of Sex" (1984), about the Willmar 8, but it is not available on videocassette.

With Babies and Banners

Union maids and rebel girls in Big Auto

1978, 45 mins., unrated, but suitable for all ages	PRINCIPAL FIGURES
Director: Lorraine Gray	Ruth Pitts, Emergency Women's Brigade
	Nellie Bessen, Emergency Women's Brigade

The subtitle of this film, "The Story of the Women's Emergency Brigade," refers to the brave and militant organization of working women and autoworkers' wives, mothers, sisters, and girlfriends who led the "outside" strike while their men occupied the Flint, Michigan, General Motors plant in the great sit-down strike of 1936–37. The documentary argues convincingly that the women's strike kitchens, day-care centers, picket lines, family aid, and community propaganda helped win the strike.

The women had double trouble, of course, since they were squeezed economically by company policy and confronted traditional sexist attitudes from their men and society, too. For example, the women who worked at buildings targeted for sit-downs were sent home so no one could accuse the remaining men of sexual improprieties. When some of the women volunteered at union headquarters, they were at first considered too "feminine" (i.e., they were on the make) or too "queer" or too intellectual. But over and over again the women demonstrated their courage and resourcefulness. When tear gas was shot into a building, the women smashed the windows to let the gas out; they fought on the propaganda front, too, with the "children's picket line" ("My daddy strikes for us little tykes. On to victory!")

This Academy Award nominee for Best Documentary combines archival footage, still photos, and contemporary interviews into a lively documentary that tells (retells) women's history "from the bottom up." Hazel Dickens sings her memorable version of the old Joe Hill IWW song "Rebel Girl" as the coda to the film.

See also: "Rosie the Riveter"; "Salt of the Earth"; "Union Maids"; "We Dig Coal."
Availability: Selected collections; AFL-CIO; ILR Media; New Day Films.

∾ The Wobblies

"Hold the fort, for we are coming . . ."

1979: 90 mins., unrated, but suitable for all
  ages
Director: Stewart Bird and Deborah Shaffer
Screenplay: Stewart Bird and Deborah
  Shaffer
PRINCIPAL FIGURES
Roger Baldwin, founder, American Civil
  Liberties Union
Joe Murphy, migratory worker
Violet and Jack Miller, migratory workers
Nels Peterson, migratory worker
Nicolas Steelink, migratory worker
Sam Krieger, migratory worker

Tom Scribner, lumberjack
Irv Hanson, lumberjack
Vaino Onga, lumberjack
James Fair, longshoreman
Irma Lombardi, silk weaver
Dominic Mignone, silk weaver
Sophie Cohen, silk weaver
Angelo Rocco, textile worker
Katie Pintek, miner's wife
Art Shields, reporter
Fred Thompson, newspaper editor, the
  Industrial Worker
Utah Phillips, folksinger

Like many documentaries about labor history, this film intercuts archival footage, old photographs, and contemporary interviews—in this case, with surviving members (in their eighties and nineties) of the Industrial Workers of the World, also known as the Wobblies and the One Big Union—into a satisfying survey of an important and (arguably) unique union. The Wobblies wanted all workers to be in one union but had to be satisfied with some of the most exploited and tough members of the American proletariat (which included many recent immigrants): their occupations were in part represented by the list of "witnesses" or interviewees for this film—especially migratory workers, lumberjacks, mill workers, and miners.

Most of these workers were unskilled or semiskilled: they felt excluded from Samuel Gompers's AFL—which one of the Wobblies said they always called the "A.F. of Hell"—in part because of his pro-war stance but mainly because of his skilled trades orientation. (Gompers called the IWW the "fungus on the labor movement.") Indeed, at the Wobbly founding convention in 1905, Big Bill Haywood said that he didn't even care if any skilled workers came into the One Big Union. The IWW Preamble Constitution proclaimed its revolutionary aims: "Instead of the conservative motto, 'A fair day's wage for a fair day's work,' we must inscribe on our banner the revolutionary watchword, 'Abolition of the wage system.'"

The heart of this documentary is the cadre of old Wobblies who still stand steadfast for their ideals. They form a narrative chorus on the highlights of Wobbly history—the Lawrence, Massachusetts, strike of women mill workers in 1912; the Paterson, New Jersey, silk workers strike of 1913; and the tragic Everett, Washington, massacre of Wobbly free-speech advocates in 1916—and provide tidbits of personal history. One rail-riding working stiff recalls their battles with "hijackers," men who tried to prey on workers, often by holding up a hundred men until they found the Wobbly organizer with a stash of cash from headquarters. The Wobblies had to send out a "flying squadron" to deal with one of these crooks: we cut the letter I in his forehead and two Ws in his cheeks, one man recalls, and then poured potassium permanganate in the wounds to signify what would happen if hijackers came around again.

Another witness recalled how Elizabeth Gurley Flynn, the Rebel Girl of Wobbly fame, asked the young women of the Lawrence strike if they wanted to have dresses "like their bosses' daughters." When they shouted "yes," she told them, "Well, you can't!" and urged them to fight on nonetheless. Still another witness told of infiltrating the scab crews that were sent out from the city to work in fields struck by the Wobblies: as the supposed scabs approached the picket line, they burst into one of the Wobbly hymns, "Hold the Fort, for We Are Coming," and had a good laugh at the employers' expense. (John Steinbeck used a similar scene when the punch-drunk Joy infiltrates the scab crew in *In Dubious Battle*.)

One minor difficulty with the film is that the names and occupations of the witnesses are introduced with their photos in the first minute of the film and are never identified again. It is hard to recall on first or subsequent viewings a single name from the list of almost twenty.

Directors Stewart Bird and Deborah Shaffer were fortunate in being able to use some animated propaganda "from the other side" (e.g., the anti-union Disney folks). Thus, we see "Little Red Henski," a cartoon featuring Alice's Egg Plant, which is disrupted by the arrival of the Little Red Henski (who looks like Lenin) who organizes the egg layers into demanding "smaller eggs" and "shorter hours." According to reviewer Melvin Dubofsky, this short film "is almost worth the price of admission in itself": Alice is played by a real actress, while a Felix the Cat look-alike is the foreman, in an early example of mixing animated and live-action modes. When Alice yells at the striking hens, "Get to work. I need those eggs," a hen replies, "You'll get your egg," as she lays one on the spot and hits Alice in the kisser with it.

As intrinsically entertaining as this cartoon is, the filmmakers use it to illustrate a tricky point in Wobbly symbols: their propaganda cartoons almost always used both the Black Cat and wooden shoe (the "sabot" of sabotage), but one of the Wobblies who is interviewed says that for them sabotaging their own workplace by burning it down, for example, would be foolish; instead, he said, they define "sabotage" as the "conscious withdrawal of efficiency" (e.g., shorter hours and smaller eggs).

Another animated short demonstrates how the war for public opinion *against* the Wobblies was won. A farmer proudly displays his prosperous-looking sacks of

"American Institutions," as a giant rat gnaws its way closer through a wall. "Bolsheviks are the rats of civilization," the farmer shouts as he smashes the Bolshevik/IWW rat with his shovel. This would be more funny if it didn't turn out to have a real-life parallel in the ferocity with which established forces attacked the Wobblies' pacifistic "free-speech fights" and other organizing drives.

The numerous important historical battles—many well known, others not—waged by the Wobblies may convince some viewers that they were more than the songbirds of the working class. Nevertheless, Wobbly Ralph Chaplin's "Solidarity Forever" (1915) is sung virtually everywhere as the "anthem" of the American labor movement.

Joyce Kornbluh's collection of political art and literature by the Wobblies, some of which is included in the film, demonstrates that their politics were usually clear and uncompromising. On the debate between "the ballot" versus "direct action," a cartoon is shown in which a politician says, "On to Washington," but a Wobbly points to a factory and says, "Here is the place where you are robbed."

Wobbly characters in film have popped up in some unlikely places (probably one or two of the band of prospectors in "The Treasure of Sierra Madre") and in some likely places (the mine workers' organizer in "Matewan"). But like the One Big Union itself, they come too often to a righteous but tragic death.

See also: "Joe Hill"; "Matewan"; ['The Treasure of Sierra Madre"].

Availability: Selected collections; AFL-CIO.

Further reading: Dubofsky, Melvin. "Film as History: History as Drama." *Labor History* 22 (1981): 136–39. A balanced review of the film.

Georgakas, Dan. "The Wobblies—The Making of a Historical Documentary." *Cineaste* 10 (Spring 1980): 14–19, 58. An in-depth interview with the film's codirectors.

Goldberg, David J. *A Tale of Three Cities: Labor Organization and Protest in Paterson, Passaic, and Lawrence, 1916–1921.* New Brunsurck, N.J.: Rutgers University Press, 1989. Reviews the competition with the A. J. Muste–founded Amalgamated Textile Workers of America and supports the claim that the IWW did not sustain poststrike organizing efforts (see Golin for a counterview).

Golin, Steve. *The Fragile Bridge: The Paterson Silk Strike, 1913.* Philadelphia: Temple University Press, 1988. Argues for the success of the IWW and its Greenwich Village intellectual allies like John Reed (see "Reds").

Gomez, Joseph A. "History, Documentary, and Audience Manipulation: A View of 'The Wobblies.'" *Labor History* 22 (1981): 141–45. A hostile review, objecting to almost everything about the film, including the projection speed of the silent archival footage.

Kornbluh, Joyce., ed. *Rebel Voices: An IWW Anthology.* Ann Arbor: University of Michigan Press, 1964. An admirably edited, thorough, and very rich collection of Wobbly writings and graphic art.

Maslin, Janet. "The Wobblies." *New York Times*, 11 Oct. 1979, C15. A brief review that considers the film a gentle, almost too gentle, depiction of the rowdy Wobbly days.

O'Connor, Harvey. *Revolution in Seattle*. New York: Monthly Review Press, 1964. A very readable memoir of the Wobblies on the Northwest coast by an ex-member and newspaper reporter.

∾ Women of Steel

Women in and out of steel

1985, 28 mins., unrated, but suitable for all ages
Director: Randy Strothman
Scripted documentary
PRINCIPAL FIGURES (ALL FORMER OR CURRENT STEELWORKERS)
Beth Destler, bottle washer for a biology lab

Sheryl Johnson, Mon Valley Unemployment Committee worker
Pat Turnell, Pizza Hut waitress
Linda Cable, former steelworker
Carolyn Demeler, former steelworker
Sherry Oratlono, current steelworker

This documentary is somewhat rare in that, with one exception, the principal figures involved in the production were laid-off female steelworkers. (The exception, Oratlono, was a millwright helper when the film was made.) The film, which the women made themselves, focuses on their lives after they broke the gender barrier at U.S. Steel's Homestead, Pennsylvania, mill, only to be laid off as the industry collapsed in the early 1980s. They were hired as the direct result of an April 1974 USWA agreement with U.S. Steel to begin a five-year plan to hire more women and minorities in the relatively high-paying jobs offered in the mills.

The film offers the testimony of women whose working and family lives took a hard fall almost immediately. A daring opening scene—for a documentary on women workers, in any case—sets in motion the downward spiral of this select group of workers: we see a woman strip off her dirty work clothes, down to her bra, and "rebuild" herself as a waitress. In concrete terms, the women went from earning twelve dollars an hour to two dollars an hour; they went from repairing tracks and laying electric cables to waitressing at Pizza Hut. (And even their waitressing jobs got worse as a result of the steel industry: Pat Turnell complains that she has to wash dishes and clean windows because her table service has slowed down.)

When the big blow in steel came in 1983—the demolition of the blast furnaces—unemployment figures climbed for both men and women, but, as the film makes clear, it was always harder for the women to get rehired whenever a company did call back some workers.

As a document on the effects of a collapsing industry on women, the film is like one continuous bad headline—an almost unrelieved tale of broken hopes and families. There are a few bright spots: Sheryl Johnson shows her unemployment commit-

One of the "Women of Steel" with a blow torch.
Courtesy Women Make Movies.

tee organizing and demonstrating and lobbying for relief; Beth Destler emphasizes how the women were able to stick together as friends and, of course, eventually work on this documentary.

The soundtrack includes several feisty songs ("I Got Trouble"; "Fight Back") by Holly Near, who has become a labor film troubadour, and what seems like a song commissioned for the film ("Women of Steel"), by Maria Hurt and CoCo Coleman.

See also: "The Life and Times of Rosie the Riveter"; "Moving Mountains"; "Roger and Me"; "Union Maids"; "Wildrose"; "The Women of Summer."
Availability: Selected collections; AFL-CIO.
Further reading: Lynd, Staughton. *The Fight against Shutdowns: Youngstown's Steel Mill Closings.* San Pedro, Calif.: Singlejack Books, 1982. Community and church groups work with organized labor to save jobs.

The Women of Summer

"The program was built out of their lives."—Esther Peterson

1986, 55 mins., unrated, but suitable for all
    ages
Directors: Suzanne Bauman and Rita Heller
Scripted documentary
PRINCIPAL FIGURES
Esther Peterson, union organizer and
    teacher, Bryn Mawr Summer School

Hilda W. Smith ("Jane"), dean, Bryn Mawr
    Summer School
Marjorie Lynch Logan, student, Bryn Mawr
    Summer School
Holly Near and Ronnie Gilbert, singers
Jennie Silverman, student, Bryn Mawr
    Summer School

The Bryn Mawr Summer School for Women Workers in Industry was established in 1921 by the president of Bryn Mawr College, M. Carey Thomas, and John D. Rockefeller, Jr., and was supported—through recruiting efforts—by such organizations as the YWCA Industrial Department, the National Consumers' League, and unions dominated by women workers (the Amalgamated Clothing Workers of America, the International Ladies' Garment Workers' Union, and the United Textile Workers of America). Hilda W. Smith, the founder and first dean of the school, wrote in the original statement of purpose that the school would "offer young women of character and ability a fuller education in order that they may widen their influence in the industrial world, help in the coming social reconstruction, and increase the happiness and usefulness of their own lives" (Schneider). In its eighteen-year history (it was replaced by the Hudson Shore Labor School in 1938), 1,610 women workers attended the school.

Esther Peterson, the recreation director of the school for several years, recalled in a recent memoir (see Kornbluh and O'Farrell) the practical and democratic nature of study sessions: "We didn't have textbooks. We'd just ask, 'What was it like when the boss said those things?' We acted out the whole thing. . . . The program was built out of their lives and it began with who they are and where they are."

This documentary history of the school is framed by a "class reunion" fifty years after most of the workers left their unusual school. Some of the alumnae from the late 1920s recalled the days when support rallies were held in Philadelphia for Sacco and Vanzetti and one of the regular Bryn Mawr faculty members was arrested. Holly Near commemorates those days in a moving song about Judge George Webster Thayer, who sentenced the men to death.

Some of the other alumnae recall the difficulties of attending the school during the Depression. They were dealing with the hungry and homeless, sometimes within their own families. Occasionally, little sisters would be openly "smuggled" in to live in the school's dormitory.

A class portrait of alumnae of the Bryn Mawr Summer School in "Women of Summer."
Courtesy Filmakers Library.

This film chronicles an early and important moment in labor education. It demonstrates how "removing" women workers from their busy homes and working lives even for a brief time strengthened their participation in the labor movement once they were back in the "real world."

Availability: Selected collections; AFL-CIO; ILR Media.
Further reading: Kornbluh, Joyce L., and Brigid O'Farrell. "You Can't Giddyup by Saying Whoa: Esther Peterson Remembers Her Organized Labor Years." *Labor's Heritage* (Spring 1994): 38–59. An oral history of an organizer and activist who worked at the Bryn Mawr Summer School.

Schneider, Florence Hemley. *Patterns of Workers' Education: The Story of the Bryn Mawr Summer School.* Washington, D.C.: American Council of Public Affairs, 1941. An early history and analysis of the eighteen years in which the school was in existence.

Working Girl

... but not a Union Maid

1988, 113 mins., R (a little sex)
Director: Mike Nichols
Screenplay: Kevin Wade
CAST
Catherine Parker = Sigourney Weaver

Tess = Melanie Griffith
Mick Dugan = Alec Baldwin
Jack = Harrison Ford
Cyn = Joan Cusack

When a New York film begins with a shot of the Staten Island ferry, one of two scenarios is likely: the film will be (1) a nostalgic elegy à la Woody Allen, with the Manhattan skyline as backdrop, or (2) a class-conscious comedy. In the case of "Working Girl," it's the latter, since the only other place sophisticated New Yorkers think is a funnier place to live than Staten Island is New Jersey. And, sure enough, we immediately see two nine-to-five "working girls" with Really Big Hair, our heroine, Tess, and her best friend, Cyn.

As in many comedies and dramas about class consciousness, our heroine wants out of the working class and into one of the jobs held by sophisticated people like her new boss, played by Sigourney Weaver, or the two Wall Street louts who work near her and keep setting her up with losers who only want sex.

What Melanie Griffith's Tess wants is a way into the class of people who *have* secretaries. Her boss is, alas, the approximate equivalent of Gordon Gekko in "Wall Street"—an acquisitions and mergers ace whose hold on her top position includes using—while pretending to mentor—Tess. Since this is a Mike Nichols film, we are not quite at the level of viciousness Oliver Stone is capable of with Gordon Gekko. In fact, Catherine's speeches of advice to Tess demonstrate a curious mixture of Wall Street savvy and Cosmo Woman snap: when confronted with a jerk at an office party, Tess compliments Catherine on how deftly she handled him. "Today's junior prick, tomorrow's senior partner," Catherine quips.

Catherine the Great provides other pertinent advice as well, since Tess has not realized how much her appearance is a class marker (her hairdo, her use of excessive amounts of jewelry, and those clothes!) because she was too busy getting herself through night school. Catherine's equivalent to the great Gekko on greed is to quote Coco Chanel: "Dress shabbily and they notice the dress. Dress impeccably and they notice the woman." When she discusses the likelihood of a marriage proposal, her mind is stuck in a groove of deals: "I've indicated that I'm receptive to an offer. I've cleared the month of June. And I am, after all, me."

As Tess studies the system, she comes up with a good merger idea, which she tries out on Catherine. Catherine, of course, will steal it, but it takes Tess a while to figure that out. The resulting comedy of money and manners involves a shared boyfriend and eventually Catherine's comeuppance.

The potential comic investigation into social class is compromised somewhat here by the classic comedy feature of one couple forming—Tess and Jack—while others break up—Jack and Catherine, Tess and Mick. We see some of Tess's Staten Island roots at Cyn's engagement party and in Tess's boyfriend, but because Griffith's acting range is so narrow, we're not convinced Tess is giving up a really bad thing to get such a good thing (an administrative position on Wall Street). In the end, office workers cheer when Tess gets her new man and her Wall Street job, but the scene is too reminiscent of the scene in "An Officer and a Gentleman" in which the working-class girl captures her officer. If this world of top guns is so attractive, then why has it been so easy to satirize it?

Critic Ben DeMott (and others) isolated one scene that epitomizes Tess's difficulties in bridging the class gap. At one point, she is on the floor helping Catherine put on ski boots. Tess has failed to get Catherine the best room at a European ski chalet. Catherine calls herself, speaking in perfect German. The world of difference between Catherine's fluent German and Tess's Staten Islandese could not be more apparent.

See also: "9 to 5"; "Wall Street."
Availability: Easy.
Further reading: DeMott, Benjamin. "In Hollywood, Class Doesn't Put Up Much of a Struggle." *New York Times*, 20 Jan. 1991, II.1, 22. Examines the unreality of "Working Girl" and other films about working-class characters that "are driven by near-total dedication to a scam—the maddening, dangerous deceit that there are no classes in America."
Harrington, Mona. "'Working Girl' in Reagan Country." *New York Times*, 15 Jan. 1989, IV.27. A feminist defense of Tess's boss Catherine and an anti-Reaganite attack on Tess.
Maslin, Janet. "Cinderella in a Business Suit." *New York Times*, 21 Dec. 1988, C22. Admires the film but acknowledges its fairy-tale aspects.
Note: Do not mistake "Working Girls" (a film about prostitutes) for this film.

Thematic Index

Films by AFRICAN-AMERICAN and
AFRICAN-CARIBBEAN Directors
"Daughters of the Dust"
"Half Slave, Half Free"
"Killer of Sheep"
"The Killing Floor"
"A Raisin in the Sun" [II]
"To Sleep with Anger"
"Sugar Cane Alley"
"Uncle Tom's Cabin"

Other Films about the
AFRICAN-AMERICAN Experience
"At the River I Stand"
"Fallen Champ"
"Harvest of Shame"
"Miles of Smiles, Years of Struggle"
"Nothing But a Man"
"A Raisin in the Sun" [I]
"Sounder"

Films about APPALACHIAN Workers
"Coal Miner's Daughter"
"Coalmining Women"
"The Dollmaker"
"Fast Food Women"
"Harlan County U.S.A."
"Matewan"
"We Dig Coal"

Films about ASIAN-AMERICANS
and ASIANS in AMERICA
"Alamo Bay"
"Come See the Paradise"
"Gung Ho"
"Iron Maze"
"Who Killed Vincent Chin?"

Films set in AUSTRALIA
"The Efficiency Expert"
"Waterfront"
"Where the Green Ants Dream"

Films about the AUTO Industry
"An American Romance"
"Black Legion"
"Blue Collar"
"Final Offer"
"Gung Ho"
"Inside Detroit"
"Rising Son"
"Sit Down and Fight"
"Tucker"
"Who Killed Vincent Chin?"
"With Babies and Banners"

BRITISH Films
"The Angry Silence"
"Business as Usual"
"Educating Rita"
"I'm All Right, Jack"
"Look Back in Anger"
"The Man in the White Suit"
"Riff-Raff"
"35 Up"

CANADIAN Films
"Final Offer"
"Moving Mountains"

Films for CHILDREN
"Breaking Away"
"The Efficiency Expert"
"The Milagro Beanfield War"
"Newsies"
"Sounder"

"Sit Down and Fight"
"The Organizer"
"The Wobblies"

Films with POSITIVE Images of Unions
  "At the River I Stand"
  "Business as Usual"
  "Final Offer"
  "Harlan County U.S.A."
  "Harry Bridges"
  "The Inheritance"
  "Matewan"
  "Moving Mountains"
  "Newsies"
  "Norma Rae"
  "Out of the Darkness"
  "Sit Down and Fight"
  "Taylor Chain" [I and II]
  "With Babies and Banners"

Films about RACISM
  "Alamo Bay"
  "At the River I Stand"
  "Black Legion"
  "Come See the Paradise"
  "Daughters of the Dust"
  "Edge of the City"
  "El Norte"
  "Iron Maze"
  "The Killing Floor"
  "Nothing But a Man"
  "Sounder"
  "Who Killed Vincent Chin?"

Films about Working-Class RESENTMENT
  "Black Legion"
  "Joe"
  "Look Back in Anger"
  "A Raisin in the Sun" [I and II]
  "Rising Son"
  "Teachers"

Films about REVOLUTION
  "Reds"
  "Spartacus"
  "To Kill a Priest"
  "Viva Zapata!"

Films Directed by Martin RITT
  "Edge of the City"

"The Molly Maguires"
"Norma Rae"
"Sounder"

SILENT Films
  "A Corner in Wheat"
  "Intolerance"
  "Metropolis"

Films about SLAVERY
  "Half Slave, Half Free"
  "Uncle Tom's Cabin"

SLEEPERS
  "Come See the Paradise"
  "Harvest of Shame"
  "The Killing Floor"
  "To Sleep with Anger"

Films about STEEL and Related Industries
  "An American Romance"
  "The Business of America"
  "Iron Maze"
  "Steel"
  "Taylor Chain" [I and II]
  "The Valley of Decision"
  "Women of Steel"

Films Mainly about STRIKES
  "Adalen 31"
  "American Dream"
  "An American Romance"
  "The Angry Silence"
  "At the River I Stand"
  "F.I.S.T."
  "Germinal"
  "Harlan County U.S.A."
  "Hoffa"
  "Last Exit to Brooklyn"
  "Matewan"
  "Newsies"
  "The Stars Look Down"
  "Salt of the Earth"
  "Strike"
  "Waterfront"
  "The Whistle at Eaton Falls"
  "The Willmar 8"

Films about the THIRD WORLD
  "The Burning Season"
  "El Norte"

"The Harder They Come"
"Macario"
"Sugar Cane Alley"
"Where the Green Ants Dream"

Films about the Struggle of Labor and
Capital from the TOP DOWN
"Desk Set"
"The Fountainhead"
"Gung Ho"
"I'm All Right Jack"
"Roger & Me"
"Sometimes a Great Notion"
"Tucker"
"Wall Street"
"Working Girl"

Films about TRUCKERS (Excluding Hoffa)
"Convoy"
"They Drive by Night"

Feature Films Made for TV
"Act of Vengeance"
"Blood Feud"
"The Burning Season"
"Half Slave, Half Free"
"The Killing Floor"
"A Raisin in the Sun" [II]
"Rising Son"
"Teamster Boss"
"The Triangle Factory Fire Scandal"
"Uncle Tom's Cabin"

Films directed by King VIDOR
"An American Romance"

"The Citadel"
"The Fountainhead"
"Our Daily Bread"

Films about Workers on the WATERFRONT
"Alamo Bay"
"Edge of the City"
"Harry Bridges"
"Never Steal Anything Small"
"On the Waterfront"
"Riffraff"
"Waterfront"

Films Focusing on WOMEN in or near the
    Workforce
"Business as Usual"
"Coalmining Women"
"Desk Set"
"The Dollmaker"
"Educating Rita"
"Harlan County U.S.A."
"The Life and Times of Rosie the Riveter"
"9 to 5"
"Norma Rae"
"A Raisin in the Sun"
"Salt of the Earth"
"Silkwood"
"Sugar Cane Alley"
"Swing Shift"
"The Triangle Factory Fire Scandal"
"Union Maids"
"We Dig Coal"
"Wildrose"
"The Willmar 8"
"With Babies and Banners"
"Working Girl"